PRINCIPLES OF SHARED RESPONSIBILITY IN INTERNATIONAL LAW

The Shared Responsibility in International Law series examines the underexplored problem of allocation of responsibilities among multiple states and other actors. The International Law Commission, in its work on state responsibility and the responsibility of international organisations, recognised that attribution of acts to one state or organisation does not exclude possible attribution of the same act to another state or organisation, but has provided limited guidance on allocation or reparation. From the new perspective of shared responsibility, this volume reviews the main principles of the law of international responsibility as laid down in the Articles on State Responsibility and the Articles on Responsibility of International Organizations, such as attribution of conduct, breach, circumstances precluding wrongfulness and reparation. It explores the potential and limitations of current international law in dealing with questions of shared responsibility in areas as military operations and international environmental law.

ANDRÉ NOLLKAEMPER is the director of the research project on Shared Responsibility in International Law (SHARES), for which he obtained an Advanced Investigator Grant of the European Research Council. He is also Professor of Public International Law at the Faculty of Law of the University of Amsterdam, where he established the Amsterdam Center for International Law (ACIL) in 1999.

ILIAS PLAKOKEFALOS is a post-doctoral researcher in the SHARES Research Project at the University of Amsterdam. He obtained his PhD from the University of Athens and has since specialized in international environmental law and the law of international responsibility.

STUDIES ON SHARED RESPONSIBILITY IN INTERNATIONAL LAW

This series produces high quality scholarship exploring questions of shared responsibility in international law. It provides new perspectives on the responsibility problems that arise from the increasing number of situations in which states, international institutions, and other actors engage in concerted action in the pursuit of common objectives. While such concerted action generally aims to provide beneficial outcomes, all too often it results in harmful ones. If that is the case, the multiplicity of actors involved in the concerted action may complicate the determination and implementation of international responsibility. Books in this series examine the grounds on which international law does and should allow for shared responsibility between all actors involved, and how it can be developed in a way that better enables the determination and implementation of shared responsibility.

The series includes both works on positive international law and works of a theoretical and interdisciplinary character.

The book series is part of the research project on Shared Responsibility in International Law (SHARES), which has been carried out at the Amsterdam Center for International Law (ACIL) of the University of Amsterdam from 2010 onwards.

General Editor

André Nollkaemper, Professor of Public International Law, University of Amsterdam

PRINCIPLES OF SHARED RESPONSIBILITY IN INTERNATIONAL LAW

An Appraisal of the State of the Art

Edited by

ANDRÉ NOLLKAEMPER

and

ILIAS PLAKOKEFALOS

Assistant editor

JESSICA N. M. SCHECHINGER

CAMBRIDGE
UNIVERSITY PRESS

CAMBRIDGE
UNIVERSITY PRESS

University Printing House, Cambridge CB2 8BS, United Kingdom

Cambridge University Press is part of the University of Cambridge.

It furthers the University's mission by disseminating knowledge in the pursuit of education, learning and research at the highest international levels of excellence.

www.cambridge.org
Information on this title: www.cambridge.org/9781107078512

First published 2014

A catalogue record for this publication is available from the British Library

Library of Congress Cataloguing in Publication data
Principles of shared responsibility in international law: an appraisal of the state of the art / Edited by André Nollkaemper and Ilias Plakokefalos.
p. cm. – (Studies on shared responsibility in international law)
ISBN 978-1-107-07851-2
1. International law. 2. Responsibility to protect (International law) 3. Strict liability. 4. Government liability (International law) I. Nollkaemper, André, editor. II. Plakokefalos, Ilias, editor.
KZ3410.P75 2014
341.26–dc23
2014016834

ISBN 978-1-107-07851-2 Hardback

CONTENTS

CONTRIBUTORS

PIERRE D'ARGENT Professor, University of Louvain (UCL); Guest Professor, University of Leiden; Member of the Brussels Bar; formerly, First Secretary of the International Court of Justice.

HELMUT PHILIPP AUST Dr. iur., Senior Research Fellow, Faculty of Law, Humboldt University Berlin.

LEÓN CASTELLANOS-JANKIEWICZ PhD Candidate and Teaching Assistant, Graduate Institute of International and Development Studies, Geneva. Former member of the SHARES Research Project (2010–2011), University of Amsterdam.

JAMES D. FRY Associate Professor of Law and Director of the LLM Programme, University of Hong Kong Faculty of Law.

ANDREA GATTINI Professor of International Law, University of Padova.

VLADYSLAV LANOVOY PhD in International Law, Graduate Institute of International and Development Studies, Geneva.

FRANCESCO MESSINEO Former Lecturer in Law, Kent Law School (Canterbury); SHARES Expert Associate.

ANDRÉ NOLLKAEMPER Professor of Public International Law at the Faculty of Law of the University of Amsterdam, and director of the SHARES Research Project.

ILIAS PLAKOKEFALOS Post-doctoral researcher in the SHARES Research Project at the University of Amsterdam.

CHRISTIAN J. TAMS Professor of International Law, University of Glasgow.

ANNEMARIEKE VERMEER-KÜNZLI Legal Counsel at the Ministry of Foreign Affairs, the Netherlands; associated researcher at the Amsterdam Center for International Law, University of Amsterdam, and SHARES Expert Associate.

ERIC WYLER Lecturer, Graduate Institute of International and Development Studies, Geneva, and Visiting Professor, Université Paris 2 Panthéon – Assas.

EDITORS' PREFACE

This is the first volume to appear in the book series *Shared Responsibility in International Law*. It was produced as part of the research project on Shared Responsibility in International Law (SHARES), which has been carried out at the Amsterdam Center for International Law (ACIL) of the University of Amsterdam from 2010 onwards.

This book series provides new perspectives on responsibility problems that arise from the increasing number of situations in which states, international institutions, and other actors engage in concerted action in the pursuit of common objectives. While such concerted action generally aims to provide beneficial outcomes, all too often it has resulted in harmful ones. If that is the case, the multiplicity of actors involved in the concerted action may complicate the determination and implementation of international responsibility. The book series examines the grounds on which international law does and should allow for shared responsibility between all actors involved, and how it can be developed in a way that better enables the determination and implementation of shared responsibility.

This first volume lays the groundwork for the series as a whole by critically reviewing the established principles of international responsibility as developed by the International Law Commission (ILC) – that are widely considered to be the state of the art in the law of international responsibility – from the perspective of shared responsibility. It discusses whether these principles allow for and support the determination and/or implementation of shared responsibility, whether they provide useful guidance for the often complex questions of distribution of international responsibility, or whether they contain obstacles. The volume also identifies any developments that might *de lege ferenda* provide for a better fit between the law of responsibility and shared responsibility.

The second volume of the series will consider, from an extra-legal perspective, how responsibility is to be distributed among multiple wrongdoing actors. Given that international law often provides no clear direction for such distribution, it considers possible grounds for distribution. This volume will engage in a fundamental inquiry into the bases and justifications for apportionment of responsibilities that could support an articulation of critique of current international law, and provide a basis for reform.

The third volume of the book series will explore the practice of shared responsibility in international law. Based on the recognition that the applicable rules and procedures for shared responsibility differ between particular issue-areas, it will map relevant practices of shared responsibility in over forty issue-areas. This will enable an assessment of the fit of the prevailing principles of international responsibility, and will provide building blocks for a proposal for critique, development, and eventually a broader theory of shared responsibility.

On the basis of the material in these first three volumes, a separate volume will consolidate the insights on the state of the law, and the grounds for development, into a new theory for shared responsibility in international law.

The present volume thus forms the essential foundation of a much broader project. It comprises eleven substantive chapters, including introductory and concluding chapters. Drafts of the chapters for this first volume were discussed at a meeting of the authors on 7 and 8 February 2013 in Amsterdam, to strengthen coherency throughout the volume.

The research leading to this book has received funding from the European Research Council under the European Union's Seventh Framework Programme (FP7/2007–2013)/ERC grant agreement n° 249499, as part of the SHARES research project carried out at the ACIL.

We thank the members of the SHARES research team as a whole for their input during various stages of the project leading up to this volume. Our particular thanks go to Jessica Schechinger for her coordinating work in support of this volume and to Laura Chafey and Belinda Macmahon for editorial assistance.

Finally, our thanks go to everyone at Cambridge University Press for their assistance during the production process of the volume.

The manuscript was finalised on 1 March 2014; later developments have not been incorporated.

André Nollkaemper and Ilias Plakokefalos
Amsterdam, 1 March 2014

ABBREVIATIONS

ACIL	Amsterdam Center for International Law
ADP	Articles on Diplomatic Protection
AFDI	Annuaire français de droit international
AFISMA	African-led International Support Mission in Mali
AIDI	Annuaire de l'Institut de Droit International
AJIL	American Journal of International Law
Ann Air & Sp L	Annals of Air and Space Law
ARIO	Articles on the Responsibility of International Organizations
ARSIWA	Articles on the Responsibility of States for Internationally Wrongful Acts
ASEAN	Association of Southeast Asian Nations
ASR	African Security Review
BYIL	British Yearbook of International Law
CAT	Convention against Torture
CEDAM	Casa Editrice Dott Antonio Milani
CERD	International Convention on the Elimination of All Forms of Racial Discrimination
CMLR	Common Market Law Reports
CRISPP	Critical Review of International Social and Political Philosophy
DRC	Democratic Republic of the Congo
DRFTPCJ	Droits: Revue française de théorie de philosophie et de cultures juridiques
EC	European Communities
ECHR	European Convention on Human Rights
ECJ	European Court of Justice
ECLI	European Case Law Identifier
ECOSOC	Economic and Social Council
ECR	European Court Reports
ECtHR	European Court of Human Rights
EIA	Ethics & International Affairs
EJIL	European Journal of International Law
ESA	European Space Agency

EU	European Union
EUR	euro
FARDC	Forces armées de la République démocratique du Congo
FRY	Federal Republic of Yugoslavia
GATT	General Agreement on Tariffs and Trade
GYIL	German Yearbook of International Law
Harv Int LJ	Harvard International Law Journal
HRLR	Human Rights Law Review
ICC	International Criminal Court
ICCPR	International Covenant on Civil and Political Rights
ICESCR	International Covenant on Economic Social and Cultural Rights
ICJ	International Court of Justice
ICLQ	International and Comparative Law Quarterly
ICSID	International Centre for Settlement of Investment Disputes
ICTY	International Criminal Tribunal for the former Yugoslavia
IECL	International Encyclopedia of Comparative Law
IGC	Intergovernmental Commission
ILC	International Law Commission
ILDC	International Law in Domestic Courts
ILM	International Legal Materials
ILR	International Law Reports
IMF	International Monetary Fund
IO	international organisation
IOLR	International Organizations Law Review
IRRC	International Review of the Red Cross
ITLOS	International Tribunal for the Law of the Sea
J Conflict & Sec L	Journal of Conflict & Security Law
JIDS	Journal of International Dispute Settlement
JIEL	Journal of International Economic Law
J Int Crim Just	Journal of International Criminal Justice
JJIL	Japanese Journal of International Law
J Phil	Journal of Philosophy
JPR	Journal of Peace Research
JSL	Journal of Space Law
L & Pol Int Bus	Law and Policy in International Business
LGDJ	Librairie générale de droit et de jurisprudence
LJIL	Leiden Journal of International Law
LOSC	United Nations Convention on the Law of the Sea
MIJIL	Michigan Journal of International Law
Mil L & L War Rev	The Military Law and the Law of War Review
MONUC	United Nations Mission in the Democratic Republic of the Congo

NATO	North Atlantic Treaty Organization
NL	The Netherlands
NPT	Non-Proliferation Treaty
NYIL	Netherlands Yearbook of International Law
NYU J Int L Pol	New York University Journal of International Law and Politics
ODIL	Ocean Development & International Law
OECD	Organisation for Economic Co-operation and Development
PAHO	Pan American Health Organization
PCIJ	Permanent Court of International Justice
Pepp L Rev	Pepperdine Law Review
PMSC	private military and security company
R2P	responsibility to protect
RBDI	Revue Belge de droit international
RCADI	Recueil des cours de l'Académie de droit international de La Haye
RGDIP	Revue géneralé de droit international public
RIAA	Reports of International Arbitral Awards
Riv Dir Int	Rivista di Diritto Internazionale
RQDI	Revue québécoise de droit international
RSDIE	Revue suisse de droit international et européen
SFDI	Société française pour le droit international
SHARES	Shared Responsibility in International Law
SJIL	Stanford Journal of International Law
SZIER	Schweizerische Zeitschrift für internationales und europäisches Recht
UK	United Kingdom
UN	United Nations
UNGAOR	United Nations General Assembly Official Records
UNPROFOR	United Nations Protection Force
UNSC	United Nations Security Council
UNTS	United Nations Treaty Series
US	United States
USD	United States dollar
Vand J Transnat L	Vanderbilt Journal of Transnational Law
VCLT	Vienna Convention on the Law of Treaties
WHO	World Health Organization
WTO	World Trade Organization
YJIL	Yale Journal of International Law
ZaöRV	Zeitschrift für ausländisches öffentliches Recht und Völkerrecht
ZöR	Zeitschrift für öffentliches Recht

TREATIES AND OTHER INTERNATIONAL LEGAL INSTRUMENTS

CASES

International courts and tribunals

National courts

1

Introduction

ANDRÉ NOLLKAEMPER

This volume explores the question of how the law of international responsibility, as authoritatively codified and developed by the International Law Commission (ILC), can be used to address situations where multiple actors contribute to harmful outcomes. In particular, it considers how and to what extent this law enables, facilitates, or obstructs determination and implementation of a responsibility that is shared between all states and/or international institutions that contribute to such harmful outcomes.

Questions that give rise to the volume include the following. If multiple states agree to reduce emissions of carbon dioxide with a view to abating climate change, yet they continue to emit carbon dioxide that causes climate change, and human displacement and environmental harm occur, can, or should, the responsibility for the harm be shared between the contributing states?[1] If states or international organisations fail to live up to the collective 'responsibility to protect' human populations from mass atrocities[2] – a responsibility that rests in part on obligations that are binding on a plurality

André Nollkaemper is Professor of Public International Law at the Faculty of Law of the University of Amsterdam, and director of the SHARES Research Project. This Introduction is in part based on P. A. Nollkaemper and D. Jacobs, 'Shared Responsibility in International Law: A Conceptual Framework' (2013) 34 MIJIL 359, and the contribution by Dov Jacobs is duly acknowledged. The research leading to this chapter has received funding from the European Research Council under the European Union's Seventh Framework Programme (FP7/2007–2013)/ERC grant agreement n° 249499, as part of the research project on Shared Responsibility in International Law (SHARES), carried out at the Amsterdam Center for International Law (ACIL) of the University of Amsterdam. All websites were last accessed on 20 March 2014.

1 The question is not entirely hypothetical. See e.g. R. Lord, S. Goldberg, and L. Rajamani (eds.), *Climate Change Liability: Transnational Law and Practice* (Cambridge University Press, 2011), at pp. 23–49. See generally M. G. Faure and P. A. Nollkaemper, 'International Liability as an Instrument to Prevent and Compensate for Climate Change' (2007) 43 ASJIL 123.

2 UN Secretary-General, 'Implementing the Responsibility to Protect: Report of the Secretary-General', UN Doc. A/63/677 (2009).

of states or organisations[3] – can we speak of a responsibility that is to be shared between the actors that failed to act?[4] If two or more states or international organisations conduct joint military operations in which some soldiers violate international humanitarian law, should responsibility be shared among these states, organisations, and individual perpetrators?[5] If states agree to cooperate, whether or not through international institutions, to conserve fish stocks beyond their exclusive economic zone but fail to realise that objective, will all of the states that collectively fail to act share in the responsibility for the failure?[6]

In this volume, we consider such questions from the perspective of positive international law. While the problem of shared responsibility clearly calls for much wider investigations, and indeed other parts of the project will approach the above questions from different angles,[7] the necessary starting point of our inquiry has to be an understanding of the law as it has been construed by the dominant actors. On this basis,

[3] D. Amnéus, *Responsibility to Protect by Military Means – Emerging Norms on Humanitarian Intervention?* (Stockholm University Press, 2008); M. Hakimi, 'State Bystander Responsibility' (2010) 21 EJIL 341, at 342–3; A. J. Vetlesen, 'Genocide: A Case for the Responsibility of the Bystander' (2000) 37 JPR 519, at 529.

[4] This question has been considered to some extent by the International Court of Justice (ICJ). *Application of Convention on Prevention and Punishment of Crime of Genocide (Bosnia and Herzegovina* v. *Serbia and Montenegro)*, Judgment, ICJ Reports 2007, 43, at para. 379 (discussing the state's responsibility for failure to prevent genocide, one of the mass atrocities that responsibility to protect (R2P) requires states to prevent); see also J. Pattison, 'Assigning Humanitarian Intervention and the Responsibility to Protect', in J. Hoffman and P. A. Nollkaemper (eds.), *Responsibility to Protect: From Principle to Practice* (Amsterdam University Press, 2012), p. 173.

[5] A. Sari, 'Jurisdiction and International Responsibility in Peace Support Operations: The *Behrami* and *Saramati* Cases' (2008) 8 HRLR 151. A similar question was raised regarding the distribution of responsibilities in the hybrid UN and African Union force in Sudan. See generally S. E. Kreps, 'The United Nations–African Union Mission in Darfur: Implications and Prospects for Success' (2007) 16 ASR 65.

[6] See e.g. United Nations Conference on Straddling Fish Stocks and Highly Migratory Fish Stocks, New York, 24 July–4 August 1995 (sixth session); Agreement for the Implementation of the Provisions of the United Nations Convention on the Law of the Sea of 10 December 1982 relating to the Conservation and Management of Straddling Fish Stocks and Highly Migratory Fish Stocks, New York, 4 August 1995, in force 11 December 2001, 2167 UNTS 3. Recently, the Sub-Regional Fisheries Commission asked for an Advisory Opinion from the International Tribunal for the Law of the Sea (ITLOS), with the aim of clarifying the responsibilities of multiple actors engaged in illegal fisheries: see *Request for an Advisory Opinion Submitted by the Sub-Regional Fisheries Commission*, Request to Render an Advisory Opinion of 28 March 2013, ITLOS Case No. 21, available at www.itlos.org.

[7] P. A. Nollkaemper and D. Jacobs (eds.), *Distribution of Responsibilities in International Law* (Cambridge University Press, 2015 *forthcoming*).

the volume will primarily inquire into the law of international responsibility as formulated by the ILC. In particular, the Articles on Responsibility of States for Internationally Wrongful Acts (ARSIWA)[8] have to be considered an authoritative formulation of international law relating to international responsibility. Courts, both international and domestic, now routinely turn to the ARSIWA when they are faced with any question of international responsibility,[9] if only for lack of an alternative, equally authoritative source. The same is not entirely true for the Articles on the Responsibility of International Organizations (ARIO),[10] which are more controversial and have not been tested in international and national courts to the same extent. However, for these latter Articles, too, it is hard to find an alternative, equally authoritative starting point for any inquiry into questions of international responsibility involving international organisations.

This volume demonstrates that while the law of international responsibility as construed by the ILC is generally highly flexible, in many respects it provides little or no guidance for solving problems of shared responsibility. In some respects, the law complicates or even impedes such solutions. As a whole, the chapters in this volume lead to the conclusion that if international law is to be helpful in addressing questions of shared responsibility, it will often be necessary to look beyond the ILC legacy. In this respect, the volume is the starting point for a further, and more fundamental, enquiry into the phenomenon of shared responsibility in international law.

This introductory chapter first summarises the processes that underlie the emergence of problems of shared responsibility, which, to some extent, are relevant in appraising the state of the law (section 1). It then explains the concept of shared responsibility (section 2) and identifies why situations in which multiple actors contribute to a harmful outcome have posed problems for international law (section 3). The chapter then sets out the framework for analysis that will be used throughout the volume to appraise the

[8] Articles on Responsibility of States for Internationally Wrongful Acts, ILC *Yearbook* 2001/II(2) (ARSIWA).

[9] S. Olleson, 'Internationally Wrongful Acts in the Domestic Courts: The Contribution of Domestic Courts to the Development of Customary International Law Relating to the Engagement of International Responsibility' (2013) 26(3) LJIL 615. UN General Assembly, 'Responsibility of States for internationally wrongful acts: Compilation of decisions of international courts, tribunals and other bodies: Report of the Secretary-General', UN Doc. A/68/72 (2013).

[10] Articles on the Responsibility of International Organizations, ILC Report on the work of its sixty-third session, UNGAOR 66th Sess., Supp. No. 10, UN Doc. A/66/10 (2011) (ARIO).

ILC legacy from the perspective of shared responsibility (section 4). The final section will explain the organisation of the volume (section 5).

1. The rise of situations of shared responsibility

The examples of situations that may lead to shared responsibility given above are not isolated incidents. As states, international institutions, and other actors increasingly engage in cooperative action, the likelihood of harm resulting from such action multiplies. Responsibility for harm caused then need not lie with any single actor, but may be shared by all actors involved.

The increase in the number of situations that appear to call for a shared responsibility is driven by interdependence between states, underlying the passage from a society of coexistence to a society of cooperation.[11] States have become increasingly dependent on each other to protect common goods, and have felt compelled to address them collectively.[12] The underlying reasons are both objective and subjective. The former are driven by factual effects across borders, such as transboundary pollution, state-supported transborder crime, and refugee flows. In other areas it is the perception that has changed, rather than the reality. The recognition that genocide is no longer acceptable is an example.[13]

Interdependence, whether perceived or real, directly influences the occurrence of situations of shared responsibility. It informs a shift towards 'global governance', thus creating an increase in the number of situations where cooperation may not deliver what was promised, and where questions of shared responsibility may arise.[14]

This pattern of interdependence-induced shared responsibility is supported by three related trends. The first is the increasing degree to which

[11] See W. Friedmann, 'Cours général de droit international public' (1969) 127 RCADI 39, at 127; G. Abi-Saab, 'Whither the International Community?' (1998) 9 EJIL 248; P.-M. Dupuy, 'International Law: Torn between Coexistence, Cooperation and Globalization. General Conclusions' (1998) 9 EJIL 278.

[12] E.-U. Petersmann, 'International Economic Law, "Public Reason", and Multilevel Governance of Interdependent Public Goods' (2011) 14 JIEL 23.

[13] Convention on the Prevention and Punishment of the Crime of Genocide, Paris, 9 December 1948, in force 12 January 1951, 78 UNTS 277.

[14] A. Buchanan and R. O. Keohane, 'The Legitimacy of Global Governance Institutions' (2006) 20 EIA 405, at 437; C. Harlow, 'Accountability as a Value in Global Governance and for Global Administrative Law', in G. Anthony (ed.), *Values in Global Administrative Law* (Oxford: Hart Publishing, 2011), p. 173.

(some) states and other actors feel morally compelled to act in relation to harm occurring elsewhere.[15] This moral stance has to some extent influenced international legal obligations to protect persons abroad, and in any case has led to an increase in situations where states and international institutions actually act abroad. An example is the notion of 'responsibility to protect' (R2P), which, because of its collective nature, raises questions concerning the distribution of obligations to act.[16]

The second supporting trend is the multiplication of actors that participate in the cooperative pursuit of public goods.[17] The fact that states now regularly defer to international organisations to 'legislate' on a wide-ranging array of topics, from cultural heritage to health and environmental law,[18] potentially leads to questions of shared responsibility between multiple organisations and/or between organisations and states. The layered nature of international organisations, which are legal persons but at the same time consist of sovereign states as members, facilitates the construction of responsibility for wrongdoing as a shared responsibility between the organisation and member states.[19] The ARIO indeed envisage that an organisation can be responsible in connection with the wrongful acts of states, for instance by adopting decisions that require states to commit acts that contravene international obligations.[20] Significantly, the Articles acknowledge that in such situations both the organisation and the state can be responsible, resulting in a situation of shared responsibility.[21]

15 A. Linklater, *The Problem of Harm in World Politics. Theoretical Investigations* (Cambridge University Press, 2011), pp. 151, 254. This is, in a domestic context, the argument of N. Elias, *The Civilizing Process*, revised edition (Oxford: Blackwell Publishing, 2000). Of course, this does not exclude other (strategic) considerations for setting up protection regimes; see e.g. B. Cronin, *Institutions for the Common Good: International Protection Regimes in International Society* (Cambridge University Press, 2003).

16 J. Pattison, *Humanitarian Intervention and the Responsibility to Protect: Who Should Intervene?* (Oxford University Press, 2010), pp. 9–11.

17 See generally on the multiplicity of actors (or 'participants') in the international legal process: R. Higgins, *Problems and Process: International Law and How We Use It* (Oxford University Press, 1995).

18 The World Trade Organization (WTO) illustrates this trend, by providing a formal negotiation forum for international trade, thus centralising discussions on this issue within one institution. In relation to this, see M. Kumm, 'The Legitimacy of International Law: A Constitutionalist Framework of Analysis' (2004) 15 EJIL 914 (arguing that 'the procedure by which international law is generated increasingly attenuates the link between state consent and the existence of an obligation under international law').

19 See generally on the layered nature of international organisations C. Brölmann, *The International Institutional Veil in Public International Law. International Organisations and the Law of Treaties* (Oxford: Hart Publishing, 2007).

20 Article 17 ARIO, n. 10.

21 Article 19 ARIO, n. 10.

The third supporting trend is the increased value attached to the accountability of contributing actors. We have seen the emergence of a culture of accountability at the international level.[22] Both in practice and in legal scholarship, more and more weight is attached to holding those who do not deliver accountable for their conduct. Many actors, including the press, civil society, and sometimes also states and international institutions, are not (always) content with putting all of the blame on just one actor, who may be the most visible wrongdoer, but extend blame to wider networks of actors who made the wrong possible. The debate on responsibility of contributing states for rendition is a case in point.[23] This development, which is part of a more general trend towards good governance and transparency,[24] has substantially increased the number of situations where questions of shared responsibility have been raised.

These developments have led to an increase in the number of situations in which it is necessary to ascertain who, among the multiplicity of actors involved in cooperation, is to answer for the failure to live up to promises and abide by agreements, and who is to provide reparation to any injured parties.

However, the mere fact that multiple actors contribute to harm does not necessarily lead to a situation in which these actors indeed share responsibility. There is safety in numbers. The very fact that states and international institutions act collectively makes it more difficult to determine who is to blame for what. The international legal order increasingly has to come to terms with a truth learned long ago in organisational theory: as the responsibility for any given instance of conduct is scattered among more actors, the discrete responsibility of every individual actor diminishes proportionately.[25]

2. The concept of shared responsibility

In this volume the concept of shared responsibility refers to situations where a multiplicity of actors contributes to a single harmful outcome,

[22] M. Bovens, *The Quest for Responsibility: Accountability and Citizenship in Complex Organisations* (Cambridge University Press, 1998); Harlow, 'Accountability as a Value in Global Governance and for Global Administrative Law', n. 14, at 173.

[23] See G. Callaghan, 'Member States Told to "Accept Responsibility" for Illegal CIA Renditions', The Parliament, 11 September 2012, available at www.theparliament.com.

[24] P. Ala'i, 'From the Periphery to the Center? The Evolving WTO Jurisprudence on Transparency and Good Governance' (2008) 11 JIEL 779.

[25] Bovens, *The Quest for Responsibility*, n. 22, p. 46.

and legal responsibility for this harmful outcome is distributed among more than one of the contributing actors. We emphasise that this definition is not identical to a particular form of responsibility recognised by the ARSIWA and the ARIO. Rather, the concept of shared responsibility as defined here is used as an external concept to assess the suitability of the principles codified and developed by the ILC in relation to situations of shared responsibility.

Leaving aside the obvious point that shared responsibility involves a multiplicity of actors, the above definition comprises three aspects: it is premised on contributions to a single harmful outcome (section 2.1), which engage the legal responsibility of the contributing actors (section 2.2), which is distributed between more than one of the contributing actors separately (section 2.3).

2.1 *Contributions to a harmful outcome*

The first defining feature of shared responsibility is that such responsibility is premised on contributions to a single harmful outcome.[26] The notion of 'contribution' will be commented upon in section 2.2; here I will address, respectively, the notion of 'harmful outcome' and the singularity of a harmful outcome.

The notion of a 'single' harmful outcome is important because it is the contribution to a single outcome that creates the basis for sharing of responsibility. If each actor contributes to a distinct harm, responsibility will lie with the individual actors for their individual contributions. In contrast, in situations where multiple actors contribute to a single harm, such harm generally will be indivisible, in the sense that the proportion of harm attributable to each contributing actor cannot be determined.

[26] The choice of the term 'harmful outcome' as a defining element of shared responsibility corresponds to the notion of outcome as a basis for responsibility in legal theory, although we do not necessarily follow the particular meanings that have been associated with outcome responsibility. See e.g. D. Miller, 'National Responsibility and Global Justice' (2008) 11 CRISPP 383; T. Honoré, *Responsibility and Fault* (Oxford: Hart Publishing, 1999), p. 27 (defining outcome responsibility in terms of responsibility for the good and bad outcomes of a person's conduct); see also P. Cane, 'Responsibility and Fault: A Relational and Functional Approach to Responsibility', in P. Cane and J. Gardner (eds.), *Relating to Responsibility* (Oxford: Hart Publishing, 2001), p. 88; B. Stern, 'A Plea for "Reconstruction" of International Responsibility based on the Notion of Legal Injury', in M. Ragazzi (ed.), *International Responsibility Today. Essays in Memory of Oscar Schachter* (Leiden: Martinus Nijhoff, 2005), p. 93.

Whether or not this is so depends largely on the test of causation, which in itself is a subject of inquiry.[27]

An outcome may be harmful in a factual sense (e.g. pollution of a watercourse, physical injury of a person, destruction of property).[28] It may also involve non-material harm, such as the violation of sovereignty of a third state.

For present purposes, whether or not an outcome is harmful is treated as a factual (and inevitably somewhat subjective) question. That is: an outcome may be harmful without necessarily being in violation of international law. In this respect the approach taken here can be distinguished from that taken by Raz, who observed that:

> one causes harm if one fails in one's duty to a person or a class of persons and that person or a member of that class suffers as a result. That is so even when one cannot be blamed for harming the person who suffered because the allocation of the loss was determined by other hands.[29]

Transposed to our topic, Raz's definition would mean that multiple actors cause harm to another person when they had a duty not to cause such harm or where international law assigns responsibility for causing such harm. In particular cases the causing of harm will indeed be wrongful, for instance because it infringes rights of states or individuals, or involves the non-realisation of collective interests of states parties to a treaty, such as genocide, climate change, or the depletion of stocks of tuna.

However, defining 'harm' in terms of wrongfulness would conflate the question of whether multiple states cause factual harm to another person, on the one hand, and the question of whether they are responsible in law for doing so. That distinction is analytically useful for studying questions of shared responsibility and will thus be maintained here.

It should be observed that a single course of conduct can lead to different levels of harm. While some levels of harm may result from the conduct of individual actors, others may result from the conduct of

[27] Chapter 2 in this volume, A. Gattini, 'Breach of International Obligations', p. 25, at pp. 28–31; Chapter 7 in this volume, P. d'Argent, 'Reparation, Cessation, Assurances and Guarantees of Non-Repetition', p. 208, at p. 222.

[28] Compare Commentary to the Articles on the Responsibility of States for Internationally Wrongful Acts, ILC *Yearbook* 2001/II(2) (ARSIWA Commentary), Commentary to Article 31, para. 6.

[29] J. Raz, *The Morality of Freedom* (Oxford University Press, 1986), p. 416. For a definition of responsibility in terms of contribution to harm, see also J. Feinberg, 'Collective Responsibility' (1968) 65 J Phil 674.

multiple actors. An example is the situation in which state A abducts a person from the territory of state B, and hands him over to state C, in which he is tortured.[30] State A's abduction independently causes harm to the person as it infringes his individual rights. But assuming that state A had knowledge of the subsequent event, the act may also be construed as a contribution to state C's act of torture – both A and C then contribute to that single harm.

2.2 *Legal responsibility for contributions*

The fact that a particular course of conduct contributes in a factual way to harm does not in itself make the author of that conduct responsible in law. In other words, holding an actor responsible is different from assigning a *causal* responsibility to that actor.[31] For the purposes of this volume, which examines the conditions, content, and implementation of shared responsibility as a matter of international law, we obviously focus on the conditions under which someone can be held responsible (in law) rather than merely on the question of whether someone caused harm. It will appear below, though, that the concept of shared causal responsibility is relevant for assessing the nature and development of shared legal responsibility.

Shared responsibility as a matter of international law arises when contributions to a harmful outcome trigger the legal responsibility of the authors of such contributions. Causal contribution is only a necessary and not a sufficient condition for legal responsibility. Shared legal responsibility rests on causal contributions that international law recognises as triggering the legal responsibility of the actor in question.

It is useful to distinguish between three situations in which this is the case. I refer to these situations as *concurrent* responsibility, *cumulative* responsibility, and *joint* responsibility. It will appear throughout the volume that each of the three types of legal responsibility raises different normative and legal questions in the determination and implementation of shared responsibility.

First, in situations of *concurrent* shared responsibility,[32] each contribution constitutes a wrongful act that by itself causes the harmful outcome.

[30] Derived from d'Argent, 'Reparation, Cessation, Assurances and Guarantees of Non-Repetition', n. 27, pp. 212.

[31] P. Pettit, 'Responsibility Incorporated' (2007) 117(1) *Ethics* 171, at 173.

[32] D'Argent, 'Reparation, Cessation, Assurances and Guarantees of Non-Repetition', n. 27, pp. 211–12.

An example is the situation where two upstream states discharge large quantities of chemicals into an international watercourse, which results in downstream harm in a third state. Each of the emissions would in itself have caused significant harm. We can consider this to be a case of shared responsibility, since multiple actors cause a single harm. Yet each individual contribution in itself is sufficient to cause the harm, and the law considers each individual contribution as wrongful.

Second, in situations of *cumulative* shared responsibility, each contribution in itself would have been insufficient to cause the eventual harm, yet international law treats it as sufficient to trigger the responsibility of the author. A state that aids a torturing state contributes to that harmful outcome, yet does not itself engage in the conduct of torture. In the approach chosen by the ILC, the responsibility of the contributing actors can either be based on a separate wrongful act (such as aid or assistance), on the one hand,[33] or on attribution of responsibility, based on direction or control, coercion or 'circumvention', on the other.[34] In both cases the eventual harm is caused in cumulation with other contributions by other actors, but each individual contribution can lead to a (shared) responsibility.

Third, a single harmful outcome may constitute what the ILC has termed 'the same wrongful act'. Article 47(1) of the ARSIWA provides that: '[w]here several States are responsible for the same internationally wrongful act, the responsibility of each State may be invoked in relation to that act.' In such cases we can also use the term *joint* responsibility. Though the terms 'shared responsibility' and 'joint responsibility' are sometimes used interchangeably,[35] the latter term is narrower than the former and is best used to refer to situations where multiple actors commit a single wrongful act and one is responsible for the acts of the other(s).[36]

Whether or not all situations of cumulative responsibility as defined above are properly considered as situations of joint responsibility is a

[33] Chapter 3 in this volume, F. Messineo, 'Attribution of Conduct', p. 60.

[34] See Articles 16–18 ARSIWA, n. 8; and Articles 14–16 ARIO, n. 10. Chapter 4 in this volume, J. D. Fry, 'Attribution of Responsibility', p. 98.

[35] E.g. R. Pierik, 'Shared Responsibility in International Law: A Normative-Philosophical Analysis', in P. A. Nollkaemper and D. Jacobs (eds.), *Distribution of Responsibilities in International Law* (Cambridge University Press, 2015 *forthcoming*). Also Fry, 'Attribution of Responsibility', ibid., p. 100.

[36] See J. Crawford, 'Third Report on State Responsibility', ILC *Yearbook* 2000/II(1), p. 74, para. 272; and d'Argent, 'Reparation, Cessation, Assurances and Guarantees', n. 27, p. 235.

question which, as a matter of positive law, is unsettled. But it would seem that not all situations of shared responsibility involve one single wrongful act. For instance, the possibility that one state aids another state in committing a wrong (in which case there would be two wrongs, not one) demonstrates that states or international organisations can share responsibility for contributing to a single harmful outcome, without this being qualified as the same wrongful act. The notion of a 'single wrongful act' will be commented upon in various contributions in this volume.[37]

In addition to these three categories where shared causal responsibility is translated into shared legal responsibility, there may be situations where actors contribute causally to harmful outcomes (and on that basis may share causal responsibility), yet do not incur shared legal responsibility. This may be so because international law does not (yet) consider such sub-threshold contributions to be significantly serious to assign responsibility. The law of international responsibility as formulated by the ILC does not provide answers to problems posed by such contributions, and in principle they are not the subject of analysis in the present volume.

However, three points are in order. First, the boundary between causal contributions that do or do not trigger responsibility is not static, and the location of the border may be a matter of controversy that is relevant to the appreciation of the state of international law. The controversial status of circumvention is a case in point.[38] Thus, whether or not a particular causal responsibility does or does not translate into legal responsibility in itself is the subject of inquiry and critique.

Second, even though sub-threshold contributions may not trigger responsibility, they may potentially be relevant in the determination of the form and degree of reparation to be provided by actors whose legal responsibility was engaged. One example is the possibility of contribution to the injury by the state that invokes responsibility.[39]

[37] See d'Argent, 'Reparation, Cessation, Assurances and Guarantees of Non-Repetition', n. 27, p. 213, 242; Chapter 8 in this volume, A.M.H. Vermeer-Künzli, 'Invocation of Responsibility', p. 251.

[38] See e.g. S. Yee, "Member Responsibility" and the ILC Articles on the Responsibility of International Organizations: Some Observations', in M. Raggazi (ed.), *Responsibility of International Organizations: Essays in Memory of Sir Ian Brownlie* (Leiden: Martinus Nijhoff, 2013), p. 325 at 332.

[39] Article 39 ARSIWA, n. 8 (providing that '[i]n the determination of reparation, account shall be taken of the contribution to the injury by wilful or negligent action or omission of the injured State or any person or entity in relation to whom reparation is sought').

Third, even though the current international law of responsibility may not address substandard causal contributions, they may well be relevant in regulatory schemes that seek to prevent questions of shared responsibility *ex post facto* arising in the first place.[40]

2.3 Distribution to individual actors

The third defining feature of shared responsibility is that the responsibility of two or more actors for their contribution to a particular outcome is *distributed between them separately*, rather than resting on them collectively.[41] If the responsibility were to rest on a collectivity, it would no longer be shared, but would instead be a responsibility of the collectivity as such.[42] Somewhat counter-intuitively, because the term may suggest otherwise, shared responsibility thus by definition is a responsibility that rests on individual actors for their contribution to a harm.

However, shared responsibility is not simply the aggregation of two or more individual responsibilities. A defining feature of shared responsibility as used in this volume, in any case in situations of cumulative and joint responsibility, is that the two or more actors stand in some relationship to each other, and their conduct or omissions mutually influence the (scope of) responsibility of the other. Indeed, an important application of the concept of shared responsibility is to situations where responsibility is based on multiple actors contributing to each other's acts and thereby to the eventual outcome.[43]

3. Shared responsibility as a challenge for international law

This volume is prompted by the gap between the number of situations in which multiple actors factually contribute to a particular harmful outcome (and thus are causally responsible), on the one hand, and the number of

[40] This is one of the reasons why the distinction between primary and secondary rules is of limited relevance, see further P. A. Nollkaemper and D. Jacobs, 'Shared Responsibility in International Law: A Conceptual Framework' (2013) 34 MIJIL 359, 412.

[41] L. May, *Sharing Responsibility* (University of Chicago Press, 1996) at p. 112.

[42] Ibid., p. 116. A major reason why in the present state of international relations exclusive collective responsibility in cases of cooperative action is not an attractive option is that the organisational structures remain too weak and the power of states too strong.

[43] Ibid., pp. 36–8.

situations where international law considers such contributions significant enough to recognise them as a ground for legal responsibility, on the other. While practice shows many examples where states and other actors together factually caused harm, it is only in rather rare situations that international law recognises that each of these contributing actors shares in the eventual responsibility.

This does not mean that international law precludes a determination of shared responsibility. The chapters in this volume will demonstrate that the principles of responsibility may often allow for (attempts) to construe a shared responsibility of multiple actors that contribute to harmful outcomes. The law as formulated by the ILC will offer substantial flexibility to address questions of shared responsibility. This holds particularly in cases of concurrent shared responsibility where harmful outcomes can result from non-coordinated individual contributions that are each internationally wrongful. An example is the downstream pollution of an international watercourse by multiple upstream states, whereby each causes significant transboundary harm. In such cases, the responsibility for the eventual harm can be allocated to individual contributors, which are unconnected as such. These situations do not give rise to major legal problems, other than that it may be difficult to determine the exact factual contributions by various actors. Each contribution can be determined on its own merits.

However, international law is not always helpful. In some cases, while not necessarily precluding the determination or implementation of shared responsibility, international law provides little or no guidance as to exactly how responsibility (or reparation) is to be allocated between multiple actors.[44] In cases of cumulative responsibility, the question of the ground upon which shares of reparation should then be divided is not easily answered. Several possible answers come to mind,[45] but international law is not particularly helpful in choosing one over the other. This is especially so for situations involving attributed responsibility.

In other cases, the law of responsibility may complicate or even inhibit determinations of shared responsibility, even though the relevant actors may provide significant causal contributions. Examples are

[44] See e.g. d'Argent, 'Reparation, Cessation, Assurances and Guarantees of Non-Repetition', n. 27, p. 249.

[45] Ibid., pp. 229–2.

the high threshold requirements for responsibility based on aid and assistance,[46] and the lack of responsibility of member states of organisations for wrongful acts committed by these organisations, even when the member states contribute to such wrongful acts, unless a number of specific conditions are fulfilled.[47]

It remains fair to say that the principles of international law on the basis of which responsibility between multiple actors should be determined or allocated are, in the words of Brownlie, 'indistinct'[48] and do not provide clear answers. There is also still much truth in the observation that Noyes and Smith made in 1988: '[t]he law of multiple state responsibility is undeveloped. The scholarly literature is surprisingly devoid of reference to the circumstances or consequences of multiple state responsibility. Judicial or arbitral decisions addressing a state's assertions that other states share responsibility are essentially unknown.'[49] While this comment is not entirely correct in light of subsequent judicial decisions of, in particular, the International Court of Justice (ICJ)[50] and the European Court of Human Rights (ECtHR),[51] it remains true that international law is often not particularly helpful in addressing questions of shared responsibility.

Our understanding of what international law does offer in situations of shared responsibility is not enhanced by a particularly rich scholarship. Although there is, of course, a sizeable amount of literature on the law of international responsibility that is relevant to shared responsibility, and on which the chapters in this volume will draw, there are very few studies that expressly address the question of how the principles of responsibility apply in cases of multiple wrongdoing actors. Handbooks

[46] See Chapter 5 in this volume, V. Lanovoy, 'Complicity in an Internationally Wrongful Act', p. 134, at pp. 151, 156.

[47] Fry, 'Attribution of Responsibility', n. 34, at pp. 113–27.

[48] I. Brownlie, *Principles of Public International Law*, 7th edn (Oxford University Press, 2008), p. 457; See also R. P. Alford, 'Apportioning Responsibility among Joint Tortfeasors for International Law Violations' (2011) 38 Pepp L Rev 233, at 240: 'there is insufficient guidance under international law with respect to questions of apportioning responsibility'.

[49] J. E. Noyes and B. D. Smith, 'State Responsibility and the Principle of Joint and Several Liability' (1988) 13(2) YJIL 225 at 224.

[50] See e.g. *Certain Phosphate Lands in Nauru (Nauru* v. *Australia)*, Preliminary Objections, ICJ Reports 1992, 240; and *East Timor (Portugal* v. *Australia)*, Judgment, ICJ Reports 1995, 90.

[51] See e.g. *Al-Jedda* v. *the United Kingdom*, App. No. 27021/08 (ECtHR, 7 July 2011) and *Ilaşcu a.o.* v. *Moldova and Russia*, App. No. 48787/99 (ECtHR, 8 July 2004).

mostly contain only a few pages dealing with the topic.[52] Very few articles exist that discuss the problem more comprehensively.[53]

If the relative number of pages devoted to the issue in a monograph is an indication, scholarly attention is certainly increasing. Eagleton did not include in his 1928 monograph on international responsibility any separate discussion of what we now call shared responsibility.[54] In Brownlie's 1983 monograph, the topic was discussed in a very short chapter of four pages.[55] In contrast, Crawford's 2013 *State Responsibility – The General Part* devotes an entire part including four chapters to problems of multiple wrongdoing states.[56] But even this latter volume does not systematically discuss each of the principles of responsibility from the angle of shared responsibility, mainly limiting itself to questions of attribution and reparation.

In recent years, a limited number of books and articles have been published that discuss particular principles of responsibility that are relevant to shared responsibility, notably complicity,[57] or which apply particular principles to particular problems of shared responsibility.[58]

52 For example, I. Brownlie, *System of the Law of Nations: State Responsibility, Part I* (Oxford: Clarendon Press, 1983). J. Crawford, *State Responsibility – The General Part* (Cambridge University Press, 2013), contains a longer discussion in Chapters 10, 12 and 20. The Oxford University Press handbook (J. Crawford, A. Pellet, and S. Olleson (eds.), *The Law of International Responsibility* (Oxford University Press, 2010)) contains only two pieces that expressly deal with the topic: C. Dominicé, 'Attribution of Conduct to Multiple States and the Implication of a State in the Act of Another State', p. 281; and A. Orakhelashvili, 'Division of Reparation between Responsible Entities', p. 647.

53 Notably S. Besson, 'La Pluralité d'Etats responsables: Vers une solidarité internationale?' (2007) 17 RSDIE/SZIER 13; Noyes and Smith, 'State Responsibility and the Principle of Joint and Several Liability', n. 49, at 225; and A. Khalfan, 'Division of Responsibility', in M. Langford and others (eds.), *Global Justice, State Duties: The Extraterritorial Scope of Economic, Social, and Cultural Rights in International Law* (Cambridge University Press, 2013) p. 298.

54 C. Eagleton, *The Responsibility of States in International Law* (New York: Columbia University Press, 1928).

55 Brownlie, *System of the Law of Nations*, n. 52, pp. 189–92.

56 Crawford, *State Responsibility – The General Part*, n. 52, part IV.

57 H. P. Aust, *Complicity and the Law of State Responsibility* (Cambridge University Press, 2013).

58 Examples include P. N. Okowa, 'Responsibility and Multiple State Actors', in *State Responsibility for Transboundary Air Pollution in International Law* (Oxford University Press, 2000); C. A. Bell, 'Reassessing Multiple Attribution: The International Law Commission and the *Behrami* and *Saramati* Decision' (2010) 42 NYU J Int L Pol 501; A. Bird, 'Third State Responsibility for Human Rights Violations' (2010) 21 EJIL 883; C. Chinkin, 'The Continuing Occupation? Issues of Joint and Several Liability and Effective Control', in P. Shiner and A. Williams (eds.), *The Iraq War and International Law* (Oxford: Hart Publishing, 2008) p. 160; M. Hakimi, 'State Bystander Responsibility'

Furthermore, the literature on the responsibility of international organisations more frequently discusses aspects of shared responsibility.[59]

On the whole, some issues remain totally uncovered: notably breach, circumstances precluding wrongfulness, invocation, and countermeasures. It also follows that comprehensive treatment, in which the existing principles are considered in their interrelationship, does not exist. The present volume aims to fill this gap.

4. A framework for assessment

The appraisal of the existing law in this volume is primarily based on the existing principles of international law relevant to shared responsibility as recognised by the ILC and in case law. However, also in view of the fact that parts of the ILC framework clearly are progressive development, the chapters also appraise the possible development of the law. They consider whether trends are identifiable, or relevant proposals have been considered, which might improve the ability of international law to address questions of shared responsibility.

This volume will appraise the various principles of shared responsibility on the basis of a single analytical framework. While not all chapters are structured on the basis of this framework, as each topic requires its own approach, all chapters discuss how a particular part of the law of responsibility can be assessed from the angle of this framework. This allows for an integral assessment in the final chapter of the volume.

(2010) 21 EJIL 341; S. Talmon, 'A Plurality of Responsible Actors: International Responsibility for Acts of the Coalition Provisional Authority in Iraq', in P. Shiner and A. Williams (eds.), *The Iraq War and International Law* (Oxford: Hart Publishing, 2008) p. 184; and S. Wittich, 'Joint Tortfeasors in Investment Law', in C. Binder and others (eds.), *International Investment Law for the 21st Century: Essays in Honour of Christoph Schreuer* (Oxford University Press, 2009) p. 707.

59 See e.g. N. Blokker, 'Abuse of the Members: Questions Concerning Draft Article 16 of the Draft Articles on Responsibility of International Organizations' (2010) 7 IOLR 35; P. Klein, 'The Attribution of Acts to International Organizations', in J. Crawford, A. Pellet, and S. Olleson (eds.), *The Law of International Responsibility* (Oxford University Press, 2010) p. 296; P. J. Kuijper and E. Paasivirta, 'EU International Responsibility and its Attribution: From the Inside Looking Out', in M. Evans and P. Koutrakos (eds.), *The International Responsibility of the European Union* (Oxford: Hart Publishing, 2013) p. 35; E. Paasivirta, 'Responsibility of a Member State of an International Organization: Where Will It End? Comments on Article 60 of the ILC Draft on the Responsibility of International Organizations' (2010) 7 IOLR 49; and A. Reinisch, 'Aid or Assistance and Direction and Control between States and International Organizations in the Commission of Internationally Wrongful Acts' (2010) 7 IOLR 63.

The analytical framework consists of two main parts. The first focuses on the question of how and to what extent particular principles enable, guide, or obstruct the determination or implementation of shared responsibility (section 4.1). The second concentrates on the degree and ways in which particular principles allow for a differentiated approach that may vary between factual and legal contexts (section 4.2).

4.1 *The enabling capacity of the ILC system*

For each of the relevant principles, the chapters will determine the extent to which they facilitate a determination or implementation of shared responsibility between multiple states and/or organisations. Do they expressly provide for shared responsibility? Are they silent, but do they nonetheless allow for the determination or implementation of shared responsibility? For instance, do the principles of attribution of conduct or attribution of responsibility allow for shared responsibility? How do the principles on determination of a breach apply in situations of shared responsibility?

A subset of this question is whether, in relation to those cases where the Articles allow for shared responsibility, they provide any guidance in terms of distribution of responsibility among multiple wrongdoing actors. This is particularly relevant for questions of attribution, complicity, and reparation, but also, in other chapters, questions may arise as to who is responsible for what.

Finally, it will be considered whether particular principles contain obstacles that might preclude the determination or implementation of shared responsibility. If so, on what grounds do such obstacles rest, and how should these grounds be assessed in light of the (detrimental) effect on shared responsibility?

To the extent that particular principles indeed limit the possibility of shared responsibility, it will be assessed whether we can identify any developments that would, *de lege ferenda*, make the principles better suited for application in situations of shared responsibility.

4.2 *Differentiation*

In exploring the principle of shared responsibility, for each of the above questions it will be considered to what extent the principles can be applied in a differentiated approach. It is to be expected that the approach to legal questions of shared responsibility will differ significantly depending on the issue-area in which they arise.[60] For this reason, it is relevant to understand and assess the general principles in terms of their openness to allowing for, and addressing, such different situations.

In addition to the general question of whether a particular principle allows for a differentiated approach,[61] three specific aspects will be considered in this context.

First, it will be examined how a particular principle interacts with primary rules that may in part overlap with the rules on responsibility, and that may be better attuned to the context of a particular issue-area. In examining any particular question of shared responsibility, it will often be necessary to assess primary and secondary rules in their mutual connection.[62]

The fact that the ILC restricted itself to secondary rules is not a compelling reason to leave aside consideration of primary rules. It appears that the ILC adopted the dichotomy between primary and secondary rules for essentially pragmatic reasons (mainly linked to the generality of secondary rules).[63] Crawford also observed that the distinction between primary and secondary obligations is 'somewhat relative'.[64]

Second, the extent to which the principle allows for a differentiation between public and private aspects of international responsibility will be examined. The common understanding is that the rules on the international responsibility of states and international organisations form a single, unitary system.[65] However, we can identify the distinct private and public law dimensions of international responsibility. While international responsibility maintains strong private law dimensions,[66] modern international law of responsibility also has a distinct public law dimension. The law of responsibility as construed by the ILC is of an objective nature, in the

60 Nollkaemper and Jacobs, 'Shared Responsibility in International Law: A Conceptual Framework', n. 40, at 415.
61 E.g. Gattini, 'Breach of International Obligations', n. 27, with respect to Articles 12–15.
62 Nollkaemper and Jacobs, 'Shared Responsibility in International Law', n. 40, at 412.
63 J. Crawford, 'The ILC's Articles on Responsibility of States for Internationally Wrongful Acts: A Retrospect' (2002) 96 AJIL 874, at 877.
64 Ibid.
65 J. Crawford and S. Olleson, 'The Nature and Forms of International Responsibility', in M. Evans (ed.), *International Law* (Oxford University Press 2003), p. 444, at p. 451.
66 H. Lauterpacht, *Private Law Sources and Analogies of International Law*, reprinted in 2002 (London: Longmans, Green and Co., 1927), p. 81; T. E. Holland, *Studies in International Law* (Oxford: Clarendon Press, 1898), p. 152.

sense that responsibility can arise regardless of damage to any particular state or organisation.[67]

Both the private and the public law dimensions are relevant for shared responsibility. As to the former, there is a remarkable overlap between the key principles of international responsibility, as partly codified by the ILC, on the one hand, and the Principles of European Tort Law – an authoritative set of principles that, to a large extent, are common to domestic systems in Europe, on the other hand.[68] The principle of joint and several responsibility, in particular – to the extent that it exists at all in general international law[69] – is of a private law nature and has its relevance in a relationship between wrongdoing and injured states. As to the latter, construing responsibility as not being based on injury to individual states also allows us better to consider questions of shared responsibility as these arise in the context of multilateral agreements which protect the collective interests of the parties. While joint responsibility in regard to transboundary environmental harm may function in a way that resembles its domestic tort law origins (for instance when two upstream riparian states cause damage to a downstream state), this is very different in settings that resemble more public law/administrative law, for instance in the context of non-compliance institutions under multilateral environmental agreements.

Third, the extent to which the principles allow for application in situations involving different types of actors will need to be assessed. In this volume we focus mainly on states and international organisations.[70]

[67] A. Pellet, 'Remarques sur une révolution inachevée. Le projet d'articles de la CDI sur la responsabilité des Etats' (1996) 42 AFDI 7, at 101; Stern, 'A Plea for "Reconstruction" of International Responsibility Based on the Notion of Legal Injury', n. 26, at 94 (noting that it would introduce a 'review of legality through the institutions of international responsibility').

[68] European Group on Tort Law, *Principles of European Tort Law: Text and Commentary* (New York: Springer, 2005) (see further European Group of Tort Law website, available at http://civil.udg.edu/php//index.php?id=129&idioma=EN).

[69] See e.g. Crawford, *State Responsibility – The General Part*, n. 52, pp. 330–1. *Eurotunnel Arbitration (The Channel Tunnel Group Ltd & France-Manche S.A. v. the Secretary of State for Transport of the Government of the United Kingdom of Great Britain and Northern Ireland and le ministre de l'équipement, des transports, de l'aménagement du territoire, du tourisme et de la mer du Gouvernement de la République française)*, Partial Award, (2007) 132 ILR 1. D'Argent, 'Reparation, Cessation, Assurances and Guarantees of Non-Repetition', n. 27, pp. 244–49.

[70] I acknowledge that the multi-layered nature of international organisations may pose additional challenges for the law of international responsibility to which the general rules of state responsibility are not *mutatis mutandis* applicable. See C. Ahlborn, 'The

Situations of shared responsibility often bring into play the responsibility of individuals and other private actors, the analysis of which is essential to comprehensively understand the issue – even though they may sometimes fly below the radar of international law. Indeed, in many examples of shared responsibility, such as climate change and atrocities committed during armed conflicts, the role of non-state actors is critical. Individuals can cause part of a proscribed outcome to which states or other actors also contribute, and their responsibility can be understood as part of a larger picture. There is merit in seeing, in the context of the genocide in Srebrenica, the responsibility of Serbia, the United Nations, the Netherlands, General Mladic and other individual perpetrators in their mutual relationship.[71]

To the extent that it is relevant, each of the principles will be reviewed in terms of its ability to differentiate between the above aspects in the determination and implementation of responsibility, thus providing the basis for a differentiated understanding of shared responsibility.

5. Structure of the volume

This volume contains eleven chapters, which by and large follow the structure of the ARSIWA and the ARIO. As noted above, the content of these Articles – though they are by no means beyond controversy – have come to dominate the practice and theory of international responsibility, and they provide the starting point for our inquiry.

Each of the chapters in the volume will discuss, to the extent relevant, the Articles pertaining to states, on the one hand, and international organisations, on the other. Due account is taken of the differences between these two categories (for instance in the determination of a breach and the attribution of responsibility), but for some questions, the principles function in a comparative way in regard to shared responsibility.

The volume starts with 'Breach of International Obligations' by Andrea Gattini (Chapter 2). Gattini demonstrates that while the definition of the objective element of a breach of an international obligation contained in the

Rules of International Organizations and the Law of International Responsibility' (2011) 8(2) IOLR 397.

[71] See generally on the interplay between responsibility of individuals and states, P. A. Nollkaemper, 'Concurrence between Individual Responsibility and State Responsibility in International Law' (2003) 52 ICLQ 615; P. S. Rao, 'International Crimes and State Responsibility', in M. Ragazzi (ed.), *International Responsibility Today. Essays in Memory of Oscar Schachter* (Leiden: Martinus Nijhoff, 2005), p. 63.

ARSIWA and the ARIO does not impede the determination of shared responsibility as such, a more varied approach to the nature of international obligations and the requirement of their breach would have enabled a better understanding of the different possible interplays of the responsibility of different actors. This holds for the role of causation, which may take a different form depending on the type of obligation at issue. Addressing questions of shared responsibility may furthermore benefit from distinguishing between various types of obligations (in particular obligations *erga omnes*, obligations of means and of result, and obligations to prevent). The chapter argues that neither the ILC nor the International Court of Justice has done much to clarify the nature of such obligations, or how they would work in cases of shared responsibility.

In Chapter 3, Francesco Messineo discusses 'Attribution of Conduct'. This chapter assesses how rules of attribution of conduct work in cases where a single course of conduct is attributed to multiple international actors. Messineo argues that multiple attribution of conduct is possible and that, when more than one subject of international law is involved in the same wrongful conduct, it is often the default answer to the question of attribution. Exclusive attribution only finds application in certain exceptional circumstances concerning organs transferred to another state or international organisation.

Chapter 4, on 'Attribution of Responsibility', by James Fry, complements Chapter 3. Whereas Chapter 3 reviews the principles relating to attribution of conduct, Chapter 4 examines situations in which the responsibility, rather than the conduct, is attributed. The principles on attribution of responsibility will generally lead to shared responsibility, since such attribution will run in parallel to attribution of conduct of the principal wrongdoer. The chapter explores the theoretical basis of attribution of responsibility and critically reviews the Articles formulated by the ILC, notably those on direction and control, coercion, and circumvention. It demonstrates that while generally the rules have been drafted to allow for shared responsibility, their common conceptual basis is not well developed, and the degree of guidance they offer (for instance, with regard to apportionment between a state or international organisation to which responsibility, on the one hand, and wrongful conduct, on the other, is attributed) is limited.

In Chapter 5, 'Complicity in an Internationally Wrongful Act', Vladyslav Lanovoy addresses complicity as a basis for shared responsibility. Where the criteria are satisfied, complicity will by definition be part of a responsibility that is shared between the complicit state and the principal wrongdoing state. The chapter argues that while the principle of complicity generally allows for shared responsibility, the requirements for responsibility for complicity have been pitched so high – particularly the requirement that the principal conduct would be internationally wrongful if committed by the aiding or assisting state or international organisation – that this may undermine the function of international responsibility to support compliance with international obligations.[72] It also argues that the regime on responsibility for complicity leaves little room for the injured party to obtain full reparation for the injury that bears an imprint of complicity, due to the fact that the ILC has provided little guidance on the causal standards governing a third party's contribution to an internationally wrongful act.

In Chapter 6, 'Circumstances Precluding Wrongfulness', Helmut Philipp Aust explores how the principles on circumstances precluding wrongfulness set forth in Articles 20 to 27 of the ARSIWA and the ARIO cope with situations in which a plurality of states and/or international organisations are implicated in the commission of a wrongful act, and one or more of them tries to rely on the circumstances. The chapter argues that although the defences have been modelled on bilateral situations, the circumstances precluding wrongfulness can cope reasonably well with situations in which all actors within a group can rely on the same circumstance precluding wrongfulness. If, however, only some of the states and/or international organisations acting together can rely on circumstances precluding wrongfulness, difficult questions arise pertaining to the issue of whether cooperating states and/or international organisations also benefit from the defence. Also, the problem arises of how to divide possible claims of reparation between the cooperating states and/or international organisations. This chapter suggests that these problems are partly caused by the ILC's decision to lump together all defences in a group of circumstances precluding wrongfulness, without differentiation between circumstances precluding wrongfulness and mere 'excuses'.

In Chapter 7, Pierre d'Argent discusses 'Reparation, Cessation, Assurances and Guarantees of Non-Repetition' as these apply in situations of shared responsibility. The chapter is structured on the basis of a fundamental distinction between situations of shared responsibility resulting from separate wrongful acts (each triggering the international responsibility of several states or organisations), on the one hand, and situations of shared responsibility resulting from the same wrongful act, on the other. As the ARSIWA

[72] SFDI, *La Responsabilité dans le système international* (Paris: Pedone, 1991), pp. 319–36.

and the ARIO limit themselves to cases where such responsibilities exist for the same internationally wrongful act, so the chapter argues, the ARSIWA and the ARIO only partly address the complexity stemming from situations of shared responsibility when it comes to the allocation of the secondary obligations of reparation, cessation, and assurances and guarantees of non-repetition. By limiting the 'plurality of responsible States' (or organisations) to cases where such responsibilities exist 'for the same internationally wrongful act', they fail to consider cases where the harmful outcome is the result of several wrongful acts for which several subjects are responsible. However, the chapter also demonstrates that although the ILC rules are silent on the matter, and thus provide little guidance, the principles relating to reparation, cessation, assurances and guarantees of non-repetition need not encounter particular problems in situations of shared responsibility, and can result in an allocation of reparation that corresponds to the role and contribution of each individual actor.

In Chapter 8, Annemarieke Vermeer-Künzli discusses 'Invocation of Responsibility' in cases of shared responsibility. The chapter is based on the premise that invocation is essential for the implementation of shared responsibility. As is the case for most other principles of responsibility, the rules on invocation were shaped by the traditional situation in which states or international organisations acted independently of each other. They therefore provide limited guidance for situations of shared responsibility. This leads to several potential problems. The fact that standing to invoke responsibility requires injury or legal interest on the basis of individualised and separate responsibility of each of the members of a plurality of responsible states and/or international organisations may force an injured state or organisation to 'fragment its claim into the smaller pieces that fit this mould'.[73] The implementation of shared responsibility by means of invocation is further complicated by specific requirements applicable to claims, such as the nationality of claims and the local remedies rule, as well as criteria for admissibility before international courts and tribunals (including the *Monetary Gold* rule).[74]

Eric Wyler and León Castellanos-Jankiewicz in Chapter 9 on 'Serious Breaches of Peremptory Norms', discuss the extent to which the assessment of the law of responsibility from the perspective of shared

[73] Vermeer-Künzli, 'Invocation of Responsibility', n. 37, p. 272.

[74] *Monetary Gold Removed from Rome in 1943 (Italy* v. *France, United Kingdom of Great Britain and Northern Ireland and United States of America)*, Preliminary Question, ICJ Reports 1954, 19 (*Monetary Gold*).

responsibility changes when the states and/or international organisations have engaged in serious breaches of peremptory norms of international law. The topic is particularly relevant since in many situations where peremptory norms may be violated, they result from multiple contributions that each individually may not meet the required gravity threshold to trigger their international responsibility for serious breaches. The chapter considers the extent to which the aggravated regime of international responsibility accommodates a multiplicity of actors who have committed or contributed to such serious breaches. Separately, the chapter outlines the shared obligations of cooperation, non-recognition, and non-assistance aimed at ending serious breaches and wiping out their effects. It is considered whether third parties and principal wrongdoers can be jointly responsible when breaching these communitarian obligations. Finally, the chapter suggests that the *erga omnes* dimension of such norms entails a shared duty to invoke serious breaches in diplomatic relations and international dispute settlement.

In Chapter 10, Christian Tams discusses 'Countermeasures against Multiple Responsible Actors'. Tams argues that the regime of countermeasures is characterised by flexibility. While developed in the bilateral, inter-state setting, it can generally be applied to instances of shared responsibility. In many cases where multiple actors bear responsibility for a harmful outcome, such actors can be targeted individually and the normal rules of countermeasures apply. However, the chapter also argues that the situation is less clear in cases where responsibility is not shared equally, but is shared in a differentiated way. In these cases the question is whether countermeasures should be available for use against actors responsible for ancillary breaches. While such responses against each of the responsible actors could enhance the effectiveness of the law of responsibility, the chapter questions whether countermeasures should be subject to specific conditions.

Chapter 11 examines on a comparative basis the questions identified above: how and to what extent do the principles enable and facilitate the determination and implementation of shared responsibility, and to what extent do they allow for a differentiated approach? The chapter thereby provides a comprehensive assessment of the extent to which the principles of international responsibility that are dominant in international legal discourse are capable of dealing with the increasing number of situations in which we can speak of shared responsibility.

2

Breach of International Obligations

ANDREA GATTINI

1. Introduction

When dealing with the objective element of the wrongful act, the International Law Commission (ILC) eventually decided that a differentiation according to the structure of the international obligation was neither necessary nor useful. However, such a differentiation might well be useful or even necessary in the context of cases of shared responsibility, both in cases in which the responsibility arises out of joint or concerted actions or omissions, and in cases in which there is no such concerted action or omission between different states, between states and international organisations, or between states and non-state actors.[1] While the definition of the objective element of a breach of an international obligation contained in Articles 12 to 15 of the Articles on Responsibility of States for Internationally Wrongful Acts (ARSIWA)[2] does not impede the determination of shared responsibility, it is maintained in this chapter that a more varied definition would have enabled a better understanding of the different possible interplays of the responsibility of different actors.

Andrea Gattini is Professor of International Law at the University of Padova. The research leading to this chapter has received funding from the European Research Council under the European Union's Seventh Framework Programme (FP7/2007–2013)/ERC grant agreement n° 249499, as part of the research project on Shared Responsibility in International Law (SHARES), carried out at the Amsterdam Center for International Law (ACIL) of the University of Amsterdam. All websites were last accessed on 20 March 2014.

1 See on these two forms of shared responsibility P. A. Nollkaemper, in Chapter 1 of this volume, 'Introduction', p. 1 at pp. 6–12; and more elaborately P. A. Nollkaemper and D. Jacobs, 'Shared Responsibility in International Law: A Conceptual Framework' (2013) 34(2) MIJIL 358, at 365–8.

2 Articles on the Responsibility of States for Internationally Wrongful Acts, ILC *Yearbook* 2001/II(2) (ARSIWA). Commentary to Articles on the Responsibility of States for Internationally Wrongful Acts, ILC *Yearbook* 2001/II(2) (ARSIWA Commentary).

After a brief comment on general issues, such as the existence of a breach and causality (section 2), the chapter will enter into a discussion relating to the varying structures of international obligations (sections 3 to 6), and will end with some thoughts, from the perspective of the concept of breach of international obligations, on the prospects for shared responsibility between states and international organisations (section 7) and states and individuals (section 8).

2. General issues

Article 12, which is the first provision of Part One, Chapter III, of the ARSIWA, deals with the breach of an international obligation. It reads as follows:

> There is a breach of an international obligation by a State when an act of that State is not in conformity with what is required of it by that obligation, regardless of its origin or character.

As has been aptly said by James Crawford, Article 12 offers just the 'bare bones'.[3] Indeed it is a difficult task to add more details, without the risk of leaving the shores of secondary norms and being submerged in the ocean of primary obligations. Nevertheless, some observations on a few general issues, which would otherwise be eclipsed, are appropriate here.

2.1 Shared obligations

A preliminary question is whether shared responsibility presupposes that all actors are bound by a shared obligation. My assumption is that the twin concepts of sovereignty and equality prevent holding a state responsible for a wrongdoing that is not attributable to it. Therefore all concerned subjects must be bound by the same obligation, or at least by formally different obligations, but with an overlapping content.[4] However, the fact that Article 12 of the ARSIWA does not give any weight to the origin or character of the

[3] See J. Crawford, *State Responsibility – The General Part* (Cambridge University Press, 2013), p. 215. For a similar characterisation of the concept of 'internationally wrongful act' see F. Latty, 'Actions and Omissions', in J. Crawford, A. Pellet, and S. Olleson (eds.), *The Law of International Responsibility* (Oxford University Press, 2010), p. 355, at p. 356: 'Notion which was deliberately left skeletal'.

[4] But see the contribution in Chapter 4 of this volume, J. D. Fry, 'Attribution of Responsibility', p. 98, at p. 114 (noting that 'it is not necessarily true that both parties can bear the same obligation').

international obligation could, in the context of shared responsibility, give rise to some complications.

In the case of a treaty obligation, the issue is sufficiently clear-cut. The starting point is that third parties can never be held responsible per se for violations of treaty rules. This would exclude from the outset any possibility of holding parties and non-parties equally responsible. Subject to what we shall see in section 7, this would also exclude the possibility of holding member states and international organisations jointly responsible for the violation of a treaty obligation, since, with the exception of mixed agreements, either the international organisation or the state(s) would not be party to the treaty in question.

In some specific cases, the treaty itself may exonerate certain parties from respecting some treaty obligations – as does, for instance, Part IV of the General Agreement on Tariffs and Trade (GATT)[5] with regard to developing countries – or it may even go so far as to exonerate some parties from respecting the core obligations of the treaty. This is famously the case for the Kyoto Protocol of 1997,[6] which, giving expression to the concept of 'common but differentiated responsibility' contained in Article 3 of the United Nations (UN) Framework Convention on Climate Change of 1992,[7] imposes the duty to abate so-called greenhouse gases only on certain categories of states, exonerating developing states from any such obligation. In both instances there is in principle no room for envisaging situations of shared responsibility between states that are subject to such obligations, on the one hand, and states that are exonerated, on the other.

In the case of customary law obligations, the answer is also sufficiently clear-cut, but exactly the opposite compared to the former example. By definition, and with the exception of regional custom, a true customary law obligation can be violated by any state or groups of states, or even by international organisations, so that the determination of shared responsibility should not pose any specific problem.

A difficulty could arise in the case of a breach of two formally different but substantially analogous obligations, such as a customary law obligation that has been codified in a treaty, or an original treaty obligation that has become customary law. In this case, a situation of shared responsibility

[5] General Agreement on Tariffs and Trade, Geneva, 30 October 1947, in force 1 January 1948, 55 UNTS 187, Part IV (GATT).

[6] Kyoto Protocol to the United Nations Framework Convention on Climate Change, Kyoto, 10 December 1997, in force 16 February 2005, 2303 UNTS 148 (Kyoto Protocol).

[7] The United Nations Framework Convention on Climate Change, New York, 9 May 1992, in force 21 March 1994, 1771 UNTS 107, Article 3.

could well arise. However, despite the substantial identity of the breach, it is possible that the responsibility of only some of the states involved in the breach could be invoked, due to some distinctive procedural features of the treaty.[8]

2.2 Causation

While it is not within the scope of this chapter to elaborate on the question of causality in the context of shared responsibility in general terms,[9] some observations on causation in relation to the breach of an international obligation are required.

As is well known, the issue of causality is dealt with variously in international legal literature and case law because of the different traditions in civil and common law countries, and because of the different approaches in civil and criminal law. It is striking that the ARSIWA touch upon the issue only in Part Two (content of responsibility), namely in Article 31, with regard to the relation between the wrongful act and the damage. Yet this is only one aspect of causality – what German doctrine calls *tatausfüllende Kausalität*, i.e. the causality that appertains to the consequences of the wrong. This must not be confused with the first question in which causality arises, an issue that appertains to the structure of the internationally wrongful act itself – what German doctrine calls *tatbegründende Kausalität.* Special Rapporteur Ago approached this latter manifestation of causality in Article 23 when dealing with the breach of an obligation to prevent an event: 'There is no breach by a State of an international obligation requiring it to prevent a given event unless, following a lack of prevention on the part of the State, the event in question occurs.'[10] The ILC made the point even clearer, by reformulating Article 23 in the following terms: 'When the result required of a State by an international obligation is the prevention, by means of its own choice, of the occurrence of a given event, there is a breach of that obligation only if, by the conduct adopted, the State does not achieve that result.'[11] The

[8] As for the related issue of the existence of circumstances precluding the wrongfulness of the conduct of only one or some of the states involved, see Chapter 6 of this volume, H. P. Aust, 'Circumstances Precluding Wrongfulness', p. 169, at pp. 190–1.

[9] On this see the contribution by P. d'Argent in Chapter 7 of this volume, 'Reparation, Cessation, Assurances and Guarantees of Non-Repetition', p. 208, at pp. 222–3.

[10] See R. Ago, 'Seventh Report on State Responsibility', ILC *Yearbook* 1978/II(1), 37, para. 19.

[11] Ibid.

reason for the proviso 'by the conduct adopted' was precisely to make explicit the necessity of a causal link.

It was not by chance that Ago approached the question at that precise point of his reports. Ago opposed the doctrinal trend that denies the relevance of attribution at all, and tends to solve all questions of attribution of responsibility as a matter of causality.[12] However, Ago was well aware that the issue of causality is particularly relevant when the state is held responsible for a breach of a duty to prevent, i.e. in relation to somebody else's injurious conduct. The ILC's eventual decision to delete all Articles dealing with the varying structure of obligations could be a signal that the ILC thought that the issue of causality belongs to the primary norms.[13] The assumption of the ILC is neither necessarily right, nor, given the distinction mentioned between the two functions of causality, would it be sufficient in situations of shared responsibility.[14] It is unfortunate that the ILC did not pay more attention to the issue, with a general provision alongside that of the *tempus delicti commissi* of Article 14.[15] This certainly could have been relevant in situations where it would have to be determined whether states that failed to achieve a particular result would share a responsibility for that failure.

It is not easy to detect from a confused and opaque international case law a coherent picture of the issue of causation. If one were to adhere to the implicit idea of the ILC that the standard of causation would vary, depending on the structure of the primary obligation breached,[16] it could perhaps be possible to distinguish the concept as follows. The 'equivalent

[12] See I. Brownlie, *System of the Law of Nations: State Responsibility* (Oxford University Press, 1983), p. 36; R. Quadri, 'Cours général de droit international public' (1964) 113 RCADI 457.

[13] This was expressly stated by the Drafting Committee in 2000, with regard to Article 31: 'The need for a causal link was usually stated in primary rules'; see ILC *Yearbook* 2000/I, 388, para. 17.

[14] For a similar criticism see B. Stern, 'The Obligation to Make Reparation', in J. Crawford, A. Pellet, and S. Olleson (eds.), *The Law of International Responsibility* (Oxford University Press, 2010) p. 562, at p. 570.

[15] For a different view see L. Castellanos-Jankiewicz, 'Causation and International State Responsibility', SHARES Research Paper 07 (2012), ACIL 2012-07 (available at www.sharesproject.nl, last accessed on 20 March 2014), for whom the lack of a provision on causation is due to various structural reasons, such as the irrelevance of fault and damage in assessing international responsibility, the agency theory, and the functional distinctions between the domestic and international legal orders (at 26 ff.).

[16] As the ILC itself apparently believes, according to the Commentary to Article 31: 'the requirement of a causal link is not necessarily the same in relation to every breach of an international obligation'; see ARSIWA Commentary, n. 2, 93, para. 10.

causal theory' – according to which every subject is held responsible for the harmful event as soon as it has put into existence a causal factor, no matter how distant in time or how determinant for the occurrence – could prevail in all those cases in which the primary obligation has a *jus cogens* character. This could be required either by the idea of the best possible protection of the victims, or by the idea of sanctioning the wrongdoers.

Apart from this particular (and admittedly to some extent debatable) case, the adequate (or efficient) causal theory seems more appropriate for all cases of negative obligations, in which the wrongful conduct typically consists of a specific act. According to this causal theory, among the possible multifarious causal factors, the one that has created the danger which has primarily led to the violation of the obligation will be selected.

Finally, the so-called 'protective purpose causal theory' (in original German, *Schutzzwecktheorie*) – according to which a certain course of conduct might be held causally relevant only if it runs counter to the specific guarantee that a subject had assumed through the obligation – seems better situated for cases of violations of positive obligations.[17] For the latter type of obligations, without such a corrective concept, a broad concept of causality would lead to unwarranted results.

The case law of the European Court of Human Rights (ECtHR or Court) clearly shows the awareness of a need to make the test of causation dependent on the type of norm. As we know, with time, and increasingly so in the last two decades, the ECtHR has drawn a whole series of positive obligations from the Articles of the European Convention on Human Rights (ECHR),[18] the text of which was strictly couched in terms of negative obligations: for instance, with regard to Articles 2, 3, or 8. In a case dealing with Article 2 of the ECHR, the applicant lamented that Italy had breached the right to life of his son, because he was killed by a group of criminals who had been granted prison leave and had tried to get hold of

[17] According to Castellanos-Jankiewicz, 'Causation and International State Responsibility', n. 15, at 47; this would be the causal test adopted by the ILC itself, as it would result from the Commentary to Article 31, where the ILC uses the phrase 'sufficient causal link that is not too remote'. The inference is, in my opinion, far from sure. For Ago, and presumably for the ILC at the time, the *conditio sine qua non* was the causal theory prevailing at least for violations of the obligation to prevent; see 'Seventh Report on State Responsibility', n. 10. For Arangio-Ruiz the general causal test was that of 'normality' and 'predictability': see G. Arangio-Ruiz, 'Second Report on State Responsibility', ILC *Yearbook* 1989/II(1), at 13.

[18] Convention for the Protection of Human Rights and Fundamental Freedoms, Rome, 4 November 1950, in force 3 September 1953, 213 UNTS 221 (European Convention on Human Rights or ECHR).

his car after a bank robbery.[19] The respondent government objected that the causal link was 'tenuous' and that the death of the applicant's son was due to a series of 'fortuitous, unforeseen and unforeseeable incidents'. The Court agreed that the occurrence was 'the result of the chance sequence of events'. This, and similar cases in which the Court insisted on the predictability of the chain of events in the particular circumstances of the case, has led some authors to hold that in the case of positive obligations, the ECtHR adopts an *ex post* foreseeability test.[20] I would go further and maintain that the Court proceeds on a case-by-case basis, taking into account the purpose of the norm allegedly violated.

It is submitted that in cases in which the responsibility arises out of joint or concerted actions or omissions, for example where some of the actors are bound by a negative obligation and some are bound by a positive one, this concept of causality, varied according to the different kinds of obligations violated, would permit better fine-tuning of the allocation of the different responsibilities of different actors.

3. The specificity of *erga omnes* obligations

Together with the different obligations that the ILC had envisaged in the first reading, to which we shall turn our attention in the next three sections, one type of obligations that is relevant for the determination of shared responsibility is that of *erga omnes* obligations. In the framework of the objective element of responsibility, Ago had thought to differentiate between international wrongful acts and international crimes, a differentiation which found expression in Article 19 as adopted on first reading.[21] Despite its popularity in some international legal literature,[22] the ILC was well advised to eventually eliminate the concept of international crimes of states, because it would have drawn inopportune, and at any rate unfounded, analogies with the different concept of international criminal

[19] *Mastromatteo* v. *Italy*, App. No. 37703/97 (ECtHR, 24 October 2002), at 164.

[20] See B. Conforti, 'Exploring the Strasbourg Case-Law: Reflections on State Responsibility for the Breach of Positive Obligations', in M. Fitzmaurice and D. Sarooshi (eds.), *Issues of State Responsibility before International Judicial Institutions* (Oxford University Press, 2004) p. 129, at p. 135.

[21] See ILC *Yearbook* 1976/II (2), at 95.

[22] In the immense literature on the subject, see the seminal collection of essays in J. H. H. Weiler, A. Cassese, and M. Spinedi (eds.), *International Crimes of State: A Critical Analysis of the ILC's Draft Article 19 on State Responsibility* (Berlin, New York: De Gruyter, 1989).

responsibility of the individual.[23] To the contrary, the ILC introduced in the Articles the notion of obligations *erga omnes.*

This category of obligations seems especially suitable for developing a general concept of shared responsibility, if we consider what the Institut de Droit International said with regard to such obligations: 'certain obligations bind all subjects of international law for the purposes of maintaining the fundamental values of the international community'.[24] While there are many studies on the consequences of a violation of obligations *erga omnes*, spurred on by the codification of the concept in Article 48 of the ARSIWA, the implications of the structure of obligations *erga omnes* as primary norms are still unexplored.

The shift from an obligation *erga omnes* to its symmetrical notion of a right *erga omnes* would appear to be particularly relevant from the perspective of shared responsibility. To give an example, the focus would not so much be on the prohibition of genocide, but on the right not to be subjected to any such egregious breach. It is curious to see that the shift, or rather the upturning, was proposed by the International Court of Justice (Court or ICJ) in the *East Timor* case at the same moment that the Court dismissed its jurisdiction for lack of the necessary third party. In the words of the Court: 'Where this [i.e. the absence of a necessary third party] is so, the Court cannot act, even if the right in question is a right *erga omnes.*'[25]

Leaving aside the profound conceptual difficulties to which this shift of perspective leads with regard to the identification of the right holder,[26] it is clear that, by employing the concept of a 'right *erga omnes*', the Court seems to imply that all states, and even international organisations, have a common obligation. But if this is the case, the dictum of the Court, drawn

[23] See Chapter 9 of this volume, E. A. Wyler and L. A. Castellanos-Jankiewicz, 'Serious Breaches of Peremptory Norms', pp. 284, at p. 287–8, 293–7.

[24] Institut de Droit International, 2005 Krakow Session, 'Obligations *erga omnes* in international law', Preamble.

[25] *East Timor (Portugal* v. *Australia)*, Judgment, ICJ Reports 1995, 90, at 102, para. 29.

[26] Whereas in the *East Timor* case the right at hand was that of self-determination, so that it would not be difficult to identify the right holder in the people entitled to self-determination, in a different case of *erga omnes* obligation, such as the prohibition of systemic violations of fundamental human rights, it would be difficult to identify the right holder, as distinct from the 'beneficiaries' of the obligation, i.e. the individuals concerned. On this point see A. Gattini, 'Alcune osservazioni sulla tutela degli interessi individuali nei progetti di codificazione della Commissione del diritto internazionale sulla responsabilità internazionale e sulla protezione diplomatica', in M. Spinedi, A. Gianelli, and M. L. Alaimo (eds.), *Le Codificazione della responsabilità internazionale degli Stati alla prova dei fatti: problemi e spunti di riflessione* (Giuffrè: Milan, 2006), p. 431.

to its extreme consequences, brings us to the conclusion that such an obligation, by its very nature, may be simultaneously violated by all states, i.e. by some through positive acts, and by all the others through omissive conduct. In other words, any breach of an *erga omnes* obligation could give rise *ipso facto* to a case of shared responsibility. In the absence of some corrective devices – one of which could be the choice of a particular causality theory, such as the adequate causality or the protective purpose causality[27] – the application of the principles of shared responsibility would lead to unexpected, and possibly unwarranted, results.

Another way to restrict somehow an otherwise overflowing notion of a 'right *erga omnes*' is to make the consequences of the violation of the norm, and consequently the issue of a possible shared responsibility, dependent on the structure and content of the norm itself. Giorgio Gaja made the convincing point that the duty to ensure compliance by other states must not necessarily apply to each *erga omnes* obligation, but that the solution could be found in the primary norm, to the extent that the norm requires the state to prevent a breach by others. For this purpose he took the example of common Article 1 of the four Geneva Conventions of 1949, which imposes on states parties the duty to 'respect and ensure respect'.[28]

Be that as it may, with its dictum in the *East Timor* case, the ICJ earned the merit of having rebuffed the common wisdom, which sees in the obligations *erga omnes* nothing more than an appropriate set of tools (or faculties) at the disposal of the states, other than the injured one, desiring to react somehow to egregious breaches of international law.

The ICJ once again had the opportunity to disavow this comfortable mindset when dealing with the consequences of Israel's breach of the Palestinian right of self-determination in the *Wall* advisory opinion of 2004.[29] It will be recalled that the Court borrowed the language of

[27] See section 2.2 above.

[28] G. Gaja, 'Do States Have a Duty to Ensure Compliance with Obligations Erga Omnes by other States?', in M. Ragazzi (ed.), *International Responsibility Today: Essays in Memory of Oscar Schachter* (Leiden: Nijhoff, 2005), p. 31, at p. 35. Geneva Convention for the Amelioration of the Conditions of the Wounded and Sick in Armed Forces in the Field (75 UNTS 31); Geneva Convention for the Amelioration of the Condition of the Wounded, Sick and Shipwrecked Members of Armed Forces at Sea (75 UNTS 85); Geneva Convention relative to the Treatment of Prisoners of War (75 UNTS 135); Geneva Convention relative to the Protection of Civilian Persons in Time of War (75 UNTS 287).

[29] *Legal Consequences of the Construction of a Wall in the Occupied Palestinian Territory*, Advisory Opinion, ICJ Reports 2004, 135, at 199 ff., paras. 154–60 (*Wall* advisory opinion). On this point see P. d'Argent, 'Compliance, Cessation, Reparation and Restitution in the Wall Advisory Opinion', in P.-M. Dupuy, B. Fassbender, M. N. Shaw, and K. P. Sommermann

Article 41 of the ARSIWA in order to detail states' obligations arising from an *erga omnes* violation committed by a third state, showing, if need be, the degree of artificiality in the distinction made by the ILC between the consequences of a grave breach of a peremptory norm and the consequences of the violation of an *erga omnes* obligation.

It is interesting to note that Article 41 of the ARSIWA is formulated in terms which already hint at a shared responsibility. Article 41(1) imposes on all states the duty to 'cooperate' in order to bring the wrongful act to an end. Article 41(2) prohibits each state from recognising as lawful the situation created by the wrongful act.[30] Obviously we cannot infer too much from this Article in order to grasp the primary obligations of states in relation to an *erga omnes* obligation, because it only deals with secondary norms, even if they are couched in terms of primary rules. Yet the model of 'positive/negative' obligations could be used here too. As states have the positive obligation to cooperate in order to bring the wrongful act to an end, it could be argued that they have an analogous positive obligation to cooperate in order to avert such an act. As states have the negative obligation not to recognise as lawful the situation created by the wrongful act, it goes without saying that they thus have *a fortiori* the negative obligation to abstain from committing such an act.

The question arises whether such obligations are not simply shared by different actors, but are joint obligations, meaning that they must be performed together, with the consequence that a violation will necessarily give rise to a case of shared responsibility. While the answer with regard to the obligation of non-recognition is surely negative, given the clear text of Article 41(2), which speaks of the obligation of each state, the answer with regard to the obligation to cooperate in Article 41(1) could be more complex. The potentialities of this paragraph are multifaceted and not yet fully explored in the literature. It is not by chance that the ILC itself was keen to specify that the norm 'may reflect the progressive development of international law',[31] and nor is it by chance that the norm has been repeatedly conjured to give legal substance to the otherwise indistinct concept of 'responsibility to protect'.[32] However,

(eds.), *Völkerrecht als Wertordung/Common Values in International Law: Festschrift für Christian Tomuschat/Essays in Honour of Christian Tomuschat* (Kehl: Engel, 2006), p. 463.

30 See Wyler and Castellanos-Jankiewicz, 'Serious Breaches of Peremptory Norms', n. 23, pp. 306–7.

31 See ARSIWA Commentary, n. 2, 114, para. 3.

32 On this point see A. Gattini, 'Responsibility to Protect and the Responsibility of International Organizations', in P. Hilpold (ed.), *Die Schutz-Verantwortung. Ein Paradigmenwechsel in der Entwickling des internationalen Rechts?* (Leiden: Nijhoff, 2013), p. 169.

the attempt made by the ILC to transform secondary norms into primary 'solidarity' obligations has met with criticism. Martti Koskenniemi, in a very critical appraisal of the ILC's treatment of the consequences of violations of obligations *erga omnes*, observed that the crux of the matter lies in the fact that any attempt at solidarity in secondary norms is doomed to fail by the lack of formulation of an agreed language about the content of the primary rules, which is due to 'the absence of a socially meaningful agreement about the direction of international cooperation'.[33] This critique would seem relevant to the possibility of inferring from the obligation to cooperate a ground for the establishment of a shared responsibility.

4. Obligations of means and obligations of result

It will be recalled that alongside some less debatable distinctions – such as composite or punctual breaches – Ago introduced a distinction between obligations of means and obligations of result. Ago's distinction did not correspond to the usual idea derived from the tradition of civil law. In civil law, an obligation of means is an obligation to endeavour, without the guarantee of the result, whereas an obligation of result is an obligation to attain a certain outcome. For Ago, instead, an obligation of means was also an obligation of result, but it was distinguishable from the latter because it specified the means through which that certain result had to be attained.[34]

Despite having been accepted by the ILC on the first reading of the Articles, the peculiar understanding of obligations of means was generally not well received by governments and in international legal literature.[35] The profound reason for the choice, however, mainly escaped the attention of commentators. Starting from the consideration that

[33] See M. Koskenniemi, 'Solidarity Measures: State Responsibility as a New International Order?' (2001) 71 BYIL 337, at 355.

[34] In the language of Ago, they were breaches of an international obligation calling for a state to adopt a particular course of conduct: see R. Ago, 'Sixth Report on State Responsibility', ILC *Yearbook* 1977/II(1), 4.

[35] See J. Combacau, 'Obligations de résultat et obligations de comportement: quelques questions et pas de réponse', in P. Reuter, *Mélanges offerts à Paul Reuter: le droit international: unité et diversité* (Pedone: Paris, 1981), p. 181. Similarly, P.-M. Dupuy, 'Reviewing the Difficulties of Codification: On Ago's Classification of Obligations of Means and Obligations of Result in Relation to State Responsibility' (1999) 10 EJIL 371; C. Economides, 'Content of the Obligation: Obligations of Means and Obligations of Result', in J. Crawford, A. Pellet, and S. Olleson (eds.), *The Law of International Responsibility* (Oxford University Press, 2010), p. 371, at p. 375.

obligations of means are positive obligations, what Ago had tried to do was to strengthen those obligations, which would otherwise float in the relatively weak and opaque realm of 'due diligence'.

The fact that a more in-depth analysis of the content of such obligations would have drawn the ILC into the tangles of primary norms, together with the decision by the ILC to focus on the objective nature of the breach for all kinds of obligations, was probably one of the main reasons why the ILC eventually decided to dispose of most of the distinctions proposed by Ago. The distinction between obligations of means and obligations of result, however, finds a firm place in the case law of the ICJ,[36] and maintains a certain relevance for a situation of shared responsibility.

Taking the obligations of means, it is clear that if Ago was right, in order to hold a state responsible, it would be sufficient to demonstrate that it did not use the tools that the norm imposed upon it to use – for instance, the adoption of a domestic statute – regardless of the fact of whether other subjects could be held responsible for the harmful outcome as well, as a consequence of a breach of whatever other rule. In a way, the question of causality would be superseded by the mere ascertainment of the failure of the state.

In contrast, if we adhere to the traditional understanding of obligations of means, inevitably the question of the kind and degree of causality comes to the fore. So, for instance, we should ask to what extent a due diligence obligation imposed on the state would have been suitable to avoid the harmful event, and to what extent the conduct of other subjects might have been conducive to the harmful event. It is obvious that in this latter conceptual framework, the distinction between obligations of means and obligations of result would be of some relevance for situations of shared responsibility. As we shall see in the next section, the partial contradiction in which the ICJ entangled itself in the *Genocide* case of 2007, with regard to the causality of the breach on the part of Serbia of the obligation to prevent the occurrence of a genocide, was due to the

[36] See *Gabčíkovo-Nagymaros Project (Hungary/Slovakia)*, Judgment, ICJ Reports 1997, 7, at 77 (*Gabčíkovo-Nagymaros*), where the Court adds the mysterious category of 'obligations of performance' alongside obligations of conduct and obligations of result; *Request of Interpretation of the Judgment of 31 March 2004 in the Case concerning Avena and Other Mexican Nationals (Mexico* v. *United States of America)*, Judgment, ICJ Reports 2009, 3, where the parties agreed, and the Court confirmed, that the obligation descending from para. 153(9) of the dispositif of the previous *Avena* judgment (see n. 76), was an obligation of result, although the parties argued on the consequences of such qualification.

Court's explicit qualification of the obligation at stake as an obligation of means.[37]

5. The obligation to prevent

According to Article 23 of the ARSIWA, adopted on first reading, there would be a violation of an obligation to prevent the occurrence of a given event 'only if, by the conduct adopted, the state does not achieve that result'.[38]

We have already evoked this provision with regard to the causality issue, as made explicit by the phrase 'by the conduct adopted'. What is also remarkable is that Ago did not conceive the obligation to prevent as a due diligence obligation, because of his understanding that all obligations, including those of due diligence, are in a way obligations of result, even if, as in the present case, the purpose of the norm is to guarantee a 'negative' result. That is the reason why various attempts to distinguish between obligations of prevention in a strict sense and obligations of due diligence, especially for the purpose of the time and consequences of their breach, are not fully convincing.[39] Article 14(3) of the ARSIWA is unmistakable in saying that the breach of an obligation to prevent occurs when the event occurs. Undoubtedly this rule becomes unpalatable under certain circumstances. This is the reason why, in most criminal codes, the concept of crimes of abstract danger (*Gefährdungsdelikte*) has been introduced, in order to punish certain dangerous conduct, regardless of the occurrence of the damaging event. However, it is difficult to transpose the concept into international law, and it may be wondered to what extent one may artificially separate certain obligations by labelling them as obligations of due diligence, for the purpose of holding the state responsible, even in the event that the apprehended result did not occur.

The difficulty with precisely assessing the content of obligations of prevention is not limited to customary international law. The obligation to prevent, albeit with different formulations, is enshrined in almost all conventions dealing with human rights and environmental protection. If one takes the well-known tri-partition of obligations with regard to human rights – i.e. the obligation to respect, the obligation to protect,

[37] *Application of the Convention on the Prevention and Punishment of the Crime of Genocide (Bosnia and Herzegovina* v. *Serbia and Montenegro)*, Judgment, ICJ Reports 2007, 43, at p. 221, para. 430 (*Genocide* case).

[38] Article 23 ARSIWA, n. 2. [39] See, however, Crawford, *State Responsibility*, n. 3, at p. 227.

and the obligation to fulfil[40] – it is easy to see that the first is an obligation to abstain from doing, and as such is immediately ascertainable, and the third is obviously an obligation to do something, and as such in most instances is dependent on a set of variables, for instance the domestic implementation of the obligation. However, the second type of obligation is not so clear-cut, and leaves room for different interpretations.

In truth, there is uncertainty and disagreement on almost every aspect of an obligation to prevent, concerning the scope of the obligation *ratione personae* (5.1), *loci* (5.2), *materiae* (5.3), and *temporis* (5.4).

5.1 Ratione personae

While the different conceptual constructions of an obligation to prevent, to which we have briefly referred previously, might have little impact in the case of a single wrongdoer, they may assume relevance in those cases where two or more states are obliged to prevent a certain 'harmful outcome'.[41] To the question of how to determine the responsibility of each state, one should add the question of whether each state would be responsible for the same violation or for a different violation, according to the qualification of their conduct. Furthermore, in most cases the violation will be caused by a failure to act, and this aspect adds another layer of complexity, i.e. the difficulty of grasping the causality of an omission.

The ICJ had to deal with this issue in its first case, the *Corfu Channel*[42] case. Albania was found responsible for having permitted a use of its territory that had caused damage to another state. In particular, the Albanian government had omitted to inform foreign ships of the presence of mines (which had possibly been laid by Yugoslavia) in its territorial waters. The Court found that 'nothing was attempted'[43] by the Albanian authorities in order to prevent the damage. The case is frequently referred to as the leading case with regard to causality and shared responsibility,[44]

[40] See H. Shue, *Basic Rights: Subsistence, Affluence, and U.S. Foreign Policy*, 2nd edn (Princeton University Press, 1996), p. 51 ff.

[41] Nollkaemper and Jacobs, 'Shared Responsibility in International Law', n. 1, at p. 367; see also Nollkaemper, 'Introduction', n. 1, p. 1, at pp. 6–9.

[42] *Corfu Channel (United Kingdom of Great Britain and Northern Ireland* v. *Albania)*, Merits, ICJ Reports 1949, 4.

[43] Ibid., at 23.

[44] See d'Argent, 'Reparation, Cessation, Assurances and Guarantees of Non-Repetition', n. 9, at p. 226 et seq. See also P. A. Nollkaemper, 'Issues of Shared Responsibility before the International Court of Justice', in E. Rieter and H. de Waele (eds.), *Evolving*

although the Court did not make explicit its thoughts on either of the two issues. However, it was not by chance that the Court reached the conclusion of Albanian responsibility for the entire damage suffered by the United Kingdom, but only through the device of switching from a general obligation to prevent to the more specific and positive (but possibly at that time, non-existent *de lege lata*) obligation to inform. In this respect, the choice of a particular obligation as a basis for a finding of responsibility, and the construction of that obligation, may have clear relevance for questions of shared responsibility.

5.2 *Ratione loci*

The solution in the *Corfu Channel* case to concentrate all responsibility on Albania could still be justified, as this was the territorial state where the wrongful damage had occurred. However, the more difficult question arises as to whether obligations of prevention could or should have an extraterritorial application. We have already encountered this question, when dealing with the concept of obligations *erga omnes*. On the one hand, it is clear that when obligations of prevention would have an extraterritorial application, this would concern all states. On the other hand, it cannot be expected that all states have the same duties with regard to the fulfilment of the obligation, especially when it implies some positive action. While the responsibility of the territorial state will generally be easy to ascertain, the same cannot be said for the other states. Without entering into the general subject of extraterritorial application here, it must be said that the case law of the ICJ, as yet, is far from providing us with clear guidelines.

One could naively think that the first and most reliable guideline would be the text of the applicable convention, as Article 29 of the Vienna Convention on the Law of Treaties[45] suggests. The ICJ held in the *Wall* advisory opinion that the International Covenant on Civil and Political Rights (ICCPR)[46] was applicable in the occupied Palestinian Territories, following the interpretation given by the UN Human Rights

Principles of International Law: Studies in Honour of Karel C. Wellens (Leiden: Martinus Nijhoff, 2011), p. 199.

[45] Vienna Convention on the Law of Treaties, Vienna, 23 May 1969, in force 27 January 1980, 1155 UNTS 331, Article 29.

[46] International Covenant on Civil and Political Rights, New York, 16 December 1966, in force 23 March 1976, 999 UNTS 171 (ICCPR).

Committee of Article 2(1) of the ICCPR.[47] Albeit with some difficulty, the Court also affirmed the extraterritorial application of the International Covenant on Economic, Social and Cultural Rights (ICESCR),[48] relying partly on Article 14 of the ICESCR and partly on the opinion of the Committee on Economic, Social and Cultural Rights.[49] The Court did not specify whether it made the extraterritorial application of the Covenants dependent on the effective control exercised by Israel as the occupying power, but from the circumstances of the case, that element could be considered present *in re ipsa*. In the *Armed Activities in the Territory of the Congo* case of 2005, the Court considered that Uganda's responsibility was engaged also for 'any lack of vigilance in preventing violations of human rights and international humanitarian law by other actors present in the occupied territory', but there the Court specified in the same paragraph that Uganda was exercising 'effective control' over the territory.[50] While the mention of humanitarian law is obvious, since its extraterritorial application is self-evident, the mention of 'human rights law', especially if it lacks a precise definition, is less evident.

It was only with the *Genocide* judgment of 2007 that the Court seems to have set a watermark. The ICJ, after having denied that Serbia committed genocide or was complicit in the commission of genocide, found nevertheless that Serbia had violated Article 1 of the Genocide Convention,[51] because it had not prevented the commission of genocide abroad. In contrast to the previous cases we have mentioned, the Court did not bother to ground the extraterritorial application on the text of the Article, and nor did it make that application dependent on the proof of effective control by the state on the activities of the wrongdoers. It is obvious why both courses were precluded for the Court. The text of the Article (and for that matter, its *travaux préparatoires*) did not provide any clue on the matter, and nor was it possible for the ICJ to find on the facts a case of effective control for the purpose of an extraterritorial application of the Convention, after having discarded it for the purpose of attribution. Therefore, the Court took the awkward path of maintaining that an

[47] *Wall* advisory opinion, n. 29, para. 109.

[48] International Covenant on Economic, Social and Cultural Rights, New York, 16 December 1966, in force 3 January 1976, 999 UNTS 3 (ICESCR).

[49] *Wall* advisory opinion, n. 29, para. 112.

[50] *Armed Activities in the Territory of the Congo (Democratic Republic of the Congo* v. *Uganda*), Judgment, ICJ Reports 2005, 168, at 231, para. 179.

[51] Convention on the Prevention and Punishment of the Crime of Genocide, Paris, 9 December 1948, in force 12 January 1951, 78 UNTS 277 (Genocide Convention), Article 1.

extraterritorial application was dependent on the 'capacity of the state to effectively influence the actions of persons likely to commit'[52] the wrongful act – quite a vague concept, which has to be assessed *in concreto*. Interestingly, the ICJ specified that this capacity is dependent not only on factual criteria (geographical distance, political links with the tortfeasors), but also on legal criteria.[53]

However, it is very difficult, if not impossible, to understand what the Court meant by 'the particular legal position [of the state] vis-à-vis the situations and persons facing the danger, or the reality' of the wrongful act.[54] This sentence is a riddle. It is unclear how the particular legal relation between a state and the potential victims of a genocide should determine our opinion on the capacity of that same state to 'effectively influence' the actions of persons, who are by definition not its own organs. Even setting aside this logical non sequitur, one is still at odds with the exact meaning of the sentence itself. On one side of the spectrum, one could think that the state of nationality has a particular duty to prevent the commission of genocide of its citizens abroad, but then one may wonder why the Court did not spell this out more clearly. On the other side, one could also imagine that the ICJ wanted to hint at the general concept of humanitarian intervention, or responsibility to protect, but in that case the 'particular legal position' would equally affect all states, and consequently it would fail as a suitable criterion to distinguish the duty to prevent of any specific state. As a whole, the vagueness with which the Court left the concept of 'capacity to effectively influence' is regrettable. One may wonder whether the ICJ would not have fared better by saying that the concept of overall control, while not sufficient for purposes of attribution, could possibly have some value in the different context of an extraterritorial application of the duty to prevent.[55] A more stringent approach by the Court to the criterion of the 'capacity of the State to effectively influence' would have had the further advantage of better focusing on the issues of shared responsibility, which inevitably arise once an extraterritorial application of a particular obligation is admitted.

A year later, the Court had a fourth occasion to clarify its thoughts on the extraterritorial application of due diligence duties, in the case that Georgia brought against the Russian Federation on the *Application of the International Convention on the Elimination of All Forms of Racial*

[52] *Genocide* case, n. 37, at 221, para. 430. [53] Ibid. [54] Ibid.

[55] For further observations on this topic see A. Gattini, 'Breach of the Obligation to Prevent and Reparation Thereof in the ICJ's Genocide Judgment' (2007) 18(4) EJIL 695.

Discrimination (CERD).[56] At the provisional measures stage, the ICJ did not consider it necessary to fully develop its argument, and it contented itself to say that 'the provisions of CERD generally appear to apply, like other provisions of instruments of that nature, to the actions of a State party when it acts beyond its territory', adding that 'in particular, neither Article 2 nor Article 5 of CERD . . . contain a specific territorial limitation'.[57] Here the Court's language is so generic that an overenthusiastic scholar might be tempted to read this passage as an endorsement of a general extraterritorial application of all human rights treaties, regardless of their structure, content, or scope, and regardless of whether or not the state was exercising effective control outside its territory.[58]

If this is the case, one could detect, in a time span of just four years, a remarkable development of the ICJ's case law on the issue of the extraterritorial application of due diligence duties, with potentially far-reaching consequences for the possible determination of shared responsibility. This development is to some extent unfortunate, because the Court did not provide any hint of what the duties of due diligence should concretely resemble.

5.3 *Ratione materiae*

Herewith we reach the issue of the content of due diligence duties. Of course, one could put forward that the scope of the obligation *ratione materiae* is dependent on the primary obligation in question, and that therefore the task of determining such content for the purpose of secondary norms is both impossible and superfluous. Admittedly, the due diligence requisites may vary in different contexts and with regard to different sets of rules. Nevertheless, the structure of the obligation must present certain common features if one is not to leave the whole matter to the discretion of the judge.

[56] International Convention on the Elimination of All Forms of Racial Discrimination, New York, 21 December 1965, in force 4 January 1969, 660 UNTS 195 (CERD).

[57] *Application of the International Convention on the Elimination of All Forms of Racial Discrimination (Georgia* v. *Russian Federation)*, Preliminary Objections, Judgment, ICJ Reports 2011, 70, at paras. 108–9.

[58] For an attempt to reconcile 'the ICJ's somewhat expansive dictum' with a more orthodox methodological approach based on classic interpretative tools, see M. Milanović, *Extraterritorial Application of Human Rights Treaties* (Oxford University Press, 2011), p. 10, note 38.

In the *Armed Activities in the Territory of the Congo* case, one can understand that the Court did not find it necessary to specify the due diligence duties incumbent on the Ugandan forces 'in preventing violations of human rights and international humanitarian law by other actors present in the occupied territory',[59] since the circumstances of the case – a military occupation in a civil war-torn region – made clear what kind of conduct was meant, from ordinary police to straight military actions. On the contrary, in the *Genocide* case, the Court's insouciance in dealing more deeply with the due diligence duties on the part of Serbia is striking, and especially so given the fact that the violation of the duty to prevent was the only charge for which the ICJ ultimately found Serbia responsible. Admittedly, the Court had a relatively easy task because it found that, in any case, the Serbian authorities 'did nothing' in order to prevent the Srebrenica genocide. But the central question of what they should actually have done to prevent the genocide, which in the Court's words had not been previously planned and which took place over just two days, lingers. The awareness of the ICJ of the weakness of this part of its judgment transpires from the astounding decision by the Court not to grant any kind of reparation to Bosnia because the genocide 'would have happened anyway', even if Serbia had risen to its obligations.[60] By doing so, the Court seems to have mixed the *tatbegründende Kausalität* with the *tatausfüllende Kausalität*, and without noticing the apparent contradiction, it turned a case of concurrent causation into one of alternative exclusive causation.[61] But if this is the case, i.e. if the Serbian conduct was ultimately irrelevant not only for the damage caused by the genocide, but for the commission of the genocide itself, one could wonder what purpose the finding of the breach did fulfil.

With regard to the duty to prevent, Ago, in his seventh report to the ILC in 1978, had given the example of an attack on a foreign embassy committed by individuals 'in circumstances which make it possible to establish that it [i.e. the attack] would certainly have succeeded and achieved its ends even if the State could not be accused of any negligence'.[62] Ago rightly reached the conclusion that the lack of causality between the conduct of the state and the event implied a lack of any breach on the part of the state. It

[59] *Armed Activities in the Territory of the Congo*, n. 50, para. 179.

[60] *Genocide* case, n. 37, para. 430 and para. 462.

[61] See Gattini, 'Breach of the Obligation to Prevent and Reparation Thereof in the ICJ's Genocide Judgment', n. 55, at 695.

[62] See Ago, 'Seventh Report on State Responsibility', n. 10, at 35, para. 14.

seems, therefore, that the ICJ wanted to make a statement of principle, and to set a principle, to the extent that in case of an egregious breach of a *jus cogens* norm, such as genocide, a state has a specific duty to prevent, regardless of its territorial application and regardless of the causal relevance of its conduct. To say this in the words of the Court, 'the obligation on each contracting State to prevent genocide is both normative and compelling'.[63] This may sound impressive, but one might wonder what use such grandiose statements of principle can have in practice.

Indeed, until now, the Court has never specified what a duty of prevention actually implies.[64] It has been argued that the concept of due diligence was used by the ICJ in the advisory opinion on the *Legality of the Threat or Use of Nuclear Weapons* in 1996, where it spoke of the 'general obligation of States to ensure that activities within their jurisdiction and control respect the environment of other States or of areas beyond national control'.[65] If this is true, the Court showed its reluctance to give more flesh to the obligation by limiting itself one year later to a mere repetition of the same formula in the *Gabčíkovo-Nagymaros* case,[66] a bilateral dispute in which the issues at stake were much more concrete. The ICJ limited itself in that case to entrusting the care to the parties to envisage a joint operational regime – to ensure the achievement of the objectives of the bilateral 1977 treaty – through a common utilisation of shared water resources in a rational and equitable manner.[67] Some authors go even further in their criticism and argue that, by choosing to frame the general obligation of territorial states as a duty 'to respect', instead of one of 'not causing damage', the Court signaled its unwillingness to see the principle of due diligence as a rule of international law,

[63] *Genocide* case, n. 37, at 220, para. 427.

[64] For a better, and more in depth, analysis of the scope of an obligation of due diligence, see the Advisory Opinion rendered by the Seabed Dispute Chamber of the International Tribunal for the Law of the Sea (ITLOS) on *Responsibilities and Obligations of States Sponsoring Persons and Entities with Respect to Activities in the Area*, Case No. 17, 1 February 2011 (2011) 50 ILM 458. The task of the Seabed Dispute Chamber was made easier by the fact that Annex III, Article 4(4) of the 1982 UN Convention on the Law of the Sea (1833 UNTS 3) takes care to specify to some extent the content of the obligation of due diligence on the part of the sponsoring state. For an appraisal of the Advisory Opinion see R. Rayfuse, 'Differentiating the Common? The Responsibilities and Obligations of States Sponsoring Deep Seabed Mining Activities in the Area' (2011) 54 GYIL 459.

[65] *Legality of the Threat or Use of Nuclear Weapons*, Advisory Opinion, ICJ Reports 1996, at 241, para. 29.

[66] *Gabčíkovo-Nagymaros*, n. 36 at 41, para. 53.

[67] Ibid., at 78, para. 140.

but rather as a principle of equity.[68] Possibly aware of this risk, the ICJ endeavoured to better substantiate the due diligence principle in the more recent *Pulp Mills*[69] case. It specified that an obligation to act with due diligence 'entails not only the adopting of appropriate rules and measures, but also a certain level of vigilance in their enforcement and the exercise of administrative control applicable to public and private operators, such as the monitoring of activities undertaken by such operators'.[70] Once again, the Court could have avoided the task of probing the effectiveness of the definition by the evaluation of concrete facts and circumstances, because it found that the two parties had undertaken such a duty only by acting through the Uruguay River Commission, which had been established by the two parties in 1975. The absence of any indication of what a general duty of prevention actually implies is bound to complicate the determination of shared responsibility in situations where two or more states fail to prevent.

5.4 *Ratione temporis*

With regard to the applicability *ratione temporis* of the duty to prevent, the ILC has provided only partial answers. Article 14(3) of the ARSIWA states, in unmistakable terms, that 'the breach of an international obligation requiring a State to prevent a given event occurs when the event occurs'. But even that apparently unmistakable statement is put in doubt by those who observe that to the extent that the obligation to prevent implies positive obligations, or can be split into separate due diligence obligations, its violation could be judged independently of the actual circumstance of the occurrence of the event. Not surprisingly, this theory is linked to the further observation that the moment *a quo* of the violation of the obligation to prevent should not be the moment when the event occurs, but should also depend on the importance of the primary obligation breached.[71] A suitable example is that of the obligation to prevent environmental damage,

[68] T. Koivurova, 'What Is the Principle of Due Diligence?', in J. Petman and J. Klabbers (eds.), *Nordic Cosmopolitanism: Essays in International Law for Martti Koskenniemi* (Leiden: Martinus Nijhoff 2003), p. 341, at p. 346.

[69] *Pulp Mills on the River Uruguay (Argentina v. Uruguay)*, Judgment, ICJ Reports 2010, 14 (*Pulp Mills*).

[70] Ibid., at 79, para. 197.

[71] See P.-M. Dupuy, 'Reviewing the Difficulties of Codification: On Ago's Classification of Obligations of Means and Obligations of Result in Relation to State Responsibility' (1999) 10(2) EJIL 366, at 384.

which, being linked to the precautionary principle,[72] can be detailed into more specific obligations, each of which can be autonomously assessed in its own right. Examples are the obligation to proceed to an environmental impact assessment, or the obligation to provide information on the risks attached to a certain dangerous activity.

It seems that the potentialities of the obligation to prevent in terms of positive obligations have escaped the attention of both the ILC and the ICJ. The narrow understanding of the obligation to prevent was clear in Ago's seventh report, in which he said that:

> where international law places an obligation on a State to prevent a certain type of event, observance of that obligation can be called in question and the responsibility of the State affirmed only if one of the events which it was the purpose of international law to prevent actually occurs.[73]

He compared the breach of the obligation to prevent to a chemical reaction, where the event is a catalysing agent, which, when put into contact with a certain substance (the state's conduct), provokes a certain reaction (the breach of the obligation).

Transposed to the topic of shared responsibility, all the preceding observations concerning the scope of application of an obligation to prevent leave the impression of too much latitude in which a court could move in charging a state for the breach of an obligation of prevention at a certain moment. The solution would be to envisage more specific and positive obligations of conduct (in Ago's meaning), but states obviously resist such a constraining option. The alternative would be to detect such obligations from general obligations of prevention, but this path entails a certain degree of arbitrariness. Further studies in this respect are needed in order to provide guidance for the case law.

6. Breach consisting of a composite act

The only category of breaches that the ILC eventually retained in a specific Article is the breach consisting of a composite act (Article 15). It is therefore interesting to analyse what relevance this type of breach could have for the issue of shared responsibility.

[72] For such a link see ITLOS's Order of 27 August 1999 in the *Southern Bluefin Tuna* cases (*New Zealand* v. *Japan*, *Australia* v. *Japan*), ITLOS Reports 1999, 274, at para. 77.

[73] Ago, 'Seventh Report on State Responsibility', n. 10, at 35, para. 14.

Ago had presented in his seventh report a single Article (Draft Article 24) on the *tempus delicti commissi*, distinguishing five different cases. As in so many instances, the ILC followed Ago's concept and terminology, but disaggregated the list into three Articles. The first Article dealt with the moment and duration of the breach of an obligation by an act of a state not extending in time; the second dealt with the moment and duration of the breach of an obligation by an act of a state extending in time; and the third dealt with the moment and duration of the breach of an international obligation to prevent a given event. In the second reading, due to the overarching goal to condense the text, the five different kinds of breaches could have been brought back under a single heading, following Ago's proposal. Curiously enough, the ILC decided to separate the issue of the extension in time of the breach of an international obligation (now Article 14 of the ARSIWA) from the issue of a composite wrongful act.

Contrary to Ago, and despite appearances, the main thrust of the ILC's Commentary is not so much on the moment and duration of the violation, but on the nature of a particular kind of obligation. As the ILC puts it, there are cases in which 'the obligation itself is defined in terms of the cumulative character of the conduct, i.e. where the cumulative conduct constitutes the essence of the wrongful act'.[74] The underlying thought of the ILC is that the violation of particular obligations, such as the prohibition of apartheid or genocide, implies the adoption of a systematic policy or practice.

The utility of having singled out this kind of violation can be doubted. The ILC points to the ECtHR's case law, according to which the rule of the exhaustion of local remedies does not apply when the state's wrongful act concerns 'a practice as such' and not just single occurrences.[75] However, the relevance of such case law is dubious.[76] The ILC evokes another interesting issue with regard to proof,[77] but again it is not clear whether and how far this issue is linked as such to that of a composite

[74] ARSIWA Commentary, n. 2, 63, para. 4.

[75] *Ireland* v. *the United Kingdom*, App. No. 5310/71 (ECtHR, 18 January 1978), at p. 64, para. 159.

[76] It will be recalled that the ICJ in the *Avena* case in 2004 rejected a similar preliminary objection by the United States with the different argument that, being a mixed claim, the aspect of Mexico's own right was predominant in its complaint: see *Avena and Other Mexican Nationals (Mexico* v. *United States of America)*, Judgment, ICJ Reports 2004, 12, at 36, para. 40.

[77] ARSIWA Commentary, n. 2, 63, para. 6. The argument runs that in order to prove a composite act, it will often be required to produce evidence of a systemic pattern.

wrongful act. It may well be that in order to prove a particular wrongful act, such as discrimination, evidence of a pattern of acts or a practice is required, but this does not change the fact that even a single act of discrimination may constitute an internationally wrongful act.

Also with regard to the topic of shared responsibility, it does not seem that the notion of a composite wrongful act could raise particular problems in general terms. The question of shared responsibility may arise when an act or omission, which taken together with the other acts or omissions is sufficient to constitute the wrongful act, is attributable to a state different from that state, or those states, to which the previous acts or omissions are attributable. Indeed, such a scenario could even be considered the prototype of shared responsibility.

However, a delicate question arises in all those cases in which the assessment of an act or omission, attributed to a certain state, and per se lawful, would change on account of the fact of having been added up with other acts or omissions that are attributable to other states. In his seventh report, Ago expressly considered the possibility that in the sequence of courses of conduct making up the composite wrong, a sequence of actions 'taken separately, may be lawful or unlawful'.[78] As an example, Ago gave the scenario of the rejection of an application for employment by a worker of a particular nationality or race, which in his view 'may not, as such, qualify as a breach of an international obligation',[79] whereas the rejection of a series of applications by persons of the same category may constitute a 'discriminatory practice' prohibited by a treaty.[80] As we have argued above, Ago's view on the specific point of discrimination could be challenged. It is telling that the ILC, in its final Commentary to Article 15, distanced itself from Ago's interpretation by giving the same example, albeit with the specification that 'an individual act of racial discrimination by a state is internationally wrongful'.[81]

Indeed, there is no hint in the ILC Commentary that the single act or omission forming the composite wrongful act could be per se lawful. The ILC's neglect of this specific issue could be explained by the fact that at that point its attention was focused on the issue of the *tempus delicti commissi* and that it possibly took for granted that the entire sequence of conduct would be attributable to a single state. However, the picture drastically changes in the event of different courses of conduct by different states.

[78] Ago, 'Seventh Report on State Responsibility', n. 10, at 47, para. 38.
[79] Ago, 'Fifth Report on State Responsibility', ILC *Yearbook* 1976/II(1), 23, para. 65.
[80] Ibid. [81] ARSIWA Commentary, n. 2, 63, para. 6.

Outside the context of attribution of responsibility, i.e. outside the situations dealt with in Articles 16 to 18 of the ARSIWA,[82] it is inconceivable that, through the concept of a composite act, a state could be made responsible only for the fact that an act or omission which is attributable to it, and which is per se perfectly lawful, is in a way causally linked to other wrongful acts or omissions attributable to other states.

Surely, what could happen is that a single wrongful act – such as an act of torture – could be seen as a part of a pattern, partly attributable to other states, and therefore constituting a grave breach of a peremptory norm of international law, triggering the consequences of Article 41 of the ARSIWA. But also in this case, we could still speak, at least in a somewhat extended meaning, of 'the same wrongful act'. The reason is that we are dealing neither with an act that would per se be lawful but for the qualification it assumes in relation to the previous acts by other subjects, nor with a course of conduct that would constitute per se a different wrong. An even better example is that of genocide. It may well be the case that the genocide is composed of different acts attributed to different states, but it is also clear that each course of conduct constitutes a wrongful act per se. The ILC might be right in saying that 'genocide is different in kind from individual acts even of ethnically or racially motivated killing',[83] but it remains that in order to be qualified as constituting part of a genocide, each single act must be committed with the relevant intent, given the requirement of *dolus specialis* in the definition of genocide.

It is noticeable that while, on the one hand, the ILC retained and even highlighted the notion of a composite wrongful act, it deleted from the Articles the germane notion of a complex wrongful act, i.e. a breach consisting of a succession of actions or omissions by the same or different organs of the state. The reasons for the deletion are clear. Regardless of the multiple participation by different organs, what matters is whether the breach actually occurred, and whether it was immediate or continuous.

7. Shared responsibility of states and international organisations

After having considered the different structure of international obligations in general terms and the possible impact of their violation in a context of shared responsibility, it is appropriate to broaden the view and

82 See Fry, 'Attribution of Responsibility', n. 4.
83 ARSIWA Commentary, n. 2, 63, para. 4.

to address particular questions relating to the breach of an international obligation that may apply in the relationship between states and international organisations.

Compared to the ARSIWA, the attention the ILC gave to the aspect of shared responsibility in the Articles on the Responsibility of International Organizations (ARIO)[84] is remarkable. Besides Part Two of the ARIO, on the responsibility of an international organisation in connection with an act of the state, and Part Five of the ARIO (Articles 58 to 63), dealing with the responsibility of a state in connection with the conduct of an international organisation, there are some other Articles whose Commentary shows that the ILC was particularly aware of issues of shared responsibility. In the Commentary to Article 3 of the ARIO, whose title reads 'International responsibility of an international organization for its internationally wrongful acts', the ILC makes the following comment:

> The fact that an international organization is responsible for an internationally wrongful act does not exclude the existence of parallel responsibility of other subjects of international law in the same set of circumstances. For instance, an international organization may have cooperated with a State in the breach of an obligation imposed on both. Another example may be that of conduct which is simultaneously attributed to an international organization and a State and which entails the international responsibility of both the organization and the State.[85]

Under Article 48 of the ARIO, entitled 'Responsibility of an international organization and one or more States or international organizations', the ILC – in contrast to what it had said in relation to the parallel Article 47 of the ARSIWA – considered joint responsibility to be the general rule, applicable in all cases of Part Two and Part Five. The ILC added to this the cases of European Union mixed agreements.[86] A possible

[84] Articles on the Responsibility of International Organizations, ILC Report on the work of its sixty-third session, UNGAOR 66th Sess., Supp. No. 10, UN Doc. A/66/10 (2011) (ARIO).

[85] Commentary to the Articles on the Responsibility of International Organizations, ILC Report on the work of its sixty-third session, UNGAOR 66th Sess., Supp. No. 10, UN Doc. A/66/10 (2011) (ARIO Commentary), p. 81, para. 6.

[86] The ILC forgot to add the most obvious example of space law (Article VI of the Treaty on Principles Governing the Activities of States in the Exploration and Use of Outer Space, including the Moon and Other Celestial Bodies, London, Moscow, and Washington DC, 27 January 1967, in force 10 October 1967, 610 UNTS 205 (Outer Space Treaty); and Article VII of the Convention on International Liability for Damage Caused by Space Objects, London, Moscow, and Washington DC, 29 March 1972, in force 1 September 1972, 961 UNTS 187 (Liability Convention), where states are jointly and severally

explanation for this remarkable switch of perspective could be that, as distinct from the ARSIWA, joint responsibility as a general rule is easier to affirm when international organisations are involved. This is so because in this context the application of joint responsibility does not touch upon the sensitive issue of sovereignty, i.e. making a state responsible for the acts or omissions of another, which is the major stumbling block for affirming joint responsibility as a general rule in all cases of shared state responsibility.

While most of the observations we have made with regard to the ARSIWA could also be repeated in the context of the ARIO, for our purposes the most interesting and innovative part of the ARIO is, of course, Part Five. The ILC envisaged various possibilities for holding a state responsible in connection with the wrongful act of an international organisation. However, despite the efforts made by the Special Rapporteur's reports and the final Commentaries, some of the situations envisaged – which are probably better assessed as cases in which the responsibility arises out of joint or concerted actions or omissions rather than cases in which there is no concerted action or omission – are far from clear when they are analysed through the lens of the breach of an international obligation.

Articles 58 and 59 of the ARIO, which deal respectively with the responsibility of a state for having aided or assisted an international organisation in the commission of a wrongful act, or having directed and controlled an organisation in the commission of a wrongful act, specify in their common paragraph 2 that '[a]n act by a State member of an international organization done in accordance with the rules of the organization does not as such engage the international responsibility of that State under the terms of this article.' Significantly, the paragraph was added in the second reading in 2011, as a consequence of the critical observations of several governments. The effect of the paragraph is to exclude in general terms the possibility of shared responsibility

responsible with international organisations operating in space. For a practical application see the Agreement between the French Government and the European Space Agency (ESA) with respect to the Centre Spatial Guyanais of 1992, renewed in 2009. Under the Agreement, the ESA assumes full liability and safeguards France from any claims for damage resulting from the launches operated for ESA programmes. France legally protects the ESA and its member states against claims arising from commercial launch activities undertaken by Arianespace, leading to third-party liability claims against France. In the latter event, Arianespace is required to reimburse the French government up to a maximum of EUR 61 million per accident. See J. Hermida, 'Risk Management in Arianespace Space Launch Agreement' (2000) 25 Ann Air & Sp L 143.

whenever member states abide by the rules of the organisation, because of the lack of any breach. In the Commentary to Article 58, the ILC somewhat grudgingly acknowledged this limitation, by adding that the insertion of the words 'as such' in paragraph 2 'does not imply that the State would then be free to simply ignore its international obligations. These obligations may well encompass the conduct of a State when it acts within an international organization.'[87] If this were the case, the ILC concludes, the state would then incur responsibility under the ARSIWA. This would open up the possibility of shared responsibility.

At first glance this observation could appear convincing, but with a closer look it is question-begging, and it may be doubted what added value the insertion of the words 'as such' provides. Assuming that the international obligation of the state is a positive one – as, for instance, in a 'Responsibility to Protect' context – and further assuming that the UN Security Council is asked to take action in order to impede or stop the violation of an *erga omnes* obligation – the voting behaviour of the Security Council's members (especially the permanent ones), which would eventually hinder the UN from taking action, is not necessarily a wrongful act. It simply means that a particular state does not wish that action to be taken by the international organisation, leaving open the question through which other means it intends to discharge its obligation to cooperate in order to stop the serious breach. It will be recalled that the ILC, in its Commentary to Article 41 of the ARSIWA, recommended states to cooperate in the framework of the UN to put an end to a grave breach of a peremptory norm, but expressly did not exclude unilateral actions.

The legal assessment of a situation in which the international obligation of the state was a negative one would be different, because its voting behaviour and its co-determining of the commission of the wrongful act by the international organisation would then be wrongful itself. The example made by the chairman of the Drafting Committee in June

[87] ARIO Commentary, n. 85, 91, para. 5. It is interesting to note that the ILC did not take notice of the ECtHR's *Behrami* judgment, in which the ECtHR had clearly stated that the voting behaviour of permanent member states within the Security Council is not subject to control by the Court. See *Agim Behrami and Bekir Behrami* v. *France*, App. No. 71412/01 (ECtHR, 2 May 2007); and *Saramati* v. *France, Germany and Norway*, App. No. 78166/01 (ECtHR, 2 May 2007), at para. 149: 'This reasoning equally applies to voluntary acts of the respondent States such as the vote of a permanent member of the UNSC in favour of the relevant Chapter VII Resolution and the contribution of troops to the security mission: such acts may not have amounted to obligations flowing from membership of the UN but they remained crucial to the effective fulfillment by the UNSC of its Chapter VII mandate and, consequently, by the UN of its imperative peace and security aim.'

2011 with regard to the scope of the new common paragraph 2 of Articles 58 and 59 of the ARIO was that of a state voting in favour of a decision by the Security Council that would lead to genocide. But then, if this were the case, one could ask what purpose the subsequent Article 61 of the ARIO, under the heading 'Circumvention of international obligations of a State member of an international organization', would have, since it seems more appropriate to capture exactly this kind of situation. Not surprisingly, the misleading example was finally deleted in the Commentary to Articles 58 and 59, so one still wonders what example the ILC had in mind when adding in paragraph 2 the proviso 'as such'.

Coming to Article 61 of the ARIO, this norm presents several problems as well, when read in the context of shared responsibility. As the ILC clarified, the wrongful act of the international organisation must have been 'caused'[88] by the conduct of the member state, but the member state's responsibility will not arise when the wrongful act of the international organisation has to be regarded as 'the unintended result' of the member state's behaviour, i.e. in the absence of *dolus*.[89] This specification indeed seems necessary; otherwise, one would end up always holding member states responsible when an international organisation committed a wrongful act. The only way to impede the international organisation from committing such a wrongful act would be for each member state to reserve a right of veto with regard to any issue, but this solution would be paradoxical and would go against the purpose of international cooperation, which lies at the core of the very existence of international organisations.[90] On the other hand, it is interesting to note that the ILC refused to include in Article 61 of the ARIO a paragraph along the lines of paragraph 2 that

[88] ARIO Commentary, n. 85, at 95, para. 7.

[89] ARIO Commentary, n. 85, at 93, para. 2. The specification of the necessity of *dolus* is very interesting, because it introduces, or one might say 'reintroduces', the element of fault in the ascertainment of international responsibility. This is being done in a different context from that in which the issue of fault has been traditionally confined: that is, the assessment of due diligence in the primary obligations to prevent.

[90] See however O. de Schutter, 'Human Rights and the Rise of International Organisations: The Logic of Sliding Scales in the Law of International Responsibility', in J. Wouters, E. Brems, S. Smis, and P. Schmitt (eds.), *Accountability for Human Rights Violations by International Organisations* (Antwerpen: Intersentia, 2010), p. 51, at p. 84, who criticises Article 61 ARIO for being too lenient towards member states, since 'the liability of the State will thus be limited whether or not the State has reserved the right to veto the decision within the internal decision-making procedures of the organization, or to block the implementation of the decision'.

was added to Articles 58 and 59, since this would have robbed Article 61 of any practical meaning.

All in all, it seems that the entire Part Five of the ARIO – with the exception of Article 62, which codifies the well-established rule of the subsidiary responsibility of member states for wrongful acts of an international organisation in some particular and well-defined instances – is more an abstract exercise *de lege ferenda* than *de lege lata*, which is still in need of many clarifications.

8. Shared responsibility of states and private actors

Another important and practical aspect of our study is the extent to which one or more states could be held responsible for the behaviour of individuals. Traditionally the issue was studied by focusing on attribution, given the prevailing view of the absence of personality under international law of individuals. In the present context, however, the investigation will focus on the objective element, i.e. the breach of an obligation.

The fact that in recent decades international law has developed concepts and rules relating to the international criminal responsibility of individuals with regard to certain crimes – where the quality of the author as state organ is irrelevant, such as in the case of genocide or other crimes against humanity – has not yet induced international law doctrine to conceive a general theoretical framework in which to put into perspective the two different kinds of responsibility. Only a few rules of thumb are readily available.[91] The first is that were an international criminal tribunal to find an individual state organ responsible for a crime, then its state would implicitly be held responsible as well, even if that finding were outside the competence of the court or tribunal. However, the reverse would not be true; the finding of responsibility of a state by an international court does not imply the criminal responsibility of any particular individual state organ.

The main reason why it is difficult to envisage a general framework of shared responsibility between states and individuals is the uncertain state of the law on the issue of direct accountability of individuals for violations of customary international law, besides the already-mentioned and well-circumscribed instances of individual criminal responsibility. As is well known, an intense debate is being fought on the issue of civil responsibility

[91] Groundbreaking: P. A. Nollkaemper, 'Concurrence between Individual Responsibility and State Responsibility in International Law' (2003) 52 ICLQ 615.

of corporations under international law for violations of human rights, either directly or in aiding and abetting such violations by host states. Official statements are quite generically ambiguous on the point,[92] doctrinal views diverge widely, and national case law is scant. As was predicted, the United States Supreme Court decision in *Kiobel* v. *Royal Dutch Shell* did not help in clarifying matters, since the Court opted to decide the case on the different issue of the jurisdictional scope of the Alien Tort Statute.[93]

[92] The circuitous and 'gluey' developments of the concept can be nicely traced in the United Nations debates. In the 1999 UN Global Compact, the principles were assumed on a purely voluntary basis; in 2003, the UN Sub-Commission for the Promotion and Protection of Human Rights concocted a breakthrough by adopting, without having been requested, a set of Draft Norms on the 'Responsibilities of Transnational Corporations and Other Business Enterprises with regard to Human Rights', Principle 1 of which reads: 'States have the primary responsibility to promote, secure the fulfillment of, respect, ensure respect of and protect human rights recognized in international as well as national law, including ensuring that transnational corporations and other business enterprises respect human rights. Within their respective spheres of activity and influence, transnational corporations and other business enterprises have the obligation to promote, secure the fulfillment of, respect, ensure respect of and protect human rights recognized in international as well as national law, including the rights and interests of indigenous peoples and other vulnerable groups' (Res. 16/003). The attempt was stopped and rebuffed by the Economic and Social Council (ECOSOC), which confirmed Res. 116/2004 of the UN Commission on Human Rights to the effect that 'Document E/CN.4/Sub.2/2003/12/Rev.2 had not been requested by the Commission and, as a draft proposal, had no legal standing, and that the Sub-Commission should not perform any monitoring function in that regard' (ECOSOC, Res. 279/2004). Finally, the UN Human Rights Council endorsed the Guiding Principles issued by Special Representative Ruggie (A/HRC/RES17/4) in 2011. In Point 3 of the Resolution, the Council '*Commends* the Special Representative for developing and raising awareness about the Framework based on three overarching principles of the duty of the State to protect against human rights abuses by, or involving, transnational corporations and other business enterprises, the corporate responsibility to respect all human rights, and the need for access to effective remedies, including through appropriate judicial or non-judicial mechanisms.' In the Commentary to Principle 11 of the Foundational Principles on the corporate responsibility to respect human rights, Special Rapporteur Ruggie had shrewdly escaped the basic question of the applicability of international law by the following terms: 'The responsibility to respect human rights is a global standard of expected conduct for all business enterprises wherever they operate. It exists independently of States' abilities and/or willingness to fulfill their own human rights obligations, and does not diminish those obligations. And it exists over and above compliance with national laws and regulations protecting human rights.'

[93] See *Kiobel* v. *Royal Dutch Petroleum et al.*, 621 F 3d 111 (S. Ct. 2013). Strongly in favour of upholding universal civil jurisdiction, see J. von Bernstorff, M. Jacob and J. Dingfelder Stone, 'The Alien Tort Statute before the US Supreme Court in the *Kiobel* Case: Does International Law Prohibit US Courts to Exercise Extraterritorial Civil Jurisdiction over Human Rights Abuses Committed Outside of the US?' (2012) 72 ZaöRV 579.

Leaving aside difficult questions relating to attribution, causality, and complicity – which are discussed in other chapters of this volume – it is clear, however, that most issues of shared responsibility between states and individuals can only arise if one concedes that also individuals, and not only states or international organisations, can be held responsible for breaches of customary international law. The amici curiae of the petitioners in the *Kiobel* case maintained that if the defendant were right, even the celebrated *Filartiga* v. *Pena Irala* case should have been rejected by the Court of Appeals of the 2nd Circuit in 1980.[94] This observation unwittingly strikes at the core of matter. Indeed, from a strict viewpoint of positive international law prevailing at that time, that case could easily have been dismissed. This overly formalistic view, however, would fail to grasp the dynamic dimension of international law creation. Just four years after *Filartiga*, the UN Convention against Torture (CAT)[95] was adopted by the General Assembly, where under Article 14 each state pledges itself to ensure civil redress for the victim against the individual torturer. The facts that it took only two and a half years for the CAT to come into force, and that it has by now been ratified by 153 states all over the world, are evidence that the idea underlying the Convention was already shared by a vast number of states at the time of *Filartiga*. The same cannot be said with regard to the responsibility of corporations for whatever violation of human rights and/or environmental protection rules. In this regard, the position of states is quite adamantly negative, and the creative role of some domestic courts simply cannot substitute the lack of state practice and *opinio juris*.

On a deeper level of analysis, a major stumbling block to envisaging a general framework of where to place the shared responsibility of states and individuals, especially juristic persons, is the difficulty in sensing the respective content of the obligations and the limits of the two kinds of responsibility. The ILC can undoubtedly be criticised for not having taken thus far any opportunity to specify the possible interactions of state and individual responsibility. The reference here goes not so much to the saving clause of Article 56 of the ARSIWA, but to the codification of the prevention of transboundary harm from hazardous activities (Draft Principles of 2001),[96] and the subsequent codification on the

[94] *Filartiga* v. *Pena Irala*, 630 F 2d 876 (2d Cir. 1980).

[95] Convention Against Torture and Other Cruel, Inhuman or Degrading Treatment or Punishment, New York, 10 December 1984, in force 26 June 1987, 1465 UNTS 85 (CAT).

[96] Draft Articles on Prevention of Transboundary Harm from Hazardous Activities, ILC *Yearbook* 2001/II(2).

allocation of loss in the case of transboundary harm arising out of hazardous activities (Draft Principles of 2006).[97] With regard to the latter, Article 4 on 'Prompt and adequate compensation' specifies in paragraph 2 that the measures of compensation foreseen by the state of origin 'should include the imposition of liability on the operator or, where appropriate, other person or entity. Such liability should not require proof of fault.' In the words of the ILC, 'state of origin' 'means the State in the territory or otherwise under jurisdiction or control of which the hazardous activity is carried out',[98] whereas the definition of 'operator' 'is based on a factual determination as to who has use, control, and direction of the object at the relevant time'.[99] In the Commentary to the Article the ILC limits itself to observing that the imposition of the primary liability on the operator, and not on the state of origin, 'is widely accepted in international treaty regimes and in national law and practice'.[100] This is surely true, but nowhere in the Draft Principles, or in the Commentaries thereto, is there an attempt to specify whether the operator's liability finds its origin in international or in domestic law, or to link the two kinds of liability/responsibility in whatsoever form. We only find a passing remark under the introductory general comment to the purpose that 'the attachment of primary liability on the operator . . . does not in any way absolve the State from discharging its own duties of prevention under international law'.[101]

In the defence of the ILC, it is true that apart from a general and, to some extent, dubious principle of 'polluter pays', there is very little, if any, guidance in customary international law with regard to responsibility for environmental damage. Moreover, and with the partial exception of compensation for nuclear damage, even under treaty law states are very careful not to get entangled in any liability scheme from which the step towards responsibility could be more easily made.[102]

[97] ILC Report on the work of its fifty-eighth session, UN Doc. A/61/10 (2006), 106 et seq.

[98] Ibid., Commentary Article 4, at 134. [99] Ibid., at 139. [100] Ibid., at 155.

[101] Ibid., at 113.

[102] For instance, in all compensation funds for oil pollution damage envisaged by the International Maritime Organization from 1971 to 2003, the liable parties have been extended from ship owners to oil receivers, but not further to flag states or importing states. Even the compensation scheme for nuclear damage leaves much to be desired. As is well known, the limitation of liability of the 1960 Organisation for Economic Co-operation and Development (OECD) Paris Convention was soon superseded by the 1963 Brussels Convention, further revised in 1982, providing for a three-tiered compensation level with the contribution of the states. To the contrary, the International Atomic Energy Agency

That does not mean, of course, that a partition of responsibility cannot be found under domestic legislation. To the extent that several domestic statutes present similar features in the handling of problems and solutions, there would be some room to re-enter the realm of international law through the device of general principles of law. An interesting example of the interplay between domestic and international law with regard to the possibilities of a shared responsibility between states and individuals could be given by space law. Article VI of the Outer Space Treaty provides in its first part that:

> States parties to the Treaty shall bear international responsibility for national activities in outer space, including the Moon and other celestial bodies, whether such activities are carried on by governmental agencies or by non-governmental entities, and for assuring that national activities are carried out in conformity with the provisions set forth in the present Treaty.

The Article is interesting because of two different features.[103] The first is that it imposes direct responsibility upon the state for everything that is done by non-governmental entities. The second is that the Article specifically prescribes the obligations of the state in relation to the activities of such non-governmental entities, namely 'authorization and continuing supervision'. This being the state of international law on the matter, nothing excludes the fact that national legislation may envisage different solutions. A survey of major domestic legislation on space activities shows that appropriate insurance or other financial guarantees by the private operators is a common requirement in order to be granted a licence, and

system is still bound by the 1963 Vienna Convention with its liability limit of USD 5 million per accident, because the 1997 Convention on supplementary compensation, which would bring the liability regimes on a par with the OECD, involving the liability of host states, has not yet entered into force, having up to this date been ratified by only four states.

[103] B. Cheng, 'Revisited: International Responsibility, National Activities, and the Appropriate State' (1998) 27 JSL 529. Article VI of the Outer Space Treaty, n. 85, however, leaves a margin of doubt on a central question, namely the identification of the 'appropriate state' that is deemed to perform the obligations mentioned. Bin Cheng comes to the convincing conclusion that, as Article VII of the Convention, under the heading of 'liability of the launching state', provides for joint liability of potentially four different states for damage caused by special objects (i.e. the state that launches; or the state that procures the launching; or the state from whose territory; or the facility from which the object is launched), thus analogically Article VI under 'appropriate state' means at the same time the state of registry of the space object operated by the individuals, the state of nationality of the individuals involved, and the state under which jurisdiction the individuals operate.

clauses of indemnification for the sums that states might be asked to pay under the 1972 Convention on International Liability for Damage Caused by Space Objects (Liability Convention) are usually provided for.[104]

9. Conclusions

In the present chapter we have tried to demonstrate that as a matter of principle, the objective element of international responsibility, i.e. the breach of an international obligation, does not pose major problems in the case of shared responsibility. What matters primarily is that the different subjects (states, international organisations, and, possibly, individuals) are bound by the obligation the breach of which is alleged. Nevertheless, problems arise as soon as we try to investigate more closely the content and structure of an international obligation. The differentiation between different types of obligations might have proved superfluous in the context of the ARSIWA, but it can be useful, or even necessary, in the context of shared responsibility. The reason for this finding is that in contemporary international law, besides the well-circumscribed hypothesis of attribution of responsibility,[105] it is still not possible to hold a state liable in the absence of a specific breach of a specific obligation attributable to it.

[104] See A. Kerrest de Rozavel and F. G. von der Dunk, 'Liability and Insurance in the Context of National Authorization', in F. G. von der Dunk (ed.), *National Space Legislation in Europe: Issues of Authorisation of Private Space Activities in the Light of Developments in European Space Cooperation* (Leiden/Boston: Martinus Nijhoff, 2011), p. 125. There is no practice as yet, but it would be interesting to see how to deal with a case in which a civil action is brought by the victim directly against the private operator before a domestic court, as allowed for by Article XI(2) of the Liability Convention (which reads: 'Nothing in this Convention shall prevent a State, or natural or juridical persons it may represent, from pursuing a claim in the courts or administrative tribunals or agencies of a launching State'), and at the same time the responsible state (or one of the responsible states) is involved in the inter-state Claims Commission envisaged under Articles XIV–XX of the Liability Convention n. 86.

[105] See Fry, 'Attribution of Responsibility', n. 4.

3

Attribution of Conduct

FRANCESCO MESSINEO

1. Introduction

Do customary international law rules on the attribution of conduct allow for the determination of shared responsibility? Imagine that an entity acting on behalf of the United Kingdom and France – say, the Intergovernmental Commission overseeing the operation of the Channel tunnel pursuant to the Treaty of Canterbury[1] – breached an obligation owed to a third party under international law. Could the conduct in question be attributed both to the United Kingdom and to France?[2] Alternatively, consider the situation of someone who is unlawfully detained by a peacekeeping force

Francesco Messineo was Lecturer in Law at the Kent Law School (Canterbury); he is Expert Associate, Research Project on Shared Responsibility in International Law (SHARES), University of Amsterdam. This chapter is partly based on my doctoral research conducted under the thoughtful supervision of Professor Christine Gray and financed by the University of Cambridge and King's College, Cambridge. I am also indebted to Dapo Akande and Professor James Crawford, as well as Professor André Nollkaemper and all colleagues at the SHARES Project. The research leading to this chapter has received funding from the European Research Council under the European Union's Seventh Framework Programme (FP7/2007–2013)/ERC grant agreement n° 249499, as part of the research project SHARES, carried out at the Amsterdam Center for International Law (ACIL) of the University of Amsterdam. Many thanks to Paolo Palchetti and Cecily Rose for helpful comments on a previous draft. The invaluable research assistance of Kathryn Greenman and François Onclin is gratefully acknowledged, as well as the contribution thereto by Kent Law School's Research Support Fund. The usual disclaimers apply. All URLs were last accessed on 6 September 2013.

1 Treaty between the United Kingdom of Great Britain and Northern Ireland and the French Republic concerning the Construction and Operation by Private Concessionaires of a Channel Fixed Link, Canterbury, 12 February 1986, 1497 UNTS 325.

2 See *Eurotunnel Arbitration (The Channel Tunnel Group Ltd and France-Manche S.A.* v. *the Secretary of State for Transport of the Government of the United Kingdom of Great Britain and Northern Ireland and le ministre de l'équipement, des transports, de l'aménagement du territoire, du tourisme et de la mer du Gouvernement de la République française)*, Partial Award, (2007) 132 ILR 1 (*Eurotunnel*).

whose soldiers are formally answering to a United Nations (UN) chain of command, but who are also effectively receiving orders from their home country.[3] Could we say that the victim is being detained both by the UN and the troop-contributing country at the same time? The answers to these questions are important. If more than one entity is responsible, any injured parties may have more avenues of redress available to them, and they may be able to request cessation of the wrongful act from multiple entities.[4]

The fact that international law recognises states and international organisations as the bearers of rights and duties means that they are 'legal persons' under international law.[5] Unlike individual responsibility under international criminal law, which directly concerns human beings, responsibility for internationally wrongful acts pertains to these abstract collective legal entities. However, states and international organisations can only act through human beings, or at least through other collective entities (including private corporations), themselves acting through human beings.[6] It follows that international law must address certain questions concerning the interaction between these actors.[7]

The aim of this chapter is to assess how rules of attribution of conduct work in the context of shared responsibility, and more specifically in cases where a single conduct is attributed to multiple international actors. This chapter does not consider in detail the basic question of how attribution rules operate in general: that is, which acts or omissions can be deemed to

3 See e.g. R. Murphy, *UN Peacekeeping in Lebanon, Somalia and Kosovo: Operational and Legal Issues in Practice* (Cambridge University Press, 2007), p. 130.

4 These issues are considered in Chapters 7 and 8 of this volume: see respectively P. d'Argent, 'Reparation, Cessation, Assurances and Guarantees of Non-Repetition', p. 208; A. M. H. Vermeer-Künzli, 'Invocation of Responsibility', p. 251.

5 This is obvious as to states, but perhaps less obvious as to international organisations. On the connection between legal personhood of international organisations and responsibility, see e.g. P. Reuter, 'Principes de droit international public' (1961) 103 RCADI 425, at 589.

6 See generally D. Anzilotti, *Teoria generale della responsabilità dello stato nel diritto internazionale* (Florence: Lumachi, 1902), reprinted in D. Anzilotti, *Scritti di diritto internazionale pubblico*, vol. II part 1 (Padua: CEDAM, 1956), p. 1, at pp. 121–48 and R. Ago, 'Third Report on State Responsibility', ILC *Yearbook* 1971/II(1), 199, at 217.

7 It cannot be excluded that other collective entities (including corporations) may be deemed to bear *international* rights and obligations, and should consequently be deemed responsible for internationally wrongful acts when they breach such obligations qua subjects of international law. A system of responsibility of corporations at the international level is, however, still embryonic (if it exists at all), because of uncertainty both as to the obligations that would be applicable to them and as to their international legal personality. The focus of this chapter on states and international organisations should not be taken as an expression of a view on this matter.

be the acts or omissions of a state or international organisation.[8] Its focus is rather on the situation where more than one state or international organisation participates in the same conduct breaching an international obligation. In these cases, international law must determine whether the attribution of an act or omission to one state or international organisation necessarily precludes the attribution of the same act or omission to another state or international organisation. Will it be possible to directly impute an internationally wrongful act to more than one collective entity at once (multiple attribution), or will attribution inevitably occur in relation to one collective entity at a time (exclusive attribution)?

The thesis espoused here is that multiple attribution of conduct is possible. Customary international law on attribution of conduct enables the determination of shared responsibility.[9] As we shall see, when more than one subject of international law is involved in the same wrongful conduct, multiple attribution is quite often the default answer to the question of attribution. Exclusive attribution (i.e. attribution to only one of the subjects potentially responsible) only finds application in certain exceptional circumstances concerning organs transferred to another state or international organisation. Indeed, international law has no difficulty with the fact that the same conduct can at the same time be seen as the act of an individual and that of a collective entity, this 'duality of responsibility' being a 'constant feature of international law'.[10] Likewise, a given conduct

[8] 'Attribution of conduct' is used here with reference to internationally wrongful acts only. In international law, the concepts of 'act of a state' and 'act of an international organisation' may vary depending on the set of rules under consideration. For instance, there is a clear distinction between those state organs that may create new obligations for a given state by signing or ratifying a treaty, and those persons (many more) that may engage the responsibility of that same state for a breach of the same treaty.

[9] The term 'shared responsibility' is used here in the sense discussed in Chapter 1 of this volume, P.A. Nollkaemper, 'Introduction', p. 1, at pp. 6–12.

[10] *Application of the Convention on the Prevention and Punishment of the Crime of Genocide (Bosnia and Herzegovina* v. *Serbia and Montenegro)*, Judgment, ICJ Reports 2007, 43, para. 173 (*Bosnian Genocide* case). See Articles on Responsibility of States for Internationally Wrongful Acts, ILC *Yearbook* 2001/II(2) (ARSIWA), Article 58; Commentary to the Articles on Responsibility of States for Internationally Wrongful Acts, ILC *Yearbook* 2001/II(2), (ARSIWA Commentary); Articles on the Responsibility of International Organizations, ILC Report on the work of its sixty-third session, UNGAOR 66th Sess., Supp. No. 10, UN Doc. A/66/10 (2011) (ARIO), Article 66; Commentary to the Articles on the Responsibility of International Organizations, ILC Report on the work of its sixty-third session, UNGAOR 66th Sess., Supp. No. 10, UN Doc. A/66/10 (2011) (ARIO Commentary). See also H. Lauterpacht, *International Law and Human Rights* (London: Stevens, 1950), at pp. 40–3; P.A. Nollkaemper,

may well 'belong' to more than one collective entity at once.[11] Quite simply, the point is that the answer to the 'whodunit' question in international law often yields two or three results at once: someone can be wrongfully detained by an individual, two states, and an international organisation, all at the same time.

It must be acknowledged that in practice, the number of cases in which multiple attribution has been recognised has been limited.[12] Moreover, it has been affirmed by some that multiple attribution is, although possible, still a minority view, with little practice to support it.[13] As we shall see below, this view finds a degree of support in some (but not all) recent pronouncements of the European Court of Human Rights (ECtHR). However, this chapter seeks to rebut these positions by providing a critical analysis of multiple attribution in light of the codification efforts by the International Law Commission (ILC). This is essential to our understanding of the most basic aspects of shared responsibility. If it were accepted that multiple attribution is a 'rare' result of the application of attribution rules, the system of international responsibility would be fundamentally ill-equipped to deal with issues of shared responsibility.[14] I am much more optimistic as to the flexibility and resilience of attribution of conduct rules as codified by the ILC.

This chapter will proceed in three steps. First, the basic framework of rules on attribution of conduct will be briefly recalled in the remainder of this introduction. This is necessary to then move on to consider how cases of potential multiple attribution of conduct may emerge in practice, and how the somewhat misnamed 'principle of independent responsibility' in fact confirms the possibility of multiple attribution, rather than denying it (section 2). Finally, we shall consider rules on the transfer of organs from one subject of international law to another. In the exceptional circumstances in which these rules apply, attribution will be to one subject of international law to the exclusion of other subjects (section 3).

'Concurrence between Individual Responsibility and State Responsibility in International Law' (2003) 52 ICLQ 615, at 618–21.

[11] This can be explained in terms of layers of responsibility, or of spheres of influence, or even by analogy with quantum physics: see A. Clapham, 'The Subject of Subjects and the Attribution of Attribution', in L. Boisson de Chazournes and M. Kohen (eds.), *Liber Amicorum Vera Gowlland-Debbas* (Leiden: Martinus Nijhoff, 2010), p. 45, at pp. 57–8 (where reference is made to Bohr's theory of complementarity regarding the wave-particle duality).

[12] P. A. Nollkaemper and D. Jacobs, 'Shared Responsibility in International Law: A Conceptual Framework' (2013) 34(2) MIJIL 359, at 383.

[13] Ibid. [14] Ibid., at 398–421.

Before proceeding any further, it must be clarified that this chapter focuses on attribution of conduct (i.e. 'direct' responsibility), not on attribution of responsibility or other cases of 'indirect' responsibility.[15] In such cases, a state or international organisation is ultimately responsible or co-responsible for an internationally wrongful act, even if the conduct is not directly attributed to it. This is what the ILC described as the 'Responsibility of a State in connection with the act of another State',[16] the 'Responsibility of an International Organization in connection with the act of a State or another International Organization',[17] and the 'Responsibility of a State in connection with the act of an International Organization'.[18] By definition, these are all cases where there is no direct attribution. Furthermore, this chapter does not deal with cases where separate acts of multiple actors result in a single injury, such as in the *Corfu Channel* case.[19] These are not relevant here because each act or omission contributing to the injury is attributed separately to its author, so there is no issue of multiple attribution of the same act or omission.

In the classic account adopted by the ILC and the International Court of Justice (ICJ or Court),[20] the aim of rules on attribution of conduct is to determine precisely when we can say that a certain conduct that is prima facie in breach of an international obligation is the conduct of a state and/or of an international organisation. General rules on attribution of conduct may be found both in the 2001 Articles on State Responsibility (ARSIWA) and in the 2011 Articles on the Responsibility of International Organizations (ARIO).[21] The ARSIWA contain eight relevant provisions (Articles 4 to 11), which are deemed to be reflective of customary international law.[22] The ARIO only contain four such provisions (Articles 6

[15] See Chapter 4 of this volume, which will consider those cases where a state or international organisation is responsible or co-responsible for an internationally wrongful act, even if the conduct is not directly attributed to it: J. D. Fry, 'Attribution of Responsibility', p. 98.

[16] Part One, Chapter IV ARSIWA, n. 10.

[17] Part Two, Chapter IV ARIO, n. 10.

[18] Part Five ARIO, n. 10.

[19] *Corfu Channel (United Kingdom of Great Britain and Northern Ireland* v. *Albania)*, Merits, ICJ Reports 1949, 4. See P. A. Nollkaemper, 'Issues of Shared Responsibility before the International Court of Justice', in E. Rieter and H. de Waele, *Evolving Principles of International Law: Studies in Honour of Karel C. Wellens* (Leiden: Martinus Nijhoff, 2011), p. 199, SHARES Research Paper 01 (2011), ACIL 2011-11, at 6 (available at www.sharesproject.nl). See also J. Crawford, 'Third Report on State Responsibility', ILC *Yearbook* 2000/II(1), at para. 268.

[20] See e.g. *Bosnian Genocide* case, n. 10, at para. 379.

[21] ARSIWA, n. 10; ARIO, n. 10.

[22] See the compilations of decisions edited by the UN Secretariat: UN Doc. A/62/62 and Corr.1 and Add.1 (2007); UN Doc. A/65/76 (2010).

to 9). The purpose of these rules is to attribute the conduct of every individual or entity acting on behalf of a state or an international organisation to that state or international organisation. The system was designed to avoid loopholes and to separate 'state' or 'international organisation' conduct from 'private' conduct.

Overall, attribution of conduct rests on three basic sets of rules. The first, and most important, concerns 'institutional links'. These apply to those actors whose conduct is automatically attributed to a state or an international organisation: all *de jure* state and international organisation organs,[23] de facto state organs,[24] other agents exercising international organisation functions,[25] and other individuals or entities exercising governmental authority.[26] These are people and entities through which states and international organisations generally operate. So long as they are acting in their capacity (even if abusing their authority), their *ex ante facto* institutional link with the state or the international organisation renders their conduct an act of that state or international organisation for the purposes of international responsibility. In this respect, it should be noted that off-duty, or private, conduct is never attributed to states or international organisations, whereas ultra vires conduct is attributed.[27]

The second set of rules on attribution is that concerning 'factual links'. Setting aside some special cases,[28] the most important type of factual link occurs when a person is acting under the instructions, direction, or control of a state or international organisation. If an institutionally linked agent (usually an organ) instructs, directs, or controls the conduct of another (private) person or group of persons at the time the conduct is carried out, that conduct will be attributable to that state or international organisation regardless of the status of those individuals. This complex rule, enshrined in Article 8 of the ARSIWA, has been the subject of a

23 Article 4 ARSIWA and Article 6 ARIO, n. 10.

24 Article 4(2) ARSIWA, as interpreted in *Bosnian Genocide* case, n. 10, at paras. 390–5. See ARSIWA Commentary, n. 10, at 42; see also I. Brownlie, *System of the Law of Nations: State Responsibility, Part I* (Oxford: Clarendon Press, 1983), p. 136; P. Palchetti, 'Comportamento di organi di fatto e illecito internazionale nel Progetto di articoli sulla responsabilità internazionale degli Stati', in M. Spinedi, A. Gianelli and M. L. Alaimo (eds.), *La codificazione della responsabilità internazionale degli stati alla prova dei fatti: problemi e spunti di riflessione* (Milan: Giuffré, 2006), p. 3, at pp. 5–6.

25 Articles 2(d) and 6 ARIO, n. 10.

26 Article 5 ARSIWA, n. 10.

27 Article 7 ARSIWA and Article 8 ARIO, n. 10.

28 Articles 9 and 10 ARSIWA, n. 10, on the absence and default of governmental authorities and on successful insurrectional and separatist movements respectively.

decades-long judicial and doctrinal debate.[29] Its application revolves around at least two focal points; 'instructions' and 'direction or control'. Instructions must be understood as comprising both specific orders and more general 'directives' that leave some discretion to the actor as to how to accomplish a certain result.[30] As to 'direction or control', the conflict between the ICJ in *Nicaragua* and the International Criminal Tribunal for the former Yugoslavia in *Tadić* as to the correct threshold of attribution underlying these words has been authoritatively solved in the *Bosnian Genocide* case, in favour of the *Nicaragua* test.[31] One of the greatest shortcomings of the ARIO is that they do not explicitly contain a rule analogous to Article 8 of the ARSIWA,[32] but the ILC explained that the definition of 'agent' in Article 2 of the ARIO is meant also to encompass this type of situation.[33]

The third and final general rule on attribution of conduct is that a state or an international organisation may adopt a certain conduct as its own after the conduct has taken place (*ex post facto*).[34] For the rule to be triggered, it is necessary that an institutionally linked actor has issued a declaration or otherwise endorsed the conduct of a person or group of persons. This rule essentially concerns cases in which attribution would not, in principle, be an issue – and so may almost be deemed a 'procedural' rule. As this could perhaps be construed as a case of 'indirect' responsibility rather than one of 'direct' multiple attribution, it will not be further

[29] See inter alia G. Bartolini, 'Il concetto di "controllo" sulle attività di individui quale presupposto della responsabilità dello Stato', in M. Spinedi, A. Gianelli and M.L. Alaimo (eds.), *La codificazione della responsabilità internazionale degli stati alla prova dei fatti: problemi e spunti di riflessione* (Milan: Giuffré, 2006), p. 25; A.J.J. De Hoogh, 'Articles 4 and 8 of the 2001 ILC Articles on State Responsibility, The *Tadić* Case and Attribution of Acts of Bosnian Serb Authorities to the Federal Republic of Yugoslavia' (2002) 72 BYIL 255; C. Kress, 'L'Organe de facto en droit international public: réflexions sur l'imputation à l'état de l'acte d'un particulier à la lumière des développements récents' (2001) 105 RGDIP 93; and P. Palchetti, *L'organo di fatto dello stato nell'illecito internazionale* (Milan: Giuffré, 2007).

[30] For instance, the ARSIWA Commentary, at 47, n. 10, speaks of general 'instructions' to carry out 'missions' abroad.

[31] *Military and Paramilitary Activities in and against Nicaragua (Nicaragua* v. *United States of America)*, Merits, ICJ Reports 1986, 14, at paras. 75, 86, 109–10 and 115; *Prosecutor* v. *Tadić* Judgment, ICTY Case No. IT-94-1-A, 15 July 1999, 38 ILM 1518, at paras. 115–45; *Bosnian Genocide* case, n. 10, paras. 402–6.

[32] See F. Messineo, 'Things Could Only Get Better: *Al-Jedda* beyond *Behrami*' (2011) 50 Mil L & L War Rev 321, at 325 and C. Ahlborn, 'The Use of Analogies in Drafting the Articles on the Responsibility of International Organizations – An Appraisal of the "Copy–Paste Approach"' (2012) 9(1) IOLR 53.

[33] ARIO Commentary, n. 10, 86. [34] Article 11 ARSIWA and Article 9 ARIO, n. 10.

considered here.[35] However, it should be noted that some perplexities may arise as to the nature of the 'acknowledgment' if the conduct in question is also attributable to another subject of international law.

2. Two types of multiple attribution

There are two types of situations where multiple attribution of conduct could theoretically arise. First, the act or omission of one person or entity may trigger attribution rules with regard to more than one subject at the same time, meaning, for instance, that the person or entity in question acts on behalf, or under the instructions, direction, or control, of more than one state or international organisation at the same time, or that it acts on behalf of one subject and under the instructions, direction, or control of another. We shall consider this type of situation in section 2.1. Second, a certain act or omission may be jointly carried out by two or more persons or entities, each of which is acting on behalf of a separate state or international organisation. In this case, there are two or more actors whose joint conduct is attributed to two or more international subjects. We shall consider this type of situation in section 2.2.[36]

2.1 Conduct carried out by one person/entity acting on behalf of more than one state/international organisation at the same time

2.1.1 Possible simultaneous application of attribution rules

Let us start with the first, and most complex, set of situations. Given a certain conduct performed by one person or entity, the application of one of the attribution rules in relation to one subject of international law does not *ipso facto* exclude the application of the same or another attribution rule in relation to the same or another subject of international law.[37] Anzilotti remarked back in 1902 that attribution of conduct

[35] But see Responsibility of international organizations: comments and observations received from international organizations, UN Doc. A/CN.4/545 (2004), at 27–8 (the agreements between the World Health Organization (WHO) and the Pan American Health Organization (PAHO) integrating PAHO's organs into the WHO are cast as a form of previous 'acknowledgment' by the WHO of PAHO's conduct as its own).

[36] The related situation where multiple international subjects engage in separate conduct independently leading to prohibited outcomes is one of potential shared responsibility, but not one of multiple attribution: see n. 19 and accompanying text.

[37] See subsections 2.1.2, 2.1.3, and 2.1.4.

Table 1 *Interactions between rules of attribution of conduct*

Conduct of one actor to whom two rules of attribution apply*	STATE ORGAN DE JURE OR DE FACTO ***Art. 4 ARSIWA***	IO ORGAN ***Art. 6 ARIO***	ENTITY EXERCISING GOVERNMENTAL AUTHORITY ***Art. 5 ARSIWA***	AGENT OR ENTITY EXERCISING IO FUNCTIONS ***Art. 6 ARIO***	ACTOR DIRECTED, INSTRUCTED OR CONTROLLED BY A STATE ***Art. 8 ARSIWA***	ACTOR DIRECTED, INSTRUCTED OR CONTROLLED BY AN IO
STATE ORGAN DE JURE OR DE FACTO ***Art. 4 ARSIWA***	Organ of two states (or joint organ)	Organ of two states/ IOs (or joint organ)	State organ exercising governmental authority of another state	A state organ exercising IO functions	State organ directed, instructed or controlled by another state	State organ directed, instructed or controlled by an IO
IO ORGAN ***Art. 6 ARIO***	*see above*	Organ of two IOs (or joint organ)	IO organ exercising governmental authority of a state	IO organ exercising functions of another IO	IO organ directed, instructed or controlled by a state	IO organ directed, instructed, or controlled by another IO
ENTITY EXERCISING GOVERNMENTAL AUTHORITY ***Art. 5 ARSIWA***	*see above*	*see above*	Entity (not an organ) exercising governmental authority of two states	Entity (not an organ) exercising the governmental authority of a state and functions of an IO	Entity (not an organ) exercising governmental authority of a state and being directed, instructed or controlled by another state	Entity (not an organ) exercising governmental authority of a state and being directed, instructed or controlled by an IO

Agent or entity exercising IO functions **_Art. 6 ARIO_**	*see above*	*see above*	*see above*	Agent or entity exercising functions of two IOs	Agent or entity exercising functions of an IO and being directed, instructed or controlled by a state	Agent or entity exercising functions of an IO and being instructed, directed or controlled by another IO
Actor directed, instructed or controlled by a state **_Art. 8 ARSIWA_**	*see above*	*see above*	*see above*	*see above*	Actor being instructed, directed or controlled by two states	Actor being instructed, directed or controlled by a state and an IO.
Actor directed, instructed or controlled by an IO	*see above*	*see above*	*see above*	*see above*	*see above*	Actor being instructed, directed or controlled by two or more IOs

* Multiple attribution does not arise if Article 6 ARSIWA or Article 7 ARIO apply (see section 3). Whenever this table refers to 'two' this could involve more than two states or IOs.

is the result of an evaluation based on law.[38] As he put it, 'the characteristic of legal attribution is that it is a pure result of the law; a will or an act are attributable to a given subject only because a legal provision says so'.[39] The ILC clarified that this legal evaluation, i.e. the operation of attribution of conduct rules, is a 'cumulative' process, meaning that the criteria are not mutually exclusive (that is, someone could be the organ of a state under Article 4, and at the same time acting under the instructions, direction, or control of that same state under Article 8).[40] But there is more. This legal process may apply at the same time with reference to more than one subject. Except for the rules on the transfer of organs considered in section 3, which constitute the only exception to this type of multiple attribution, nothing in the text of the ILC Articles prevents the contemporaneous application of the rules to more than one subject of international law. This leads to a number of possible interactions between rules of attribution of conduct, some examples of which are considered in Table 1.

Table 1 shows those situations in which the conduct of one actor could be deemed to be the conduct of two or more states and/or international organisations at the same time because of the contemporaneous application of two rules of attribution. While such simultaneous application may potentially involve more than two rules at the same time, the table only considers permutations between two attribution rules at a time, thereby illustrating twenty-one cases of possible simultaneous application between the main rules on attribution of conduct of states and international organisations. Indeed, extra layers of complexity may arise where three or more rules apply at once: for instance, when a joint organ of two or more states and/or international organisations is instructed, directed, or controlled by another state and/or international organisation, or where a joint organ of two or more states and/or international organisations instructs, directs, or controls the act of another state's (or international organisation's) organ. These cases may potentially lead to the attribution to three or more subjects at once. Rather than listing all possible cases, the aim of Table 1 is simply to illustrate that this type of multiple attribution is conceptually possible and wholly consistent with the framework of attribution rules as codified by the ILC.

38 Anzilotti, *Teoria generale della responsabilità dello stato nel diritto internazionale*, n. 6.

39 D. Anzilotti, *Corso di diritto internazionale*, 4th edn, vol. I (Padua: CEDAM, 1955), p. 222.

40 ARSIWA Commentary, n. 10, at 39.

However, this does not mean that all the cases considered in Table 1 are equally well established in theory and practice, nor that all situations mentioned therein will always entail multiple attribution. First, if the rule on transferred organs considered in section 3 applies, attribution will be to only one subject. This important limiting factor is highlighted in Table 1, but whenever the rule does not find application (for example, because the transfer of the organ was not complete, as we shall see below), attribution will be to both subjects of international law involved. Furthermore, it must be recognised that courts have at times had difficulty with recognising the concept of multiple attribution. Nonetheless, in my view the overall balance of the available practice considered in this chapter supports the possibility of multiple attribution. We shall now consider certain examples identified in Table 1.

2.1.2 Joint organs established ad hoc: *Hess*, *Eurotunnel*, and *Nauru*

Let us start by considering how attribution rules on state and/or international organisation organs may potentially interact with each other. Two types of cases clearly emerge from practice. First, an entity or person may be established ad hoc by two or more states and/or international organisations as their joint organ: for instance, the Coalition Provisional Authority that operated in Iraq between 2003 and 2004. Second, an organ of a state and/or international organisation may also act as an organ of another state and/or international organisation: for instance, organs of the Pan American Health Organization also act as organs of the World Health Organization by virtue of an agreement between the two international organisations.[41]

An older case concerning the European Convention on Human Rights (ECHR) exemplifies that it has not always been recognised that acts of joint organs could be attributed to all states involved. In the *Hess* case, one of the questions was whether the detention of a Nazi war criminal in Spandau prison following the Nuremberg trials could be attributed to the United Kingdom, given that the prison had been established in 1945 by

[41] UN Doc. A/CN.4/545 (2004), n. 35, at 27–8 ('[a]s a step towards integration, WHO and PAHO concluded an agreement in 1949 whereby the Pan American Sanitary Conference . . . and the Pan American Sanitary Bureau, would serve respectively as the Regional Committee and the Regional Office of the World Health Organization for the Americas. PAHO thus acts at the same time as a component of both the United Nations and the inter-American systems').

the Allied *Kommandatura*, which was at the time a joint organ comprised of four Governors from the United States, the United Kingdom, the Soviet Union, and France, taking decisions on a consensual basis.[42] According to the European Commission, the consequent responsibility had to be deemed indivisible, because 'the responsibility for the prison ... [was] exercised on a Four Power basis' and the United Kingdom acted 'only as a partner in the joint responsibility which it shares with the three other Powers'; therefore, such 'joint authority [could] not be divided into four separate jurisdictions'.[43]

However, it is now clear that in the case of a joint organ, attribution will plainly be to all subjects that established the joint organ. This was clarified by the ILC in the ARSIWA Commentaries.[44] For example, the Coalition Provisional Authority in Iraq could be seen as a joint organ of the coalition partners, so that any action or omission of that joint organ could be attributed directly to all coalition partners.[45] The rule was affirmed in the *Eurotunnel* arbitration award, which established that the Intergovernmental Commission (IGC) overseeing the Channel Tunnel Fixed Link was indeed a joint organ of France and the United Kingdom, and that 'if a breach of the Concession Agreement [had] resulted from action taken by the IGC both States would be responsible accordingly'.[46]

Some support for the rule may also be found in the *Certain Phosphate Lands in Nauru* case before the ICJ.[47] The United Nations had granted a trusteeship jointly to the United Kingdom, New Zealand, and Australia over the territory of Nauru and constituted them into an 'Administering Authority' which was in practice run by Australia on behalf of the three countries.[48] Could Nauru bring a case against Australia when such a

[42] *Hess* v. *the United Kingdom*, App. No. 6231/73 (ECtHR, 28 May 1975). To be precise, the question was couched in terms of 'jurisdiction' under Article 1 ECHR, which comprises both attribution issues and other issues.

[43] Ibid., at 74.

[44] ARSIWA Commentary, n. 10, at 44 (the conduct of 'a single entity which is a joint organ of several States ... is attributable to [all] States').

[45] See generally S. Talmon, 'A Plurality of Responsible Actors: International Responsibility for Acts of the Coalition Provisional Authority in Iraq', in P. Shiner and A. Williams (eds.), *The Iraq War and International Law* (Oxford: Hart Publishing, 2008), p. 185.

[46] *Eurotunnel*, n. 2, para. 179 (the Tribunal went on to consider certain omissions of the IGC as well as the states concerned as being in breach of the Concession agreement: see para. 395).

[47] *Certain Phosphate Lands in Nauru (Nauru* v. *Australia)*, Preliminary Objections, ICJ Reports 1992, 240 (*Nauru* case). See Crawford, 'Third Report', n. 19, paras. 270–1.

[48] Ibid., *Nauru* case, paras. 41–7. The territory had been a Trusteeship also under the League of Nations system.

claim, in Australia's view, was 'in substance, not a claim against Australia itself but a claim against the Administering Authority in relation to Nauru'?[49] An aspect of this question concerned the attribution of the conduct of the Administering Authority, a joint organ of the United Kingdom, New Zealand, and Australia, to Australia. The Court held that Australia could indeed be sued independently. While the question of the nature and content of Australia's liability would be reserved for the merits, in the Court's view it was clear 'that Australia had obligations under the Trusteeship Agreement, in its capacity as one of the three States forming the Administering Authority, and [that] there [was] nothing in the character of that Agreement which debar[red] the Court from considering a claim of a breach of those obligations by Australia'.[50] In other words, the conduct of the joint organ was at least partly attributable to Australia as one of the states forming it.

In sum, both the *Eurotunnel* arbitration and the *Nauru* case constitute recent and consistent indications that the act of a joint organ may be attributable to each state (or international organisation) comprising that organ.[51] This is further confirmation of the theoretical assumptions underpinning Table 1; the rules on attribution of conduct apply cumulatively, and a certain entity may be purposefully constituted to jointly exercise governmental functions belonging to more than one state at a time, or institutional functions of more than one international organisation at a time.

2.1.3 Organs belonging to more than one state/international organisation: the case of the European Union

Attribution rules on state and/or international organisation organs may also interact with each other when there is no ad hoc joint organ. As we said above, an organ of a state or international organisation may at times also act as an organ of another state and/or international organisation (or more). In this case, its conduct would be attributed to both states and/or international organisations, unless the rules on transferred organs (to be considered in section 3) apply. For example, consider the position of customs officials of member states of the European Union (EU), who act simultaneously as organs of their state and of the EU. Can their acts be attributed both to the EU and to the member state under international law?

[49] Ibid., para. 39. [50] Ibid., para. 48.

[51] See Nollkaemper, 'Issues of Shared Responsibility before the International Court of Justice', n. 19, at 7–8.

The literature on the responsibility of member states for acts arising from the EU legal order is vast,[52] but the question addressed here is quite narrow. We are not interested in 'piercing the veil' issues, nor in assessing whether member states are responsible for decisions of the EU, or vice versa. Nor are we considering all potential cases of indirect responsibility of either member states or the EU for aiding/abetting, coercing each other, or even circumventing their international obligations through each other.[53] The question considered in this example is rather whether the implementation of EU acts by member states can be directly attributed to both the EU and the member state concerned, or whether it must be attributed exclusively either to the EU or to a member state. Because the customs union is a matter of exclusive EU competence where binding EU directives and regulations apply,[54] the acts and omissions of customs officials at the borders of EU member states constitute a perfect example of this issue.[55]

In its comments to the ILC during the drafting of the ARIO, the European Commission took the view that when implementing a binding act of the EU, organs of member states act as de facto organs of the EU, so that 'the conduct of the organ of a member State would be attributed [to

[52] See e.g. P. Eeckhout, 'The EU and its Member States in the WTO – Issues of Responsibility', in L. Bartels and F. Ortino (eds.), *Regional Trade Agreements and the WTO Legal System* (New York: Oxford University Press, 2006), p. 449; M. D. Evans and P. Koutrakos (eds.), *The International Responsibility of the European Union: European and International Perspectives* (Oxford: Hart Publishing, 2013), pp. 35–74, 295–312 and 359–60; S. Talmon, 'Responsibility of International Organizations: Does the European Community Require Special Treatment?', in M. Ragazzi (ed.), *International Responsibility Today: Essays in Memory of Oscar Schachter* (Leiden: Martinus Nijhoff, 2005), p. 405; J. W. van Rossem, 'Interaction between EU Law and International Law in the Light of *Intertanko* and *Kadi*: The Dilemma of Norms Binding the Member States but not the Community' (2009) 40 NYIL 183.

[53] See Nollkaemper, 'Introduction', n. 9, as well as Chapter 4 in this volume, Fry, 'Attribution of Responsibility', n. 15.

[54] See Article 3(1)(a) and Articles 28–33 of the Treaty on the Functioning of the European Union; see also Council Regulation (EEC) No. 2913/92 of 12 October 1992 establishing the Community Customs Code, as subsequently amended, and Regulation (EC) No. 450/2008 of the European Parliament and of the Council of 23 April 2008 laying down the Community Customs Code (Modernised Customs Code).

[55] The fundamental assumption made here is that attribution of conduct in this context does not constitute a *lex specialis* for the purposes of Article 64 ARIO, n. 10, i.e. that the rules in ARIO would fully apply here. But see F. Hoffmeister, 'Litigating against the European Union and its Member States – Who Responds under the ILC's Draft Articles on International Responsibility of International Organizations?' (2010) 21 EJIL 723, for the contrary view.

the EU]'.[56] This position was essentially based on certain substantive points of (internal) EU law that were accepted by a number of World Trade Organization (WTO) panel reports.[57] In fact, the European Commission had called for a specific rule to be added to the ARIO stating that acts of member states implementing binding rules of regional organisations should only be attributed to the international organisation in question.[58] In refuting this view, Special Rapporteur Gaja relied on the decisions of the European Court of Human Rights in *Bosphorus*[59] and the European Court of Justice in *Kadi*[60] as authorities which 'examined the implementation of a binding act that left no discretion' and 'clearly [did] not lend support to the proposal of considering that conduct implementing an act of an international organization should be attributed to that organization'.[61]

Indeed, the WTO panel reports relied upon by the European Commission could perhaps be taken as simply reflecting the procedural issues specific to those cases, in which the EU was the only respondent, also on behalf of its member states (even in relation to measures adopted only by member states). As the panel made clear in *Biotech*, this acceptance of responsibility by the EU was what mattered, because the complaining parties had directed their complaints to the EU and it, in turn, '*never contested* that, for the purposes of this dispute, the challenged member State measures [were] attributable to it under international law'.[62] Cast in these terms, this was more of a procedural acceptance of attribution under Article 9 of the ARIO than a statement against the possibility of

[56] G. Gaja, 'Seventh Report on Responsibility of International Organizations', UN Doc. A/CN.4/610 (2009), at p. 12.

[57] See *European Communities – Protection of Trademarks and Geographical Indications for Agricultural Products and Foodstuffs*, Panel Report, 15 March 2005, WT/DS174/R, para. 7.98 and para. 7.725; see also, *European Communities – Selected Customs Matters*, Panel Report, 16 June 2006, WT/DS315/R, and Appellate Body Report, 13 November 2006, WT/DS315/AB/R; *European Communities – Measures Affecting the Approval and Marketing of Biotech Products*, Panel Report, 29 September 2006, WT/DS291/R (*Biotech*), para. 7.101.

[58] Hoffmeister, 'Litigating against the European Union and its Member States', n. 55, at 728–9.

[59] *Bosphorus Hava Yollari Turizm Ve Ticaret Anonim Şirketi* v. *Ireland*, App. No. 45036/98 (ECtHR, 30 June 2005) (*Bosphorus*), at para. 153.

[60] *Kadi and Al Barakaat International Foundation* v. *Council of the European Union and Commission of the European Communities*, European Court of Justice, joined cases C-402/05 P and C-415/05 P, [2008] 3 CMLR 41 (*Kadi*), at para. 314.

[61] Gaja, 'Seventh Report', n. 56, p. 13. [62] *Biotech*, n. 57, para. 7.101 (emphasis added).

multiple attribution of conduct.[63] By contrast, the question of multiple attribution had been specifically raised in another WTO case, previously brought by the United States against both the European Communities and two of its member states – *Customs Classification of Certain Computer Equipment*. The solution adopted therein was somewhat in favour of potential multiple attribution.[64]

Be that as it may, it seems that both the European Commission and the Special Rapporteur looked at the question from an odd angle. If, according to EU law, certain organs of member states are assigned certain functions of the EU – namely, the implementation of EU measures under Article 291(1) of the Treaty on the Functioning of the European Union – each act of implementation becomes a situation in which the organs of the state are *de jure*, and not de facto, organs of the EU for the purposes of Article 5 of the ARIO. They are also, at the same time, organs of their member states. Let us assume that the rules on transferred organs that we shall analyse in section 3 do not apply in this context, because state organs implementing EU binding acts are not 'transferred' to the EU when implementing EU acts.[65] The result is that both Article 4 of the ARSIWA and Article 5 of the ARIO would apply at the same time: there is no need to choose between attribution to the EU and attribution to the member state, and the authority of *Bosphorous* and *Kadi* is not necessary here. The same would hold true in other cases where the internal rules of an international organisation assign certain of its functions to organs of member states without any transfer of that organ from the state to the international organisation.

2.1.4 Other cases: state/international organisation functions and instructions, direction, or control

So far, we have only discussed the simultaneous application of rules of attribution concerning organs, but Table 1 above contains many more examples of potential multiple attribution engaging the other attribution

63 See P. J. Kuijper, 'Introduction to the Symposium on Responsibility of International Organizations and of (Member) States: Attributed or Direct Responsibility or Both?' (2010) 7 IOLR 9, at 20.

64 *European Communities – Customs Classification of Certain Computer Equipment*, Report of the Panel of 5 February 1998 WT/DS62/R, 22 June 1998, para. 8.16, as interpreted by Hoffmeister, 'Litigating against the European Union and its Member States', n. 55, at 732 (but the author then reaches the conclusion that the subsequent WTO reports mentioned above overruled this approach).

65 See ibid., at 727. But see also Kuijper, 'Introduction to the Symposium on Responsibility of International Organizations and of (Member) States', n. 63, at 16.

rules. These other rules cannot be analysed here in detail, but two particular situations must be considered.

First, the framework proposed in Table 1 assumes that it is possible for an entity to exercise the governmental authority of two or more states at the same time under the terms of Article 5 of the ARSIWA. How can this situation arise? In the ARSIWA Commentaries, the threshold for the application of Article 5 is that of being 'empowered, if only to a limited extent or in a specific context, to exercise specified elements of governmental authority'.[66] Examples of situations triggering the rule are 'parastatal' entities, such as 'former State corporations' that have been 'privatized but retain certain public or regulatory functions': for example, a national railway that is authorised to levy fines on customers.[67] In turn, the concept of 'governmental authority' is not clearly defined. The Commentaries acknowledge that 'beyond a certain limit, what is regarded as "governmental" depends on the particular society, its history and traditions'.[68] Given the nature of this enquiry, the question is whether it is possible to reach the conclusion that a certain entity is acting in the exercise of the governmental authority of two or more states at the same time. Although there is little judicial practice confirming this, it seems that nothing in principle prevents a situation such as this from arising. For example, a private military and security company (PMSC) could be entrusted by two or more states with certain governmental functions. If the United States and the United Kingdom governments acting together, rather than the United States government alone, had contracted those companies that were 'providing services' at the Abu Ghraib prison,[69] the question would have arisen as to whether the conduct of the PMSC could be attributed to both – and an affirmative answer would have been likely.[70]

Second, Table 1 assumes that it is possible for a person or entity to be under the instructions, direction, or control of two or more states and/or international organisations at the same time. At first sight, this may seem to imply that 'effective' control can be 'effective' in relation to more than

[66] Ibid. [67] ARSIWA Commentary, n. 10, p. 42. [68] Ibid., p. 43.

[69] See the US Court of Appeal judgment in *Saleh* v. *Titan Corp.*, 580 F 3d 1 (D.C. Circuit 2009).

[70] On responsibility of PMSCs generally, see e.g. F. Francioni and N. Ronzitti (eds.), *War by Contract: Human Rights, Humanitarian Law, and Private Contractors* (Oxford University Press, 2011); C. Hoppe, 'Passing the Buck: State Responsibility for Private Military Companies' (2008) 19 EJIL 989; C. Lehnardt, 'Private Military Companies and State Responsibility', in S. Chesterman and C. Lehnardt (eds.), *From Mercenaries to Market: The Rise and Regulation of Private Military Companies* (Oxford University Press, 2007), p. 139.

one subject of international law at the same time. As briefly noted above, the rule in Article 8 of the ARSIWA is split into at least two components: 'instruction' and 'direction or control'. The complex question of what 'effective control' means and what degree of control triggers the 'direction or control' threshold only applies to the second of these two elements of Article 8. While it may be true that 'effective' control can only be exercised by one subject at a time, the rule on 'instructions' can lead to multiple attribution. It is perfectly possible for someone to have received general instructions to carry out a certain conduct by a state and/or international organisation, and then to be under the more specific 'effective' control of another state and/or international organisation when carrying out the orders. It is also possible for someone to have received similar instructions from two or more states. Multiple attribution would ensue in all these cases. As an example, consider the conduct of the captain of a vessel who, following the combined instructions received by both Italian and Maltese authorities, disembarks a group of shipwrecked refugees in Libya. Having acted under the instructions of the authorities of both governments, his conduct would be attributed to both Italy and Malta, and could engage the responsibility of both countries for any breach of *non-refoulement* obligations under international law.

Finally, a general point must be made concerning all cases considered in Table 1. All attribution of conduct rules, especially as interpreted in the *Bosnian Genocide* case,[71] must rely on the existence of institutionally linked actors (organs), which are either acting themselves or instructing, directing, or controlling the acts of others (in the case of factual links).[72] It follows that once it is established that joint organs may exist and indeed give rise to multiple attribution of conduct, as we have discussed above, the fact that joint organs may also give rise to joint factual links of instruction, direction, or control is a necessary logical consequence. Therefore, for instance, if the Intergovernmental Commission overseeing the Channel Tunnel Fixed Link instructed, directed, or controlled a private actor, multiple attribution of conduct to France and the United Kingdom would ensue by operation of Article 8 of the ARSIWA combined with (two instances of) Article 4 of the ARSIWA. The ARSIWA Commentaries seem to explicitly recognise that someone might be operating under the joint instructions of two states at a time.[73]

[71] *Bosnian Genocide* case, n. 10. [72] ARSIWA Commentary, n. 10, at 38.
[73] ARSIWA Commentary, n. 10, at 44.

2.2 *Conduct jointly carried out by two or more persons/entities acting on behalf of different states/international organisations*

All the cases of multiple attribution we have analysed so far concern conduct carried out by one person or entity acting on behalf of more than one subject of international law at the same time. We must now consider the other case of multiple attribution of conduct, which arises when the same conduct is carried out jointly by two or more actors, each of whom is acting on behalf of a different state and/or international organisation. This is, admittedly, a rare occurrence. Consider, for instance, two soldiers belonging to different coalition partners in Iraq jointly patrolling a certain area in a tank at the beginning of the conflict in 2003. For the purposes of this example, let us assume that the tank was being operated jointly by the two soldiers and that a civilian was unlawfully killed by a weapon fired by the tank, so that we can identify one harmful conduct as the cause of the death. Could this conduct be attributable to both states?

The answer to this question is affirmative. In this case, the question is not one of simultaneous application of rules of attribution of conduct concerning one actor, but of the simple application of the rules in relation to each subject of international law concerned. Each of the two soldiers in the example is plainly a state organ under Article 4 of the ARSIWA, and nothing in the text of the rules (nor in the authorities from which they are derived) seems to suggest that cooperation between different subjects of international law cannot lead to multiple attribution in cases like this.

The complexity, however, arises when trying to define the relevant conduct: i.e. the one act or omission that is carried out jointly and constitutes an internationally wrongful act. It is difficult to understand precisely what constitutes the 'joint' conduct of two or more actors. In many other cases, one could well reach the conclusion that there is not 'one' conduct in breach of international law, but 'two' (or more) courses of conduct that are each independently attributable to only one of the two states – a situation somewhat similar to *Corfu Channel* (the difference being that the time, place, and obligation breached would be the same, rather than different). For instance, if the two soldiers mentioned above were jointly patrolling a street in Baghdad on foot, and they unlawfully killed a civilian together, it would be entirely possible to conceptualise the event as two separate internationally wrongful acts rather than one internationally wrongful act attributable to two states. As we shall see, Article 47(1) of the ARSIWA operates in such a way that the final result would be identical (both states would be responsible), but in some scenarios there may be one indivisible conduct that is attributable to two state organs acting together without the previous establishment of a joint organ. As will be discussed in Chapters 7 and 8 of this volume, this may have consequences in terms of invocation of responsibility and the remedies available.

Indeed, courts have occasionally had some difficulty with this type of situation, precisely in the context of invocation of responsibility. For instance, the European Court of Human Rights declared Saddam Hussein's 2006 application against twenty-one European states inadmissible because, among other reasons, the applicant had not specified which of the coalition partners was responsible for the alleged violations of his human rights.[74] Although the ECtHR employed the language of Article 1 of the ECHR (i.e. the concept of 'jurisdiction'), the point was also made that there was not sufficient evidence of attribution of conduct; Hussein had not demonstrated how the command structures operated, nor which of the respondent states had been involved in his arrest and detention.[75] This should be taken as an important practical warning concerning attempts to invoke responsibility based on multiple attribution of conduct. The ECtHR implicitly said that when invoking the multiple responsibility of several actors, the claimant must be able to prove that a link of attribution exists with each of them: that is, that they must have genuinely acted together. Although Hussein's claim was rejected, the judgment should not necessarily be read as preventing future claims based on the joint exercise of power.

2.3 *The principle of independent responsibility*

The main textual argument in favour of multiple attribution is that both the ARSIWA and the ARIO clearly recognise the possibility that one wrongful act may implicate the responsibility of a plurality of international subjects at the same time. Crucially, however, such plurality is reduced to bilateral relationships where issues of invocation of responsibility are concerned.[76] The 'principle of independent responsibility'[77] is enshrined in Article 47(1) of the ARSIWA:

[74] *Saddam Hussein* v. *Albania and others (Admissibility)*, App. No. 23276/04 (ECtHR, 14 March 2006).

[75] Ibid., 224–5. [76] See generally Crawford, 'Third Report', n. 19, paras. 263–83.

[77] ARSIWA Commentary, n. 10, at 124.

> Where several States are responsible for the same internationally wrongful act, the responsibility of each State may be invoked in relation to that act.

Article 48(1) of the ARIO clarifies how the rule works when international organisations are involved:

> Where an international organization and one or more States or other international organizations are responsible for the same internationally wrongful act, the responsibility of each State or international organization may be invoked in relation to that act.

These rules establish the independence of each bilateral legal relationship between each injured state and/or international organisation and each responsible state and/or international organisation. They are also a clear recognition that states may act jointly, and so may international organisations, or states and international organisations. In this case, they would each be separately responsible for the same wrongful act of which they are 'co-authors'.[78]

This principle of independent responsibility has been linked by some authors to the principle of exclusive responsibility, that is: conduct is, in principle, only to be attributed to one actor.[79] In their view, the fact that the system of international responsibility was designed with bilateral relations and obligations in mind would make it ill-equipped to deal with the multiple attribution of conduct to more than one actor at once. In my view, however, questions of invocation should be considered wholly separately from questions of attribution of conduct. While it is true that international responsibility has often been understood as a bilateral affair, the system of international responsibility is evolving from one in which individual (bilateral) causes of action (*à la* Brownlie) were the focus of discussions on responsibility (at least among Anglo-American lawyers),[80] to one in which breaches are considered as 'violations' of 'the law' – something approaching a 'general law of wrongs' in international law.[81] In this Copernican revolution, collective action in breach of obligations

[78] D'Argent, 'Reparation, Cessation, Assurances and Guarantees of Non-Repetition', n. 4, pp. 241–4; Vermeer-Künzli, 'Invocation of Responsibility', n. 4, p. 271.

[79] See Nollkaemper and Jacobs, 'Shared Responsibility in International Law: A Conceptual Framework', n. 12.

[80] See Brownlie, *System of the Law of Nations*, n. 24, pp. 189–92. Continental lawyers often begged to differ: see e.g. Reuter, 'Principes de droit international public', n. 5, at 583–618.

[81] See generally J. Crawford, *The International Law Commission's Articles on State Responsibility: Introduction, Text and Commentaries* (Cambridge University Press, 2002), pp. 1–60.

would be best understood in terms of joint 'violations' of the 'rules', rather than separate breaches of bilateral obligations. But even if one adopted a strictly 'bilateral' approach, precisely the fact that invocation of responsibility remains possible towards each of the parties to whom conduct is attributed constitutes proof that the same conduct *can* be attributed to multiple parties. In other words, the underdevelopment of the system of invocation of responsibility when multiple actors are concerned[82] does not impinge upon the basic framework of attribution, which permits multiple attribution.

As the ARSIWA Commentaries put it, 'the situation can arise where a single course of conduct is at the same time attributable to several States and is internationally wrongful for each of them'.[83] Substantially the same concept was expressed by the Commentaries to the ARIO, according to which 'one could also envisage conduct being simultaneously attributed to two or more international organizations, for instance when they establish a joint organ and act through that organ'.[84] As we have seen, states and international organisations may also act together by giving joint instructions to the same actor. Indeed, 'attribution of a certain conduct to an international organization does not imply that the same conduct cannot be attributed to a State; nor does attribution of conduct to a State rule out attribution of the same conduct to an international organization'.[85] This is unsurprising. As we recalled above, attribution of conduct is the result of an evaluation based on law, not on fault or causality issues, and attribution rules are structured in an open fashion.[86] All of them can be applied contemporaneously to one or more subjects of international law, so that the same conduct may be deemed to have been performed by a state and an international organisation, more than one state, more than one international organisation, etc. Furthermore, conduct might arise through the concurrent action or omissions of two or more persons acting each on behalf of one state and/or international organisation.

One may legitimately wonder about the origin of the contrary idea, whereby attribution is exclusively to one subject of international law at a time. It would be interesting to investigate whether this might perhaps be a fallacy deriving from domestic law analogies. For instance, in both English and French law the concept of 'control' is used when disentangling cases of

[82] This will be analysed in Chapter 8, Vermeer-Künzli, 'Invocation of Responsibility', n. 4.

[83] ARSIWA Commentary, n. 10, at 124. [84] ARIO Commentary, n. 10, at 83.

[85] Ibid., at 83. [86] See n. 17.

potential multiple attribution in order to find the *one* responsible party.[87] But the premise of domestic private law is completely different from that of international responsibility for internationally wrongful acts, and thus such domestic law analogies are likely to be misleading.[88]

3. Exclusive attribution of transferred organs

3.1 Organs transferred to a state

Multiple attribution does not occur in all circumstances where a single conduct could potentially be attributed to multiple international actors. The rule on transferred organs constitutes an exception to the rule on multiple attribution, in the sense that it is designed to prevent multiple attribution of conduct from occurring if certain requirements are met.

Suppose that, at the request of the receiving government, thirty Italian police officers working in Bologna are sent for a few months to San Marino to be employed in a special anti-fraud operation of the Sammarinese police. There, they participate in the activities of the local police. In particular, following the orders of a local judge, they carry out the seizure of some documents in the Sammarinese branch of a Swiss bank. Switzerland holds this act to be a violation of the obligations arising under a multilateral treaty signed inter alia by both Italy and San Marino. Can Switzerland claim that the seizure of the documents is attributable to Italy under international law? Could it claim it is attributable to San Marino? If one applied the rules on attribution that we considered above, and what we just said about multiple attribution, the answer would plainly be yes to both questions. Italian police officers are *de jure* organs of the Italian Republic (Article 4 of the ARSIWA). In this instance, they are also acting under the

[87] See e.g. *Mersey Docks and Harbour Board* v. *Coggins & Griffiths (Liverpool) Ltd and McFarlane* [1946] 2 All ER 345 and H. Capitant, F. Terré, and Y. Lequette, *Les Grands arrêts de la jurisprudence civile, Tome 2. Obligations, Contrats spéciaux, Sûretés*, 12th edn (Paris: Dalloz, 2008), pp. 463–5.

[88] See J. Crawford, 'The System of International Responsibility', in J. Crawford, A. Pellet, and S. Olleson (eds.), *The Law of International Responsibility* (Oxford University Press, 2010), p. 17, at pp. 21–2 (international responsibility forms 'a single system, without any precise comparator in national legal systems'); A. Pellet, 'The Definition of Responsibility in International Law', in J. Crawford, A. Pellet, and S. Olleson (eds.), *The Law of International Responsibility* (Oxford University Press, 2010), p. 3, at p. 13 (highlighting the similar view by Kelsen and Arangio-Ruiz); Reuter, 'Principes de droit international public', n. 5, at 584–95 (on the 'unity of the theory of responsibility', which is neither criminal nor civil). Contra, see Brownlie, *System of the Law of Nations*, n. 24, p. 23.

instructions, direction, or control of the Sammarinese authorities (Article 8 of the ARSIWA). This would be a textbook example of dual attribution, were it not for the operation of one rule we have not yet analysed: Article 6 of the ARSIWA. This provides that:

> The conduct of an organ placed at the disposal of a State by another State shall be considered an act of the former State under international law if the organ is acting in the exercise of elements of the governmental authority of the State at whose disposal it is placed.

According to the Commentaries, if in our example Italy actually puts its police officers at the disposal of San Marino and they exercise Sammarinese governmental authority, their conduct will be attributed only to San Marino, and not to Italy.[89] However, because this is an exception to the general rule allowing for dual attribution, it must be narrowly construed. According to the ILC, there is a transfer of attribution from one state to another only in the 'limited' and 'precise situation' where organs of a state are 'effectively put at the disposal' of another, 'so that the organ may temporarily act for [the latter's] benefit'.[90]

Under the limited circumstances in which it applies, Article 6 of the ARSIWA acts as a rule on the transfer of attribution (and thus, often, also responsibility) when organs are transferred. According to the Commentaries, the two key elements of this rule are 'being placed at the disposal' of the receiving state and exercising elements of the governmental authority thereof 'with the consent, under the authority of and for the purposes of the receiving State'.[91] Back in 1971, Special Rapporteur Ago had described in detail why this was to be an exceptional rule. In many cases, the transfer of an organ to another state was not actual, but only nominal, in that the lending state maintained authority over the lent organ. These 'apparent' loans could not lead to a transfer of attribution, because 'the organ will in fact still be acting under the control and in accordance with the instructions of the State to which it belongs'.[92] A case of such an apparent loan was relevant in *Attorney General* v. *Nissan* before the UK House of Lords in 1969.[93] British troops had requisitioned Mr Nissan's hotel in Nicosia during their participation in a truce mission at the request of the Cyprus government, which later became a UN peacekeeping operation. According to the British government, the troops

[89] ARSIWA Commentary, n. 10, at 44. [90] Ibid. [91] Ibid.

[92] Ago, 'Third Report', n. 6, at 199–274, 272. See also ARSIWA Commentary, n. 10, at 44.

[93] *Attorney-General* v. *Nissan* [1969] UKHL 3; [1970] 1 AC 179; (1969) 44 ILR 359.

were acting as agents of Cyprus first, and as agents of the UN later, and as such their conduct was not attributable to the United Kingdom. Their Lordships instead held that UK troops remained 'soldiers of Her Majesty' subject to UK command throughout the time, and their conduct should thus be attributed to the United Kingdom.[94] Because the transfer of the organ had not been a complete one, the United Kingdom was still responsible:

> From the documents it appears further that, though national contingents were under the authority of the United Nations and subject to the instructions of the commander, the troops as members of the force remained in their national service. The British forces continued, therefore, to be soldiers of Her Majesty. Members of the United Nations force were subject to the exclusive jurisdiction of their respective national States in respect of any criminal offences committed by them in Cyprus.[95]

In fact, Article 6 of the ARSIWA permits dual attribution in at least two cases. First, when organs are not fully transferred, and the sending state still partly controls the transferred organ, attribution will be to both states under Article 4 (for the sending state) and Article 8 of the ARSIWA (inasmuch as it is controlled by the receiving state), respectively. Second, in certain cases lent organs would act as organs of two states at the same time. If a state lends one of its organs to another state, Ago argued, it may still happen that the latter's 'demands' are not 'so exacting as to prevent the organ from continuing to act simultaneously, though independently, as an organ of its own State'.[96] A case-by-case analysis would then be necessary to disentangle the question of whose authority is being exercised at any given time, if it is possible to do so. According to the ILC, for Article 6 of the ARSIWA to apply, not only has the transferred organ to be entrusted with governmental functions of the receiving state,[97] it also has to act 'in conjunction with the machinery of that State and under its exclusive direction and control, rather than on instructions from the sending State'.[98] If that is so, attribution becomes exclusive to the receiving state.

A very interesting example of transferred organs concerns the Principality of Andorra.[99] Before a treaty of 1993 settled its status as a state (it has been a member of the United Nations since July 1993),

[94] Ago, 'Third Report', n. 6, at 199–274, 271.
[95] *Attorney-General* v. *Nissan*, n. 93, at 376. [96] Ibid., at 268.
[97] ARSIWA Commentary, n. 10, at 45. [98] Ibid., p. 44.
[99] See *Drozd and Janousek* v. *France and Spain*, App. No. 12747/87 (ECtHR, 26 June 1992) (*Drozd* case).

Andorra was a *sui generis* entity proximate to statehood. Its territory has long been under the joint sovereignty of two co-princes: the President of the French Republic and the Spanish Bishop of Urgel.[100] In application of an ancient custom, France and Spain seconded some of their own judges to the *Tribunal de Corts* of the Principality. Mr Drozd and Mr Janousek were prosecuted by the Tribunal and sentenced to imprisonment for armed robbery; they then instituted proceedings against France and Spain before the ECtHR. The ECtHR considered that one question to be decided was whether 'the acts complained of by Mr. Drozd and Mr. Janousek [could] be attributed to France or Spain or both, even though they were not performed on the territory of those States'.[101] The answer was in the negative, because in the view of the ECtHR this was what we would call a complete transfer of organs from France and Spain to Andorra. While sitting in Andorran courts, the judges did not do so 'in their capacity as French or Spanish judges', but acted 'in an autonomous manner' and without any 'supervision' by France or Spain.[102]

Drozd and Janousek and Article 6 of the ARSIWA were relied upon as authorities by the British government before the High Court in the *Al-Saadoon* case.[103] The government argued that British troops in Iraq were put at the disposal of the Iraqi government in the sense of Article 6 of the ARSIWA so that their conduct (the detention of Al-Saadoon and another person charged with war crimes and their imminent transfer to Iraqi authorities) would be attributable to Iraq rather than the United Kingdom, just as the conduct of French and Spanish judges operating in Andorra was only attributable to Andorra. The High Court correctly held the two situations distinguishable, because a complete transfer had not occurred. In the Court's view, 'Article [6] deals with a *limited situation* in which the organ is *acting under the exclusive direction and control of the state at whose disposal it is placed*'.[104] This was not the case in the circumstances under analysis. It was 'plainly' wrong to say 'that the

[100] See J. Crawford, *The Creation of States in International Law*, 2nd edn (Oxford: Clarendon Press, 2006), p. 197.

[101] *Drozd* case, n. 99, para. 91. [102] Ibid., para. 96.

[103] See *R. (Al-Saadoon)* v. *Secretary of State for Defence (High Court)* [2008] EWHC 3098 (Admin), at paras. 75–81, overruled on the point of attribution by *R. (Al-Saadoon)* v. *Secretary of State for Defence (Court of Appeal)* [2009] EWCA Civ 7, [2009] 3 WLR 957, at paras. 32–40. See also *Al-Saadoon and Mufdhi* v. *the United Kingdom (Admissibility)*, App. No. 61498/08 (ECtHR, 30 June 2009); *Al-Saadoon and Mufdhi* v. *the United Kingdom*, App. No. 61498/08 (ECtHR, 2 March 2010).

[104] *R. (Al-Saadoon)* v. *Secretary of State for Defence (High Court)*, n. 103, para. 80 (emphasis added).

British forces have no autonomous role in the matter of the claimants' detention or transfer into the custody of [Iraqi authorities]', because it was still 'in their power to refuse to transfer the claimants'.[105] The Court of Appeal disagreed on this point, and deemed that the British forces were acting as 'agents' of Iraqi courts.[106] However, it did not reach this conclusion by applying the criterion of Article 6 of the ARSIWA. It stated that the United Kingdom 'was not exercising, or purporting to exercise, any autonomous power of its own as a sovereign state'[107] and therefore it was not exercising 'jurisdiction' for the purposes of Article 1 of the ECHR. Interestingly, the ECtHR, seized of the same matter, did not even address the question of attribution, taking it for granted that the detention and possible transfer of Al-Saadoon was attributable to the United Kingdom.[108]

The cases mentioned so far show that issues of attribution when organs are transferred are very complex to assess. The correct construction seems to be that of the High Court in *Al-Saadoon*: that is, the recognition that 'direction and control' by the receiving state's authorities are necessary for a complete transfer of attribution to occur. However, it is important not to confuse this requirement of 'direction and control' with the 'direction *or* control' of Article 8 of the ARSIWA. The point of Article 6 of the ARSIWA is not to establish if there can be attribution, but how to disentangle a situation of potential dual attribution. Article 6 has nothing to do with a factual link of instructions, direction, or ('effective') control over non-state actors. The question is rather whether the receiving state has actually formed an institutional link with the transferred organ. The transfer of organs creates a situation where an institutional link is temporarily created with the receiving state and severed with the sending one. All on-duty conduct of transferred organs, even if ultra vires, will be attributed as if they were the receiving state's organs only, and this is irrespective of a factual link of instructions, direction, or control, with each specific conduct considered.[109]

There is obviously an overlap here. We have seen in the discussion of Table 1 that multiple attribution may arise when an organ belongs to more

105 Ibid., para. 79.

106 *R. (Al-Saadoon)* v. *Secretary of State for Defence (Court of Appeal)*, n. 103, para. 40.

107 Ibid., para. 32.

108 *Al-Saadoon and Mufdhi* v. *the United Kingdom (Admissibility)*, n. 103, especially at paras. 84–9.

109 ARSIWA Commentary, n. 10, at 44 ('what is crucial for the purposes of Article 6 is the establishment of a functional link between the organ in question and the structure or authority of the receiving state'). See also ILC *Yearbook* 1974/I, at 43–61, 55.

than one subject of international law at a time. We have also discussed the example of member states' customs officials implementing binding EU regulations and thus acting at the same time as an organ of their member state and of the European Union.[110] In those cases, too, Article 6 of the ARSIWA might potentially have applied as an exception to multiple attribution, but we assumed that it would not. The threshold of 'being put at the disposal' of the EU is not nearly met because customs officials do not answer to European Union organs, but remain fully in the line of command of their member state. There is not even an attempt at integrating them into the EU machinery as such: they simply exercise functions of the European Union at the same time as exercising governmental functions of their member state. The default rule of multiple attribution applies, and the exception of Article 6 of the ARSIWA is not triggered.

It should be added that the same rule in Article 6 of the ARSIWA also applies by analogy to the rare situation of an organ or agent of an international organisation transferred to a state for the exercise of governmental authority thereof. While this was clear in Ago's third report and in the ARSIWA adopted on first reading,[111] the final version of the ARSIWA is not explicit on the point, although the Commentaries mention the issue.[112] The symmetrical situation of organs put at the disposal of international organisations by both states and international organisations is fully considered by the ARIO, as we shall see.

3.2 *Organs transferred to an international organisation*

3.2.1 'Effective control' in Article 7 ARIO

We have just seen that under Article 6 of the ARSIWA, when states put their organs at the disposal of another state, the acts of the transferred or lent organs are attributed to the receiving state 'if the organ is acting in the exercise of elements of the governmental authority of the State at whose disposal it is placed'. We have also seen that it is probably correct to extend the application of this rule to organs transferred from international organisations to states, although a more specific provision in this respect would have been welcome. But what happens when organs are transferred from

[110] See section 2.1.3.

[111] ILC *Yearbook* 1974/II(1), at 269–90, 286 (text of Article 9 includes organs 'placed at the disposal of a State . . . by an international organization').

[112] ARSIWA Commentary, n. 10, at 45.

states or international organisations to an international organisation? In a textual departure from the ARSIWA, Article 7 of the ARIO provides that:

> The conduct of an organ of a State or an organ or agent of an international organization that is placed at the disposal of another international organization shall be considered under international law an act of the latter organization if the organization exercises effective control over that conduct.

It is recalled that Article 6 of the ARSIWA instead provides that:

> The conduct of an organ placed at the disposal of a State by another State shall be considered an act of the former State under international law if the organ is acting in the exercise of elements of the governmental authority of the State at whose disposal it is placed.

Despite this striking difference between the two formulations, the text of Article 7 of the ARIO 'generally' met with a 'positive reaction' by states.[113] Even the notorious *Behrami* case of the European Court of Human Rights paid initial lip service to the first draft of the provision,[114] and the International Monetary Fund, otherwise quite critical of the work of the ILC on international organisations, endorsed the Article.[115]

However, while there may be agreement on the formula 'effective control over that conduct', its exact meaning is not very clear. Is the word 'control' in Article 8 of the ARSIWA, interpreted by the ICJ in *Bosnian Genocide* as 'effective control', the same 'effective control' under consideration here, that is, the criterion to attribute conduct of organs transferred to international organisations? Or does 'effective control' have a different meaning in Article 7 of the ARIO? More generally, was it really a good idea to use the words 'effective control' in Article 7 of the ARIO? The drafting history of Article 6 of the ARSIWA, on organs transferred to states, will shed some light on this problem.

3.2.2 The drafting history of Article 6 ARSIWA and 'effective control' in Article 7 ARIO

The question of organs transferred or lent to international organisations had already been addressed by Ago in his third report on state responsibility, when he discussed what would later become Article 6 of the

113 Gaja, 'Seventh Report', n. 56, at 11.

114 *Agim Behrami and Bekir Behrami* v. *France and Ruzhdi Saramati* v. *France, Germany and Norway*, App. No. 71412/01 and App. No. 78166/01 (ECtHR, 2 May 2007), at 93.

115 UN Doc. A/CN.4/556 (2005), at 25.

ARSIWA.[116] Ago started by mentioning the role of the UN and troop-contributing states in Korea (the 1950 UN operation under American unified command) and the Congo (the 1961 operation under UN command),[117] and concluded that both in the context of states lending organs to other states, and in that of states lending organs to international organisations, the receiving state or organisation 'must be held responsible for any violations of international law committed by the organ placed at its disposal, when the acts of that organ are genuinely performed in the name and on behalf of the beneficiary and in accordance with orders issued by the beneficiary alone'.[118]

In Ago's view, therefore, the rule had to be the same for what has now become Article 6 of the ARSIWA and what was to become Article 7 of the ARIO. According to him, in both cases what mattered was 'effective control'.[119] By this he meant that the transferred organ should not only be integrated into the organisation of the receiving state (or its 'machinery', in Ago's terminology),[120] but also clearly under the authority of the receiving state as opposed to the sending one. The Commentaries adopted by the ILC in 1974 clearly spoke of a 'functional link' being established 'with the machinery of the beneficiary State'.[121] This functional link derives from being 'placed at the disposal' of the receiving state and it is a link akin to that established by a state with its organs – that is, an institutional one – because 'the organ in question acts in the exercise of functions appertaining to the State at whose disposal it has been placed . . . and is required to obey any instructions it may receive from that State and not instructions from the State to which it belongs'.[122] It was clear then that such an institutional link was to be accompanied by a lack of interference from the sending government: the efficacy of control resided not in a factual link akin to Article 8 of the ARSIWA, but in the fact that the transfer between states was real, i.e. the organic link was severed with the sending state, however temporarily.

The discussion in 1974 therefore constituted a crucial moment, because it was then that 'effective control' was first used in this context, and first defined as an exclusive institutional link with the receiving state. In other words, 'effective control' as Ago used it in 1971 added nothing more than the idea of exclusivity of the transfer of an organ – and the ILC was wise to

[116] Ago, 'Third Report', n. 6, 199, at 268 and 271–4. [117] Ibid., at 272–3.
[118] Ibid., at 273–4. [119] ILC *Yearbook* 1974/I, 43, at 60.
[120] Ago, 'Third Report', n. 6, 199, at 267. [121] ILC *Yearbook* 1974/II(1), 269, at 287–8.
[122] Ibid., at 288.

phrase it in Article 6 of the ARSIWA in terms of 'being placed at the disposal', rejecting Ago's initial formulation.[123] 'Effective control' here had nothing at all to do with Article 8 of the ARSIWA or factual links.

3.2.3 Why the wording of Article 7 ARIO is misleading

In sum, in 1974 the ILC considered 'effective control' as a criterion to avoid dual attribution, and decided to replace it with that of 'being at the disposal of', which was meant to convey the same idea. Therefore, it is somewhat surprising to see that a similar question is arising today with reference to Article 7 of the ARIO. Why should the rule on organs transferred to international organisations be phrased differently from that of organs transferred to states? And why should it be phrased in terms of both 'being at the disposal of' *and* 'effective control', if the two were interchangeable concepts back in 1971?

The term 'effective control' in Article 7 of the ARIO clearly owes its debt to the arguments that Ago put forward in 1971 in his third report.[124] In the Commentaries to the ARIO, Gaja sought to link the 'effective control' test in what is now Article 7 of the ARIO to the formulation of Article 6 of the ARSIWA, and justified his proposed change of the latter's formulation by reference to the unsuitability of the language of 'governmental authority' in the context of international organisations.[125] But this is slightly unpersuasive. There *is* an equivalent for 'exercise of elements of governmental authority' in the context of international organisations, as the ARIO now recognise in Article 2(d): the concept of 'functions' of the international organisation. In fact, in order to maintain an analogy *mutatis mutandis* between Article 6 of the ARSIWA and Article 7 of the ARIO, the latter should have been drafted as follows: 'The conduct of an organ of a State or an organ or agent of an international organization that is placed at the disposal of another international organization shall be considered under international law an act of the latter organization if the organ or agent is acting in the exercise of the functions of the international organization at whose disposal it is placed.'

The Commentaries to the ARIO nonetheless affirmed the intention to keep the analogy with Article 6 of the ARSIWA, and explained that the point was not establishing if there was attribution, but choosing between

[123] See Ago, 'Third Report', n. 6, 199, at 274 and ILC *Yearbook* 1974/I, 43, at 60.
[124] Ago, 'Third Report', n. 6, 199, at 273. [125] ARIO Commentary, n. 10, at 87–8.

two subjects, if it were possible to do so.[126] This suggests that the 'effective control' test of Article 7 of the ARIO was not the same 'control' of Article 8 of the ARSIWA, *Nicaragua*, and *Bosnian Genocide*. In this context, one should interpret 'effective control' as a criterion determining when exclusive (rather than multiple) attribution can occur: the transfer of attribution follows the transfer of the organ only if the original institutional link with the sending state (or international organisation) has been (temporarily) severed. This is what a *mutatis mutandis* application of Article 6 of the ARSIWA would mean, and this is what the ILC should have adopted and clarified.[127]

However, there is an important obstacle to this construction of 'effective control' in Article 7 of the ARIO as being equivalent to Article 6 of the ARSIWA: and that is the text of Article 7 of the ARIO. The words 'effective control *over that conduct*' unequivocally suggest a factual link, not an institutional one. The ARIO Commentaries explicitly recognise as much by saying that the criterion 'is based according to Article 7 on the factual control that is exercised over the *specific conduct* taken by the organ or agent placed at the receiving organization's disposal'.[128] These words evoke the 'effective control' threshold advanced in *Bosnian Genocide* and *Nicaragua*, even if they employ it for a different purpose. The literal interpretation of the words 'effective control over that conduct' would imply that, in order for a transfer of attribution to occur under Article 7 of the ARIO, we must analyse every single conduct and adopt the criterion of 'control' akin to that in Article 8 of the ARSIWA before establishing that attribution has transferred from a state to an international organisation.

Thus, a crucial difference would seem to emerge between Article 6 of the ARSIWA and Article 7 of the ARIO. While Article 6 of the ARSIWA, before transferring attribution, requires the creation of an institutional link akin to that of Articles 4 or 5 of the ARSIWA to be established with the receiving state (the exercise of functions of the receiving state), Article 7 of the ARIO would only require a factual link akin to Article 8 of the ARSIWA: that is, a link of control at the time of the conduct. This interpretation, which is certainly possible under the current formulation of Article 7 of the ARIO, would yield a quite striking result. It would

126 Ibid., at 88.

127 Before the ARIO project commenced, similar views on the applicability of (what is now) Article 6 ARSIWA to this situation were expressed by L. Condorelli, 'Le Statut des forces des Nations Unies et le droit international humanitaire' (1995) 78 Riv Dir Int 881.

128 ARIO Commentary, n. 10, at 87–8 (emphasis added).

mean that organs transferred from states could never temporarily become organs or agents of an international organisation, thereby creating an institutional link with the international organisation, because a factual link with the international organisation would need to be established every time before attribution could be transferred. Of course, there could be good policy reasons for such a choice: for example, a preference for attribution of conduct (and thus responsibility) to states rather than international organisations, given that states usually have more financial means at their disposal than international organisations. Another possible reason for this difference could be that the premise behind Article 7 of the ARIO is precisely that states in fact never completely transfer their organs to international organisations, so that control would always to a certain extent be concurrent. But the intentions of the Commission did not seem to be these, at least initially. The difference between Article 7 of the ARIO and Article 6 of the ARSIWA seems to have occurred more by accident than by design.

3.2.4 Article 7 ARIO in practice

The complex relationship between Article 7 of the ARIO and Article 6 of the ARSIWA that we have just discussed leads to the conclusion that Article 7 of the ARIO was wrongly formulated, and that the criterion of 'effective control' in this context is misleading. According to some, it is also unsupported by state or international organisation practice.[129] It is important to reiterate that under the construction proposed here, 'effective control over the conduct' in Article 7 of the ARIO should not have the same meaning as the criterion to establish a factual link which bears a similar name in Article 8 of the ARSIWA. The drafting history of the two provisions points in this direction, although admittedly the text of Article 7 of the ARIO does not.[130] The transfer of attribution from a state or an international organisation to an international organisation should occur every time that the transferred organ is both functionally

[129] See e.g. K.M. Larsen, 'Attribution of Conduct in Peace Operations: The "Ultimate Authority and Control" Test' (2008) 19 EJIL 509, at 518, and the comments by the International Labour Organization in UN Doc. A/CN.4/568/Add.1 (2006), at 14–15 (according to the International Labour Organization, Article 7 ARIO fails to distinguish between a 'secondment' and a 'loan' of a state official to an international organisation; in its view, attribution would only arise when a 'secondment' occurs).

[130] One may also argue that, when analysing ILC codification texts, the role of the drafting history should be held in much higher regard than the 1969 Vienna Convention on the Law of Treaties (1155 UNTS 331) allows for treaties.

integrated in the receiving organisation and has ceased to be so with regard to the sending state or international organisation: if not, multiple attribution would ensue.

In any event, because of the rarity of situations in which states actually relinquish control over their organs, Article 7 of the ARIO is seldom triggered, regardless of how it is interpreted. In his seventh report, Gaja underlined that multiple attribution may well ensue from the fact that the threshold in Article 7 of the ARIO is high. Indeed, certain types of state/international organisation cooperation may render it difficult to assess who has control precisely because the conduct in question should be attributed to all cooperating actors.[131] Ago had reached a similar conclusion back in 1971, when discussing the *Nissan* case mentioned earlier.[132] As we saw, at some point the UK operation in Cyprus became part of a UN force. Despite this, the Court maintained attribution to the United Kingdom because 'the ... forces ... had not ceased to be British soldiers'.[133]

Most of the available practice on Article 7 of the ARIO is indeed from peace operations under UN auspices – either run directly by the United Nations (peacekeeping operations) or simply authorised by the UN Security Council but run by member states. As I have discussed elsewhere,[134] while in *Behrami* the ECtHR had wrongly applied an 'ultimate authority and control' test to this type of situation and had a priori excluded the possibility of dual attribution when peace support operations were concerned, both mistakes have recently been consigned to history by the subsequent Grand Chamber decision in *Al-Jedda*, which confirmed that dual attribution is possible.[135]

A similarly contradictory succession of authorities concerns the Netherlands, where the conduct of the United Nations Protection Force (UNPROFOR) (Dutchbat) during UN peace support operations in Bosnia came before Dutch courts. Successive courts have reached opposite conclusions as to attribution of conduct. In 2008, the District Court in The Hague held that the conduct of the Dutch contingent in

[131] Gaja, 'Seventh Report', n. 56, at 9. [132] See n. 93 and accompanying text.

[133] See Ago, 'Third Report', n. 6, at 199, 271–2 (note 420).

[134] Messineo, 'Things Could Only Get Better: *Al-Jedda* beyond *Behrami*', n. 32.

[135] *Al-Jedda* v. *the United Kingdom*, App. No. 27021/08 (ECtHR, 7 July 2011), at para. 80 ('The Court does not consider that, as a result of the authorisation contained in Resolution 1511, the acts of soldiers within the Multi-National Force *became attributable to the United Nations or – more importantly, for the purpose of this case – ceased to be attributable to the troop-contributing nations*'; emphasis added).

Dutchbat at the time of the Srebrenica genocide should be attributed to the United Nations only, and not to the Netherlands. Interestingly, the Court first referred to Article 6 of the ARSIWA, and said it was applicable by analogy.[136] It then said that the Dutch contingent was 'ranked within the UN command structure',[137] and therefore its actions were attributable only to the United Nations.[138] As a consequence, 'even gross negligence or serious failure of supervision on the part of the forces made available to the UN must in principle be attributed exclusively to this organization'.[139] A different conclusion on attribution would be warranted, the Court added, if the forces were found to act under the sole command of Dutch authorities 'cutting across' UN command.[140] This was a significant reversal of the 'effective control' rule in Article 7 of the ARIO. The Hague District Court held that in the case of 'parallel instructions' from both home and the United Nations, attribution would still be to the UN only, rather than to both the state and the UN, as the application of Article 6 of the ARSIWA by analogy (ostensibly the basis of the Court's decision) would dictate. In the Court's view, only a strong intervention of the lending state would determine attribution to the lending state, and attribution to the UN would be automatic in all other cases. In sum, the Court held that a strong presumption of UN attribution existed, although such presumption was not quite as strong as that of the UN Secretariat, which is ready to accept UN attribution even 'where the United Nations command and control structure [has] broken down'.[141] However, in July 2011, the Dutch Court of Appeal reversed this decision. It found that the Dutch peacekeepers were under the 'effective control' of authorities in The Hague, rather than the United Nations, and that attribution could potentially be to both the United Nations and the Netherlands.[142] In September 2013, the Dutch Supreme Court confirmed the Court of Appeal's decision, and reiterated that 'international law, in particular Article 7 DARIO in conjunction with

[136] *Hasan Nuhanović* v. *The Netherlands*, ECLI:NL:RBSGR:2008:BF0181 (10 September 2008), at para. 4.8, available at http://uitspraken.rechtspraak.nl/.

[137] Ibid., para. 4.9. [138] Ibid., para. 4.11. [139] Ibid., para. 4.13.

[140] Ibid., para. 4.14.11. [141] UN Doc. A/CN.4/637/Add.1 (2011), at 13–14.

[142] *Hasan Nuhanović* v. *The Netherlands*, ECLI:NL:GHSGR:2011:BR0133 (5 July 2011), at para. 5.3; also ILDC 1742 (NL 2011). See B. Boutin, 'Responsibility of the Netherlands for the Acts of Dutchbat in *Nuhanović* and *Mustafić*: The Continuous Quest for a Tangible Meaning for 'Effective Control' in the Context of Peacekeeping' (2012) 25 LJIL 521; P. A. Nollkaemper, 'Dual Attribution: Liability of the Netherlands for Conduct of Dutchbat in Srebrenica' (2011) 9 J Int Crim Just (2011) 1143.

Article 48(1) DARIO, does not exclude the possibility of dual attribution of given conduct'.[143] The Supreme Court also affirmed the Court of Appeal's legal finding that effective control could be exercised by two entities (a state and an international organisation) at the same time and with reference to the same conduct.[144]

The main result of *Al-Jedda* and the Dutch cases is that the rule on transferred organs in Article 7 should be reaffirmed, while acknowledging that its application is confined to those rare cases in which true transfers of organs have occurred – which is seldom the case in the context of military operations under UN auspices. When transfers are incomplete or only on paper, multiple attribution may ensue.

4. Conclusions

One of the key cases of shared responsibility in international law arises when two or more states or international organisations carry out together a single harmful conduct. According to the general rules on responsibility for internationally wrongful acts, the same conduct can be attributed to more than one subject of international law at the same time. In the framework proposed here, multiple attribution of conduct may arise in two sets of circumstances: either because the conduct is carried out by one person or entity to whom more than one rule of attribution applies, so that they are deemed to be acting on behalf of more than one state and/or international organisation at the same time; or because the conduct is carried out by two or more persons or entities each acting on behalf of a different state and/or international organisation. However, there are two important exceptions to multiple attribution of conduct: Article 6 of the ARSIWA, on the transfer of organs to states, and Article 7 of the ARIO, on the transfer of organs to international organisations. Despite the difference in text, the drafting history of codification efforts at the International Law Commission leads to the conclusion that these two rules should be interpreted as being analogous. In order for the presumption of dual attribution to be rebutted, a transfer of organs from a state and/or international organisation to another state and/or international organisation would need to satisfy two requirements. First, the

[143] *The Netherlands* v. *Hasan Nuhanović*, ECLI:NL:HR:2013:BZ9225 (6 September 2013), at para. 3.11.2; see also para. 3.9.4.

[144] See ibid., para. 3.11.2, read in conjunction with para. 3.5.2.

transferred organ must have exercised functions of the receiving state and/or international organisation; second, the sending state and/or international organisation must not have maintained control over the conduct of the organ. In all other cases of incomplete transfers of organs, multiple attribution may well ensue. The resulting framework is one in which multiple attribution is the default rule, not the exception, when states or international organisations act jointly.

4

Attribution of Responsibility

JAMES D. FRY

1. Introduction

Independent responsibility remains the general principle in the law of international responsibility, as established by the 2001 Articles on Responsibility of States for Internationally Wrongful Acts (ARSIWA) and later confirmed by the 2011 Articles on the Responsibility of International Organizations (ARIO).[1] Independent responsibility prescribes that each state or international organisation is responsible only for its own internationally wrongful conduct.[2]

However, both sets of Articles leave open the possibility of attributing responsibility to party A for internationally wrongful conduct committed by party B, often called 'attribution of responsibility',[3] or 'attributed responsibility'. The possibility of attributed responsibility is parallel to

James D. Fry is Associate Professor of Law and Director of the LLM Programme, University of Hong Kong Faculty of Law. The author thanks Liu Yang for his research assistance. The research leading to this chapter has received funding from the European Research Council under the European Union's Seventh Framework Programme (FP7/2007–2013)/ERC grant agreement n° 249499, as part of the research project on Shared Responsibility in International Law (SHARES), carried out at the Amsterdam Center for International Law (ACIL) of the University of Amsterdam.

[1] See Articles on Responsibility of States for Internationally Wrongful Acts, ILC *Yearbook* 2001/II(2) (ARSIWA); Commentary to the Articles on Responsibility of States for Internationally Wrongful Acts, ILC *Yearbook* 2001/II(2) (ARSIWA Commentary); Articles on the Responsibility of International Organizations, ILC Report on the work of its sixty-third session, UNGAOR 66th Sess., Supp. No. 10, UN Doc. A/66/10 (2011) (ARIO); Commentary to the Articles on the Responsibility of International Organizations, ILC Report on the work of its sixty-third session, UNGAOR 66th Sess., Supp. No. 10, UN Doc. A/66/10 (2011) (ARIO Commentary).

[2] J. Crawford, *The International Law Commission's Articles on State Responsibility, Introduction, Text and Commentaries* (Cambridge University Press, 2002), pp. 91, 145.

[3] See generally ibid.; ARIO Commentary to Article 1, para. 4, n. 1.

the normal situation of responsibility based on attribution of conduct.[4] This is to say that responsibility can be both direct and attributed (or indirect). The combination of attributed responsibility to one state or international organisation, on the one hand, and attribution of responsibility or conduct to another, on the other, might lead to multiple attribution (of responsibility, conduct, or both).

Attribution of responsibility may arise in several types of situations of 'shared responsibility', a concept that refers to the responsibility of multiple actors for their contribution to a single harmful outcome.[5] Attribution of responsibility may arise out of situations where states or international organisations act independently in causing a collective injury to a third party.[6] While state A can be held responsible for the internationally wrongful act committed (according to rules of attribution of conduct), state B may nevertheless also be attributed responsibility for state A's conduct without the conduct being attributed to state B.[7] In this sense, the attribution is multiple. The possibility may even arise that both parties are jointly responsible for the conduct attributable solely to another.[8] For example, under the mixed agreements between the European Union (EU) and its member states that fail to provide a clear division of power, both parties will be jointly responsible for a breach, without determining the attribution of conduct.[9] This indicates that the EU or the member states shall be responsible even if the breach can be attributed to the other.

It may seem that attribution of responsibility also may occur where multiple wrongdoers acted together in causing the harm. However, this is not necessarily true. By participating in the common enterprise, a state or international organisation is already involved in the wrongful conduct, and responsibility in such situations may be direct rather than attributed.

[4] Article 2 ARSIWA, n. 1. Attribution of conduct is discussed in Chapter 3 of this volume, F. Messineo, 'Attribution of Conduct', p. 60.

[5] Chapter 1 of this volume, Nollkaemper, 'Introduction', n. 1, at pp. 6–12.

[6] Ibid., at pp. 9–10; also P.A. Nollkaemper and D. Jacobs, 'Shared Responsibility in International Law: A Conceptual Framework' (2013) 34(2) MIJIL 359, at 368–9.

[7] ARIO Commentary to Chapter II, 'Attribution of conduct to an international organization', at para. 2, n. 1.

[8] G. Gaja, 'Second Report on the Responsibility of International Organizations', UN Doc. A/CN.4/541 (2004), para. 8.

[9] *Parliament* v. *Council*, European Court of Justice, case C-316/91 (1994) ECR I-653, at I-661–2. See also the oral pleadings to the World Trade Organization panel on *European Communities – Customs Classification of Certain Computer Equipment*, Report of the Panel of 5 February 1998, WT/DS62/R, WT/DS67/R, WT/DS68/R, where the EC asserted responsibility for infringements.

While in both the ARSIWA and the ARIO attributed responsibility would seem to provide for determinations of shared responsibility, the question of how the existing rules on attribution of responsibility indeed successfully allow for multiple attribution calls for further analysis. This chapter develops the notion of attribution of responsibility within the context of shared responsibility.[10]

No significant practice has been observed in relation to attribution of responsibility, and therefore the points made here are somewhat theoretical and speculative, just as many of the significant parts of the ARSIWA and the ARIO are theoretical and speculative. Nevertheless, the analysis may still be useful inasmuch as the ARSIWA and the ARIO can influence the progressive development of international law in this area, supported by the tremendous attention that the international legal community has given to these instruments.

This chapter will examine in which situations responsibility may be attributed to a state or international organisation and how this may support a determination of shared responsibility. For the convenience of description, occasionally this chapter refers to parties bearing shared responsibility as 'jointly responsible'. To avoid confusion with its domestic counterpart, joint responsibility is defined to occur where responsibility arises out of the acts of multiple actors that result in a single injury, and is distributed to them separately rather than collectively.[11] 'Joint' in this context is purely descriptive, and does not aim to be given any particular legal consequence.[12] Whenever 'joint responsibility' or 'jointly responsible' are mentioned below, the terms should be assumed to be in accordance with the above definition.

This chapter first analyses the concept of 'attribution of responsibility' and whether it leaves open the possibility of multiple attribution (section 2), and then analyses the ARSIWA and the ARIO concerning the plurality of responsible states and/or international organisations (section 3). The chapter then moves on to a discussion of the relevant Articles under the ARSIWA and the ARIO on attributed responsibility (aid or assistance, direction and control, coercion and circumvention), and identifies

[10] For the basic tenets of shared responsibility, see Nollkaemper and Jacobs, 'Shared Responsibility in International Law', n. 6.

[11] See Nollkaemper, 'Introduction', n. 1, at p. 10, and further Nollkaemper and Jacobs, 'Shared Responsibility in International Law', n. 6, at p. 368.

[12] Ibid., Nollkaemper and Jacobs.

potential contributing and restraining factors with regard to a determination of shared responsibility (section 4).

2. The concept of attribution of responsibility

2.1 The concept of attribution

Attribution is a legal mechanism for handling the collectivity of subjects of international law. It sets out the conditions that have to be satisfied in order to determine that a state or another subject of international law has performed a particular act.[13] According to the International Law Commission (ILC) Commentary to the ARSIWA, attribution of conduct should be determined by international law rather than by causality, making it a normative operation.[14] This view is not without objections from commentators who believe that attribution should be a factual operation.[15] A better view might be that the two ideas are perfectly consistent with each other. Adopting a normative approach simply imposes legal sense on the factual link between the conduct and the state, and it does not in any way deny the latter. To put it plainly, we can take the concept of attribution to mean a probe into the question of 'who did it'. It aims to identify the state to which the internationally wrongful act is attached for the purpose of responsibility,[16] even though it says nothing about whether responsibility should actually attach or not – there is still the issue of breach to consider.[17]

The ILC clearly deems causation irrelevant to the determination of international responsibility, as can be seen from the absence of causation

[13] L. Conforelli and C. Kress, 'The Rules of Attribution: General Considerations', in J. Crawford, A. Pellet, and S. Olleson (eds.), *The Law of International Responsibility* (Oxford University Press, 2010), p. 221. 'Attribution of Conduct' is discussed in Chapter 3 of this volume: see n. 4.

[14] Crawford, *The International Law Commission's Articles on State Responsibility*, n. 2, at p. 91.

[15] G. Arangio-Ruiz, 'Second Report on State Responsibility', ILC *Yearbook* 1989/II(1), at 48–53. See also Chapter 2 in this volume, A. Gattini, 'Breach of International Obligations', at p. 29.

[16] Crawford, *The International Law Commission's Articles on State Responsibility*, n. 2, at p. 92. See also Conforelli and Kress, 'The Rules of Attribution', n. 13, at p. 221.

[17] It should also be noted that the role of attribution is not limited to the international responsibility context, but rather acts as the foundation for the international legal system as a whole. See Crawford, *The International Law Commission's Articles on State Responsibility*, n. 2, at pp. 222–3; see also J. Crawford, 'First Report on State Responsibility', ILC *Yearbook* 1998/II(1), 33.

from the constitutive elements of internationally wrongful conduct.[18] As the rules currently stand, causation in the law of international responsibility is limited to the determination of reparations.[19] In this sense, the role of causation is to supply the link between the internationally wrongful conduct and the damage caused. Since the ILC excluded damage from the constitutive element of responsibility, causation is of limited utility in determining responsibility. However, d'Aspremont argues that causation can possibly exist in other stages, implicit in attribution of conduct, which arises as the causal link between the conduct and the breach, substituting the traditional causation between breach and injury.[20] However, this is not real 'causation'. Intuitively, if one says 'A causes B', B has to be something different from A. It is hard to assert that a state's conduct 'causes' an 'internationally wrongful conduct', because the latter actually is a conceptualisation of the former by the ILC, which means both are the same thing. This would be the same as saying that 'the killing causes the murder', which does not make sense. Therefore, it is unlikely that, in the ILC's framework, causation will ever play a role in determining responsibility.[21] However, such potential confusion with causation can only possibly occur for attribution of conduct. As shown below, attribution of responsibility does not arise as a link between the conduct and the perpetrator, but provides a nexus between different perpetrators. This critical point also excludes causation from the realm of attribution of responsibility.

2.2 Attribution of responsibility as distinct from attribution of conduct

In both attribution of responsibility and attribution of conduct, attribution serves to identify a party who is either potentially responsible

[18] For a detailed analysis of the reason for such absence of causation in international responsibility, see L. Castellanos-Jankiewicz, 'Causation and International State Responsibility', SHARES Research Paper 07 (2012), ACIL 2012-07, available at www.sharesproject.nl (last accessed on 20 March 2014). Compare Gattini, 'Breach of International Obligations', n. 15, at pp. 28–31.

[19] Ibid., Castellanos-Jankiewicz, 'Causation and International State Responsibility', at 5.

[20] J. d'Aspremont, 'The Articles on the Responsibility of International Organizations: Magnifying the Fissures in the Law of International Responsibility' (2012) 9(1) IOLR 15, at 21.

[21] Causation may be relevant for the determination of breach, but this falls outside the scope of this chapter. For more on causation and breach, see Gattini, 'Breach of International Obligations', n. 15, at pp. 28–31.

(attribution of conduct)[22] or responsible (attribution of responsibility). In fact, the ILC has indicated that 'the idea of the implication of one state in the conduct of another is analogous to problems of attribution (of conduct)'.[23] The ILC did not elaborate on how they are 'analogous', but it seems that attribution of responsibility and attribution of conduct are functionally equivalent, in that both are a pathway towards responsibility. However, attribution of responsibility differs greatly from attribution of conduct. Attribution of conduct and attribution of responsibility apply to different factual patterns, function independently of each other, and possess distinct theoretical bases.

The literature hardly discusses the concept of attribution of responsibility. One line of thought equates attribution of responsibility to the concept of derived responsibility, stating that attribution of responsibility occurs where one state is responsible for the conduct of another state, while the latter state is simultaneously responsible for its own conduct.[24] The idea of derived responsibility can be traced to sole arbitrator Max Huber in *British Claims in the Spanish Zone of Morocco 1923–1925*. The arbitration involved the dependency relationship of a protectorate, and the arbitrator held that since the protected state did not act independently in the international domain and any measures taken by third states concerning the protected state necessarily would affect the rights of the protector state, the protector state should take up the responsibility for the protected state.[25] This chapter accepts such a concept of attribution of responsibility, except that this latter state might not always bear responsibility for its own conduct – for example, in the situation of circumvention of international obligations under Article 17 of the ARIO.

Before elaborating on these differences in detail, it is necessary to emphasise one basic characteristic of attribution of responsibility. For the state or international organisation bearing attributed responsibility, there should be 'conduct', as it is used in the general sense. However, two points should be made. First, the conduct need not be internationally wrongful conduct. Attribution of responsibility is independent from

22 The point with 'potentially' is that breach still has to be proven.

23 Crawford, *The International Law Commission's Articles on State Responsibility*, n. 2, at p. 147

24 D. Amoroso, 'Moving Towards Complicity as a Criteria of Attribution of Private Conducts: Imputation to States of Corporate Abuses in the US Case Law' (2011) 24 LJIL 989.

25 *British Claims in the Spanish Zone of Morocco (Great Britain/Spain)* (1924) 2 RIAA 615, at 648.

internationally wrongful conduct. Second, while there should be conduct, this is not necessarily conduct by the actor to whom responsibility is attributed. Given that attribution of responsibility concerns the relationship, factual or legal, between the party who commits the wrong and the party to which responsibility is attributed, there can be some doubt over whether the latter party actually committed a course of 'conduct'. This is a critical issue, because it in essence delimits the scope of attributed responsibility. For example, the provision of aid or assistance would not be considered a proper case for attribution of responsibility, since the state or international organisation providing such aid actually committed an internationally wrongful act of its own.

2.2.1 Different factual contexts

Attribution of responsibility necessarily involves more than one party, since if there is only one wrongdoer, direct reference to attribution of conduct would be sufficient for responsibility purposes. Such a multiparty model of attributed responsibility is confirmed by the ILC. Even though there is no explicit mention of 'attribution of responsibility' in the ARSIWA, arguably it is implicit in its Chapter IV, entitled 'Responsibility of a state in connection with the conduct of another state',[26] where a state bears responsibility for the internationally wrongful act not committed by itself. Moreover, the fact that both the ARSIWA and the ARIO provide separate chapters on attribution of conduct and attribution of responsibility suggests that they constitute distinct rules, functioning within their respective domains. In other words, attribution of responsibility involves independent acts of multiple parties causing a collective injury, whereas attribution of conduct often, but not necessarily, will involve the situation of a single wrongdoer.[27]

2.2.2 Different sphere of operation

The above conceptualisation of attribution of responsibility is not built upon attribution of conduct, and presumably also is without prejudice to attribution of conduct. The ILC designed the concept of attribution of

[26] It is also called 'indirect responsibility' or 'responsibility for the act of another' by Roberto Ago; see R. Ago, 'Eighth Report on State Responsibility', ILC *Yearbook* 1979/II(1), at 4, para. 2.

[27] The possibility of multiple attribution of conduct is explained by Messineo, 'Attribution of Conduct', n. 4, at pp. 62–3, 67–83.

conduct as one of the constitutive elements of an internationally wrongful act, which entails international responsibility. However, attribution of responsibility provides a different route to determining responsibility, which is independent of the determination of whether there is an internationally wrongful act. This is compatible with the opinion of Giorgio Gaja that responsibility does not always need to be based upon attribution of conduct:

> There is no need to devise special rules on attribution in order to assert the organization's responsibility ... Responsibility of an organization does not necessarily have to rest on attribution of conduct to that organization. It may well be that an organization undertakes an obligation in circumstances in which compliance depends on the conduct of its member States.[28]

Even though this observation addresses responsibility of international organisations, state responsibility runs parallel to this. For any particular state, attribution of responsibility also does not depend on attribution of the conduct to that state.[29]

An example of the independence of attribution of responsibility from attribution of conduct can be found in Article 6(1) of Annex IX to the 1982 United Nations (UN) Convention on the Law of the Sea (LOSC or Convention),[30] which provides that '[p]arties which have competence under Article 5 of this Annex shall have responsibility for failure to comply with obligations or for any other violation of this Convention.' No reference to attribution of conduct is made here. Neither is it likely that attribution of conduct is implicitly presumed, because what matters for responsibility is competence, rather than conduct. The inclusion of the word 'competence' in the LOSC is essential. Given that competence over particular conduct is not always clearly divided between a state party and an international organisation that is a party to the Convention, either the state party or the international organisation could be held responsible for the breach not committed by itself, as long as the matter

[28] Gaja, 'Second Report', n. 8, para. 11. See also C. Yamada, 'Revisiting the International Law Commission's Draft Articles on State Responsibility', in M. Ragazzi (ed.), *International Responsibility Today: Essays in Memory of Oscar Schachter* (Leiden: Martinus Nijhoff, 2005), p. 121.

[29] Crawford, *The International Law Commission's Articles on State Responsibility*, n. 2, at p. 145.

[30] United Nations Convention on the Law of the Sea, Montego Bay, 10 December 1982, in force 16 November 1994, 1833 UNTS 3 (LOSC).

falls within its competence. This is further supported by paragraph 2 of the same Article, which provides that failure by the organisation or its member states to provide information, or the provision of contradictory information, concerning who has responsibility in respect of any specific matter, shall result in joint and several liability. Therefore, it does not matter who actually committed the wrongful conduct.

Mixed agreements between the European Union and its member states also represent a typical example.[31] Responsibility can be attributed without attribution of conduct to the same subject, because the European Union or member states can be held responsible for the conduct of the other. As the European Court of Justice stated in *Parliament* v. *Council*, which concerned a mixed cooperation agreement, 'in those circumstances, in the absence of derogations expressly laid down in the Convention, the Community and its member States as partners of the ACP States are jointly liable to those latter States for the fulfilment of every obligation arising from the commitments undertaken'.[32]

Of course, it cannot be denied that responsibility and conduct both can be attributed to one party. Nevertheless, attribution of responsibility and attribution of conduct do not necessarily correspond to each other, in that the effective functioning of each does not depend on the other.

2.2.3 Distinct theoretical bases

As described above, attribution of conduct is a legal operation, addressing the factual link between the conduct and the state or international organisation through a normative approach. Such an instrumental approach, though widely accepted by ILC members, is not free from objections. For example, Brownlie not only labelled the concept of imputability (attribution) 'superfluous',[33] but also pointed out that 'imputability (attribution) implies a fiction where there is none, and conjures up the idea of vicarious liability where it cannot apply'.[34] For Brownlie, what truly matters is whether there is a breach of an international obligation, depending on

31 For more information on mixed agreements, see e.g. C. Hillion and P. Koutrakos (eds.), *Mixed Agreements Revisited* (Oxford: Hart Publishing, 2010); and J. Heliskoski, *Mixed Agreements as a Technique for Organizing the International Relations of the European Community and its Member States* (Leiden: Kluwer Law International, 2001).

32 *Parliament* v. *Council*, n. 9, at I-660–1, recital 29.

33 I. Brownlie, *System of the Law of Nations, State Responsibility, Part I* (Oxford: Clarendon Press, 1983), p. 36.

34 Ibid.

which the content of attribution will vary.[35] It seems that Brownlie views attribution of conduct as an artificial tool, the content of which may change as the relevant obligation changes. The same cannot be said of attribution of responsibility, because attributed responsibility is based upon solid grounds of its own. Asking the question why responsibility can be attributed to a particular party is, in a theoretical way, asking why states or other international law subjects can bear responsibility. The answer, as this chapter demonstrates below, lies with the theory of control. This is a significant difference between attribution of responsibility and attribution of conduct.

2.3 *Basis of attribution of responsibility*

2.3.1 States

The earliest theory of attribution of responsibility is the 'representation theory' of Anzilotti. Anzilotti argued that an injured state could not claim responsibility against a represented state because the latter state did not carry out international relations by itself. Rather, it was the representing state that bore the responsibility indirectly.[36] This theory was later replaced by the 'control theory', which holds that for indirect responsibility to attach, it is necessary that the unlawful act is within the freedom of decision of the controlling state.[37] According to Eagleton's idea that power breeds responsibility, states are only willing to accept responsibility for actions if they have authority over such actions.[38] Such authority assumes that the responsible state has the power to prevent unlawful acts within its own territory.[39] The degree of such responsibility is proportional to the scope of the authority exercised.[40] If one seeks the origin for such authority, it should be the necessary corollary of the sovereignty and autonomy of states.[41] What is inherent within this power to prevent is actually the authority over the conduct taking place within its territory, for which responsibility is incurred, and such authority is manifested in the form of control.[42] In this sense, control

[35] Ibid. [36] Ago, 'Eighth Report on State Responsibility', n. 26, at 5. [37] Ibid., at 17.

[38] C. Eagleton, *The Responsibility of States in International Law* (New York University Press, 1928), p. 152.

[39] Ibid. This ability to prevent unlawful acts is inherent in Articles 29 and 30 of both the ARSIWA and the ARIO concerning the duty of performance and non-repetition.

[40] Eagleton, *The Responsibility of States in International Law*, n. 38, at p. 152. [41] Ibid.

[42] The 'control' is used in the general sense, and should not be confused with 'effective control'.

over conduct can provide a basis for attribution of responsibility for states.

Upon closer analysis, Eagleton's notion of control is limited to the influence exercised over conduct. To put it differently, Eagleton argues for control as the basis for attribution of conduct. Accordingly, if he were to claim control as the basis for responsibility, he also must be assuming a connection between wrongful conduct and responsibility. However, since attributed responsibility can be responsibility without wrongful conduct, it seems that Eagleton's control theory is not directly applicable.

However, this does not mean that control cannot serve as a basis for responsibility. It is important to note that 'responsibility without wrongful conduct' does not mean there is no wrongful conduct at all; otherwise there would be no responsibility. What it actually means is that a state can be attributed responsibility for the conduct of another. In other words, there was no wrongful conduct of the state or international organisation on its own. In order to attribute responsibility for the wrongful conduct of another, it is possible that control is directly established between states rather than between the state and the conduct. If such control necessarily affects the autonomy of the state, then it is possible to argue that what Eagleton called 'authority over actions', rather than the actions per se, is transferred. Therefore, a link can be established between the controlling state and the conduct of the actual perpetrating state, whereby the former state bears responsibility. In this sense, control and autonomy of states are two sides of the same coin: namely, who bears authority over the conduct. The control theory provides the rationale for Chapter IV of the ARSIWA.[43]

2.3.2 International organisations

Given that control can constitute the basis for state responsibility, is it correct to say the same for international organisations, simply because they, like states, have acquired international legal personality?[44] Generally, it is believed that since international organisations have the necessary powers transferred to them by their member states, they can accordingly

[43] J. D. Fry, 'Coercion, Causation, and the Fictional Elements of Indirect State Responsibility' (2007) 40 Vand J Transnat L 611, at 617.

[44] *Reparation for Injuries Suffered in the Service of the United Nations*, Advisory Opinion, ICJ Reports 1949, 174.

be attributed responsibility just like states.[45] However, a word of caution must be provided here. States and international organisations are not equivalent. While states are considered identical and equal sovereigns regardless of their domestic political institutions and cultures, for example, international organisations are not necessarily created equal, and show great diversity depending on these same factors.[46] Therefore, it might be argued that for different international organisations, control is derived from different sources, and it is reasonable to question whether there can be a uniform source of control as a basis for responsibility for all international organisations. Indeed, it has been observed that for some international organisations, control can be derived from the transfer of power by member states, such as the European Union, although it is difficult to claim so for others.[47] This largely exposes the inadequacy of the ARIO, and is addressed later in this chapter.

2.4 A further distinction

A necessary question at this point is the following: how is control as the basis of attribution of responsibility different from control in attribution of conduct? It is clear that control also has a role to play in attribution of conduct. The most typical is that 'effective control' is the test for attribution of conduct in cases of secondment of organs: for example, in peacekeeping operations.[48] However, even though attribution of conduct and attribution of responsibility both rely on control, this does not necessarily negate the distinction between them, because in these two scenarios, control actually aims at different objects. In attribution of conduct, control is exercised over the conduct committed, while in attribution of responsibility, control is over the state or international organisation. Attribution of conduct is symbolised by a transfer of conduct. Once an act is committed, it is transferred from the actual committer to the state or organisation to which the conduct is attributed. By exercising effective

[45] C. Ahlborn, 'The Use of Analogies in Drafting the Articles on the Responsibility of International Organizations – An Appraisal of the "Copy–Paste Approach"' – (2012) 9(1) IOLR 53, at 63.

[46] J. Wouters and J. Odermatt, 'Are All International Organizations Created Equal?' (2012) 9(1) IOLR 7, at 12.

[47] N. Nedeski and P. A. Nollkaemper, 'Responsibility of International Organizations "in Connection with Acts of States"' (2012) 9(1) IOLR 33, at 38–9.

[48] Gaja, 'Second Report', n. 8, at 19.

control, the seconding party actually makes the conduct its own, even though the organ that commits the wrong already is seconded to another state or international organisation. In other words, the conduct is transferred from the seconded party to the seconding party. However, in attribution of responsibility, control exercised by one party over another does not affect the fact that the perpetrator still is the seconding party. In essence, attributed responsibility represents an effort to substitute transfer of conduct with transfer of authority. In the former case, the controlling party will be regarded as the perpetrator of the conduct, but the same is not true in the latter case. This particularity of attributed responsibility can be explained by the fact that it proposes to address relationships, either legal or factual, between states, rather than conduct. Such a relationship does not affect attribution of conduct, but it can influence the authority over the conduct, which originally is retained by the influenced party, but is transferred due to the relationship between the two parties.

This distinction is well reflected in the analysis of the conduct of peacekeeping operations. Some argue that in this case the element of control actually has made the conduct 'collective', meaning it is attributable to both parties.[49] The choice of the ILC to prescribe the effective control test in determination of the attribution of conduct[50] has been attacked, particularly for its ignorance of the legal institutional link between the peacekeeping operation and the United Nations itself, which would render the conduct attributable to the United Nations instead.[51] Such a conflict between alternative ways of attributing conduct would be avoided if effective control were to become a legal basis for attribution of responsibility to the contributing member states, avoiding the question of whether the conduct is attributable as well.[52]

[49] J. d'Aspremont, 'Abuse of the Legal Personality of International Organizations and the Responsibility of Member States' (2008) 4 IOLR 91, at 115.

[50] Gaja, 'Second Report', n. 8, at 19. See also Chapter 3 of this volume, Messineo, 'Attribution of Conduct', n. 4, at pp. 88–96, where he argues that Article 7 of the ARIO should be interpreted as saying that the effective control test would only require that a factual link be established whenever there is a transfer of an organ between a state and an international organisation, thereby eliminating the necessity to create any institutional link.

[51] A. Sari, 'UN Peacekeeping Operations and Article 7 ARIO: The Missing Link' (2012) 9(1) IOLR 77, at 82.

[52] See Messineo, 'Attribution of Conduct', n. 4, at pp. 88–96, where he argues that in the case of transfer of an organ from a state to an international organisation, there is good reason for the conduct of the organ to be attributed to the state.

2.5 *The possibility of multiple attribution*

2.5.1 The view of the ILC

For shared responsibility – which would involve the responsibility of each of the multiple parties – to stand, it is necessary that the possibility of multiple attribution is left fully open, so that each party can either be attributed responsibility or bear responsibility based on attribution of conduct. The question, therefore, is whether attribution of responsibility to one state or international organisation necessarily precludes the responsibility of another state or international organisation.

An answer comes from the Committee on Accountability of International Organizations (IO) of the International Law Association: 'The responsibility of an IO does not preclude any separate or concurrent responsibility of a State or of another IO which participated in the performance of the wrongful act'.[53] The Committee does not say whether the same holds true for the responsibility of a state.

The ILC does not explicitly state its view on this particular point, so it requires more analysis to say whether the ILC supports multiple attribution of responsibility. Paragraph 1 of Article 47 of the ARSIWA, entitled 'Plurality of Responsible States', stipulates that '[w]here several States are responsible for the same internationally wrongful act, the responsibility of each State may be invoked in relation to that act.'[54] Similarly, paragraph 1 of Article 48 of the ARIO provides as follows: 'Where an international organization and one or more States or other international organizations are responsible for the same internationally wrongful act, the responsibility of each State or organization may be invoked in relation to that act.'[55] Both Articles provide for the right of the injured state or international organisation to invoke responsibility against each one of the responsible states or international organisations individually. This might leave open the possibility of multiple attribution of responsibility, but the ILC does not say so explicitly.

[53] International Law Association Committee on Accountability of International Organisations, Report of the Seventieth Conference held in New Delhi, 2–6 April 2002, at 16

[54] Article 47(1) ARSIWA, n. 1.

[55] Article 48(1) ARIO, n. 1. See on these Articles also Chapter 8 of this volume, A. M. H. Vermeer-Künzli, 'Invocation of Responsibility', p. 251, and Chapter 9, E. A. Wyler and L. A. Castellanos-Jankiewicz, 'Serious Breaches of Peremptory Norms', p. 284, at pp. 289, 290, 307.

Such a possibility of multiple attribution of responsibility is supported by the *Nauru* case, where the International Court of Justice (ICJ or Court) rejected Australia's argument that it could not be sued individually by Nauru, but could only be sued jointly with the other two states that also were in charge of administering the trust territory.[56] The situation involving international organisations is more complicated by the possibility that a state or international organisation bears only subsidiary responsibility, in which case such subsidiary responsibility can only be invoked if the primarily responsible state or international organisation has not provided reparation.[57] Article 48(2) of the ARIO does not distinguish expressly between a state that is a member of the international organisation involved and one that is not. The former is a perfectly clear situation, as is confirmed by Article 62 of the ARIO, which provides that where a member state is responsible, such responsibility is presumed to be subsidiary.[58] This is largely due to the fact that international organisations should bear responsibility on their own and member states cannot be held responsible simply because of their membership.[59] However, the ARIO do not provide any examples of non-member states bearing subsidiary responsibility.

Given that Article 47 of the ARSIWA and Article 48 of the ARIO address the invocation of responsibility, which is the consequence of responsibility rather than the establishment of responsibility per se, what the two Articles provide cannot be directly used for analysis of a rule of multiple attribution of responsibility. However, their significance lies in the fact that they do not exclude, and therefore indirectly recognise, the possibility of two or more states or international organisations being responsible for the same internationally wrongful act. The 'sameness' in this context emphasises that it is only one internationally wrongful act that is being addressed, as opposed to separate internationally wrongful acts. It should not be forgotten that in this case both attributed responsibility and responsibility based on attribution of conduct can be built upon this single wrongful conduct. Therefore, shared responsibility possibly could be built upon this by investigating under what conditions one party may incur responsibility for its involvement in the internationally wrongful conduct of another party. That is a necessary starting

[56] *Certain Phosphate Lands in Nauru (Nauru* v. *Australia)*, Preliminary Objections, ICJ Reports 1992, 240, at 255–62 (*Nauru*).

[57] Article 48(2) ARIO, n. 1. [58] Ibid., Article 62(2).

[59] ARIO Commentary to Article 62 at para. 2, n. 1.

point for further analysis of multiple attribution of responsibility and shared responsibility. The consequence of such multiple attribution of responsibility is thus a 'joint responsibility'.[60] It is the aim of this chapter only to address the relationship between the injured parties and the responsible parties, rather than the relationship between the multiple responsible parties.

It is necessary to recall that the definition of attribution of responsibility, as responsibility for the conduct of another, means that there cannot be situations where all of the parties bear attributed responsibility, because the conduct must at least be attributed to one party. For that particular party, responsibility can hold if the two requirements of breach and attribution of conduct are satisfied. Accordingly, there is no reason to deny the possibility that responsibility can be attached to parties other than the one bearing attributed responsibility.

2.5.2 Limitations on multiple attribution

There exist certain limitations on the responsibility of the parties other than those to which responsibility is attributed: for example, coercion, where the coerced party bears at most a limited degree of responsibility;[61] or circumvention, through which responsibility is inapplicable to the party carrying out the circumvention because its international legal personality is being abused.[62] Moreover, in cases where an organisation bears primary responsibility, the subsidiary responsibility only can be invoked to the extent that the primary responsibility does not lead to reparation.[63]

3. Default rules of attribution of responsibility

This section explores the various grounds of attributed responsibility to see if they promote or hamper shared responsibility. Although 'control' explains how the authority over conduct is transferred, it is in itself not sufficient for responsibility to be attributed, because it does not address the source of illegality. If attributed responsibility is responsibility without wrongful conduct, where does the wrongfulness come from? If a state does nothing wrong, why attribute responsibility to it? In other words, attribution of responsibility may seem reasonable because a state or international organisation cannot be held responsible without first

[60] Nollkaemper and Jacobs, 'Shared Responsibility in International Law', n. 6, at 366–70.
[61] See section 3.3. [62] See section 3.5.2. [63] Article 48(2) ARIO, n. 1.

incurring an obligation.[64] Since attributed responsibility is the responsibility for the wrongful conduct of another, the reasonable corollary should be that the 'wrongful conduct of another' also is wrongful for the party attributed responsibility. Indeed, the ILC has prescribed that in all of the scenarios incurring attributed responsibility, both parties should bear the same international obligations, except in the case of coercion.[65] Coercion constitutes an exception simply because it is so powerful as an 'extreme' case of attributed responsibility that the ILC deems it appropriate to attach responsibility even when the coercing party does not bear the same international obligation.[66]

Even though the ILC only lists coercion as an exception, it is not necessarily true that both parties can bear the same obligation.[67] Although both states and international organisations are international legal persons, they do not necessarily have an equal scope of competence. For example, international organisations generally are not able to participate in most treaties in which states participate. Accordingly, the international obligation of a state can be broader than that of an international organisation. Therefore, in the case of an international organisation providing assistance or exercising control over another international organisation or state in committing an internationally wrongful act, it may be difficult to attribute responsibility to the controlling international organisation. A fairly practical solution would be to rely on the rule of circumvention as is stipulated in Articles 17 and 61 of the ARIO.

Another essential element for attribution of responsibility – control over the state or international organisation – must be established through an analysis of the legal or factual relationship. However, the notion of a legal or factual relationship is so broad that it is hard to understand what it actually means. Indeed, the only thing that is known is that such a relationship would encroach on the autonomy of the state or international organisation affected. The ILC did provide specific manifestations of such a relationship in the ARSIWA and the ARIO, including aid or assistance,

[64] This idea is developed from Article 34 of the Vienna Convention on the Law of Treaties, which stipulates that a treaty 'does not create either obligations or rights for a third State without its consent'. Vienna Convention on the Law of Treaties, Vienna, 23 May 1969, in force 27 January 1980, 1155 UNTS 331, Article 34 (VCLT).

[65] Article 17(b) ARSIWA, n. 1; Articles 15(b) and 58(b) ARIO, n. 1.

[66] Crawford, *The International Law Commission's Articles on State Responsibility*, n. 2, at p. 147.

[67] Compare Gattini, 'Breach of International Obligations', Chapter 2 in this volume, n. 15, at p. 26.

direction and control, coercion, and, in the case of international organisations, circumvention of obligations. It is not clear why the ILC listed only these scenarios, and whether or not this list is exhaustive. In light of this, by simply analysing these Articles, the conclusions that can be drawn concerning whether attribution of responsibility provides for the possibility of shared responsibility are incomplete. There might well be other situations of attribution of responsibility yet to be formulated. This chapter mainly focuses on the rules as they currently exist. However, section 2 has already explained that attribution of responsibility does not hamper multiple attribution, although it does provide certain limitations. With the potential scenarios of attributed responsibility listed by the ILC, it is possible to at least get a sense of how attribution of responsibility works towards shared responsibility in these specific situations, thus enabling a search for clues that could lead to a more coherent analysis.

The following section first addresses scenarios common to both the ARSIWA and the ARIO, such as aid or assistance, direction and control, and coercion, ending with a discussion of the common elements, such as knowledge and breach of an identical obligation.[68] It then moves on to look at the special scenario in the case of international organisations, namely circumvention. It is important to note that the title of the respective Chapters in the Articles all contain 'in connection with'. What is needed for the purpose of attributed responsibility, then, is to know to what extent they also provide for responsibility 'for' the conduct of another entity. In all of the following scenarios, it is assumed that the conduct is attributable to only one party,[69] and it is the responsibility of the other party that is at issue. Since control is established as the basis for attribution of responsibility, the subsections that follow test whether control can be identified for the purpose of attributing responsibility.

3.1 *Aid or assistance*

The first scenario is aid or assistance.[70] Article 16 of the ARSIWA and Articles 14 and 58 of the ARIO provide for responsibility where one

[68] 'Coercion' does not require that the coercing state or international organisation be bound by the same obligation as the coerced party. However, it is worth including it for the purpose of comparison.

[69] ARIO Commentary, n. 1, at 158.

[70] For a critical analysis on whether aid or assistance fits shared responsibility, see Chapter 5 in this volume, V. Lanovoy, 'Complicity in an Internationally Wrongful Act', at p. 134.

state or international organisation assists another state or international organisation in committing an internationally wrongful act. Two requirements for responsibility have been stipulated: first, that the state or international organisation has knowledge of the circumstances of the internationally wrongful act; and second, that the assisted act would be internationally wrongful if committed by the assisting state or international organisation.[71] What constitutes aid or assistance is not defined. Given that a separate chapter of this book deals with aid or assistance,[72] only a few issues potentially relevant to attribution of responsibility are addressed here.

This chapter asserts that aid or assistance is not related to attributed responsibility. The difficulty with its being so categorised is that aid or assistance is formulated to provide for a separate wrong itself, rather than responsibility in connection with the conduct of the assisted party.[73] If so, then the responsibility will be direct rather than attributed. As early as 1978, the ILC produced what was then Article 27 concerning aid or assistance:

> Aid or assistance by a State to another State, if it is established that it is rendered for the commission of an internationally wrongful act carried out by the latter, itself constitutes an internationally wrongful act, even if, taken alone, such aid or assistance would not constitute the breach of an international obligation.[74]

This view has been passed down to the current Articles. Article 16 of the ARSIWA and Articles 13 and 58 of the ARIO all provide that the assisting party is responsible 'for doing so',[75] such as the act of assisting or aiding. This view has also gained further support among scholars.[76] In light of this view, the assisting party bears responsibility for its own conduct, rather than the conduct of the assisted state. Accordingly, the paradigm situation is that both the assisting and assisted parties each are responsible for their own distinct acts.

[71] Article 16 ARSIWA, n. 1; Articles 14 and 58 ARIO, n. 1.

[72] See Lanovoy, 'Complicity in an Internationally Wrongful Act', n. 71.

[73] E.g., B. Graefrath, 'Complicity in the Law of International Responsibility' (1996) 29 RBDI 370, at 371.

[74] ILC *Yearbook* 1978/II(2), 99.

[75] Article 16 ARSIWA, n. 1; Articles 14 and 58 ARIO, n. 1.

[76] D'Aspremont, 'Abuse of the Legal Personality of International Organizations', n. 49, at 98. See also S. Talmon, 'A Plurality of Responsible Actors: International Responsibility for Acts of the Coalition Provisional Authority in Iraq', in P. Shiner and A. Williams (eds.), *The Iraq War and International Law* (Oxford: Hart Publishing, 2008), p. 185, at p. 218.

Moreover, aid or assistance does not provide for a satisfactory tool for (multiple) attribution of responsibility. The content of aid or assistance does not indicate an element of control which, as noted earlier, is an essential condition of attribution of responsibility. Since the assisted party bears primary responsibility while the assisting state has merely a supporting role,[77] the latter will only be responsible to the extent that its own conduct has contributed to the internationally wrongful act.[78] Provision of aid does not necessarily entail control over the assisted party, though such assistance can be conditional on the receiving party not performing certain acts. However, promises to that effect simply are the 'consideration' for rendering assistance, and they do not signify control over the receiving party that will lead to a transfer of authority.

It has been argued that aid or assistance is rather flexible and inclusive, so it can be interpreted either to indicate subsidiary complicity or co-perpetrator status.[79] This view finds support in the Commentary to Article 16 of the ARSIWA, where the ILC explained that it is not necessary that the aid or assistance makes an 'essential contribution' to the commission of an internationally wrongful act. Rather, it is simply sufficient that the conduct 'contributed significantly'.[80] This means that providing aid or assistance is a matter of degree of involvement. However, even if it reaches the extent that it becomes 'a veritable co-author of the principal internationally wrongful act',[81] without which the harm would not have been incurred,[82] the greater role it plays in the causal link still does not change the fact that the assisting party has no control over the assisted party.[83]

3.2 *Direction and control*

Article 17 of the ARSIWA provides that a state that directs and controls another in the commission of an internationally wrongful act is responsible

[77] Ibid. [78] Ibid.

[79] Crawford, *The International Law Commission's Articles on State Responsibility*, n. 2, at p. 50.

[80] Ibid. [81] ILC *Yearbook* 1978/II(2), at 104, para. 18.

[82] This seems to imply a 'but-for' test. For a critique of the but-for test in determining the link between the potentially responsible state and the harm caused, see Fry, 'Coercion, Causation, and the Fictional Elements of Indirect State Responsibility', n. 43, at 634–7. See also Gattini, 'Breach of International Obligations', n. 15, at pp. 28–31.

[83] It also has been argued that joint responsibility would apply in this context: see J. Quigley, 'Complicity in International Law: A New Direction in the Law of State Responsibility' (1986) 57 BYIL 77, at 120.

for the act itself. Article 15 of the ARIO is largely modelled upon this, except that the controlled or directed entity could be a state as well as another international organisation. There is no clear definition for direction and control. According to the ILC, 'control' refers to the 'domination over the commission of wrongful conduct and not simply the exercise of oversight, still less mere influence or concern',[84] and 'directs' connotes more than mere incitement or suggestion, but rather 'actual direction of an operative kind'.[85] Moreover, it is necessary that direction and control are actually exercised over the internationally wrongful act,[86] with mere possession of power to direct and control being insufficient.[87] Therefore, what is required is not only normative control in general, but also factual control and direction over the particular act. The principle of direction and control fits well into the idea of 'control' as a basis for attribution of responsibility. It is the controlled party that commits the internationally wrongful act, but the responsibility of the controlling party can be incurred. This would seem to fit this chapter's own control argument. However, there are issues that need further clarification for such a principle to involve shared responsibility.

3.2.1 Potential ambiguities

First, there seems to be ambiguity as to whether direction and control provides derived or direct responsibility. It has been assumed that direction and control concerns derived responsibility.[88] However, could it also be simply direct responsibility for the directing and controlling party, with the internationally wrongful conduct attributed to it?[89] Since the conduct of a state or international organisation can only be committed through its organs, what is the difference between controlling a state or international organisation and controlling its organs?[90] Such ambiguity is further emphasised by the ILC's statement that 'a State which directs and controls another in the commission of an internationally wrongful

[84] Crawford, *The International Law Commission's Articles on State Responsibility*, n. 2, at p. 154.

[85] Ibid. [86] Ibid. [87] Ibid.

[88] Crawford, *The International Law Commission's Articles on State Responsibility*, n. 2, at p. 147.

[89] Attribution of conduct to the directing and controlling state or international organisation possibly can be established through Article 6 of the ARSIWA or Article 7 of the ARIO, n. 1.

[90] A. Reinisch, 'Aid or Assistance and Direction and Control between States and International Organizations in the Commission of Internationally Wrongful Acts' (2010) 7 IOLR 63, at 77.

act is responsible for the act *itself*, since it controlled and directed the act *in its entirety*'.[91] This casts some doubt on the possibility of responsibility being shared. The question, then, is as follows: does the controlling and directing party take over the whole conduct and become solely responsible? As discussed above, the difference between the two concerns the transfer of conduct. Is the unlawful conduct that is transferred to the directing and controlling party of a nature such that the influenced party can retreat with clean hands? This is not entirely clear. However, it is possible to find some hints by looking at the responsibility of the directed and controlled party. As the ILC stated, the mere fact of being under someone's direction and control does not exempt the influenced party of its responsibility,[92] because, in contrast with coercion, the directed and controlled party is not completely deprived of any freedom to decline.[93] Such responsibility can well arise directly with the unlawful conduct actually attributed to it. Moreover, the directed or controlled party cannot use the defence of 'superior orders',[94] for otherwise it would be like using 'internal law' between the two parties to avoid international obligations, which generally is not accepted. Therefore, direction and control does not provide an all-or-nothing solution to responsibility. It has been argued that such ambiguity is 'insignificant' in practice,[95] possibly because the injured party may choose between the two as a basis for claiming damages.

3.2.2 Difficulties in the case of the international organisation–state relationship

In the context of an international organisation, the only form of direction and control that an international organisation can exercise over its member states is through binding decisions upon its member states.[96] It is assumed that member states have no choice but to comply with the decision. This would lead to a certain overlap with Article 17 of the ARIO concerning circumvention of obligations. The ILC has argued that such an overlap would be partial and would not cause any inconsistency, because that Article has wider coverage to include cases where a binding

[91] ARSIWA Commentary to Article 17, para. 1, n. 1 (emphasis added).
[92] Crawford, *The International Law Commission's Articles on State Responsibility*, n. 2, at p. 155.
[93] Ibid. [94] ARSIWA Commentary to Article 17, para. 9, n. 1.
[95] Reinisch, 'Aid or Assistance and Direction and Control between States and International Organizations', n. 91, at pp. 63, 77.
[96] ARIO Commentary to Article 15, para. 4, n. 1.

decision requires a state to carry out a lawful act.[97] However, given that a decision of an international organisation is normative rather than factual, an international organisation cannot exercise factual direction and control as stipulated by the ILC's Commentaries, which require that there is more than simply the power to direct and control, but also factual direction and control. Therefore, it is doubtful whether direction and control is applicable for holding an international organisation responsible for the conduct of its member states.

On the other hand, direction and control exercised by a member state over its international organisation also creates ambiguity. It has been acknowledged under Article 59(2) of the ARIO that 'an act by a State member of an international organization done in accordance with the rules of the organization does not as such engage the international responsibility of that State under the terms of this article'. This may not affect non-member states, but it is somewhat ambiguous for member states. What is the distinction between a member state acting in accordance with the rules of the organisation and the member state exercising control? It can be hard to determine whether direction and control has been exercised in borderline cases. Unless the criteria concerning the situations giving rise to direction and control are further clarified, the utility of this rule is severely limited.

3.3 *Coercion*

Article 18 of the ARSIWA provides that a state that coerces another state to commit an internationally wrongful act shall bear responsibility for the act. Articles 16 and 60 of the ARIO extend the principle to international organisations. Coercion is not defined, but it is insufficient to establish coercion simply when 'compliance with the obligation is made more difficult or onerous, or that the acting State is assisted or directed in its conduct'.[98] Instead, coercion must satisfy an even higher threshold, which the ILC even equated to *force majeure*, giving the coerced state no choice but to submit to the coercion.[99] This means that the coerced party is completely under the control of the coercing party, leading to the responsibility of the latter.

[97] Ibid., para. 5. [98] ARSIWA Commentary to Article 18, para. 2, n. 1.

[99] Crawford, *The International Law Commission's Articles on State Responsibility*, n. 2, at p. 156.

As has been confirmed by the ILC, the responsibility of the coercing party towards the victim does not derive from the act of coercion itself, but rather from the wrongful conduct by the coerced state.[100] However, it is difficult to say that responsibility can be shared between the coercing and the coerced party, because the coerced party may lose the ability to bear responsibility as a result of the coercion.[101] If coercion reaches the degree of *force majeure*, the responsibility of the coerced state or international organisation vis-à-vis the injured victim will be precluded.[102] Indeed, the ILC has described the coerced state as being 'deprived of its sovereign capacity of decision'.[103] By analogy, it also might be said that a coerced international organisation similarly will lose its international legal personality. Therefore, only the coercing state or international organisation will be left even capable of responsibility, creating a scenario of indirect responsibility. The obstacle lies with the extremely high threshold of coercion. Moreover, in practice, in contrast with aid or assistance and direction and control, coercion of a member state by an international organisation is difficult to establish from the fact that the state is complying with the rules of the latter, because it is deemed highly unlikely by the ILC that coercion can arise out of such compliance.[104] For non-member states, the possibility is simply 'theoretical' because it is difficult to exercise coercion outside the headquarters of an international organisation.[105]

3.4 *Common requirement of knowledge*

In both the ARSIWA and the ARIO, the requirement of knowledge is common to all three 'traditional' scenarios of attributed responsibility. This may be seen as problematic, because incorporating subjective elements like knowledge into the constitutive elements of responsibility

[100] ARSIWA Commentary to Article 18, para. 1, n. 1.

[101] Fry, 'Coercion, Causation, and the Fictional Elements of Indirect State Responsibility', n. 43, at 629.

[102] Article 23 ARSIWA, n. 1; Article 23 ARIO, n. 1.

[103] ILC *Yearbook* 1979/II(2), 102, para. 25. The author of this chapter has critiqued this idea as being contradictory because the coerced state cannot retain the necessary sovereignty to commit an internationally wrongful act for indirect responsibility to apply and at the same time be deprived of sovereignty so that responsibility falls completely on the part of the coercing state: see Fry, 'Coercion, Causation, and the Fictional Elements of Indirect State Responsibility', n. 43, at 629.

[104] ARIO Commentary to Article 60, para. 3, n. 1.

[105] P. J. Kuijper, 'Introduction: Attributed or Direct Responsibility or Both?', Symposium on Responsibility of Organizations and of (Member) States (2010) 7 IOLR 9, at 25.

is a deviation from the basic premise of objective responsibility underlying both the ARSIWA and the ARIO, as Article 2 of the ARSIWA does not prescribe any subjective constitutive element for an internationally wrongful act. Indeed, it has been argued that the whole concept of internationally wrongful acts as developed by the ILC aims to eradicate subjective elements entirely.[106]

However, the ILC is not taking such an absolute position. Instead, it recognises that sometimes a breach of an international obligation may depend on knowledge or intent of the state.[107] For example, Article II of the Genocide Convention prescribes that 'genocide means any of the following acts committed with intent to destroy, in whole or in part, a national, ethnical, racial or religious group'.[108] The inclusion of subjective elements in the Articles of Chapter IV signifies some inconsistency among the different Articles of the ARSIWA itself. A possible reason for the ILC to include in Chapter IV such a requirement of knowledge could be the desire to introduce one more element for responsibility, so as to prevent overly broad determinations of responsibility. It would be unfair for the party providing aid or assistance to assume the risk that such aid or assistance will be used for unlawful purposes,[109] particularly if it does not even know of the circumstances that would lead to such unlawful conduct. However, does the party exercising direction and control, or coercion, suffer the same unfairness if no requirement of knowledge was included? Perhaps not. It is difficult to direct, control, or coerce without knowledge of the circumstances, rendering the requirement with no practical significance in these two scenarios.

Even if one accepts the appropriateness of the subjective element being inserted, there still remains the question of the degree of knowledge required for attributed responsibility to apply. This issue is important because the degree of knowledge is related to the scope of responsibility to be attributed.

Knowledge is a matter of fact and needs proof from evidence produced, and arguably it is not easy to prove. However, in practice it is not

106 D'Aspremont, 'The Articles on the Responsibility of International Organizations', n. 20.

107 Crawford, *The International Law Commission's Articles on State Responsibility*, n. 2, at p. 81.

108 Convention on the Prevention and Punishment of the Crime of Genocide, Paris, 9 December 1948, in force 12 January 1951, 78 UNTS 277 (Genocide Convention), Article II.

109 Crawford, *The International Law Commission's Articles on State Responsibility*, n. 2, at p. 147.

always necessary to prove actual knowledge. Two judicial decisions have accepted a less rigorous standard of knowledge. In the *Corfu Channel* case, the responsibility of Albania was based on the obligation to notify of the mines, which in turn depended on the knowledge of the mine-laying. Having examined the indirect evidence, the International Court of Justice said that the mine-laying activity could not have occurred without Albania's knowledge.[110] Therefore, the Court did not directly find knowledge on the part of Albania, but inferred such knowledge. Moreover, there is also some support for an even less exacting requirement. In *Ilaşcu* v. *Moldova and Russia*, the European Court of Human Rights held Russia responsible for all of the conduct, including the applicants' transfer to the *Transdniestria* regime, and the subsequent ill-treatment by the police where 'the agents of the Russian government knew, or at least should have known, that fate which awaited them'.[111] Including constructive knowledge would seemingly curtail the effects of inserting the subjective element in the first place, but it is important to note that the subjective requirement should not always be considered absolute. Indeed, the ILC has proceeded on the assumption that different primary rules can provide for different standards of knowledge for responsibility purposes.[112] The two cases mentioned here are examples where the knowledge is specifically discussed. However, it is still not clear whether they apply universally regardless of which of the three scenarios is relevant.

3.5 *Circumvention*

While parallel rules between the ARSIWA and the ARIO can be assumed concerning direction, control, and coercion, this does not cover all of the situations where shared responsibility might occur between an international organisation and its member states. The relationship between an international organisation and its member states cannot be completely modelled on inter-state relations. While states generally are considered equal sovereigns, there is a normative and vertical relationship between

110 *Corfu Channel (United Kingdom of Great Britain and Northern Ireland* v. *Albania)*, Merits, ICJ Reports 1949, 4, at 22.

111 *Ilaşcu* v. *Moldova and Russia*, App. No. 48787/99 (ECtHR, 8 July 2004), paras. 384–5.

112 Crawford, *The International Law Commission's Articles on State Responsibility*, n. 2, at p. 13. For a detailed survey of areas where the subjective requirement can be loosened, see H. P. Aust, *Complicity and the Law of State Responsibility* (Cambridge University Press, 2011), pp. 244–8.

an international organisation and its member states, since the former can exert binding or non-binding decisions on the latter.[113] Equally true is the influence that a member state is able to exercise over its international organisation.[114] The ARIO address this situation. Articles 17 and 61 of the ARIO provide for responsibility of an international organisation or its member states for circumventing its own obligations through the other. For the international organisation, responsibility can be attributed via either binding decisions or non-binding recommendations and authorisations.[115] For member states, responsibility can be attributed via taking advantage of the independent legal personality of the international organisation.[116] Circumvention literally means 'to get around'. An international organisation or member state may try to rely on the other to perform certain activities that are in breach of its own international obligation. This is what Articles 17 and 61 of the ARIO aim to prevent. The rationale is that an international organisation or member state cannot do via another entity what it cannot do itself.[117] Accordingly, the Articles do not require that the act is internationally wrongful for the influenced member state(s) or international organisation.[118]

3.5.1 Responsibility of international organisations

In the case of binding decisions made by an international organisation, member states generally will obey the obligation to comply with such decisions. The member states can thus be said to be under the normative control of the international organisation in carrying out wrongful acts, giving rise to attributed responsibility for the latter. The ILC has noticed that a binding decision can possibly overlap with 'direction and control', and in extreme cases can reach the extent of coercion.[119] This section assumes that compliance with the binding decision of the international organisation necessarily leads to circumvention.[120] However, that would

[113] ARIO, Commentary to Chapter IV, 'Responsibility of an international organization in connection with the act of a State or another international organization', para. 3, n. 1.

[114] This part should in essence be classified as state responsibility, yet it is not covered by the ARSIWA. Part V of the ARIO aims to fill such a responsibility gap.

[115] Articles 17(1) and (2) ARIO, n. 1. [116] Ibid., Article 61(1).

[117] N. Blokker, 'Abuse of the Members: Questions Concerning Draft Article 16 of the Draft Articles on Responsibility of International Organizations' (2010) 7 IOLR 35, at 39.

[118] Articles 17(c) and 61(b) ARIO, n. 1.

[119] ILC Report on the work of its sixty-first session, UN Doc. A/64/10 (2009), at 85–6, para. 3 and 87, para. 2. See section 4.2.2.

[120] ARIO Commentary to Article 17, para. 7, n. 1.

result in circumvention in every situation where a binding decision is made. The key is whether the act is a breach of an international obligation for the international organisation. When member states themselves act as agents of the organisation and do not enjoy any discretion in the implementation of a binding wrongful measure of the organisation, it is widely recognised that the organisation concerned can be held responsible if a wrongful act is committed. There is no reason why a state cannot be similarly held responsible if an international organisation acts upon the agency of the state.[121]

However, the responsibility is not always shared. First, the responsibility of the international organisation can be established even before any act is actually committed by its member states, without even the possibility of incurring responsibility for the state. Second, as is stipulated by the ARIO, even when that act is actually committed by the member state, responsibility can be attributed to the international organisation regardless of whether the act committed actually is internationally wrongful for the member state. Therefore, the member state may or may not be held responsible for its act. If the member state that executes the binding decision is also committing a wrong, then shared responsibility can be said to occur where both the international organisation and the member state can be held responsible. Otherwise, only the international organisation will be responsible.

In the case of non-binding decisions (for example, authorisations and recommendations), it is additionally required that the act is actually committed, and that there is a causal link between the authorisation or recommendation and the act. It is true that Article 17(b) of the ARIO stipulates that in such cases responsibility can be attributed to the international organisation. However, the responsibility does not rest on a solid basis because it is questionable why an international organisation should be responsible for its non-binding decision. To what extent is circumvention possible if member states retain the freedom to choose whether to commit the authorised or recommended act? There is no sufficient 'control' on the side of the organisation to lead to its responsibility. However, the ILC explains that the freedom of member states is only theoretical, because 'an authorization often implies the conferral by an organization of certain functions to the member or members concerned so that they would exercise these functions instead

[121] D'Aspremont, 'Abuse of the Legal Personality of International Organizations', n. 49, at 105.

of the organization'.[122] The ILC also tried to limit the responsibility that an international organisation might shoulder by introducing another requirement of a causal link between the authorisation or recommendation and the actual committal of the wrong, but even such a link cannot be at the same level of control as binding decisions.

3.5.2 Responsibility of states

The idea of holding states responsible for the acts of the international organisation seems to be 'against a historical trend' of states transferring power to an international organisation and making the latter bear responsibility independently.[123] However, where the member states make use of the separate legal personality of the international organisation to achieve what they cannot do themselves, it is hard to argue that the member states can hide behind the veil of the international organisation. Such an abuse of legal personality of international organisations is analogous to the doctrine of 'piercing the corporate veil'. As explained in the ILC's Commentary, three requirements must be satisfied in such a situation: first, the international organisation has competence regarding the relevant subject matter;[124] second, there is a significant link between the conduct of the circumventing member state and the conduct of the international organisation; and third, the act committed must also constitute a breach of an international obligation for the member state.[125]

As is pointed out by the ILC, the rationale behind circumvention is taking advantage of the legal personality of the international organisation.[126] However, arguably 'taking advantage of' is not strong enough to indicate control over the state or international organisation for the purpose of attributed responsibility. 'Taking advantage of' can occur in two different stages. A distinction should be drawn between the provision of competence at the point of the establishment of the international organisation and abusing such competence during the decision-making process. In the former case, it can well be argued that the international organisation simply is an instrument for the member states for the purpose of the circumvention of obligations. Although the international organisation is a prima facie independent person, it is in the control of its member states.

[122] ARIO Commentary to Article 17, para. 8, n. 1.

[123] E. Paasivirta, 'Responsibility of a Member State of an International Organization: Where Will It End? Comments on Article 60 of the ILC Draft Articles on the Responsibility of International Organizations' (2010) 7 IOLR 49, at 51.

[124] ARIO Commentary to Article 61, paras. 6–8, n. 1. [125] Ibid. [126] Ibid.

Therefore, even normal decision-making processes can manifest such control exercised by the member states towards their goal of circumventing obligations. In contrast, during the decision-making stage, merely taking advantage seems insufficient because the distinction between a member state's normal participation and abusing legal personality is not clear-cut. D'Aspremont argues that the criteria should be 'effective and overwhelming control',[127] which deprives the international organisation of autonomy of expressing a distinct will of its own.[128] Only if the rule moves towards such a higher threshold can it provide attributed responsibility for the member states, but the responsibility is not shared, since the legal personality of the controlled organisation is abused.

4. Conclusions

To conclude, the above analysis should be put into the shared responsibility context. It follows from the above that the concept of attributed responsibility may allow for a determination of shared responsibility.

The criteria for responsibility based on attribution of conduct and attribution of responsibility are different. Under shared responsibility, due to the fact that responsibility essentially is shared between multiple wrongdoers, a court will have to decide the responsibility of each individual entity, given, of course, that there are no established rules on joint and several responsibility. The court will determine the responsibility of the actual perpetrator according to the general rules applicable to situations of single wrongdoers under the ARSIWA and the ARIO, with both attribution of conduct and breach of an international obligation required. However, the party bearing attributed responsibility will be assessed according to a different set of criteria, including knowledge of the circumstances and the special link – based on control – between the influenced party and itself, such as aid, direction, coercion, or circumvention. It is doubtful whether these criteria provide an equally rigorous threshold for establishing responsibility. If they do not, and intuitively it would seem not, then it might create unfairness favouring one responsible party over another because of the different levels required for establishing responsibility. This problem does not exist with cases

[127] D'Aspremont, 'Abuse of the Legal Personality of International Organizations', n. 49, at 100.

[128] Ibid., at 105.

where there is a single wrongdoer, because determinations of responsibility there require an all-or-nothing approach, and the responsibility will be placed on only one party.

Attributed responsibility presumes control, and thereby enables shared responsibility between the controlling and the controlled entity. However, at one level of control, responsibility ceases to be shared. Generally, the categories of attributed responsibility indicate different degrees of control between the parties, which is manifest by the legal or factual relationship between the parties. The degree ranges within a continuum, with aid or assistance, direction and control, coercion, and circumvention in order, from weak to strong. If such a nexus is taken to the extreme, such as with coercion, the influenced party may even lose its international legal personality, thereby removing a prerequisite for responsibility on the international level. This is supported by the ILC's recognition of the coerced state as being 'deprived of its sovereign capacity of decision'.[129] Given that one party would be prevented from bearing responsibility, responsibility could not be shared between the parties.

The possibility of shared responsibility triggered by attributed responsibility raises a major problem in terms of quantification of responsibility. This is of particular interest for third parties. Under shared responsibility, the injured party may claim against any of the wrongdoers involved on the basis of Article 47 of the ARSIWA and Article 48 of the ARIO. This was accepted in the *Nauru* case, where the ICJ ruled that the mere fact that Australia was not alone in exercising the administrative authority did not render the claim against Australia inadmissible *in limine litis*.[130] However, it should be noted that the Court's decision on this issue, like the Articles on plural responsible parties, was more qualitative than quantitative in determining responsibility. For example, the ICJ could decide whether Australia was responsible, but it would have been difficult for the Court to decide to *what extent* it was responsible. In the *Nauru* case, the ICJ was able to get away from the quantification issue because the parties finally agreed to withdraw the case. However, if the parties had requested the Court to decide on this, supposedly there were no rules for the ICJ to rely on so as to allow an apportionment. Therefore, if an injured party brings a claim against only part of the multiple wrongdoers, it would appear that a court might only be able to decide on responsibility qualitatively rather than quantitatively, again,

[129] ILC *Yearbook* 1979/II(2), at 102, para. 25. [130] *Nauru*, n. 56, at 259.

unless there is a well-recognised principle of joint and several responsibility. As previously mentioned, this is already an issue outside the shared responsibility context. Nevertheless, in the context of shared responsibility, the difficulty will appear more in a quantitative sense. In other words, it is not a question of whether or not any of the wrongdoers can be held responsible. Rather, the issue is what proportion of responsibility each party will bear.

The issue of quantification thus provides an obstacle to the determination of shared responsibility in cases of attribution of responsibility. The difficulty of determining allocation between responsible parties is that attribution of responsibility essentially provides only the nexus between parties associated with an internationally wrongful act, and a nexus can be difficult to quantify. To be clear, both parties are not the actual perpetrators of the internationally wrongful act. For example, the internationally wrongful act may be committed by the directed party, but the directed party is under the direction of the directing party. It is the *direction* that created the nexus between the parties, but such a nexus is difficult, if not impossible, to quantify. In order to quantify whether the directing party's influence was 80 per cent or 20 per cent, for example, an outside indicator needs to be introduced that is applicable to all parties – an indicator such as intention, similar to determining fault within the context of tort law. Among the indirect responsibility scenarios, aid or assistance is probably different from the other categories because it is essentially a scenario where both parties actually commit some act towards the ultimate harm, and an analytical approach that focuses on intent or causation in relation to each may be a useful tool for appropriately distributing responsibility. For the other forms of indirect responsibility, it might be a little more difficult to come up with a means for distributing responsibility. There are currently no readily available approaches for such a purpose.

This also means that this conception of attribution of responsibility does not lend itself easily to a distribution of responsibility among multiple wrongdoers. One possible route is to assess each party's contribution to the damage, which resembles a causal analysis. However, this will encounter significant difficulties. The ILC deems causation irrelevant to the determination of international responsibility, as can be seen from the absence of causation from the constitutive elements of internationally wrongful conduct.[131] Rather, causation in the law of

[131] For a detailed analysis of the reason for such absence of causation in international responsibility, see Castellanos-Jankiewicz, 'Causation and International State Responsibility', n. 18.

international responsibility is limited to the determination of reparations.[132] Therefore, it is unlikely that causation will ever play a role in determining the distribution of responsibility, unless it is a factor that is part of particular primary obligations.

If one were to try to create better rules to provide a way for apportionment in the context of shared responsibility, the effort probably would start with clarifying 'several' responsibility, not just 'joint and several' responsibility, even though it is somewhat difficult to talk about one without the other. As this chapter does not deal with damages, the apportionment referred to here is limited to apportionment of responsibility, which is an assessment on the contribution of each actor towards the ultimate single harm.[133] It is even questionable whether a general principle of 'joint and several' responsibility exists in international law, and therefore focusing just on 'several' responsibility seems premature. A few thoughts are shared here concerning joint and several responsibility, inasmuch as making progress on that front is directly related to making progress with multiple attribution of responsibility.

The conditions for the application of joint and several responsibility are not entirely clear in either the ARSIWA or the ARIO. On the contrary, the Commentary to Article 47 of the ARSIWA, which relates to the 'Plurality of responsible States', says:

> The general rule in international law is that of separate responsibility of a State for its own wrongful acts and paragraph 1 reflects this general rule. Paragraph 1 neither recognizes a general rule of joint and several or solidary responsibility, nor does it exclude the possibility that two or more States will be responsible for the same internationally wrongful act. Whether this is so will depend on the circumstances and on the international obligations of each of the States concerned.[134]

Therefore, it is necessary to emphasise several aspects of attributed responsibility that will provide some support for the establishment of joint and several responsibility.

Two ICJ cases seem to support the existence of joint and several responsibility. First, there is the *Oil Platforms* case, where the Iran–Iraq War was hampering the United States' commerce in the Gulf, and it was seen as being difficult to assess the individual impact of Iran and

[132] Ibid., at 5.

[133] Nollkaemper and Jacobs, 'Shared Responsibility in International Law', n. 6, at 367.

[134] Crawford, *The International Law Commission's Articles on State Responsibility*, n. 2, at pp. 272–3.

Iraq on that commerce. In a Separate Opinion, ICJ Judge Bruno Simma conducted a comparative analysis of the tort law of various states in relation to joint and several liability, and he concluded that the principle rises to the level of a general principle of law within the meaning of Article 38(1) of the ICJ Statute.[135] The essence of joint and several responsibility is that each of the wrongdoers may have a claim brought against them alone for the full amount of the injury, leaving questions of percentages of contribution to the injury to be sorted out between the wrongdoers,[136] just as with joint and several liability in the context of domestic tort law. Some hint of apportionment can also be found in cases of reduced responsibility, where the injured state has contributed to its own injury. For example, as ICJ Judge Philadelpho Azevedo noted in his dissent in the *Corfu Channel* case, when the injured state contributes to the occurrence of its own injury, 'the conduct of the victim can be taken into account by reducing the degree of responsibility (amount of responsibility) [of the offending state] and consequently apportioning the damages'.[137] If apportionment can be achieved between the wrongful party and the injured party, there presumably is no reason why the same cannot apply between different wrongful parties.

Concerning the different aspects of attributed responsibility to be emphasised to support the existence of joint and several responsibility, it is first important to note how attribution of conduct is not necessarily at issue, because attribution of responsibility does not depend on attribution of conduct. A scenario of attributed responsibility can be contrasted with the *Oil Platforms* case, where it could only be determined that the conduct was attributable either to Iran or Iraq. In that case, even though Judge Simma proposed a joint and several responsibility doctrine, the Court still could not circumvent an exact finding on attribution of conduct, especially without a clearly established rule on multiple attribution of conduct. This is because both Iran and Iraq were committing the internationally wrongful act, and therefore the Court had no reason to deviate from an analysis on attribution of conduct.

135 *Oil Platforms (Islamic Republic of Iran* v. *United States of America)*, Judgment, ICJ Reports 2003, 161, at 354–8 (Separate Opinion Judge Simma).

136 See e.g. *Eurotunnel Arbitration (The Channel Tunnel Group Ltd & France-Manche S.A.* v. *the Secretary of State for Transport of the Government of the United Kingdom of Great Britain and Northern Ireland and le ministre de l'équipement, des transports, de l'aménagement du territoire, du tourisme et de la mer du Gouvernement de la République française)*, Partial Award, (2007) 132 ILR 1, at 60.

137 *Corfu Channel*, n. 110, at 4, 95.

The second aspect of attributed responsibility to be highlighted here is that both parties necessarily have some share (though not necessarily in the form of actually committing the international wrongful act) in the harmful results. On the one hand, the influencing party will not bear any responsibility without the conduct being committed by the influenced party. On the other hand, the internationally wrongful act will not be committed without the influence exerted by the influencing party. This creates a close nexus between the parties, with each playing a necessary part towards the final harm caused. Therefore, it is not reasonable to diminish the responsibility of either party to zero and to burden the other with the full amount of responsibility.

The third aspect of attributed responsibility has practical significance. If no rule of apportionment is provided, one of the multiple wrongdoers runs the risk of bearing more responsibility for its contribution to the final harm than what is fair. This problem is particularly acute in the case of attributed responsibility. For all the categories of attributed responsibility mentioned in the ARSIWA and the ARIO, it is the controlled party that actually commits the wrongful act, and the influence exercised by the controlling party is operating in the background. It will be more difficult for the injured state or an international organisation to see the nexus between the parties. What is more convenient is to claim directly against the party who actually committed the internationally wrongful act. Therefore, a lack of several responsibility, where the party paying the reparation can claim against the other wrongdoers, will worsen the situation of the controlled party, leading to unfairness towards the controlled party.

It follows from the above that the rules on attributed responsibility should be further clarified by placing greater emphasis on treating the parties bearing direct responsibility and the parties bearing attributed responsibility together. As presently constituted, the ARSIWA and the ARIO rules in relation to attributed responsibility envisage only one-way influence, with the basic model of one dominant powerful party 'controlling' the other, except for perhaps aid or assistance. If the flow of influence actually is uni-directional, then it seems quite natural that only the dominant party will bear the responsibility.[138] However, if it can be

[138] E.g. C. Dominicé, 'Attribution of Conduct to Multiple States and the Implication of a State in the Act of Another State in the Law of International Responsibility', in J. Crawford, A. Pellet, and S. Olleson (eds.), *The Law of International Responsibility* (Oxford University Press, 2010), p. 280 at pp. 284, 288 (arguing for independent responsibility concerning

shown that the influenced party also has had some role in the commission of the internationally wrongful act, it can be easier to argue for a shared responsibility among the parties. The mixed agreements mentioned earlier in this chapter are an excellent example of shared responsibility involving attributed responsibility, with the possibility that the responsibility for the conduct of either the European Union or its member states can be attributed to the other, although the EU might try to claim exclusive responsibility of its own. The basis for attribution of responsibility there is the mutual consent to the agreement, without too much dominance by one over the other, although this characterisation of the relationship is likely to be contested.

In sum, for attribution of responsibility without the conduct also being attributed, the rules are readily available in the ARSIWA and the ARIO, even though it is possible to question the reasonableness of a part of them as belonging to the attributed responsibility family – for example, aid or assistance, in terms of control as the basis of responsibility. Indeed, as the ILC stated, '[t]he assisting state will only be responsible to the extent that its own conduct has caused or contributed to the internationally wrongful act.'[139] This implies that the assisting state bears responsibility only for its own conduct. Moreover, even where attributed responsibility is possible, multiple attribution is not necessarily feasible, given that the party bearing attributed responsibility may take over the whole responsibility – for example, with coercion and circumvention. It is not difficult to see the dilemma inherent in multiple attribution of responsibility. On the one hand, sufficient control is required as the basis for attributed responsibility. On the other hand, control cannot be so thorough that the controlled party is completely deprived of its autonomy. Among all of the scenarios involving attributed responsibility that are analysed in this chapter, the one on 'direction and control' is the most likely scenario for multiple attribution and, in turn, for shared responsibility, even though this chapter has been quite critical of 'direction and control'.

direction and control, with only the controlling state being responsible, 'for it is either that the state is responsible for the act of another carried out under its direction or control, or the dependent state maintains a certain degree of freedom, in which case it is responsible for its own conduct'). See also Fry, 'Coercion, Causation, and the Fictional Elements of Indirect State Responsibility', n. 43, at 639 (arguing that in the case of coercion, only the coercing state would be responsible, even though it may still be argued that even a coerced state has some degree of freedom that one could say justifies the consideration of the coerced state's responsibility).

139 Crawford, *The International Law Commission's Articles on State Responsibility*, n. 2, at p. 148.

5

Complicity in an Internationally Wrongful Act

VLADYSLAV LANOVOY

1. Introduction

The one-dimensional breach is no longer the dominant feature of the law of international responsibility. Increasingly, the breach of an international obligation is the product of complicity by other states and international organisations that operate in complex and often non-transparent schemes and arrangements. The idea of holding a subject of international law responsible beyond its conduct that amounts to the breach of its own international obligation is relatively recent. It accompanies the maturity of the international community and the gradual move towards a shared responsibility framework in international law.[1] The responsibility for complicity emerges as a tool to promote respect for legality and the rule of law in international relations.[2] It is also an avenue for the injured party to seek redress from those states or international organisations that contribute to the commission of an internationally wrongful act.

This chapter explores the principles and standards that the International Law Commission (ILC) elaborated in Article 16 of the Articles on the Responsibility of States for Internationally Wrongful Acts (ARSIWA)[3]

Vladyslav Lanovoy has a PhD in International Law, Graduate Institute of International and Development Studies, Geneva. The research leading to this chapter has received funding from the European Research Council under the European Union's Seventh Framework Programme (FP7/2007–2013)/ERC grant agreement n° 249499, as part of the research project on Shared Responsibility in International Law (SHARES), carried out at the Amsterdam Center for International Law (ACIL) of the University of Amsterdam.

[1] P. A. Nollkaemper and D. Jacobs, 'Shared Responsibility in International Law: A Conceptual Framework' (2013) 34(2) MIJIL 359, at 390.

[2] H. P. Aust, *Complicity and the Law of State Responsibility* (Cambridge University Press, 2011), pp. 50–96.

[3] See Articles on Responsibility of States for Internationally Wrongful Acts, ILC *Yearbook* 2001/II(2) (ARSIWA); Commentary to the Articles on Responsibility of States for Internationally Wrongful Acts, ILC *Yearbook* 2001/II(2) (ARSIWA Commentary).

and Articles 14 and 58 of the Articles on the Responsibility of International Organizations (ARIO).[4] These provisions are almost identical in their content. Hence, the analysis will primarily rely on Article 16 of the ARSIWA and will point to the peculiarities in the application of its sister provisions under the ARIO. This chapter does not address situations of complicity towards the maintenance of unlawful situations resulting from the commission of serious breaches of peremptory norms.[5]

As in any domestic legal order, the responsibility for complicity plays a vital role as the gatekeeper between lawful and unlawful forms of cooperation. Article 16 of the ARSIWA formulates the criteria for making this distinction as follows:

> *Aid or assistance in the commission of an internationally wrongful act*
> A State which aids or assists another State in the commission of an internationally wrongful act by the latter is internationally responsible for doing so if:
>
> (a) that State does so with knowledge of the circumstances of the internationally wrongful act; and
> (b) the act would be internationally wrongful if committed by that State.

In the *Bosnian Genocide* case, the International Court of Justice (ICJ or Court) held that responsibility for aid or assistance under Article 16 of the ARSIWA is a rule of customary international law.[6] In examining whether Serbia was responsible for complicity in genocide under Article III(e) of the Genocide Convention,[7] the Court looked by analogy into the requirements of Article 16 of the ARSIWA. In doing so, the Court cast doubt on the ordinary meaning of some of the conditions set forth in the text of Article 16.[8]

[4] Articles on the Responsibility of International Organizations, ILC Report on the work of its sixty-third session, UNGAOR 66th Sess., Supp. No. 10, UN Doc. A/66/10 (2011) (ARIO); Commentary to the Articles on the Responsibility of International Organizations, ILC Report on the work of its sixty-third session, UNGAOR 66th Sess., Supp. No. 10, UN Doc. A/66/10 (2011) (ARIO Commentary).

[5] See the contribution to this volume, Chapter 9, by E. A. Wyler and L. A. Castellanos-Jankiewicz, 'Serious Breaches of Peremptory Norms', p. 284. See also in Chapter 2 of this volume, A. Gattini, 'Breach of International Obligations', p. 25, at pp. 34–5, 53.

[6] *Application of the Convention on the Prevention and Punishment of the Crime of Genocide (Bosnia and Herzegovina* v. *Serbia and Montenegro)*, Judgment, ICJ Reports 2007, 43, at 217, para. 420 (*Bosnian Genocide*).

[7] Convention on the Prevention and Punishment of the Crime of Genocide, New York, 9 December 1948, in force 12 January 1951,78 UNTS 277 (Genocide Convention).

[8] *Bosnian Genocide*, n. 6, at p. 113, para. 166 and p. 216, para. 419 et seq.

This chapter examines the extent to which the provisions on complicity allow for the determination of shared responsibility and equitable allocation of legal consequences. It highlights instances from practice and *opinio juris* to show that the current regime on responsibility for complicity contains more questions than answers.[9] From the perspective of shared responsibility, three overarching aspects of the ILC's codification on complicity will be examined. First, Article 16 of the ARSIWA and its sister provisions in the ARIO cast doubt on basic postulates of the modern law of responsibility, including the notion of responsibility without fault. Similarly, the boundaries between responsibility for complicity and cognate concepts such as due diligence and joint and several responsibility are relatively elusive. Second, the requirements for responsibility for complicity, in particular its opposability criterion (i.e. the requirement that the [principal] conduct would be internationally wrongful if committed by the aiding or assisting state or international organisation), undermine the legality function of international responsibility.[10] Third, the current regime on responsibility for complicity leaves little room for the injured party to obtain full reparation for the injury that bears an imprint of complicity. Part of the problem stems from the ILC's failure to provide guidance on the causal standards governing a third party's contribution to an internationally wrongful act.

Section 2 of this chapter briefly outlines the codification history of responsibility for complicity and its interaction with the treaty norms that prohibit complicity. Section 3 discusses the requirements of responsibility for complicity. It assesses the material and cognitive elements of complicity, and makes an argument against the opposability requirement as an obstacle to a more far-reaching framework of shared responsibility. Section 4 questions the extent to which Article 16 of the ARSIWA and its sister provisions in the ARIO can accommodate concerns of shared responsibility in terms of distribution of responsibility and equitable allocation of legal consequences.

[9] See e.g. Aust, *Complicity and the Law of State Responsibility*, n. 2, at pp. 97–191; A. Felder, *Die Beihilfe im Recht der völkerrechtlichen Staatenverantwortlichkeit* (Zurich: Schulthess, 2007); J. Quigley, 'Complicity in International Law: A New Direction in the Law of State Responsibility' (1986) 57 BYIL 77; B. Graefrath, 'Complicity in the Law of International Responsibility' (1996) 29 RBDI 370.

[10] SFDI, *La Responsabilité dans le système international* (Paris: Pedone, 1991), pp. 319–36.

2. The emergence and codification of responsibility for complicity

In 1939, Roberto Ago considered any common consideration of different entities implicated in the same wrongdoing to be inconceivable.[11] Ago's *propos* flowing from a contractual dimension of the law of international responsibility took only a few decades to fall into disrepute.[12] As part of his seventh report to the ILC in 1978, then as a Special Rapporteur, he introduced the following provision:

> *Article 25: Complicity of a State in the internationally wrongful act of another State*
> The fact that a State renders assistance to another State by its conduct in order to enable or help that State to commit an international offence against a third State *constitutes an internationally wrongful act* of the State, which thus *becomes an accessory to the commission of the offence* and incurs international responsibility thereby, *even if the conduct in question would not otherwise be internationally wrongful.*[13]

During the ensuing discussions, Ago stressed that 'the Commission ought to show intellectual courage in dealing with [complicity]'.[14] He was aware that '[t]he rule partook more of the progressive development of international law rather than of its codification, but he believed that, if there was one case in which the Commission should carry out progressive development, it was surely the case [of complicity]'.[15] The rule emerged as a prime example of 'multilateralization, or universalization, of the relations of responsibility'.[16] Codifying this form of responsibility meant moving beyond the monolithic view of the breach.[17] It also meant

[11] R. Ago, 'Le Délit international' (1939) 68 RCADI 415, at 523 ('[c]e qui paraît inconcevable en droit international, c'est toute forme de complicité, de participation, ou de provocation au délit').

[12] See G. I. Tunkin, *Theory of International Law* (Cambridge, MA: Harvard University Press, 1974), p. 403 ('there is no exact indication that the concepts of guilt and complicity are inapplicable to a state as a subject of international law'); N. Ushakov, *Основания Международной Ответственности Государств* (Moscow: International Relations, 1983), pp. 145–54; B. Graefrath and E. Oeser, 'Teilnahmeformen bei der völkerrechtlichen Verantwortlichkeit' (1980) 29 *Staat und Recht* 45.

[13] R. Ago, 'Seventh Report on State Responsibility', ILC *Yearbook* 1978/II(1), at 60 (emphasis added).

[14] ILC *Yearbook* 1978/I, at 240, para. 21 (Ago). [15] Ibid.

[16] L.-A. Sicilianos, 'The Classification of Obligations and the Multilateral Dimension of the Relations of International Responsibility' (2002) 13 EJIL 1127, at 1127.

[17] ILC *Yearbook* 1999/II(2), at 69, para. 251. Cf. E. Klein, 'Beihilfe zum Völkerrechtsdelikt', in I. von Münch (ed.), *Staatrecht, Völkerrecht, Europarecht: Festschrift für Hans-Jürgen Schlochhauer zum 75. Geburtstag am 28. März 1981* (Berlin: Walter de Gruyter, 1981), p. 429.

that international law would regulate the implication of multiple entities in the commission of an internationally wrongful act. The regulation of complicity is a step towards a more transparent global governance and reinforces respect for the rule of law. According to Vaughan Lowe, the notion of complicity 'heralds the extension of legal responsibility into areas where States have previously carried moral responsibility but the law has not clearly rendered them responsible for the acts that they facilitate'.[18]

In Ago's view, complicity was the only real form of participation in an internationally wrongful act.[19] Following criticisms received from states and some ILC members regarding the terminology used by Special Rapporteur Ago, the term 'complicity' mutated into a more neutral notion of providing 'aid or assistance' for an internationally wrongful act.[20] Substantive changes were introduced into former draft Article 27, which was adopted on the first reading of the ARSIWA:

> *Article 27: Aid or assistance by a State to another State for the commission of an internationally wrongful act*
> Aid or assistance by a State to another State, if it is established that it is rendered for the commission of an internationally wrongful act, carried out by the latter, itself constitutes an internationally wrongful act, even if, taken alone, such aid or assistance would not constitute a breach of an international obligation.[21]

The amendments introduced by the time of the second reading of the ARSIWA affected the scope of the provision and its practical consequences.[22] 'Complicity' in the original draft Article 25 and its successor draft Article 27[23] had a broader scope of application than in the current Article 16 of the ARSIWA and Articles 14 and 58 of the ARIO.[24] Notably, the language of the original draft Articles 25 and then 27 allowed the complicit state to be held responsible in those situations where it was not bound by the same obligation as that breached by the aided or assisted state.[25] At the same time, earlier drafts of the provision contained a stringent cognitive requirement suggesting that the aid or assistance had to be rendered specifically for the commission of an internationally wrongful act. The Commentary to current Article 16 of the ARSIWA still refers to 'complicity', implying its use as a synonym for

[18] V. Lowe, *International Law* (Oxford University Press, 2007), p. 121.
[19] Ago, 'Seventh Report on State Responsibility', n. 13, at 60, para. 76.
[20] ILC *Yearbook* 1978/I, at 223–41. [21] Ibid., at 269, para. 2.
[22] J. Crawford, 'Second Report on State Responsibility', ILC *Yearbook* 1999/II(1), at 45–57.
[23] ILC *Yearbook* 1987/II(2), at 102. [24] Ibid., at 99–105. [25] Ibid.

'aid or assistance', but the reach of this form of responsibility is clearly distinct from its original meaning in Ago's draft.[26]

The stringency of the conditions set forth in the ARSIWA and ARIO provisions and their Commentaries is to some extent remedied by the fact that several international treaties expressly prohibit complicity.[27] The ILC was aware of this phenomenon, as this form of responsibility effectively leaped the artificial barrier between primary and secondary norms.[28] While the intention of the ILC was mainly to examine the principles of attribution and the consequences of the breach of an international obligation, the ordinary meaning of the terms used in Article 16 of the ARSIWA and its sister provisions in the ARIO implies recognition of the general rule not to aid or assist in the wrongful act of another state.

Recently, Olivier Corten questioned whether there is room and need for an independent application of Article 16 of the ARSIWA, as the examples from the practice of complicity fall under a particular primary rule that prohibits such conduct.[29] The general rule on responsibility for complicity would, accordingly, carry only 'une vocation didactique ou symbolique, même s'il ne ferait en théorie que répéter une interdiction déjà présente par ailleurs'.[30] This statement is questionable. Firstly, while the available practice can thus far be linked to a particular treaty norm that prohibits complicity, responsibility for complicity can be incurred in respect of any breach of an international obligation. Secondly, the same conduct may result in a direct violation of a treaty obligation regulating complicity and concurrently facilitate the commission of a parallel breach of another international obligation.[31] Thirdly, most of the primary norms dealing

[26] ARSIWA Commentary, n. 3, Article 16, para. 11. Cf. *Bosnian Genocide*, n. 6, at 216, para. 419. For a continued use of the term 'complicity', see e.g. Quigley, 'Complicity in International Law', n. 9, at 77; Graefrath, 'Complicity in the Law of International Responsibility', n. 9, at 370; Klein, 'Beihilfe zum Völkerrechtsdelikt', n. 17, at 425.

[27] E.g. Convention on the Prohibition of the Use, Stockpiling, Production and Transfer of Anti-Personnel Mines and on their Destruction, Oslo, 18 September 1997, in force 1 March 1999, 2056 UNTS 211, Articles 1(1)(c); Convention on Cluster Munitions, Dublin, 30 May 2008, in force 1 August 2010, 2688 UNTS, Article 1(c); Genocide Convention, n. 7, Article III(e); and Charter of the United Nations, San Francisco, 26 June 1954, in force 24 October 1945, 1 UNTS 16, Article 2(5).

[28] ARSIWA Commentary, n. 3, Article 16, para. 2.

[29] O. Corten, 'La "Complicité" dans le droit de la responsabilité internationale : un concept inutile' (2011) 57 AFDI 57, at 60–7.

[30] Ibid., at 60.

[31] *Oil Platforms (Islamic Republic of Iran* v. *United States of America)*, Further Response to the United States of America Counter-claim submitted by the Islamic Republic of Iran, 24 September 2001, paras. 7.50–1.

with complicity are directly applicable to states, and not to international organisations. Fourthly, and most importantly, primary regimes merely prohibit states from aiding, assisting, or otherwise facilitating unlawful conduct. They are often silent as to what constitutes complicit conduct, how responsibility for such conduct arises, and what legal consequences it entails. Responsibility for complicity, therefore, lies between primary and secondary norms.

The scope of responsibility for complicity depends on the view one holds of the international legal order. If it is regarded as the reproduction of bundles of bilateral sovereign relations, then complicity's effectiveness as a basis for responsibility is limited, and criteria such as the opposability or intention become justified. If, however, the international legal order today is considered to be concerned with the sanctity of international obligations, the rule of law, and transparency in global governance, then a slightly revised model of responsibility for complicity is appropriate. This chapter discusses some of the early signs of such a model.

3. The constituent elements of responsibility for complicity

The rule on responsibility for complicity garnered considerable support within the ILC and the United Nations (UN) Sixth Legal Committee.[32] However, analysis of the comments reveals varying, if not contradictory, views on the content of responsibility for complicity.[33] For example, while the United States insisted that the provision should expressly refer to the requirement of intent,[34] the Netherlands argued for retention of the actual and constructive standards of knowledge within the provision.[35] Out of around forty states that provided comments, Sweden was, to the best of the author's knowledge, the only state that expressly argued for a limitation that is currently contained in paragraph (b) of Article 16.[36]

[32] Comment by Mali, ILC *Yearbook* 1980/II(1), at 101; Comment by Mexico, ILC *Yearbook* 2001/II(1), at 51; Comment by Japan, ILC *Yearbook* 1999/II(1), at 107; Comments by the United Kingdom and United States, ILC *Yearbook* 1998/II(1), at 129; ILC *Yearbook* 2001/II(1), at 52.

[33] Comments by Denmark on behalf of the Nordic countries (Finland, Iceland, Norway, Sweden, and Denmark) and the Republic of Korea, ILC *Yearbook* 2001/II(1), at 52. See Aust, *Complicity and the Law of State Responsibility*, n. 2, at pp. 169 et seq.

[34] Comment by the United States, ILC *Yearbook* 1998/II(1), at 129.

[35] Comment by the Netherlands, ILC *Yearbook* 2001/II(1), at 52.

[36] Comment by Sweden, ILC *Yearbook* 1981/II(1), at 77. See also subsequent comment by the United States, ILC *Yearbook* 2001/II(1), at 51.

Germany and Switzerland had objections to the existence of a proper legal basis for the rule on responsibility for complicity, let alone its constituent elements.[37] Serbia raised similar objections in its pleadings in the *Bosnian Genocide* case.[38]

The following subsection discusses the elements of responsibility for complicity in Article 16 of the ARSIWA and Articles 14 and 58 of the ARIO from the perspective of shared responsibility. First, the material element of complicity will be looked at and the scope of complicity will be distinguished from due diligence and joint or several responsibility. Next, the cognitive dimension and the opposability requirement of responsibility for complicity will be addressed.

3.1 *Material element of complicity and its scope*

As different forms of complicity proliferate in international affairs, it is crucial to inquire whether these need to be of a specific character, degree, or extent in order to trigger international responsibility. To borrow the words of the Irish High Court, '[t]he issue of "participation" [in the alleged wrongdoing] is not a black and white issue. It may well be ... a matter of "substance and degree".'[39] Complicity may involve different financial, technical, and military or other contributions.

The usual scenario of complicity arises where state A actively provides military, economic, or technical assistance to state B, at the request of the latter, and with the specific purpose of committing an internationally wrongful act. For example, in the context of the ongoing hostilities in Syria, different states have allegedly been providing ammunition and other assistance to the Syrian government, which could subsequently be used in the commission of violations of international humanitarian law and human rights law.[40] Other states have struggled in their decision-making on whether or not to arm the opposition movement.[41] Austria,

[37] Comment by Germany and Switzerland, ILC *Yearbook* 1998/II(1), at 128.

[38] *Bosnian Genocide*, n. 6, Oral Proceedings, CR 2006/40, at 50–1; CR 2006/43, at 63–5; Jurisdiction, Counter-Memorial of the Federal Republic of Yugoslavia of 22 July 1997, at 336.

[39] *Edward Horgan* v. *An Taoiseach and others*, Irish High Court, Application Declaratory Relief, Case No. 3739P (2003), para. 174.

[40] E.g. 'Syria: Who's Backing Who?', *The Guardian*, 11 October 2012; 'Turkey Accuses Russia of Supplying Syria with Munitions', *The Guardian*, 11 October 2012.

[41] See P. A. Nollkaemper, 'A Shared Responsibility Trap: Supplying Weapons to the Syrian Opposition', cross-posted on the *SHARES Blog* and *EJIL Talk*, 17 June 2013. See also e.g. Council of the European Union, 'Council Declaration on Syria', 27 May 2013; 'Sending

for instance, has referred to Article 16 of the ARSIWA as a basis for potential responsibility if those states were to provide arms to the rebels.[42] The ICJ also used Article 16 of the ARSIWA as a benchmark for evaluating the collaboration between Serbia and the Republika Srpska, technically a non-state entity. The Court found that although Article 16 of the ARSIWA 'concerns a situation characterized by a relationship between two States, [and] is not directly relevant to the present case, it nevertheless merits consideration'.[43]

Other scenarios of complicity may occur where state A provides assistance pursuant to an existing treaty with state B, but knowing that the assistance is no longer being used in accordance with that treaty.[44] Holding states responsible for complicity in these scenarios may be problematic.[45] First, it is uncertain whether a state has the duty to inquire whether its aid or assistance is being diverted from its original purpose as set out in the treaty. States are expected to rely on the good faith commitment of their counterparts.[46] Second, the state continues to be bound to perform its obligation to deliver specific assistance, although it has the right to suspend the operation of that obligation or the treaty as a whole. Such suspension of assistance may avoid the finding of complicity. The same cannot be said about the state that simply protests against the unlawful use of its aid or assistance, while continuing to deliver that same aid or assistance.[47]

Complicity can also originate on the basis of cooperation under less formal arrangements or memoranda of understanding between states or inter-agencies.[48] These may allow for a non-scrutinised exchange of

Missiles to Syrian Rebels, Qatar Muscles In', *The New York Times*, 29 June 2013; 'US Says it will give Military Aid to Syria Rebels', BBC News, 14 June 2013; 'US Considers Syria Policy as John Kerry Seeks Ways to Help Civil War Rebels', *The Guardian*, 12 June 2013; and 'France and Britain Push Syrian Arms', *International Herald Tribune*, 15 March 2013.

42 'Austrian Position on Arms Embargo in Syria', *The Guardian*, 15 May 2013.

43 *Bosnian Genocide*, n. 6, at 217, para. 420.

44 See examples of the United States cutting military aid to Indonesia on the occasion of intervention in East Timor and to Turkey after its invasion of Cyprus, cited in Quigley, 'Complicity in International Law', n. 9, at 90.

45 See also Quigley, ibid., at 123 (on the bill before the United States Senate proposing to reduce aid from the US to Israel because of the amount it spent on civilian settlements in the West Bank and Gaza strip).

46 *Affaire du Lac Lanoux (France* v. *Spain)*, Award, (1957) 12 RIAA 281, at 313.

47 Quigley, 'Complicity in International Law', n. 9, at 124; G. Nolte and H. P. Aust, 'Equivocal Helpers – Complicit States, Mixed Messages and International Law' (2009) 58 ICLQ 1, at 19.

48 F. Messineo, 'The Abu Omar Case in Italy: "Extraordinary Renditions" and State Obligations to Criminalize and Prosecute Torture under the UN Torture Convention' (2009) 7 J Int Crim Just 1023.

intelligence, operational collaboration, common training, and exchanges of technical equipment that is used, for example, for the commission of human rights violations by other states.[49] Less conventional forms of assistance include the provision of export credit guarantees[50] or helping a state to circumvent the requirements of UN Security Council resolutions.[51] In the context of collaboration between states and international organisations, aid or assistance can also take 'the form of providing funds to the organization for its extrabudgetary technical cooperation activities or hosting its headquarters, offices or meetings'.[52]

During the discussion of the provision on responsibility for complicity in the ILC, Paul Reuter suggested excluding remote forms of assistance from the scope of international responsibility.[53] Another member of the ILC, Nikolai Ushakov, was of the view that

> participation must be active and direct. It must not be too direct, however, for the participant then became a co-author of the offence, and that [is] beyond complicity. If, on the other hand, participation [is] too indirect, there might be no real complicity. For instance, it would be difficult to speak of complicity in an armed aggression if the aid and assistance given to a State consisted in supplying food to ensure the survival of the population for humanitarian reasons.[54]

However, Article 16 of the ARSIWA and Articles 14 and 58 of the ARIO do not contain any content-based limitation of complicit conduct. The

[49] See e.g. *R.* v. *Hape*, 2007 Supreme Court of Canada 26; *Canada (Justice)* v. *Khadr*, 2008 Supreme Court of Canada 28; *Amnesty International Canada* v. *Canada (Chief of the Defence Staff) (F.C.)*, 2008 Federal Court 336; *Amnesty International Canada* v. *Canada (Chief of the Defence Staff) (F.C.A.)*, 2008 Federal Court of Appeal 401. See also Open Society Foundation, 'Globalizing Torture: CIA Secret Detention and Extraordinary Rendition', February 2013.
El-Masri v. *The Former Yugoslav Republic of Macedonia*, App. No. 39630/09 (ECtHR, 13 December 2012), para. 239.

[50] E.g. Qinghai Project, described in A. Gowlland Gualtieri, 'The Environmental Accountability of the World Bank to Non-State Actors: Insights from the Inspection Panel' (2001) 72 BYIL 213, at 238; Ilisu Dam construction project, described in Aust, *Complicity and the Law of State Responsibility*, n. 2, at pp. 148–9.

[51] *Legal Consequences for States of the Continued Presence of South Africa in Namibia (South West Africa) Notwithstanding Security Council Resolution 276 (1970)*, Advisory Opinion, ICJ Reports 1971, 16, at 66, para. 133.

[52] Comment by International Labour Organization, UN Doc. A/CN.4/568/Add.1 (2006), at 25.

[53] ILC *Yearbook* 1978/I, at 229, para. 5 (Reuter) ('[Reuter] doubted whether assistance that was materially too remote could be regarded as complicity').

[54] ILC *Yearbook* 1978/I, at 239 (Ushakov).

ILC's Commentaries are silent on the nature of the aid or assistance as such.[55] It follows that whether material, legal, political, or otherwise, the aid or assistance generates responsibility insofar as it can be established that it facilitates or contributes to the commission of the internationally wrongful act by another entity. That being said, the degree and extent of complicity is an important benchmark at the stage of allocation of legal consequences between the aiding or assisting entity and the aided or assisted one.[56]

The degree and extent of complicity are also essential to distinguish it from the scenario of joint responsibility.[57] For instance, Brownlie suggested that assistance in the context of aggression could lead to a finding of joint responsibility:

> [T]he supply of weapons, military aircraft, radar equipment, and so forth, would in certain situations amount to 'aid or assistance' in the commission of an act of aggression but would not give rise to joint responsibility. However, the supply of combat units, vehicles, equipment and personnel, for the specific purpose of assisting an aggressor, would constitute a joint responsibility.[58]

Brownlie implies that the distinction between assistance as an ancillary or derivative form of responsibility, and assistance as amounting to joint responsibility, is determined by the content of 'assistance' and the intention of the assisting party. These criteria are not conclusive. Contrary to joint responsibility, where the actor itself commits the wrongful act, in the scenario that we are concerned with responsibility follows from knowingly contributing to the wrongful act of another. The complicit conduct may in itself be lawful and the legal consequences only unfold once the principal wrongful act is committed.[59] In theory, the distinction is one of attribution. Whereas in the scenario of joint or several responsibility the act causing the injury is concurrently attributable to two or more states, in the situation of complicity no attribution of the principal wrongful act to the complicit entity takes place. In practice, however, it may be more difficult to distinguish complicity from a fully fledged commission of the wrongful act in situations where multiple actors contribute to the commission of the

[55] See J. Crawford, *State Responsibility: The General Part* (Cambridge University Press, 2013), p. 402.

[56] See section 4. See also ILC *Yearbook* 1978/II(2), at 104, para. 20.

[57] Ibid., para. 18.

[58] I. Brownlie, *System of the Law of Nations: State Responsibility Part 1* (Oxford: Clarendon Press 1983), p. 191.

[59] Ago, 'Seventh Report on State Responsibility', n. 13, at 58, para. 72.

same wrongful act, and in a similar manner. If their joint contributions are each essential for the commission of the wrongful act, they may be held jointly or severally liable.[60] If, however, their contributions only facilitate the commission of the wrongful act but are not its essential conditions, then they may be held responsible for complicity. For instance, in the case of intervention in Iraq, numerous allied states contributed with different military equipment and troops to the Coalition Provisional Authority, run by the United States and the United Kingdom.[61] Had it been established that the intervention was unlawful, it would have been factually complicated to draw a distinction between complicity and the joint responsibility of those states.

Finally, it is questionable whether the material element of complicity is limited to active conduct or whether it can also consist of omissions. In the *Bosnian Genocide* case, the ICJ ruled that the failure to comply with an obligation to prevent a given event implies behaviour of omission on behalf of the state, whereas complicity consists of an affirmative or positive action.[62] If the scope of Article 16 of the ARSIWA were indeed confined to positive actions, this would replace the general qualification of the internationally wrongful act, which originates either from actions or omissions. In respect of aid or assistance arising out of omissions, Olivier Corten and Pierre Klein questioned the usefulness 'of the notion of complicity, which it appears, can always be substituted with the far more manageable concept of due diligence'.[63] They argued that:

> [e]ither the notion of complicity is interpreted as requiring the establishment of a specific intention on the part of the accomplice, and it will therefore be far more convenient to turn to the concept of due diligence,

[60] Of course, the notion of joint and several responsibility itself is not well established in international law: see S. Talmon, 'A Plurality of Responsible Actors: International Responsibility for Acts of the Coalition Provisional Authority in Iraq', in P. Shiner and A. Williams (eds.), *The Iraq War and International Law* (Oxford: Hart Publishing, 2008), p. 185, and Chapter 7 by Pierre d'Argent in this volume, P. d'Argent, 'Reparation, Cessation, Assurances and Guarantees of Non-Repetition', p. 208, at pp. 244–49.

[61] See C. Chinkin, 'The Continuing Occupation? Issues of Joint and Several Liability and Effective Control', in P. Shiner and A. Williams (eds.), *The Iraq War and International Law* (Oxford: Hart Publishing, 2008), p. 161; Talmon, 'A Plurality of Responsible Actors', n. 60, at 185–230.

[62] *Bosnian Genocide*, n. 6, at 222, para. 432. See also Crawford, *State Responsibility*, n. 55, pp. 403–5.

[63] O. Corten and P. Klein, 'The Limits of Complicity as a Ground for Responsibility: Lessons Learned from the *Corfu Channel* Case', in K. Bannelier et al. (eds.), *The ICJ and the Evolution of International Law* (London: Routledge, 2011), p. 314, at p. 332.

> which does not require such an element of intention. Or the notion of complicity is interpreted as not requiring the establishment of such a specific intention, but this notion then appears equivalent to – or could be even said to merge with – the concept of due diligence.[64]

Some reservations are in order in respect of this argument. Certainly, the ICJ ruled that complicity in genocide 'always requires that some positive action has been taken to furnish aid or assistance'.[65] However, it is unclear whether the Court's reasoning meant to extend by implication to Article 16 of the ARSIWA, or whether its validity is confined to complicity in genocide pursuant to Article III(e) of the Genocide Convention.[66]

Conceptually, the obligations of due diligence differ from the situations of responsibility for complicity arising out of omissions. Three elements shed light on a thin red line between responsibility for complicity through omission and responsibility that arises from a failure of due diligence. First, compliance with a due diligence obligation requires some degree of effective control to be exercised, whether legally or illegally, over the territory, from inside or outside its borders.[67] This is not a relevant criterion for determining whether a state has been complicit in an internationally wrongful act. Moreover, depending on the character of the primary norm, the degree of vigilance that is required may vary.[68] Second, if we follow the reasoning of the Court, the 'capacity to influence effectively [the events leading to the breach]' now emerges as an applicable standard for the obligation to prevent,[69] whereas complicity requires 'full knowledge of facts'.[70] Third, while complicity requires actual knowledge of the circumstances of the assisted wrongful act, the failure to fulfil a

[64] Ibid., at p. 331. [65] *Bosnian Genocide*, n. 6, at 222, para. 432.

[66] ILC *Yearbook* 1978/I, at 270, para. 5 (Schwebel); M. Milanović, 'State Responsibility for Genocide: A Follow-Up' (2007) 18 EJIL 669, at 680–4.

[67] *Bosnian Genocide*, n. 6, Oral Proceedings, CR 2006/17, at 43–4, para. 305 (according to Brownlie, extraterritorial application of the Genocide Convention without any limit would render it 'chaotic and extra-legal'). See also A. Gattini, 'Breach of the Obligation to Prevent and Reparation Thereof in the ICJ's Genocide Judgment' (2007) 18 EJIL 695, at 699.

[68] *United States Diplomatic and Consular Staff in Tehran (United States of America* v. *Iran)*, Judgment, ICJ Reports 1980, 3, at 31–2, paras. 63 and 67; *Armed Activities on the Territory of the Congo (Democratic Republic of the Congo* v. *Uganda)*, Judgment, ICJ Reports 2005, 168, at 226 and 231, paras. 160 and 178; *Pulp Mills on the River Uruguay (Argentina* v. *Uruguay)*, Judgment, ICJ Reports 2010, 14, at 79, para. 197.

[69] *Bosnian Genocide*, n. 6, at p. 221, para. 430; Declaration of Judge Skotnikov, at 10. See also P.-M. Dupuy, 'Crimes sans châtiment ou mission accompli?' (2007) 111 RGDIP 242, at 244 (noting 'un usage à éclipses de l'obligation de diligence due').

[70] *Bosnian Genocide*, n. 6, at 223, para. 432.

state's due diligence obligation arises upon constructive knowledge or risk that the breach will occur.[71]

The documented examples of complicity through omission are rare compared to those consisting of positive action. In Ago's view, even in cases where a state concludes a treaty with another state ensuring that it will remain neutral in the event of the latter's act of aggression against a third state, responsibility for complicity would unfold.[72] Indeed, there is no logical objection to accepting that under certain circumstances a mere formal promise may constitute aid or assistance in the sense of Article 16, as long as it contributes to the internationally wrongful act.[73] Likewise, a state may grant explicit authorisation for flights over its territory, but may also simply not object to the use of its airspace, provided that it has knowledge of the ultimate use of the airspace for the commission of an internationally wrongful act.[74] Similarly, a state may knowingly fail to inform its officials that sensitive information and intelligence sharing is used by another state for the commission of human rights violations.[75] The measures taken by several states in countering terrorism are instructive as regards instances of complicity by omission.[76] These include authorisations for overflight and landing rights, refuelling facilities for aircraft, placing at the disposal of other states unregulated access to ports and military bases, passive receipt or passage of information extracted under torture,[77] and facilitating the abduction of persons by agents of another state.[78]

[71] Ibid., at 221, para. 431. [72] ILC *Yearbook* 1978/I, at 240, para. 26 (Ago).

[73] M. L. Padeletti, *Pluralità di Stati nel fatto illecito internazionale* (Milan: Giuffrè Editore, 1990), p. 76; P. Klein, 'The Attribution of Acts to International Organizations', in J. Crawford et al. (eds.), *The Law of International Responsibility* (Oxford University Press, 2010), p. 296, at p. 307.

[74] See e.g. 'Iran Supplying Syrian Military via Iraqi Airspace', *The New York Times*, 4 September 2012. See also Aust, *Complicity and the Law of State Responsibility*, n. 2, at pp. 228–30; and Human Rights First, 'Enablers of the Syrian Conflict: How Targeting Third Parties Can Slow the Atrocities in Syria', March 2013.

[75] S. Borelli, 'Rendition, Torture and Intelligence Cooperation', in H. Born et al. (eds.), *International Intelligence Cooperation and Accountability* (London: Routledge, 2011), p. 98.

[76] M. Scheinin and M. Vermeulen, 'International Law: Human Rights Law and State Responsibility', in H. Born et al. (eds.), *International Intelligence Cooperation and Accountability* (London: Routledge, 2011), p. 252.

[77] United Kingdom House of Lords/House of Commons, Joint Committee on Human Rights, 'Allegations of UK Complicity in Torture', Twenty-third Report of Session 2008–2009, HL Paper 152, HC 230, published on 4 August 2009, para. 38.

[78] D. Marty, 'Secret Detentions and Illegal Transfers of Detainees Involving Council of Europe Member State: Second Report' (Strasbourg: Council of Europe Parliamentary Assembly, 2007), paras. 11, 39 and 105; UN Human Rights Council, 'Joint Study on

Several scholars have questioned the extent to which a vote, or its absence, by a member of an international organisation could amount to aid or assistance in the commission of an internationally wrongful act.[79] Whether affirmative or negative, the vote is not tangible or physical assistance for the purported wrongful act. Special Rapporteur Giorgio Gaja expressed the view that:

> [a] distinction between States which vote in favour and the other States would not always be warranted. This would reflect also a policy reason, because giving weight to that distinction could negatively affect the decision-making process in many organizations, because the risk of incurring responsibility would hamper the reaching of consensus.[80]

Comments originating from a number of states and international organisations led Special Rapporteur Gaja to conclude that 'the influence that may amount to aid or assistance could not simply consist in participation in the decision-making process of the organization according to the pertinent rules of the organization'.[81] Unless state conduct goes clearly beyond the rules of the organisation and its decision-making procedures, responsibility for rendering aid or assistance to the internationally wrongful act would not arise.[82] Factors such as 'the size of the membership and the nature of the involvement [of the member state]' may affect the consideration of responsibility.[83] For example, China observed in the Sixth Committee that given that the decisions and

Global Practices in Relation to Secret Detention in the Context of Countering Terrorism', UN Doc. A/HRC/13/42 (2010), at 81–5.

79 See J. M. Cortés Martín, *Las Organizaciones Internacionales: Codificación y Desarrollo Progresivo de su Responsabilidad Internacional* (Sevilla: Instituto Andaluz de Administración Pública, 2008), pp. 298–312; D. Sarooshi, *International Organizations and their Exercise of Sovereign Powers* (Oxford University Press, 2005), p. 64; A. Geslin, 'Réflexions sur la répartition de la responsabilité entre l'organisation internationale et ses Etats membres' (2005) 109 RGDIP 539.

80 G. Gaja, 'Fourth Report on Responsibility of International Organizations: Addendum', UN Doc. A/CN.4/564/Add. 2 (2006), at 13, para. 93.

81 G. Gaja, 'Seventh Report on Responsibility of International Organizations', UN Doc. A/CN.4/610 (2009), at 25, para. 74.

82 Article 58(2) ARIO, n. 4. See R. Higgins, 'The Legal Consequences for Member Status of Non-fulfilment by International Organizations of their Obligations towards Third Parties: Provisional Report' (1995) 66 AIDI 388. Cf. P. Klein, *La Responsabilité des organisations internationales dans les ordres juridiques internes et en droit des gens* (Brussels: Bruylant, 1998), p. 485.

83 ARIO Commentary, n. 4, Article 58, para. 4; P. Palchetti, 'Sulla responsabilità di uno Stato per il voto espresso in seno ad un'organizzazione internazionale' (2012) 2 Riv Dir Int 352, at 364 and 368.

actions of an organisation are generally under the control of its members or depend upon their support, those states that vote in favour or that apply such a measure should assume international responsibility.[84] The responsibility could thus vary depending on the evidence of the actual degree of participation in the voting procedures.[85] For example, a state may direct the adoption of a decision that leads to a violation of an international obligation; control the proceedings that lead to the adoption of the decision (for instance, when its representative chairs the meetings or has a casting vote); exercise a veto in the process leading to a decision that could prevent the commission of the wrongful act; or be part of the minority in the decision-making process by abstaining or voting against the decision.[86] Apart from the last scenario, where the member state has little influence on the decision-making process that leads to the commission of an internationally wrongful act, responsibility for complicity could unfold.

In the *Application of the Interim Accord of 13 September 1995*, the ICJ hinted that this question of degree of contribution could have arisen if Greece's conduct were evaluated in the absence of an express obligation in Article 11 of the Interim Accord.[87] The Court stressed that the question before it was 'not whether the decision taken by NATO at the Bucharest Summit with respect to the Applicant's candidacy was due exclusively, principally, or marginally to the Respondent's objection'.[88] In different factual circumstances, the Court could have considered the degree of contribution of a particular vote or absence thereof towards the commission of the internationally wrongful act.[89]

In sum, the ILC's provisions on responsibility for complicity do not contain a content-based limitation. Any contribution insofar as it is clearly linked to the commission of the principal wrongful act would constitute aid or assistance. This arguably includes omissions. The question of

[84] Comment by the People's Republic of China, UN Doc. A/C.6/60/SR.11 (2005), para. 53; Comment by Belarus, UN Doc. A/C.6/60/SR.12 (2005), para. 51.

[85] Cortés Martín, *Las Organizaciones Internacionales*, n. 79, at p. 300. [86] Ibid.

[87] *Application of the Interim Accord of 13 September 1995 (The Former Yugoslav Republic of Macedonia* v. *Greece)*, Judgment, ICJ Reports 2011, 1, at 25, para. 70.

[88] Ibid.

[89] See e.g. 'Statement of Intention by the Republic of Bosnia and Herzegovina to institute legal proceedings against the United Kingdom before the International Court of Justice, issued by the Mission of Bosnia' (1994) 43 ICLQ 714. Cf. *Bosnian Genocide*, n. 6, Provisional Order of 8 April 1993, ICJ Reports 1993, 3, at 6, para. 2(m) (where the Court stated that the embargo should be interpreted so as not to preclude the right to self-defence).

responsibility then revolves around the causal link and the extent to which the specific aid or assistance, whether active or passive, facilitates the commission of an internationally wrongful act. In connection with its material element, responsibility for complicity differs from responsibility arising out of the violation of due diligence obligations, and the situations of joint or several responsibility. While the establishment of responsibility for complicity is technically derivative or ancillary in relation to the principal wrongdoing, it constitutes a separate internationally wrongful act from the principal wrongdoing.[90] In this sense, responsibility for complicity is to a large extent premised on the logic of independent responsibility, and leaves little room for genuine shared responsibility.

3.2 The cognitive element of complicity

There is no doubt that states are 'monstres froids, n'ont pas d'âmes et donc pas non plus d'état d'âme'.[91] As Brierly put it, '[states] have no wills except the wills of the individual human beings who direct their affairs'.[92] This holds true in respect of international organisations. Following lengthy discussions, the ILC decided that the place of fault in the domain of international responsibility was limited to settling the extent of legal consequences deriving from an injury.[93] In other words, '[i]n the absence of any specific requirement of a mental element in terms of the primary obligation, it is only the act of the State that matters, independently of any intention'.[94] However, the provisions on aid or assistance do not fit this logic.

The text of Article 16 of the ARSIWA refers to 'knowledge of the circumstances of the internationally wrongful act' that the aiding or assisting entity must have in order to incur responsibility. By contrast, the ILC's Commentary indicates that the aiding or assisting state incurs responsibility only if it 'intended, by the aid or assistance given, to facilitate the occurrence of the wrongful conduct'.[95] During the process

[90] ARSIWA Commentary, n. 3, Chapter IV, para. 5.

[91] P.-M. Dupuy, 'Faute de l'État et fait internationalement illicite' (1987) 5 DRFTPCJ 51.

[92] J. Brierly, *The Law of Nations*, 6th edn (Oxford: Clarendon Press, 1963), p. 55.

[93] J. Crawford, 'First Report on State Responsibility', ILC *Yearbook* 1998/II(1), at 27–30, paras. 108–11 and 118. Cf. R. Ago, 'La colpa nell'illecito internazionale', in *Scritti giuridici in onore di Santi Romano*, 3 vols. (Padua: CEDAM, 1940), vol. 3, pp. 177–206.

[94] ARSIWA Commentary, n. 3, Article 2, para. 10; A. Ouedraogo, 'L'Évolution du concept de faute dans la théorie de la responsabilité internationale des États' (2008) 21 RQDI 129.

[95] ARSIWA Commentary, n. 3, Article 16, para. 5.

of elaboration of the ARSIWA and the ARIO, a number of states and international organisations expressed doubts as to the clarity of the requirement of 'knowledge of the circumstances', and that the 'aid be used with the view to the commission of the internationally wrongful act'.[96] The ILC did not elucidate this important aspect in Articles 14 and 58 of the ARIO.[97] Hence the mystery remains as to whether responsibility for complicity as construed by the ILC is not a reminiscence of fault, so diligently assassinated by Anzilotti and hesitantly resurrected by Ago and Arangio-Ruiz.[98] To paraphrase the former ILC member Satya Pal Jagota, the smoke of the cigarette may have left the room, but the ashes remain.[99]

Although the ICJ framed the interpretation of knowledge in the *Bosnian Genocide* case as requiring 'full knowledge of facts' on behalf of Serbia, it is not clear whether the assisting state needs to know of the actual intention of the assisted state in all circumstances, or only where the norm breached requires a particular *mens rea*.[100] It seems that the Court leaned towards the latter:

> There cannot be a finding of complicity against a State unless at the least its organs were aware that genocide was about to be committed or was under way, and if the aid and assistance supplied, from the moment they became so aware onwards, to the perpetrators of the criminal acts or to those who were on the point of committing them, enabled or facilitated the commission of the acts. In other words, an accomplice must have given support in perpetrating the genocide with full knowledge of the facts.[101]

[96] See e.g. Comments by the United Kingdom and United States, ILC *Yearbook* 1998/II(1), at 128–9; Comments by Denmark, on behalf of the Nordic Countries (Finland, Iceland, Norway, Sweden, and Denmark), Republic of Korea, United Kingdom, United States, and the Netherlands, all reproduced in ILC *Yearbook* 2001/II(1), at 52.

[97] See G. Gaja, 'Eighth Report on Responsibility of International Organizations', UN Doc. A/CN.4/640 (2011), at 16–18, paras. 45–9 ('[i]n view of these conflicting comments [e.g. the EU and the World Bank suggesting a clear reference to intention, whereas Cuba, for instance, suggested a presumption of knowledge of the circumstances], it seems preferable not to include in the commentary . . . a discussion of the relevance of intention on the part of the assisting or aiding international organization').

[98] See Ago, 'Le Délit international', n. 11, at 486; A. Gattini, 'La Notion de faute à la lumière du projet de convention de la Commission du droit international sur la responsabilité internationale' (1992) 3 EJIL 253; G. Perrin, 'Le Problème de la faute dans la responsabilité internationale de l'Etat', in *Im Dienst an der Gemeinschaft: Festschrift für Dietrich Schindler zum 65. Geburtstag* (Basel: Verlag Helbing & Lichtenhahn, 1989), p. 127.

[99] A. Gattini, 'Smoking/No Smoking: Some Remarks on the Current Place of Fault in the ILC Draft Articles on State Responsibility' (1999) 10 EJIL 397, at 397.

[100] *Bosnian Genocide*, n. 6, at 222, para. 432.

[101] Ibid.

Helmut Philipp Aust presents the problem in the following way: 'how might it be possible to distinguish between a State which is pursuing its normal course of business and a State which is about to abuse its rights or to render aid or assistance with a view to further the commission of an internationally wrongful act by another State?'[102] Construing intent as one of the conditions for responsibility for complicity is at odds with the general framework of international responsibility of states and international organisations. In this respect, the ILC's Commentary to Article 2 of the ARSIWA is instructive:

> A related question is whether fault constitutes a necessary element of the internationally wrongful act of a State. This is certainly not the case if by 'fault' one understands the existence, for example, of an intention to harm. In the absence of any specific requirement of a mental element in terms of the primary obligation, it is only the act of a State that matters, independently of any intention.[103]

In most cases, it is difficult, if not impossible, to establish that a state did not only know that its assistance would be used for a violation of an international obligation of another state, but that it had been providing assistance for that purpose.[104] The ILC discussed an example of this scenario that occurred in 1958, when Germany allowed US military bases to be set up in its territory.[105] These bases were used to send US aircraft to Lebanon for a military intervention.[106] Ago was of the opinion that this situation would fall within the boundaries of complicity, although it was unlikely that Germany desired the US intervention in Lebanon.[107] Paolo Palchetti has argued that the expression 'with the view to facilitate' as used in the ILC's Commentary to Article 16 of the ARSIWA simply means that the act of aiding and assisting must be *deliberate* in character, without any requirement that the aiding or assisting state be aware of the ultimate purpose of the act that it is assisting.[108] Neither is it necessary to show that the aiding or assisting

[102] Aust, *Complicity and the Law of State Responsibility*, n. 2, at p. 83. See also ARSIWA Commentary, n. 3, Article 16, para. 5.
[103] Ibid.
[104] Graefrath, 'Complicity in the Law of International Responsibility', n. 9, at 375. Cf. Crawford, *State Responsibility*, n. 55, at pp. 405–8.
[105] Ago, 'Seventh Report on State Responsibility', n. 13, at 58–9, para. 73. [106] Ibid.
[107] Ibid.
[108] P. Palchetti, 'State Responsibility for Complicity in Genocide' in P. Gaeta (ed.), *The UN Genocide Convention – A Commentary* (Oxford University Press, 2009), p. 380, at p. 389.

entity intended for the wrongful act to be committed, nor that it wanted that particular outcome.[109]

If state A sends its drones to state B, the latter being continuously reproached by international organisations and other states for using drones in extrajudicial executions, a foreseeable consequence of such action is that state A cannot invoke its absence of knowledge of the circumstances surrounding the internationally wrongful act. In cases where state A supports state B in the commission of an internationally wrongful act, the assessment of the knowledge of the *circumstances* does not entail the connivance of the content, specific form, or modalities of the wrongful act as such.[110] In line with our example, state A only needs to know the circumstances of the wrongdoing, i.e. that its drones will be used to commit extrajudicial killings by state B. State A need not know that the drones will be used to kill a particular individual or the modalities of such executions. It is also possible that state A may provide drones to state B for the lawful purpose of a topographic survey of a remote region. If, then, these drones are unexpectedly used for an unlawful activity, state A bears no responsibility.

The test of 'knowledge of the circumstances of the wrongful act' finds some expression in practice.[111] In 2009, the UN Legal Counsel expressed an opinion regarding the collaboration of the UN Mission in the Democratic Republic of the Congo (MONUC) and the Forces armées de la République démocratique du Congo (FARDC) that supports the knowledge of the circumstances test:

> If MONUC has reason to believe that FARDC units involved in an operation are violating one or the other of those bodies of law [international humanitarian law, human rights law and refugee law] and if, despite MONUC's intercession with the FARDC and with the Government of the DRC, MONUC has reason to believe that such violations are still being committed, then MONUC may not lawfully continue to support that operation, but must cease its participation in it completely . . . MONUC may not lawfully provide logistic or 'service' support to any FARDC operation if it has reason to believe that the FARDC units involved are violating any of those bodies of

109 Ibid. See also Quigley, 'Complicity in International Law', n. 9, at 108–17; Padeletti, *Pluralità di Stati nel fatto illecito internazionale*, n. 73, at pp. 226–7. Cf. Graefrath, 'Complicity in the Law of International Responsibility', n. 9, at 375. Cf. ILC *Yearbook* 1999/I, at 68, para. 4 (Economides).

110 Cf. *Corfu Channel (United Kingdom of Great Britain and Northern Ireland* v. *Albania)*, Judgment, ICJ Reports 1949, 4; Dissenting Opinion by Judge Azevedo, at pp. 85–6.

111 V. Lowe, 'Responsibility for the Conduct of Other States' (2002) JJIL 1, at 8.

> law ... This follows directly from the Organization's obligations under customary international law and from the Charter to uphold, promote and encourage respect for human rights, international humanitarian law and refugee law.[112]

Several actions taken with regard to the participation of different states in the conflict in Syria in 2013 may suggest that the *intention* requirement is immaterial, particularly where the pattern of violations is widespread and systematic.[113] For example, in June 2012, a Russian ship taking weaponry to the Syrian regime was not able to proceed to its final destination. It was stopped in the United Kingdom's territorial waters and had to return to Russia after the British insurers Standard Club cancelled the ship's insurance.[114] On that occasion, a Foreign and Commonwealth Office spokesman said:

> [w]e are aware of a ship carrying a consignment of refurbished Russian-made attack helicopters heading to Syria. We are working closely with international partners to ensure that we are doing all we can to stop the Syrian regime's ability to slaughter civilians being reinforced through assistance from other countries.[115]

Similarly, Turkey intercepted a Russian plane heading to Syria and allegedly transporting weaponry.[116] Neither the United Kingdom nor Turkey seem to have verified whether Russia actually intended the shipments to be used by the Syrian regime, and for what specific purposes. These and other reactions by states to prevent complicity in a wrongful act merge legal and policy considerations. Likewise, it is not always clear whether they are premised on the responsibility for complicity or a specific primary rule. For instance, the reactions of the European Union member states to shipments of weaponry to Syria could fall concurrently under the

[112] ARIO Commentary, n. 4, Article 14, para. 6.

[113] Human Rights Council, 'Report of the Independent International Commission of Inquiry on the Syrian Arab Republic', UN Doc. A/HRC/24/46 (2013); Human Rights Council, 'Report of the Independent International Commission of Inquiry on the Syrian Arab Republic', UN Doc. A/HRC/23/58 (2013); 'Syria: Who's Backing Who?', *The Guardian*, 11 October 2012; 'Arms Shipments Seen from Sudan to Syria Rebels', *The New York Times*, 12 August 2013; and 'In Turnabout, Syria Rebels Get Libyan Weapons', *The New York Times*, 21 June 2013.

[114] 'Russian Arms Shipment Bound for Syria Foiled by Britain's Insurers', *The Guardian*, 19 June 2012.

[115] Ibid.

[116] 'Turkey Accuses Russia of Supplying Syria with Munitions', *The Guardian*, 11 October 2012.

arms trade embargo, but could also be fuelled by considerations of the general rule on the responsibility for aid or assistance.

In the *El-Masri* judgment, the European Court of Human Rights (ECtHR) emphasised that:

> the Macedonian authorities not only failed to comply with their positive obligation to protect the applicant from being detained in contravention of Article 5 of the Convention, but they actively facilitated his subsequent detention in Afghanistan by handing him over to the CIA, despite the fact that they *were aware or ought to have been aware of the risk of that transfer.*[117]

Although the ECtHR does not state it expressly, it seems to rely on Article 16 of the ARSIWA – or on a similar rationale – as a partial basis for Macedonia's responsibility. If this reading of the Court's rationale is correct, then the ECtHR seems to subscribe to a more lenient interpretation of knowledge, whether actual or constructive.

Knowledge of the circumstances of the wrongful act thus appears to be a more objective and practical test than the requirement of intent. In ascertaining knowledge of the circumstances of the internationally wrongful act, the following criteria may be relevant: (a) the notoriety of facts where 'the circumstances were such as called for some reaction, within a reasonable time';[118] (b) the special interest of the aiding or assisting state in the region;[119] and (c) the geographical proximity.[120] Other relevant indicators include the existence of legal proceedings involving the state recipient of aid or assistance, or other independent inquiries into the allegations of complicity.[121] The nature of the aid or assistance and of the breach itself, whether instantaneous or continuous in character, may further influence the examination of whether the state or international organisation knew, or had reasons to know, about the relevant circumstances of the wrongful act. If, for the first act in the chain of continuous breach, one cannot presume that the state knew that it was contributing to the commission of the wrongful act, this assumption is reversed from the

117 *El-Masri*, n. 49, para. 239 (emphasis added).

118 *Temple of Preah Vihear (Cambodia* v. *Thailand)*, Judgment, ICJ Reports 1962, 6, at 23.

119 *Fisheries (United Kingdom* v. *Norway)*, Judgment, ICJ Reports 1951, 116, at 139.

120 *Bosnian Genocide*, n. 6, at 221, para. 430; *Armed Activities on the Territory of the Congo*, n. 68, at 230–1, paras. 174–80.

121 *El-Masri*, n. 49, at para. 157; A. Boivin, 'Complicity and Beyond: International Law and the Transfer of Small Arms and Light Weapons' (2005) 87 IRRC 467, at 470.

moment the violation extends in time and the state fails to suspend its aid or assistance. Furthermore, in situations where violations of *jus cogens* norms are implicated, or where the illegality of particular conduct by the recipient state has been declared prior to the decision by the aiding or assisting state to contribute, the presumption of knowledge is justified.[122]

In this sense, a more lenient approach to the cognitive or subjective element of complicity as compared to the requirement of intention would facilitate the establishment of shared responsibility between multiple actors. To be effective, knowledge of the circumstances of the wrongful act could be proven not only on the basis of material evidence, but also indirect evidence. Unless the substantive norm breached expressly requires the showing of intention, knowledge of the circumstances of the wrongful act is a sufficient standard for triggering the responsibility of the complicit entity.

3.3 The opposability element of the obligation breached

The developments occurring in the law of responsibility – including the more far-reaching rules on invocation and enforcement of responsibility – have reinforced the idea that the international legal order has an interest in the observance of the law. In the past, it was 'perfectly legitimate in international law to regard the idea of the breach of an obligation as the exact equivalent of the idea of impairment of the subjective right of others'.[123] Today, in many areas of international law, the respect for strictly bilateral relations has an impact on third parties, and depends upon their conduct. 'As interaction increases, more bilateral disputes will have peripheral effects'.[124]

Under Article 34 of the Vienna Convention on the Law of Treaties, a bilateral obligation does not create any duties for third states.[125] Article 16 of the ARSIWA and its sister provisions in the ARIO reproduce this logic. They limit the responsibility to situations where both the aiding or

[122] Graefrath, 'Complicity in the Law of International Responsibility', n. 9, at 377; Lowe, 'Responsibility for the Conduct of Other States', n. 111, at 14.

[123] R. Ago, 'Second Report on State Responsibility', ILC *Yearbook* 1970/II(1), 192.

[124] M. W. Reisman, *Nullity and Revision: The Review and Enforcement of International Judgments and Awards* (Cambridge University Press, 1974), pp. 331–2.

[125] Vienna Convention on the Law of Treaties, Vienna, 23 May 1969, in force 27 January 1980, 1155 UNTS 331, Article 34. See also D. J. Bederman, 'Third Party Rights and Obligations in Treaties', in D. B. Hollis (ed.), *The Oxford Guide to Treaties* (Oxford University Press, 2012), p. 328.

assisting entity, and the aided or assisted entity, are bound by the same international obligation. The original Article 25 and the former draft Article 27 of the ILC's state responsibility project did not contain any such limitation. As we alluded to earlier, only one state specifically requested the ILC to consider bringing such a limitation within the scope of the provision.[126] Special Rapporteur James Crawford convinced the ILC that the rule on responsibility for aid or assistance could not 'be applied to bilateral obligations in an unqualified form':[127]

> Take a case where finance or goods are to be provided pursuant to a treaty by State A to State B, and State A realizes that to comply with the treaty will produce a breach of State B's obligation to State C. Under international law both treaties are presumably valid, although this is without prejudice to the international responsibility of State B. In such circumstances, why should State A be the judge of State B's compliance? If State B insists upon performance of its treaty with State A, is State A entitled to refuse? Yet under [former] Article 27, it would appear that if State A knowingly provides the assistance, it is responsible to State C.[128]

The Special Rapporteur's footnote attached to the preceding comment raises an important issue as to the justification of the opposability requirement:

> It might be argued that State A's intention here is not to injure State C, but rather to comply with State B's obligation. Refined judgments of the 'intention' of States, based on casuistical doctrines such as 'double effect', are not a very secure basis for State responsibility. A broad rule such as that specified in [former] Article 27 [current Article 16] could only work satisfactorily if it were open to the assisting State to justify its assistance, e.g., on the ground of an equally valid moral or legal duty. But to enact a principle of justification would plainly involve legislating in the field of the primary rules of responsibility.[129]

This assertion raises a question about the validity of treaties. Crawford seems to admit that the treaty between state A and state B is valid. If state A concludes another treaty with state C on the agreement that it shall not

[126] See e.g. Comment by Sweden, ILC *Yearbook* 1981/II(1), at 77 ('[a]ssuming, for example, that State A, by treaty with State B has undertaken not to increase the size of its navy beyond a certain level, would it be unlawful for a third State to sell warships to State A, if that level is thereby exceeded?').

[127] Crawford, 'Second Report on State Responsibility', n. 22, at 51, para. 186. See also Crawford, *State Responsibility*, n. 55, pp. 409–10.

[128] Ibid., 'Second Report on State Responsibility'. [129] Ibid., at footnote 360.

provide state B with particular assistance, this does not necessarily imply that the initial treaty between state A and state B is invalid. If the validity of both treaties is recognised, then one is faced with the question of conflict of norms. The question is whether, by complying with the terms of the first treaty, i.e. rendering the aid or assistance prescribed therein to state B, state A is not facilitating the commission of the internationally wrongful act against state C. As Reuter explains:

> si le fait illicite réside dans la conclusion du traité (le deuxième en date) on pourrait toujours imaginer que la répartition adéquate soit l'élimination de ce traité; il pourrait en être ainsi si le deuxième était conclu de mauvaise foi et que les circonstances soient telles que l'autre partie à ce traité puisse être considérée comme un complice de la violation de l'obligation déjà souscrite par A, ce qui sera rarement le cas.[130]

The matter could be looked at differently in the context of international responsibility.[131] For example, if state A (a persistent objector to claims to extended security zones at sea)[132] assists state B (which has acquiesced in such claims) to engage in unlawful military activities within the security zone of state C, state A would incur no responsibility under current Article 16 of the ARSIWA.[133] In the author's view, this outcome is unacceptable, given that state A is fully aware that its assistance will contribute to the breach of an obligation binding state B vis-à-vis state C.[134] The wrongfulness of state A's conduct derives from the wrongful character of state B's conduct and the knowledge thereof by state A.

[130] P. Reuter, *Introduction au droit des traités* (Paris: Presses Universitaires de France, 1995), p. 99. See also H. Lauterpacht, 'Contract to Breach a Contract', in E. Lauterpacht (ed.), *International Law: Being the Collected Papers of Hersch Lauterpacht, The Law of Peace, Parts VII–VIII*, 4 vols. (Cambridge University Press, 1978), vol. IV, p. 340, at p. 374.

[131] Cf. *Case concerning the difference between New Zealand and France concerning the interpretation or application of two agreements concluded on 9 July 1986 between the two States and which related to the problems arising from the Rainbow Warrior Affair*, Decision, (1990) 20 RIAA 217, at 251, para. 75 ('in international law there is no distinction between contractual and tortious responsibility'). See also A. Orakhelashvili, 'Division of Reparation between Responsible Entities', in J. Crawford et al. (eds.), *The Law of International Responsibility* (Oxford University Press, 2010), p. 646, at p. 652.

[132] See N. Klein, *Maritime Security and the Law of the Sea* (Oxford University Press, 2011), p. 58 ('[s]ecurity or exclusion zones in maritime space are generally accepted for use during armed conflict'). These zones can extend beyond the territorial sea of the coastal state.

[133] Lowe, 'Responsibility for the Conduct of Other States', n. 111, at 7.

[134] *Gabčikovo-Nagymaros Project (Hungary/Slovakia)*, Judgment, ICJ Reports 1997, 7 at p. 38, para. 47.

In line with the fundamental principle of good faith, the prohibition of the abuse of rights, and the principle that no state should procure injury to the rights of another, it would only be reasonable to attach legal consequences to state A's actions. Article 16(b) of the ARSIWA appears to be a safety valve for an otherwise complicit state or international organisation that can argue that it is bound by a different rule from the one breached by the principal wrongdoer.[135] Crawford clarifies that what in fact is required by Article 16(b) is not the identity of norms or sources of the obligation, but rather the wrongfulness of the conduct.[136] In his view, '[w]ithout the inclusion of paragraph (b), ARSIWA Article 16 could become a vehicle by which the effects of well-publicized bilateral obligations are given universal extension'.[137]

This strict 'bilateralisation' of complicity in the current Article 16 of the ARSIWA is regrettable.[138] First, the opposability of the obligation on the aiding or assisting state, and on the aided or assisted state, perpetuates a particular vision of reciprocal normativity in international law.[139] Second, it shuts the door to the development or extension of responsibility for wrongdoings committed in collaboration between states and entities other than states, which are rarely if ever bound by the same obligations. It suffices to consider the scenario of the *Kosovo* advisory opinion,[140] and to assume that the 'authors of the declaration of independence' were aided or assisted by third states. Had the ICJ deemed such declaration to be not in conformity with international law, could one raise the question of whether the aiding or assisting states bear responsibility for undermining the sovereignty and territorial integrity of Serbia?

Likewise, the requirement of opposability makes little sense in Articles 14 and 58 of the ARIO.[141] It is difficult to find examples where the organisation is bound by the same obligation as its member states. Cuba

[135] Aust, *Complicity and the Law of State Responsibility*, n. 2, pp. 264–5.

[136] Crawford, *State Responsibility*, n. 55, at p. 410. [137] Ibid.

[138] See Crawford, 'Second Report on State Responsibility', n. 22, Annex (providing a brief comparative review on liability for inducing a breach of contract as a civil wrong).

[139] See C. Gutiérrez Espada, *El hecho ilícito internacional* (Madrid: Dykinson S.L., 2005), pp. 215–20; Aust, *Complicity and the Law of State Responsibility*, n. 2, pp. 249–65; ILC *Yearbook* 1999/I, at 68, para. 5 (Economides).

[140] *Accordance with International Law of the Unilateral Declaration of Independence in Respect of Kosovo*, Advisory Opinion, ICJ Reports 2010, 403.

[141] Compare Chapter 2 of this volume, Gattini, 'Breach of International Obligations', n. 5, pp. 49–54.

suggested deleting this requirement and ensuring 'the progressive development of a rule establishing that States and international organizations are duty-bound not to facilitate the commission of an act in breach of international law'.[142] The Russian Federation criticised this requirement for the reason that 'some actions could be taken only by States and not by international organizations'.[143]

As Lukashuk, a former member of the ILC, rightly noted at the time of the second reading of the ARSIWA, the requirement of opposability is

> a typically private-law approach to responsibility. If an entity, while assisting another entity, breached the obligations stemming from a contract concluded with a third party, it was not considered to be liable. Even in private law, however, such acts were not deemed to be acts of good faith, something that would be all the more unacceptable in public law. The specific nature of international law and international responsibility certainly had to be borne in mind. Many States had pointed that out in the Sixth Committee, stating that the responsibility of States under international law had a sui generis quality and was neither civil nor criminal. It was on that basis that several States, including Israel, had called for the deletion of the provision that the obligation breached must also be binding upon the State that provided assistance.[144]

To accept the regulation of complicity as it appears in the provisions codified by the ILC is to recognise that there is nothing wrong with aiding or assisting a breach of an international obligation by which one is not bound. To use a metaphor, there is nothing wrong with giving the keys to the car without the car itself. This is a dangerous move, not only because it reinforces an overly restrictive notion of responsibility and legal interest, but it also fails to capture the social need of the system as a whole. The proper tests of knowledge and causation avoid opening the floodgates of responsibility for complicity, which was the apparent justification for adding the requirement of opposability in the text of Article 16(b) of the ARSIWA and its sister provisions.

The requirement of opposability is an overly formalistic tool for preserving the bilateralist structure of international responsibility. It

[142] Comment by Cuba, UN Doc. A/CN.4/636 (2011), at 16.

[143] Comment by the Russian Federation, UN Doc. A/C.6/60/SR.12 (2005), at 11, paras. 67–9. See also Comment by Israel, UN Doc. A/C.6/60/SR.16 (2005), at 9, para. 55; Comment by Guatemala, UN Doc. A/C.5/60/SR.12 (2005), at 17, para. 103.

[144] ILC, *Yearbook* 2001/I, at 42, para. 52 (Lukashuk).

creates an additional barrier for complicity to operate as a basis for shared responsibility. This requirement finds no clear support in practice and *opinio juris*, and was heavily criticised during the discussion of the ARIO. Instead of the opposability requirement, a more effective way to regulate the scope of responsibility for complicity would be to clarify its material and cognitive elements and to develop a proper causal analysis.

4. Distributing responsibility and allocating the legal consequences between the complicit and the principal entities

Complicity stands apart from the standard cause-and-effect analysis, which applies to any given relationship between the wrongful act and the injury.[145] It is unsettled in positive law whether the complicit conduct in a wrongful act of another generates the presumption of shared responsibility, and, if so, what its modalities are.[146] This is evident in the contradictions of the ILC on the distribution of responsibility and the allocation of legal consequences between the complicit and the principal wrongdoers.[147] In essence, two causal operations take place in the situation of complicity.[148] First, a causal link must be established between the complicit conduct and the breach of an international obligation by the principal wrongdoer. Second, for the purposes of the implementation of responsibility, the causal link must be shown between the aid or assistance and the injury deriving from the principal wrongful act. It is at this second stage that the injured party will have the onus of showing that the injury, and not only the underlying wrongful act, finds some trace in the complicit conduct.

145 See Ago, 'Le Délit international', n. 11, 417 et seq. Cf. Klein, 'Beihilfe zum Völkerrechtsdelikt', n. 17, at 433 (raising concern about the absence of a predetermined causal standard in cases of complicity in the internationally wrongful act).

146 See C. Dominicé, 'Attribution of Conduct to Multiple States and the Implication of a State in the Act of Another State', in J. Crawford et al. (eds.), *The Law of International Responsibility* (Oxford University Press, 2010) pp. 281–9; Orakhelashvili, 'Division of Reparation between Responsible Entities', n. 131, at pp. 647–6.

147 ARSIWA Commentary, n. 3, Article 16, paras 4 and 10. See also Article 31 ARSIWA, para. 10; G. Arangio-Ruiz, 'Second Report on State Responsibility', ILC *Yearbook* 1989/II(1), at 15, para. 46. See also Chapter 7 in this volume, d'Argent, 'Reparation, Cessation, Assurances and Guarantees of Non-Repetition', n. 60 at pp. 215–16.

148 B. Stern, 'The Obligation to Make Reparation', in J. Crawford et al. (eds.), *The Law of International Responsibility* (Oxford University Press, 2010), p. 562, at p. 570.

Regarding the first aspect of causal analysis, Article 16, in line with its Commentary, requires that the aid or assistance 'contributed significantly to' the commission of the internationally wrongful act.[149] The Commentary adopted on the first reading contained the following clarification: 'the aid or assistance must have the effect of making it *materially* easier for the State receiving the aid or assistance in question to commit an internationally wrongful act'.[150] At the same time, the ILC points out that the aid or assistance need not be essential for the commission of the wrongful act.[151] During the second reading of the ARSIWA, Bruno Simma warned the ILC that:

> the substantial or essential element was virtually absent . . . [it] was a real problem, namely, how to be more precise and specific about the interrelationship between the aid provided to the State and the wrongful act it committed. To do so, it was important either to restrict the notion of complicity to the most serious breaches of international law and, in particular, the violation of obligations *erga omnes*, and then to be less restrictive on the link between aid and the wrongful act, or to confine oneself to forms of aid which were essential and then require a causal link between the aid and the wrongful act or, lastly, to emphasize the positive and active nature of the link, i.e., the existence of a specific link between the aid and the wrongful act.[152]

It is questionable whether requiring more than a simple factual link between the complicit conduct and the principal wrongful act is appropriate for the purposes of finding responsibility for complicity. Amidst comments received on the transposition of Article 16's content to the ARIO, the UN Office of Legal Affairs underscored 'the fundamental difference between States and international organizations, whose aid and assistance activities in an ever-growing number and diversity of areas, often constitute their core functions'.[153] In this vein, the International Monetary Fund (IMF) argued, for instance, that its programme of assistance can never be 'essential, or contribute significantly, to a particular wrongful conduct of a member State', as it is within the mandate of the organisation to assist its members

[149] ARSIWA Commentary, n. 3, Article 16, para. 5. See also section 3.1 above.

[150] ILC *Yearbook* 1978/II(2), at 103 (original emphasis).

[151] Quigley, 'Complicity in International Law', n. 9, at pp. 121–2; Crawford, 'Second Report on State Responsibility', n. 22, at 50, para. 182.

[152] ILC *Yearbook* 1999/I, at 79, para. 41 (Simma).

[153] Comment by UN Office of Legal Affairs, UN Doc. A/CN.4/637/Add.1 (2011), at 19, para. 5.

'in addressing their balance of payments problems'.[154] The IMF would be unable to supervise the behaviour of the borrowing states even by loan conditionality.[155] This functional justification will not necessarily excuse the prima facie responsibility of the organisation. Even if it is part of the mandate of an international organisation to provide aid or assistance, it cannot do so insofar as it knows of the circumstances of the wrongful act of the receiving state. The ILC itself seems to undermine the degree-based approach when stating that the responsibility could unfold even when 'the assistance may have only been an incidental factor in the commission of the primary act, and may have contributed only to a minor degree, if at all, to the injury suffered'.[156]

This comment by the ILC brings us to the second aspect of causal analysis. This concerns the question of the causal link between the complicit conduct and the injury that flows from the principal wrongful act. Are the existing causal standards adequate to respond to situations of complicity? The ILC's silence in this regard is all the more problematic because it represents some leeway for otherwise complicit states and international organisations to escape their obligation of reparation *vis-à-vis* an injured party.

One uniform test of causation is not known in international law.[157] Most frequently, courts and tribunals, when examining causation, look at its factual and legal facets. In terms of the former, international courts and tribunals generally require the existence of a proximate cause between the breach of an obligation by a state and the injury suffered.[158] This is also known as in-fact causation or an objective criterion of causation.[159] It implies that only those injuries that are in a proximate relationship to the

[154] Comment by IMF, UN Doc. A/CN.4/582 (2007), at 10.

[155] See A. Reinisch, 'Aid or Assistance and Direction and Control between States and International Organizations in the Commission of Internationally Wrongful Acts' (2010) 7 IOLR 63, at 68.

[156] ARSIWA Commentary, n. 3, Article 16, para. 10.

[157] See also Chapter 2 in this volume, Gattini, 'Breach of International Obligations', n. 5, at pp. 28–31.

[158] F. V. García Amador, 'Sixth Report on State Responsibility', ILC *Yearbook* 1961/II(1), 6; Arangio-Ruiz, 'Second Report on State Responsibility', n. 147, at 12–16, paras. 34-51. See Brownlie, *System of the Law of Nations*, n. 58, at p. 224; C. Gray, *Judicial Remedies in International Law* (Oxford: Clarendon Press, 1987), pp. 33–9

[159] B. Cheng, *General Principles of Law as Applied by International Courts and Tribunals* (reprint 2006) (Cambridge University Press, 1953), p. 245. See also *Guidance Regarding Jus ad Bellum Liability*, Eritrea–Ethiopia Claims Commission, Decision No. 7, (2007) 26 RIAA 1, at 12–15.

wrongful act lead to reparation.[160] According to the US–German Mixed Claims Commission:

> It matters not whether the loss be directly or indirectly sustained so long as there is a clear, unbroken connection between Germany's act and the loss complained of. It matters not how many links there may be in the chain of causation connecting Germany's act with the loss sustained, provided there is no break in the chain and the loss can be clearly, unmistakably, and definitely traced, link by link, to Germany's act. But the law cannot consider . . . the 'causes of causes and their impulsions one on another'. Where the loss is far removed in causal sequence from the act complained of, it is not competent for this tribunal to seek to unravel a tangled network of causes and of effects, or follow, through a baffling labyrinth of confused thought, numerous disconnected and collateral chains, in order to link Germany with a particular loss. All indirect losses are covered, provided only that in legal contemplation Germany's act was the efficient and proximate cause and source from which they flowed.[161]

The problem with the application of this reasoning to situations of complicity is that complicit conduct as such is never the proximate cause of the injury. It is always the principal wrongful act that constitutes the proximate cause of the injury. Technically, complicity occasions the harm, rather than causes it. 'In the case of assistance to a wrongful act, the participant would neither cause the principal to act nor would the latter act in consequence of this assistance.'[162] Hence, the central question with respect to linking the complicit conduct to the injury suffered is one of foreseeability (i.e. the legal facet of causal analysis).[163] This is constructed on the assumption that the injury is a logical consequence of an act insofar as it could have been foreseen.[164] For instance, in the *Naulilaa* case, the Arbitral Tribunal resorted to the foreseeability test, holding Germany liable for all the damage that it could have foreseen, even though the link between the unlawful act and the actual damage was

160 *Antippa (the Spyros) case* v. *Germany*, Case No. 285, (1926) 7 Greco–German Mixed Arbitral Tribunal 23–8. See also Arangio-Ruiz, 'Second Report on State Responsibility', n. 147, at 27–39.

161 *Administrative Decision No. II*, United States–German Mixed Claims Commission, Award, (1923) 7 RIAA 29.

162 Aust, *Complicity and the Law of State Responsibility*, n. 2, at p. 212.

163 See *Houston Contracting Company* v. *National Iranian Oil Company*, Award, (1988) 20 Iran–US Claims Tribunal Reports 3; *Behring International Inc.* v. *Iran*, Award, (1991) 27 Iran–US Claims Tribunal Reports 218.

164 P. Okowa, *State Responsibility for Transboundary Air Pollution in International Law* (Oxford University Press, 2001), pp. 179 et seq.

not really a 'direct' one.[165] Transposing the rationale of the Tribunal in the *Samoan Claims* case, the complicit entity would be liable for its share of the injury if, at the time of its decision to grant aid or assistance, it could have reasonably foreseen the injury from the principal wrongful act for which it was rendering aid or assistance.[166]

If the entity could have reasonably foreseen the injury from the principal wrongful act for which it was rendering aid or assistance, the question then is whether its share is deducted from the responsibility of the principal state or international organisation. The ILC's Commentary suggests that 'international practice and the decisions of the international tribunals do not support the reduction or attenuation of reparation for concurrent causes'.[167] Taken literally, this means that complicity – which is best construed as a concomitant, concurrent, or parallel cause – would have no involvement in the reparation due by the principal wrongdoer to an injured party. This could lead to potential issues of double recovery. Holding the principal wrongdoer

> liable for full compensation would be neither equitable nor in conformity with a proper application of the causal link criterion. The solution should be the repayment of partial damages, in proportion to the amount of the injury presumably to be attributed to the wrongful act and its effects, the amount to be awarded to be determined on the basis of the criteria of normality [proximate cause] and predictability [foreseeability].[168]

[165] *Responsabilité de l'Allemagne à raison de dommages causés dans les colonies portugaises du Sud de l'Afrique*, Award, (1928) 2 RIAA 1011, at 1032–3 (*Naulilaa*). The notion of directness has not disappeared from the causal terminology as applied by the international dispute settlement mechanisms. See different contributions in R. B. Lillich and D. J. Bederman, *The Iran–United States Claims Tribunal: Its Contribution to the Law of State Responsibility* (New York: Transnational Publishers, 1998).

[166] Cheng, *General Principles of Law as Applied by International Courts and Tribunals*, n. 159, pp. 249–50, citing 'Joint Report No. II of August 12, 1904' in connection with *Samoan Claims (Germany, Great Britain, United States)*, Award (1902) 9 RIAA 15, at 23–7. See also *Lighthouse Arbitration (France* v. *Greece)*, Award, (1956) 23 ILR 352; A. Rovine and G. Hanessian, 'Toward a Foreseeability Approach to Causation Questions at the United Nations Compensation Commission', in R. B. Lillich (ed.), *The United Nations Compensation Commission* (New York: Transnational Publishers, 1995), p. 234, at pp. 239 and 247.

[167] ARSIWA Commentary, n. 3, Article 31, para. 12. See *United States Diplomatic and Consular Staff in Tehran*, n. 68, at 29–32; *Corfu Channel*, n. 110, Compensation Judgment, ICJ Reports 1949, at 244, 250. See also *CME Czech Republic BV (The Netherlands* v. *Czech Republic)*, Partial Award, (2001) 9 ICSID Reports 113, at 231, para. 583; UN Compensation Commission, Report and Recommendations made by the Panel of Commissioners Concerning the First Installment of 'F2' Claims, UN Doc. S/AC.26/1999/23 (1999), para. 38.

[168] Arangio-Ruiz, 'Second Report on State Responsibility', n. 147, at 14, para. 44.

A reduction of reparation due by the principal wrongdoer is appropriate whenever 'an identifiable element of injury can properly be allocated to one of several concurrently operating causes alone'.[169] Hence, the principal wrongdoer must show that a given part of the injury flowing from its wrongful act was due to the contribution of the aiding or assisting entity. This may, however, be difficult to establish where concurrent causes are of the same nature, i.e. different contributors to the wrongdoing provide the same kind of assistance. Assume that states A and B knowingly provide materials designed for environmental pollution to state C, which will construct a dam on the border with state D in breach of its international obligation. If it is impossible to identify whether the materials of state A or state B constituted the necessary or ultimate cause of the internationally wrongful act, then both state A and state B are subject to international responsibility, and any ensuing reparations would have to be split accordingly between state C on the one hand, and states A and B on the other. It follows that the aiding or assisting state will be held responsible 'if on the facts it can be established that its conduct materially contributed to the damage suffered by the [injured state], even if other factors and causal agents also enter into the equation'.[170] To assume otherwise on considerations of lack of proximity to the injury would undermine the *effet utile* of the rule on complicity.

At a minimum, this lenient causal link is appropriate in situations where the damage is indivisible.[171] Regardless of whether complicit conduct leads to a quantifiable estimate of material damage, it always contributes to a moral damage or legal injury.[172] Satisfaction or guarantees of non-repetition may well be the appropriate form of reparation in these circumstances.[173] Relaxing the stringency of the causal relationship

[169] ARSIWA Commentary, n. 3, Article 31, para. 13.

[170] Okowa, *State Responsibility for Transboundary Air Pollution in International Law*, n. 164, at 188. See also ARSIWA Commentary, n. 3, Article 16, para. 10; A. Tunc (ed.), *International Encyclopedia of Comparative Law* (Leiden: Martinus Nijhoff, 1983), vol. XI Torts, at 68–70; H. L. A. Hart and A. M. Honoré, *Causation in the Law*, 2nd edn (Oxford: Clarendon Press, 1985).

[171] See *Dix Case*, Award (1903–1905) 9 RIAA 119, at 121. See also Talmon, 'A Plurality of Responsible Actors', n. 60, pp. 217 et seq.; Felder, *Die Beihilfe im Recht der völkerrechtlichen Staatenverantwortlichkeit*, n. 9, pp. 277–8.

[172] B. Stern, 'A Plea for "Reconstruction" of International Responsibility Based on the Notion of Legal Injury', in M. Ragazzi (ed.), *International Responsibility Today: Essays in Memory of Oscar Schachter* (Boston/Leiden: Martinus Nijhoff, 2005), p. 93.

[173] ARSIWA Commentary, n. 3, Article 16, para. 1; *Ilaşcu a.o.* v. *Moldova and Russia*, App. No. 48787/99 (ECtHR, 8 July 2004), paras. 484 et seq. See Chapter 7 in this volume, d'Argent, 'Reparation, Cessation, Assurances and Guarantees of Non-Repetition', n. 60.

in proportion to the relief sought would ensure that spreading responsibility does not divert it.[174]

5. Conclusions

The constituent elements and standards of responsibility for complicity as formulated in Article 16 of the ARSIWA and Articles 14 and 58 of the ARIO leave a number of theoretical and practical questions unanswered. Considering that 'codification does not necessarily eliminate the possibility of gaps',[175] this chapter has argued that the ILC's framework constitutes a partial, but incomplete, response to complicit behaviour in international law. To succeed in reducing black sites of non-law in the twenty-first century, the rule on responsibility for complicity needs to be officially divorced from the *probatio diabolica* of 'intention', extended to cover any action or omission that causally contributes to the wrongful act, and stretched beyond the limited logic of *pacta tertiis* as it operates in the law of treaties. Finally, the ICJ's application of Article 16 of the ARSIWA to the collaboration between states and non-state actors gives rise to new prospects for the rule to remedy the gaps in the existing modes of attribution of conduct.[176]

In terms of the implications of this analysis for shared responsibility, complicity allows different actors that contribute to the same internationally wrongful act to bear responsibility. However, the modalities for the distribution of responsibility and, even less, the allocation of legal consequences between the complicit and the principal entity, are relatively unclear. The situation becomes even more complex when multiple actors contribute to the commission of the same internationally wrongful act. This chapter also shows that the application of the existing causal standards to the allocation of legal consequences in the scenarios of complicity might lead to inequitable results. The model of responsibility for complicity, operating without the requirements of intent and opposability, would arguably constitute a more effective mechanism

[174] Aust, *Complicity and the Law of State Responsibility*, n. 2, p. 89.

[175] H. Lauterpacht, *The Function of Law in the International Community* (reprint) (Oxford University Press, 2012), p. 66.

[176] *Bosnian Genocide*, n. 6, para. 419 et seq.; Crawford, 'Second Report on State Responsibility', n. 22, para. 165; E. Savarese, 'Complicité de l'Etat dans la perpétration d'actes de génocide: Les Notions contiguës et la nature de la norme' (2007) 53 AFDI 280, at 285.

for bringing complicit entities to account. Such a model would also enhance the effectiveness of complicity as a form of shared responsibility in international law. As instances and forms of complicity in the relations between states, international organisations, and non-state actors grow in numbers and complexity, the law will need to catch up with the speed of events.

6

Circumstances Precluding Wrongfulness

HELMUT PHILIPP AUST

1. Introduction

> There is behaviour that is right; and there is behaviour that, though wrong, is understandable and excusable. The distinction between the two is the very stuff of classical tragedy. No dramatist, no novelist would confuse them. No philosopher or theologian would conflate them.[1]

With these remarks, Vaughan Lowe criticised the International Law Commission (ILC) for having failed to translate adequately the differing degrees of wrongfulness and responsibility into its system of 'defences' for violations of the law. As is well known, the ILC has labelled these defences as 'circumstances precluding wrongfulness'. It thus aspired to introduce a measure of conceptual clarity and uniformity into a field that was previously characterised by considerable diversity – justifications, excuses, defences, circumstances precluding responsibility – all these categories could be found in the works of scholars as well as in judicial practice.[2] What these categories meant to cover was a diverse field of different grounds which could exculpate, or 'defend', states from claims for wrongful behaviour. These grounds included notions that are quite

Helmut Philipp Aust Dr. iur. is Senior Research Fellow at the Faculty of Law, Humboldt University Berlin. I would like to thank the editors and the other participants at the authors' seminar for useful comments and suggestions. Any errors are mine. The research leading to this chapter has received funding from the European Research Council under the European Union's Seventh Framework Programme (FP7/2007–2013)/ERC grant agreement n° 249499, as part of the research project on Shared Responsibility in International Law (SHARES), carried out at the Amsterdam Center for International Law (ACIL) of the University of Amsterdam.

[1] V. Lowe, 'Precluding Wrongfulness or Responsibility: A Plea for Excuses' (1999) 10 EJIL 405, at 406.

[2] S. Szurek, 'The Notion of Circumstances Precluding Wrongfulness', in J. Crawford, A. Pellet, and S. Olleson (eds.), *The International Law of Responsibility* (Oxford University Press, 2010), p. 427, at p. 428.

characteristic for the international legal order, such as 'self-help' and 'self-defence', but also concepts frequently found in domestic private law, such as *force majeure*, distress, and necessity.

The provisions on 'circumstances precluding wrongfulness' (Articles 20 to 27 of the Articles on the Responsibility of States for Internationally Wrongful Acts (ARSIWA) and the Articles on Responsibility of International Organizations (ARIO), respectively) have found widespread acceptance in international practice.[3] This practice, however, is essentially limited to 'bilateral' situations, i.e. the classic scenario in which one state advances a claim against another state (or other bilateral settings such as investment claims). In contrast, it is mostly uncharted territory as to how these circumstances come to be applied in situations of 'shared responsibility'.[4] In more concrete terms, how can the circumstances set forth in Articles 20 to 27 of the ARSIWA and the ARIO cope with situations in which a plurality of states and/or international organisations are implicated in the commission of a wrongful act, and one or more of them try to rely on the circumstances?[5] Could it be that the circumstances are characterised by an emphasis on 'bilateral' situations

[3] Ibid., at pp. 428–9. For an overview of judicial practice see the 'Materials on the Responsibility of States for Internationally Wrongful Acts', compiled by the UN Secretariat, UN Legislative Series, UN Doc. ST/LEG/SER.B/25 (2012), at 154 et seq.

[4] For a definition of the concept of shared responsibility as used for this volume, see Chapter 1, P. A. Nollkaemper, 'Introduction', p. 1, at pp. 6–12; as well as P. A. Nollkaemper and D. Jacobs, 'Shared Responsibility in International Law: A Conceptual Framework' (2013) 34(2) MIJIL 359.

[5] This chapter does not, in general, deal with the reverse situation in which a state/international organisation invokes a circumstance precluding wrongfulness against a plurality of states acting together. This scenario does not pose particular problems for all of the circumstances set forth by the ILC in the Articles on Responsibility of States for Internationally Wrongful Acts, ILC *Yearbook* 2001/II(2) (ARSIWA), Articles 20–27. For example, with respect to consent, it is clear that consent given by a state/international organisation can only authorise conduct vis-à-vis that state. With respect to self-defence, the determining factor for the question against which states' measures of self-defence can be taken depends entirely on the applicable primary rules of the *jus ad bellum*. The notions of *force majeure*, distress, and necessity are generally indifferent towards the conduct of the state/international organisation which is affected by the relevant conduct. Therefore, it is difficult to envisage problems that are specifically related to issues of shared responsibility in this context. The only circumstance where particular problems arise in this reverse scenario is Article 22 of the ARSIWA and the Articles on the Responsibility of International Organizations, ILC Report on the work of its sixty-third session, UNGAOR 66th Sess., Supp. No. 10, UN Doc. A/66/10 (2011) (ARIO), Article 22 (countermeasures). On the problems related to the taking of countermeasures against a multitude of responsible states, see the contribution in Chapter 10 of this volume, C. J. Tams, 'Countermeasures against Multiple Responsible Actors', p. 312.

and, hence, cannot adequately deal with the complexity of 'shared responsibility'?

These questions have so far not received a lot of attention. Although there is only a limited amount of practice on which we can draw, it is worthwhile to expound these questions further. Several grounds have been noted for the growing number of cases that create situations of 'shared responsibility', amongst which one can find the growing interdependence of today's world, the greater heterogeneity of actors, and an increasing 'moralization' of international relations which leads to a greater emphasis on questions of responsibility and accountability.[6] If this assessment is correct, it will most likely only be a matter of time until a state and/or an international organisation will rely on one of the circumstances precluding wrongfulness in a case in which multiple responsible actors are involved.[7]

Scenarios for the individual defences set forth in the ARSIWA and the ARIO that involve issues of 'shared responsibility' can be easily imagined: consider the case of state A expressing its consent to the deployment of the military forces of state B on its territory. Would the 'defence' of consent under Article 20 of the ARSIWA also cover the conduct of a state C that deploys military advisors for the troops of state B? How does 'self-defence' under Article 21 of the ARSIWA accommodate situations of collective self-defence? Which states can rely on the exculpatory effect of Article 22 of the ARSIWA when they take collective countermeasures in order to induce a wrongdoing state to cease its wrongful conduct? How can *force majeure* (Article 23 of the ARSIWA) preclude the wrongfulness of a 'joint organ' of two states if, for instance, the two states have set up joint border patrols and an aeroplane deployed in this context is carried by heavy wind into the airspace of a third state? Can distress (Article 24 of the ARSIWA) exculpate both an international organisation and a troop-contributing member state if – in a situation of dual attribution – a soldier of a peacekeeping force can only save his life by the commission of an act prohibited by international humanitarian

[6] See generally Nollkaemper and Jacobs, 'Shared Responsibility in International Law', n. 4.

[7] Although one should note the general reluctance of states to rely on circumstances precluding wrongfulness which, as P. Okowa argues, is due to the fact that such reliance constitutes a prima facie acknowledgement of wrongful conduct. See 'Defences in the Jurisprudence of International Tribunals', in G. S. Goodwin-Gill and S. Talmon (eds.), *The Reality of International Law – Essays in Honour of Ian Brownlie* (Oxford: Clarendon Press, 1999), p. 389, at p. 389.

law? And might several member states of an international organisation rely on 'necessity' under Article 25 of the ARSIWA in order to justify a humanitarian intervention in a third state?

These examples may highlight that circumstances precluding wrongfulness might well come to apply in situations of shared responsibility. It is the purpose of this chapter to critically analyse how well the ILC's work is equipped for dealing with such situations. To this end, the next section will first give a brief overview of the conceptual background for this discussion (section 2). Thereafter, we will turn towards the individual defences codified by the ILC with a view to their suitability for situations of shared responsibility (section 3). The fourth section will summarise the various challenges we will have come across in this discussion. Section 5 will offer some considerations as to how these shortcomings could be remedied. In particular, it will be argued that the conceptual basis of the circumstances regime should be reconsidered. A differentiation between circumstances that truly preclude wrongfulness and other defences that merely 'excuse' state or international organisation behaviour might help to remedy some of the deficiencies that we will come across in the course of this chapter. Finally, a brief conclusion will be given.

2. The conceptual background

2.1 'Shared responsibility'

According to the definition underlying this volume, responsibility is shared when multiple actors are responsible for their contribution to a single harmful outcome.[8] A specific manifestation of such shared responsibility arises when multiple actors are responsible for their contribution to a single harmful outcome and the contributions cannot causally be attributed to individual actors.[9] The following remarks will assess the impact of several modes of shared responsibility on the application of the circumstances precluding wrongfulness. Preceding this discussion, it is useful to briefly set out what these modes are and thereby also to clarify the terminology employed in this chapter. The chapter will concentrate on three dimensions of shared responsibility. First, by 'joint conduct', a situation is referred to in which two or more

[8] Nollkaemper, 'Introduction', n. 4, at pp. 6–12; see further Nollkaemper and Jacobs, 'Shared Responsibility in International Law', n. 4, at 366–8.

[9] Ibid.

states and/or international organisations act together 'on the same footing'. This category therefore signals that all those actors would incur responsibility for violating a given obligation. Second, by 'multiple attribution', a situation is envisaged in which one form of conduct or omission is attributed to two or more states and/or international organisations.[10] Thirdly, 'complicity' situations deal with what is set out in Article 16 of the ARSIWA, i.e. aid or assistance rendered by one state and/or international organisation to another state and/or international organisation for the commission of a wrongful act. These three modes are not exhaustive of the concept of 'shared responsibility'. However, they may suffice so as to give examples for the present purposes.

In situations of attribution of responsibility (as to which see in more detail Chapter 4 of this volume), it would seem to be highly unlikely that the circumstances could apply to the benefit of the state which is, for instance, directing or controlling another state in the commission of an internationally wrongful act (Article 17 of the ARSIWA), or even coercing another state (Article 18 of the ARSIWA). In particular, structural considerations militate in this regard. The concept of attribution of responsibility presupposes that the two elements of an internationally wrongful act under Article 2 of the ARSIWA are already met by the state that has engaged in wrongful conduct, and not necessarily by the state to which responsibility is attributed.[11] In the most likely scenarios, circumstances precluding wrongfulness would thus intervene on the first level, i.e. pertaining to the conduct of the state which was directed, controlled, or coerced by another state, and not on the second level of the state to which responsibility is attributed. That said, there may be exceptional scenarios in which a state organ might have been forced to coerce the organ of another state to commit an internationally wrongful act in a situation of distress. Such 'chains' of justification are conceivable but are, apparently, of a rather theoretical nature.

2.2 General features of the circumstances precluding wrongfulness

The list of defences set forth in Articles 20 to 27 of the ARSIWA covers quite a large ground, and has accordingly been labelled a 'grab bag'.[12]

[10] See Chapter 3 of this volume, F. Messineo, 'Attribution of Conduct', p. 60, at pp. 62–3, 67–83.

[11] See Chapter 4 of this volume, J. D. Fry, 'Attribution of Responsibility', p. 98.

[12] R. Rosenstock, 'The ILC and State Responsibility' (2002) 96 AJIL 792, at 794.

Hence, one is well advised to be cautious about identifying overarching structural principles for these very diverse defences. Nonetheless, the work of the ILC is characterised by some considerations which need to be kept in mind when we discuss the application of these defences in situations of shared responsibility.

2.2.1 The development of the circumstances regime

With respect to the historical development of the defences of international law, it can be noted here that ever since international law had begun to comprise a distinct field of international responsibility, defences have formed part of this field of the law.[13] This becomes apparent from the work of the Preparatory Commission for the 1930 Hague Conference for the codification of international law, which formulated a number of bases of discussion for 'circumstances under which states can decline their responsibility'. The concrete grounds mentioned by the Commission were self-defence, reprisals, provocative attitudes of an injured person, and acts of the armed forces in the suppression of a riot or insurrection.[14] Just as with the later work of the first ILC Special Rapporteur on this topic, F. V. García Amador,[15] these bases of discussion were still characterised by the initial focus of the law of state responsibility on the question of reparations for injuries to aliens.[16]

When the ILC recalibrated its work under the stewardship of Roberto Ago, its second Special Rapporteur on the topic, towards drafting a general framework for the legal consequences attached to wrongful conduct,[17] the question of the defences became particularly important. Now the codification was not 'only' about finding common ground for justifying violations of the law in an important, but relatively narrow, specific field of international law. According to the approach proposed

[13] See, with further references, F. Paddeu, 'A Genealogy of *Force Majeure* in International Law' (2012) 82 BYIL 381, at 405. On the historical reasons for the absence of a law of state responsibility before the end of the nineteenth century, see C. Tomuschat, 'International Law: Ensuring the Survival of Mankind on the Eve of a New Century' (1999) 281 RCADI 9, at 269.

[14] Cf. Szurek, 'The Notion of Circumstances Precluding Wrongfulness', n. 2, pp. 427–8.

[15] F. V. García Amador, 'First Report on State Responsibility', ILC *Yearbook* 1956/II, 203 et seq.; 'Third Report on State Responsibility', ILC *Yearbook* 1958/II, 50 et seq.

[16] On the development of the ILC's codification work, see generally J. Crawford, 'Introduction', in J. Crawford (ed.), *The International Law Commission's Articles on State Responsibility* (Cambridge University Press, 2002), p. 1, at pp. 1–4.

[17] R. Ago, 'Working Paper', ILC *Yearbook* 1963/II, 251, at 253.

by Ago and ultimately adopted by the ILC, the defences would now apply across the whole range of international legal obligations.[18] This generalising approach has been criticised for various reasons.[19] Why should, potentially, the same defence of 'distress' – a highly personalised notion – be able to justify the violation of a bilateral commercial treaty just as well as rules that are more closely related to issues of global public policy, such as the obligation to prevent genocide? To be fair, the ARSIWA set forth that none of the defences 'preclude the wrongfulness of any act of a State which is not in conformity with an obligation arising under a peremptory norm of general international law'.[20] As the Commentary makes clear, 'one State cannot dispense another from the obligation to comply with a peremptory norm, e.g. in relation to genocide or torture, whether by treaty or otherwise'.[21] In addition, the ILC has included the general disclaimer that a *lex specialis* may exist that would then dispense with the application of the general rules laid down in its two sets of Articles.[22] It would exceed the scope of this chapter to discuss specific emanations of the *lex specialis*.[23] It suffices to mention here that in the context of human rights law, several modifications apply. In order to justify conduct that prima facie infringes upon human rights guarantees, states generally have to argue within the bounds of what the relevant human rights agreement prescribes. The argument of necessity, for instance, is already factored into the general principle of proportionality, which needs to be respected when state action infringes upon human rights. In addition to this test, it would not seem that states could additionally also rely on the principle of necessity as provided for by Article 25 of the ARSIWA.[24]

2.2.2 Preclusion of wrongfulness

With respect to the general rules as laid down by the ILC, a number of structural features stand out. It was Roberto Ago who introduced the

[18] Commentary to the Articles on Responsibility of States for Internationally Wrongful Acts, ILC *Yearbook* 2001/II(2) (ARSIWA Commentary), reprinted in Crawford, *The International Law Commission's Articles*, n. 16, Introduction to Chapter V of Part One, para. 2.

[19] For general critique of the approach see A. Pellet, 'Can a State Commit a Crime? Definitely, Yes!' (1999) 10 EJIL 425.

[20] Article 26 ARSIWA, n. 5. [21] ARSIWA Commentary, n. 18, Article 26, para. 6.

[22] Article 55 ARSIWA, n. 5.

[23] Cf. Okowa, 'Defences in the Jurisprudence of International Tribunals', n. 7, p. 390.

[24] See further C. Ryngaert, 'State Responsibility, Necessity and Human Rights' (2010) 41 NYIL 79.

notion of 'circumstances precluding wrongfulness'.[25] How this notion operates can only be understood with reference to the cornerstone of the ILC codification, to be found in Article 1 of the ARSIWA. According to this provision, '[e]very internationally wrongful act entails the international responsibility of that State'. Article 2 of the ARSIWA further defines the notion of 'internationally wrongful act' by stipulating that there is such an act 'when conduct consisting of an action or omission (a) is attributable to the State under international law' (the subjective criterion) and '(b) constitutes a breach of an international obligation of the State' (the objective criterion).[26] The defences laid down in the ARSIWA are said to dispense with the objective element, i.e. the breach of an international obligation. Accordingly, if a defence is successfully relied upon by a state or international organisation, the conduct in question is no longer wrongful in character.

The ILC has been criticised for this construction of the defences.[27] The major criticism in this regard is that only some of the grounds for justification would effectively preclude wrongfulness. This would be the case for the defences of consent, self-defence, and, according to most commentators,[28] also reliance on the right to take countermeasures. However, for the

[25] At the same time, one should note that there have been some variations to Ago's work on defences over time. In particular, as Andrea Gattini has meticulously argued, it can be established from his early writings on issues of fault in the law of state responsibility that, according to Ago, *force majeure* was a defence which related to a lack of fault on the part of the respective state. Only later as Special Rapporteur did these differentiations disappear, arguably for the reason that Ago did not wish to see the question of fault openly discussed in the ILC. Instead, the inclusion of *force majeure* and – at the time – fortuitous event would have served as a reintroduction of fault into the law of state responsibility, albeit in a disguised and negative form. See with further references A. Gattini, 'La Notion de faute à la lumière du projet de convention de la Commission du droit international sur la responsabilité internationale' (1992) 3 EJIL 253, at 271–2.

[26] On the questionable terminology with respect to the objective and subjective elements, see A. Gattini, *Zufall und force majeure im System der Staatenverantwortlichkeit anhand der ILC-Kodifikationsarbeit* (Berlin: Duncker & Humblot, 1991), p. 44.

[27] See Lowe, 'Precluding Wrongfulness or Responsibility', n. 1; T. Christakis, 'Les "Circonstances excluant l'illicéité: une illusion optique?"', in *Droit du pouvoir – pouvoir du droit. Mélanges en l'honneur de Jean Salmon* (Brussels: Bruylant, 2007), p. 223; A. de Hoogh, *Obligations Erga Omnes and International Crimes* (The Hague: Kluwer, 1996), pp. 221–4.

[28] See H. Lesaffre, 'Circumstances Precluding Wrongfulness in the ILC Articles on State Responsibility: Countermeasures', in J. Crawford, A. Pellet, and S. Olleson (eds.), *The International Law of Responsibility* (Oxford University Press, 2010), p. 469, at p. 469. This is also the view of the ICJ: see *Gabčíkovo-Nagymaros Project (Hungary/Slovakia)*, Judgment, ICJ Reports 1997, 7, para. 82.

other three grounds set forth in the ILC's work, conceptual reasons as well as an analysis of international practice would instead speak for the view that *force majeure*, distress, and necessity cover conduct that is still wrongful, yet in some form is excused or leads to attenuated forms of responsibility.[29] This can be seen, for instance, in the international practice of states that assumes that some form of compensation is owed if a state relies on the state of necessity.[30]

For Special Rapporteur Ago, it was impossible to conceive of a wrongful act that would not entail the 'disadvantageous consequences' that usually ensue.[31] According to Ago, '(i)t is difficult to see what would be the point of making such a characterization. Imposing an obligation while at the same time attaching no legal consequences to breaches of it would in fact amount to not imposing the obligation in question at all.'[32] To hold otherwise would have required Ago and the ILC to change the formulation of what was to become Article 1 of the ARSIWA. Until the very end of the work of the Commission on the ARSIWA, such a reformulation was not a realistic option. Likewise, when the ILC worked on the ARIO, its decision to model those rules as closely as possible on the ARSIWA 'precluded' it from revisiting this conceptual question. While this approach can, of course, be criticised for a lack of imagination, it is also understandable that, in light of the meagre available practice on the responsibility of international organisations, the ILC did not want to reinvent the wheel in this regard.[33]

2.2.3 The distinction between primary and secondary rules

For various reasons, the inclusion of the circumstances precluding wrongfulness in the ILC's codification work is at odds with the conceptual decision to include only the so-called 'secondary rules' of international law, i.e. only to deal with those questions that concern the

[29] Such a distinction was also considered by J. Crawford, 'Second Report on State Responsibility', UN Doc. A/CN.4/498/Add.2 (1999), paras. 228–9, but was not adopted by the Commission.

[30] Cf. Christakis, 'Les "Circonstances excluant l'illicéité"', n. 27, p. 265.

[31] R. Ago, 'Eighth Report on State Responsibility', ILC *Yearbook* 1979/II(1), 28, para. 52.

[32] Ibid.

[33] For a critical assessment of the ILC's approach in this regard, see C. Ahlborn, 'The Use of Analogies in Drafting the Articles on the Responsibility of International Organizations – An Appraisal of the "Copy–Paste" Approach' (2012) 9(1) IOLR 53. An advance version is available as SHARES Research Paper 13 (2012), ACIL 2012–14, at www.sharesproject.nl (last accessed on 20 March 2014).

consequences of the commission of a wrongful act.[34] As the defences would effectively render the conduct in question lawful, they could be regarded as operating on the level of the primary rules which, by definition, cannot be concerned with the consequences of wrongful conduct, as there is none in the light of their intervention. While the distinction between primary and secondary rules may be useful for heuristic purposes, its importance should not be overstated. The ILC's codification work also features other examples of rules which are not easy to categorise into one or the other domain and nevertheless fulfil useful functions for the regime of international responsibility.[35]

Nonetheless, this critique touches upon an important issue for the questions that interest us here and which, as we shall see immediately below, makes the application of the circumstances somewhat unpredictable in situations of shared responsibility. States cooperate in all kinds of conceivable scenarios and a large part of international law is in place to precisely enable cooperation.[36] Frequently, it is difficult to distinguish between lawful and thus socially welcome forms of cooperation, on the one hand, and, on the other, situations in which aspects of this cooperation exhibit elements of wrongfulness. At times, the motives and the factual basis for one state or international organisation among a group of actors to take a given form of action will not be readily apparent to all the actors involved. Whether or not circumstances precluding wrongfulness can be relied upon by one or more states or international organisations in such a group may thus change the legal assessment on the basis of which those actors committed themselves to the collective endeavour. Put differently, the circumstances precluding wrongfulness may operate as a kind of 'magic touch',[37] rendering wrongful conduct lawful.

The problems associated with this state of affairs are exacerbated by the fact that most situations in which circumstances precluding wrongfulness will be relied upon will not be adjudged in forms of judicial

[34] Cf. P. Malanczuk, 'Countermeasures and Self-Defence as Circumstances Precluding Wrongfulness in the International Law Commission's Draft Articles on State Responsibility' (1983) 43 ZaöRV 705, at 709.

[35] An example is the provision on complicity in Article 16 ARSIWA, n. 5.

[36] *Drozd and Janousek* v. *France and Spain*, App. No. 12747/87 (ECtHR, 26 June 1992), para. 110; see also G. Nolte and H. P. Aust, 'Equivocal Helpers – Complicit States, Mixed Messages and International Law' (2009) 58 ICLQ 1, at 12; C. Chinkin, 'The Continuing Occupation? Issues of Joint and Several Liability and Effective Control', in P. Shiner and A. Williams (eds.), *The Iraq War and International Law* (Oxford: Hart, 2008), p. 161, at p. 182.

[37] Christakis, 'Les "Circonstances excluant l'illicéité"', n. 27, p. 223.

dispute settlement. Rather, the involved states and/or international organisations will have to determine for themselves whether the conditions for the applicability of a circumstance precluding wrongfulness have been met.

This is a general problem with the law of international responsibility.[38] But when a state or international organisation invokes a circumstance precluding wrongfulness, there is an additional 'entry point' for the problem of self-judgment, since not only does compliance with the original obligation need to be assessed, but also the conduct of the state and/or international organisation that relies on a defence. If we then take into account that situations of shared responsibility are by definition characterised by the involvement of more than just two actors, it becomes apparent that there is growing potential for disagreement.

While one might say that this is a factual problem pertaining to the ascertainment of legal rules in international law, it nonetheless characterises the environment in which the application of the circumstances precluding wrongfulness takes place, even more so when a multitude of actors is involved. Therefore it is understandable that the ILC formulated some limits to the circumstances precluding wrongfulness.[39] For instance, it is affirmed that 'a distinction must be drawn between the effect of circumstances precluding wrongfulness and the termination of the obligation itself. The circumstances in Chapter V operate as a shield rather than a sword'.[40] By their character as exceptions, the circumstances precluding wrongfulness all share a potentially intricate relationship with the ideal of an international rule of law.[41] They are escape routes from responsibility and, for this reason, deserve to be interpreted narrowly.

[38] See, with further references, H. P. Aust, 'The Normative Environment for Peace – On the Contribution of the ILC's Articles on State Responsibility', in G. Nolte (ed.), *Peace through International Law? The Role of the International Law Commission* (Berlin: Springer, 2009), p. 13, at pp. 23–8.

[39] One explicit limit set forth by the ARSIWA and ARIO respectively is the affirmation that the peremptory norms of general international law (*jus cogens*) form the outer boundary of what the circumstances can preclude in terms of wrongfulness. See Article 26 ARSIWA and ARIO, n. 5; on the evolution of this provision see M. Forteau, *Droit de la sécurité collective et droit de la responsabilité internationale* (Paris: Pedone, 2006), pp. 395 et seq.

[40] ARSIWA Commentary, n. 18, Introduction to Chapter V, para. 2.

[41] Rosenstock, 'The ILC and State Responsibility', n. 12, at 794: 'They [the circumstances precluding wrongfulness, HPA] demonstrate the related view of most states that freedom to look out for themselves should have, or as a fact of life does have, at least equality with, if not outright priority over, community mechanisms or concerns.'

3. Testing the circumstances precluding wrongfulness

With these general observations in mind, it is now time to turn to the individual defences set forth in Articles 20 to 27 of the ARSIWA and the ARIO and to test how well they are equipped for application in situations of shared responsibility.

3.1 Consent

The defence of consent is an expression of the concept of state sovereignty and 'lies at the very foundation of international law'.[42] The idea behind including consent as a defence in the ILC's work is that consent given to a certain course of conduct 'precludes the wrongfulness of that act in relation to the consenting State'.[43] In order to preclude wrongfulness, the consent must be 'valid', which refers to a number of conditions pertaining to the modalities of its expression. For instance, the consent must be 'freely given and clearly established'.[44] For our purposes, it is important to note that Article 20 'is concerned with the relations between the two States in question'.[45] The ILC included this clarification in its Commentary in order to stress that where more than one state needs to consent to given conduct in order to make it lawful, the consent of only one state would not suffice to preclude the wrongfulness of the act. Arguably, this clarification works the other way too. If state A consents to the stationing of troops by state B, it is to be assumed prima facie that this consent only covers troops from state B and that state B is not authorised, for example, to 'subcontract' other states. In general, the limits of the expressed will determine what forms of conduct, and by whom, will be susceptible to falling within the scope of application of Article 20 of the ARSIWA and the ARIO.[46] At least with respect to the provision in the ARSIWA, the reason for this limitation can ultimately be seen in the connection of consent with state sovereignty. When the expressed will is

[42] A. Abass, 'Consent Precluding State Responsibility: A Critical Analysis' (2004) 53 ICLQ 211, at 225; see also G. Nolte, *Eingreifen auf Einladung. Zur völkerrechtlichen Zulässigkeit des Einsatzes fremder Truppen im internen Konflikt auf Einladung der Regierung* (Berlin: Springer, 1999), pp. 133–40.

[43] ARSIWA Commentary, n. 18, Article 20, para. 1.

[44] Ibid., para. 6.

[45] Ibid., para. 9.

[46] A. Ben Mansour, 'Circumstances Precluding Wrongfulness in the ILC Articles on State Responsibility: Consent', in J. Crawford, A. Pellet, and S. Olleson (eds.), *The International Law of Responsibility* (Oxford University Press, 2010), p. 439, at p. 444.

the outer limit for the determination of consent, it is not to be presumed lightly that a state that has been authorised to engage in certain conduct via consent can jointly implement this authorisation together with other actors. The giving of consent towards another state may, irrespective of the form in which it finds expression, resemble the conclusion of a bilateral agreement. Also in this case, the beneficiary of such an agreement would not be entitled to extend the reach of the agreement towards third parties without the consent of the partner with which it entered into the agreement. While this reasoning appears to be relatively straightforward at first sight, it raises a number of questions for situations of shared responsibility.

Consider, for instance, the case of complicity, as laid down in the provision on 'aid or assistance' in Article 16 of the ARSIWA.[47] According to the concept of complicity underlying this provision, responsibility can only arise when aid or assistance has been given in the commission of a wrongful act. If the effect of consent under Article 20 of the ARSIWA is to preclude the wrongfulness of the given conduct, it would accordingly not be unlawful for state C to assist state B in the above-mentioned example. Following this reasoning, it would be conceivable that state C could assist state B with military advice or the provision of military equipment. A problem which is raised by such a scenario is the distinction between complicity-based responsibility and joint responsibility (i.e. where two states act more or less on the same footing).[48] In other words, where does responsibility for complicity end, and joint responsibility begin? Would the presence of those military advisors on the territory of state A still be covered by the consent of state A? The logic behind Article 20 of the ARSIWA seems to imply that state B could avail itself of the support of other states. The effects of the consent of state A would extend to merely 'supporting states'. However, state B would not be free to join hands with third states contributing to the conduct in question to the extent that they could no longer be regarded as mere 'accomplices', but rather as main actors themselves. Accordingly, we are faced here with problems that are primarily due to uncertainties surrounding the concept of complicity in international law.

[47] See generally H. P. Aust, *Complicity and the Law of State Responsibility* (Cambridge University Press, 2011); see also Chapter 5 of this volume, V. Lanovoy, 'Complicity in an Internationally Wrongful Act', p. 134.

[48] I. Brownlie, *State Responsibility* (Oxford University Press, 1983), p. 191; Lanovoy, 'Complicity in an Internationally Wrongful Act', n. 47.

Nonetheless, the suitability of the circumstances precluding wrongfulness is tested by such a borderline case between complicity and joint responsibility.

While it is certainly possible to distinguish cases on this basis, this construction might lead to considerable uncertainty for all actors involved. The state that expresses its consent will not know with absolute certainty what forms of the conduct to which it has consented may be 'contracted out' to third states. Conversely, state B may not know how far it can go in securing the support of other states for the conduct for which it has been authorised by state A. Finally, state C must take careful consideration as to whether it can take the risk of supporting state B without becoming responsible for conduct which goes beyond mere aid or assistance.

These uncertainties may, of course, be remedied by a previous agreement between all actors involved. State A may clearly establish that it is giving consent only to state B and that no other states may become involved. It may also express its consent to states B and C together in the first place. However, in how many situations will states actually conclude such agreements before these thorny questions arise?[49]

That these questions may have great practical relevance becomes apparent in the light of the 2013 military intervention by France in Mali. Upon the expression of an invitation to intervene militarily in the state, in order to support the interim government of Mali in its fight against insurgents and alleged terrorists, France launched an armed intervention on 11 January 2013. In this context, it has enjoyed the support of various other states. Algeria, for example, has opened its airspace for overflights of French military aircraft and has thus substantially supported the French intervention in Mali. It is uncontroversial that this act of support by Algeria is covered by the invitation from Mali expressed to France. Depending on the concrete facts of the case, it might be more difficult to judge whether the consent of the government of Mali also extends to the several other African states that have announced their support of France in its intervention, and to European allies of France, such as the United Kingdom and Germany, which have declared – to varying degrees – their support of the French intervention.[50] Similar questions arise with respect to the alleged support of the United

[49] See also Abass, 'Consent Precluding State Responsibility', n. 42, at 216.

[50] See UN Doc. S/RES/2085 (2012) on the planned deployment of the 'African-led International Support Mission in Mali' (AFISMA).

States with regard to intelligence matters and targeting. From a political perspective, it appears highly unlikely that the government of Mali would object to such forms of support, but the case may highlight the potential for disagreements over the reach of the consent expressed.

An example relied upon by Special Rapporteur Giorgio Gaja in the course of the preparation of the ARIO may show that forms of *clearly* expressed consent towards a plurality of actors can also be found in international practice. In 2005, the government of Indonesia invited the European Union, five member states of the Association of Southeast Asian Nations (ASEAN), and Norway and Switzerland to deploy the 'Aceh Monitoring Mission',[51] which had the mandate to supervise the peace process in the Indonesian province of Aceh. Accordingly, it was clearly determined which actors could rely on the Indonesian consent – a situation that is different from the early phases of the Mali intervention, in which consent was expressed solely to the French government, which then relied on the support of other states.

In the absence of such a clear and specific agreement of the Aceh Monitoring Mission type, several uncertainties that are related to the defence of consent make it difficult for all actors involved to assess reliably whether their conduct will be covered by Article 20 of the ARSIWA or the ARIO, or whether they may potentially be faced with a claim for reparation.

3.2 *Self-defence*

For some, it was a questionable decision to include self-defence in the list of circumstances precluding wrongfulness, as self-defence would not fall into this category. Rather, it would be a right, pure and simple, and, for that matter, even an 'inherent right', as Article 51 of the United Nations (UN) Charter stipulates.[52] Accordingly, self-defence would operate on the level of the primary rules of international law and could not simultaneously belong to the category of secondary rules that the ILC was

[51] G. Gaja, 'Fourth Report on the Responsibility of International Organizations', UN Doc. A/CN.4/564 (2006), para. 13.

[52] See, with further references, Forteau, *Droit de la sécurité collective et droit de la responsabilité internationale*, n. 39, pp. 405 et seq.; for the view that self-defence under Article 51 also constitutes a circumstance precluding wrongfulness, see L.-A. Sicilianos, *Les Reactions décentralisées à l'illicite – Des contre-mesures à la légitime défense* (Paris: Presses Universitaires de France, 1990), p. 43.

purporting to codify.[53] The eventual inclusion of self-defence in the set of Articles was justified on the basis that, as the ILC Commentary formulates, 'self-defence may justify non-performance of certain obligations other than that under Article 2(4) of the Charter provided that such non-performance is related to the breach of that provision'.[54] Although self-defence as set forth in Article 21 of the ARSIWA and the ARIO thus operates as a separate defence, the conditions for its exercise remain those which are laid down in Article 51 of the UN Charter, as the proviso 'in conformity with the Charter of the United Nations' makes clear.[55]

This connection between UN Charter law and the law of international responsibility will accordingly determine how the defence of Article 21 of the ARSIWA and the ARIO has to be applied in situations of shared responsibility. Article 51 of the UN Charter guarantees the individual as well as the *collective* right of self-defence: the latter deals exactly with the situation in which one or more states come to the rescue of a state that has had to endure an 'armed attack' in the sense of Article 51. Accordingly, collective self-defence potentially brings about situations of shared responsibility, whether in the form of joint conduct or of complicity-type situations. In any case, it involves a plurality of states acting together and relying collectively on the specific circumstance of self-defence.

It is therefore worthwhile to look more closely at the requirements for the exercise of collective self-defence as they have developed in international judicial practice. In this respect, guidance can be obtained from the *Nicaragua* judgment of the International Court of Justice (ICJ or Court), where it is stipulated that:

> it is also clear that it is the State which is the victim of the armed attack which must form and declare the view that it has been so attacked. There is no rule

[53] See T. Christakis and K. Bannelier, 'La Légitime défense en tant que "circonstance excluant l'illicéité"', in R. Kherad (ed.), *Légitimes défenses* (Paris: LGDJ, 2007), p. 233; J.-M. Thouvenin, 'Circumstances Precluding Wrongfulness: Self-Defence', in J. Crawford, A. Pellet, and S. Olleson (eds.), *The International Law of Responsibility* (Oxford University Press, 2010), p. 455, at p. 460.

[54] ARSIWA Commentary, n. 18, Article 21, para. 2; Christakis and Bannelier argue that the inclusion of Article 21 of the ARSIWA was not necessary as the right to take counter-measures would effectively deal with the situation envisaged by the ILC. See Christakis and Bannelier, 'La Légitime défense en tant que "circonstance excluant l'illicéité"', n. 53, pp. 253–4. Only with respect to self-defence affecting third states do they envisage a separate meaning of Article 21 ARSIWA: ibid., at 255–6.

[55] ARSIWA Commentary, n. 18, Article 21, para. 6.

> in customary international law permitting another State to exercise the right of collective self-defence on the basis of its own assessment of the situation. Where collective self-defence is invoked, it is to be expected that the State for whose benefit this right is used will have declared itself to be the victim of an armed attack ... There is no rule permitting the exercise of collective self-defence in the absence of a request by the State which regards itself as the victim of an armed attack.[56]

This finding of the Court is also an important guideline for the application of Article 21 of the ARSIWA and the ARIO in situations of shared responsibility. It is clear that in order to rely on this defence, the relevant state must have been asked by the attacked state to do so. Accordingly, of a group of states seeking to rely on Article 21 of the ARSIWA/ARIO, only those that were specifically authorised to join the efforts of self-defence may successfully do so. It has been a matter of controversy whether the Court was right in this regard,[57] especially with respect to the customary international law form of self-defence (as the ICJ was precluded from applying Article 51 directly for jurisdictional reasons).[58] However, as Christine Gray has observed, 'any other approach would allow the third state to pronounce on the existence of an armed attack and to decide that it was going to use force even against the wishes of the victim state'.[59] The requirement of a request for assistance has the same underlying rationale as the defence of consent in Article 20 of the ARSIWA. It serves to protect the autonomy, and thereby the sovereignty, of the attacked state, which shall not be forced into a coalition with other states against its will.[60]

[56] *Military and Paramilitary Activities in and against Nicaragua (Nicaragua* v. *United States of America)*, Merits, ICJ Reports 1986, 14, paras. 196 et seq.

[57] Ibid., Dissenting Opinion by Judge Jennings, at 544–5.

[58] See, with further references, A. Randelzhofer and G. Nolte, 'Article 51', in B. Simma, D.-E. Khan, G. Nolte, and A. Paulus (eds.), *The Charter of the United Nations – A Commentary*, 3rd edn (Oxford University Press, 2012), p. 1397, at para. 48.

[59] C. Gray, *International Law and the Use of Force*, 3rd edn (Oxford University Press, 2008), p. 184.

[60] Similar considerations apply to the form with which the UN Security Council sometimes authorises only member states 'co-operating' with a certain government to 'use all necessary means'. Thereby, the Security Council preserves the autonomy of the victim of an armed attack (as in the case of the Iraqi invasion of Kuwait: see UN Doc. S/RES/687 (1991)), or of a state engulfed in the fight against piracy (as in the case of the authorisations to fight piracy off the coast of Somalia: see UN Doc. S/RES/1816 (2008), op. para. 7). Although not included in the defences as codified by the ILC, acting on behalf of an authorisation of the UN Security Council can also be seen as a circumstance precluding wrongfulness: see Forteau, *Droit de la sécurité collective et droit de la responsabilité internationale*, n. 39, p. 392.

In this regard, the problematic questions are ultimately not rooted in the domain of international responsibility. Due to its *renvoi* to the UN Charter system,[61] the law of international responsibility will follow the results of the interpretation of Article 51 of the UN Charter. Likewise, the potentially difficult interplay between self-defence and the law of neutrality will have to be addressed by the primary rules[62] whose effects will only be translated into the domain of the secondary rules concerning responsibility.[63] For instance, the concept of 'benevolent neutrality' (or 'non-belligerency') may be understood as a special rule concerning aid and assistance for states lawfully defending themselves against an armed attack.[64] Originally developed in the course of the Second World War as a means to justify the so-called 'Destroyer Deal' between the United States and the United Kingdom,[65] it has been criticised for undermining the traditional law of neutrality, and being an inadmissible 'half-way house' between neutrality and belligerency.[66] It is true that benevolent neutrality is not recognised in situations in which no authoritative determination of wrongfulness has been made with respect to an ongoing armed conflict between two states. For the rather seldom-found situation in which the UN Security Council has made a determination as to which state has committed an aggression or is responsible for a breach of the peace,[67] benevolent neutrality becomes an option. It then allows third states to support victims of unlawful uses of force while allowing them to retain the benefits of neutrality. Arguably, self-defence under Article 22 of the ARSIWA could help to integrate those normative concepts into the law of international responsibility which are part of the normative environment of self-defence

[61] Ibid., at p. 406.

[62] Crawford, 'Second Report on State Responsibility', n. 29, para. 300.

[63] Cf. Thouvenin, 'Circumstances Precluding Wrongfulness', n. 53, pp. 460–1.

[64] Cf. S. Neff, *The Rights and Duties of Neutrals – A General History* (Manchester University Press, 2000), p. 193; H. P. Aust, 'Article 2(5)', in B. Simma, D.-E. Khan, G. Nolte, and A. Paulus (eds.), *The Charter of the United Nations – A Commentary*, 3rd edn (Oxford University Press, 2012), paras. 25–7.

[65] See R. H. Jackson, 'Address to the Inter-American Bar Association, Havana, Cuba, 27 March 1941' (1941) 35 AJIL 348; on the background influence of Hersch Lauterpacht, see E. Lauterpacht, *The Life of Hersch Lauterpacht* (Cambridge University Press, 2011), pp. 177–8.

[66] See, among others, Y. Dinstein, *War, Aggression, and Self-Defence*, 5th edn (Cambridge University Press, 2011), p. 180; for contemporaneous critique, see E. M. Borchard, 'War, Neutrality and Non-Belligerency' (1941) 35 AJIL 618.

[67] See, for instance, UN Doc. S/RES/660 (1990) on the Iraqi invasion of Kuwait.

under the UN Charter.[68] To hold otherwise would potentially sow a seed of fragmentation between these two fields of international law – something that Article 59 of the ARSIWA ('[t]hese articles are without prejudice to the Charter of the United Nations') seeks to prevent.[69] The *renvoi* to the primary rules on the matter is of course no panacea. In few questions are opinions as divided as with respect to the conditions of the exercise of the right of self-defence.

A special form of shared responsibility may arise if collective self-defence is carried out in the framework of an international organisation that was founded to organise the self-defence of its members, such as the North Atlantic Treaty Organization (NATO). In this regard, it is questionable whether the organisation also could rely on the right to self-defence with respect to the attack on one of its members.[70] The Commentary adopted by the ILC remains obscure in this regard and only notes that this question will have to be addressed by the applicable primary rules.[71] In general, it would appear that the relevant international organisation would benefit from the right of self-defence of its member states which have, through the founding of the organisation, transferred certain of their powers to it, which the international organisation could then exercise in the name of its members. Guidance on these questions will ultimately also depend on the provisions on the responsibility of international organisations in connection with wrongful acts of a state and/or international organisation. These are set forth in Articles 14 to 17 of the ARIO, which will help to determine whether or not the conduct of an international organisation in connection with the exercise of self-defence by one of its member states triggers responsibility.

3.3 Countermeasures

The inclusion of countermeasures in the chapter on circumstances precluding wrongfulness was another controversial decision of the

68 See also Thouvenin, 'Circumstances Precluding Wrongfulness', n. 53, at p. 461, stating that 'certain actions in self-defence can be carried out by States who are formally at peace'.

69 ARSIWA Commentary, n. 18, Article 59, para. 2: 'The articles are in all respects to be interpreted in conformity with the Charter of the United Nations.'

70 G. Gaja, 'Fourth Report on the Responsibility of International Organizations', n. 51, para. 19.

71 Commentary to the Articles on the Responsibility of International Organizations, ILC Report on the work of its sixty-third session, UNGAOR 66th Sess., Supp. No. 10, UN Doc. A/66/10 (2011) (ARIO Commentary), Commentary to Article 21(3).

ILC.[72] It was generally a matter of debate whether the sets of Articles should include provisions on countermeasures in the first place. Critics argued that doing so would legitimise this – in their view – rather primitive means of enforcing international law.[73] The ILC decided to retain the provisions on countermeasures and defined them as 'measures which would otherwise be contrary to international obligations of the injured State *vis-à-vis* the responsible State if they were not taken by the former in response to an internationally wrongful act by the latter in order to procure cessation and reparation'.[74] In addition, however, the ILC pointed out that like 'other forms of self-help, countermeasures are liable to abuse and this potential is exacerbated by the factual inequalities between States'.[75]

If countermeasures are already controversial in their own right, the subject of a major debate that continues to the present day is whether states that are not directly injured states in the sense of Article 42 of the ARSIWA should also have the right to adopt countermeasures.[76] Although they are not the only conceivable means of taking countermeasures in the context of 'shared responsibility', collective countermeasures are arguably the best test case in this regard. The ILC opted for a differentiated and vague compromise solution. It first made mention of the possibility of the invocation of responsibility by a state other than the injured state in Article 48 of the ARSIWA. In a second step, the ILC was more circumspect in allowing such non-injured states to adopt countermeasures. The question is ultimately left hanging in the air by the saving clause of Article 54 of the ARSIWA and Article 57 of the ARIO, which stipulates that the Chapter on countermeasures

> does not prejudice the right of any State, entitled under Article 48, paragraph 1 to invoke the responsibility of another State, to take lawful measures against that State to ensure cessation of the breach and reparation in the interest of the injured State or of the beneficiaries of the obligation breached.

[72] See also Chapter 10 of this volume, Tams, 'Countermeasures against Multiple Responsible Actors', n. 5.

[73] See, with further references, D. J. Bederman, 'Counterintuiting Countermeasures' (2002) 96 AJIL 817.

[74] ARSIWA Commentary, n. 18, Introduction to Chapter II of Part Three, para. 1.

[75] Ibid., para. 2.

[76] See M. Akehurst, 'Reprisals by Third States' (1970) 44 BYIL 1, at 15–16; M. Koskenniemi, 'Solidarity Measures: State Responsibility as a New International Order?' (2001) 72 BYIL 337, at 344.

By referring to 'lawful measures', the ARSIWA do not take a position on the question of whether or not countermeasures in the collective interest are sanctioned by the international legal order. This equivocation was ascribed by Special Rapporteur James Crawford to the reticence of states to allow for such measures and a mixed picture emerging from state practice.[77] The most comprehensive study on this question so far has come to a slightly different result, and has argued that it would have been very possible to affirm the existence of a basis in customary international law for taking countermeasures in the collective interest.[78] In any case, Articles 48 and 54 of the ARSIWA constitute the outer limit for precluding the wrongfulness of measures of 'self-help' in the collective interest. As the available practice on countermeasures in the collective interest shows, such countermeasures are taken both by individual states[79] as well as by collectives of states, or states acting in conjunction with an international organisation. The latter practice is of special relevance for the topic of shared responsibility. Examples from this practice include the reaction of Western states against the imposition of martial law in Poland in 1981 when landing rights for the Polish airline LOT were suspended; temporary import prohibitions concerning goods from Argentina in 1982 in the context of the Falklands conflict; measures adopted against Iraq in 1990 before the UN Security Council adopted sanctions; and the reaction of Western states against the former Yugoslavia in 1998 when European Commission member states froze assets and imposed a flight ban for Yugoslav airlines in reaction to the escalating Kosovo crisis.[80] More recent practice arguably includes the extended sanctions programme of the European Union against Iran which goes beyond what the relevant UN Security Council resolutions

77 See the comments of governments in UN Doc. A/CN.4/515 (2001), at pp. 87 et seq.; see further A. Pellet, 'Les Articles de la CDI sur la responsabilité internationale des Etats pour fait internationalement illicite suite – et fin?' (2002) 43 AFDI 1, at 20.

78 C. J. Tams, *Enforcing Obligations Erga Omnes in International Law* (Cambridge University Press, 2005), p. 246; for an overview of the practice, see ibid., pp. 207 et seq.; and M. Dawidowicz, 'Public Law Enforcement without Public Law Safeguards? An Analysis of State Practice on Third-Party Countermeasures and their Relationship to the UN Security Council' (2006) 77 BYIL 333. See also E. Katselli, *The Problem of Enforcement in International Law: Countermeasures, the Non-Injured State and the Idea of the International Community* (London: Routledge, 2010).

79 The ILC Commentary refers, for example, to the measures taken by the United States against Uganda in 1978, and against South Africa in 1986, as well as by the Netherlands against Suriname in 1982. See ILC ARSIWA Commentary, n. 18, Article 54, paras. 3–4.

80 Ibid., para. 3.

require, as it stipulates a comprehensive oil embargo against Iran.[81] It emerges from this practice that groups of states and international organisations acting collectively also rely on the justificatory function of the concept of countermeasures.

Once one is willing to accept the lawfulness of the concept of countermeasures in the collective interest as such, the implication is that Article 22 of the ARSIWA is also reasonably well-equipped to deal with situations of shared responsibility, as there are no apparent reasons why states could not do collectively what they are entitled to do individually. The problematic issues, however, lie elsewhere: what obligations under international law qualify as obligations *erga omnes*?[82] And what procedural and substantive requirements have to be observed when a group of states and/or international organisations resort to taking such countermeasures in the collective interest? Of these problems, the measures adopted by the European Union against Iran are a good example. It is far from certain whether Iran is effectively in breach of its obligations under the Non-Proliferation Treaty (NPT).[83] While it is reasonable to assume that there have been violations of the safeguards agreement Iran entered into with the International Atomic Energy Agency, it is doubtful whether the obligations contained in this agreement are *erga omnes* obligations, since they are frequently described as being rather technical in character.[84] Also, if one considers the alleged quality of the NPT as a 'world order treaty',[85] this does not necessarily justify an extension of the range of obligations emanating from this regime for the violation of which non-injured states and/or international organisations may take countermeasures.

Yet another question is how to deal with the situation in which state A takes countermeasures against state B for the violation of an obligation the latter owed to state A. If state A can rely on Article 22 of the ARSIWA, it would also be possible for state C to furnish 'aid or assistance' to state A for the commission of the act, which would be wrongful had it not been

[81] See EU Council Decision 2012/35/CFSP of 23 January 2012 and EU Council Regulation 267/2012 of 23 March 2012; on these measures see further P.-E. Dupont, 'Countermeasures and Collective Security: The Case of the EU Sanctions against Iran' (2012) 17 J Conflict & Sec L 301.

[82] *Barcelona Traction, Light and Power Company, Limited (Belgium* v. *Spain)*, Second Phase, ICJ Reports 1970, 3, para. 33.

[83] Dupont, 'Countermeasures and Collective Security', n. 81, at 326.

[84] Ibid., at 329.

[85] On this concept see C. Tomuschat, 'Obligations Arising for States without or against their Will' (1993) 241 RCADI 248, at 269.

undertaken in response to the previous conduct of state B. This situation is comparable to the scenarios we have surveyed above with respect to consent. Here also, the crucial question would be when the conduct of state C would lose its character as mere 'aid or assistance' and cross the threshold of triggering the independent responsibility of state C. Where this would be the case as, for instance, the contribution of state C would be too substantial to consider it as mere support, the question of the wrongfulness of the conduct of state C would then depend on whether state C could rely on the right to take countermeasures in the collective interest, as just discussed. Where this would not be the case – as, arguably, in the great majority of cases – state C would then commit a wrongful act and could not avail itself of the defence of countermeasures under Article 22 of the ARSIWA. This shows, again, that states have to carefully determine whether or not to participate in conduct with a cooperating state that is only deemed lawful because of the intervention of one of the circumstances precluding wrongfulness. Because in most situations no forms of judicial dispute settlement will be available, states take this decision at their own risk and in light of the fact that all actors will judge the legality of their conduct for themselves.[86]

3.4 Force majeure

Force majeure is defined by the ILC as 'the occurrence of an irresistible force or an unforeseen event, beyond the control of the State, making it materially impossible in the circumstances to perform the obligation'.[87] It is similar to the 'supervening impossibility of treaty performance' as laid down in Article 61 of the Vienna Convention on the Law of Treaties (VCLT).[88] However, the scope of the two has to be distinguished. Whereas Article 61 of the VCLT is a ground for the suspension or termination of treaty obligations, *force majeure* is only concerned with the preclusion of the wrongfulness of a given act and leaves intact the underlying obligation which has to be complied with as soon as the

86 Cf. *Air Service Agreement of 27 March 1946* (*United States of America* v. *France*), (1978) 18 RIAA 417, at para. 81.

87 Article 23 ARSIWA/ARIO, n. 5.

88 1155 UNTS 331. See further S. Szurek, 'Circumstances Precluding Wrongfulness in the ILC Articles on State Responsibility: *Force Majeure*', in J. Crawford, A. Pellet, and S. Olleson (eds.), *The International Law of Responsibility* (Oxford University Press, 2010), p. 475, at p. 475.

situation of *force majeure* has ceased.[89] Article 23(2) of the ARSIWA further sets forth that *force majeure* cannot be relied upon if the state in question has contributed to the situation or has – by way of contract or agreement, for instance – assumed the risk of that situation occurring.

The quite substantial available practice on *force majeure* is limited to bilateral situations.[90] It can be imagined, however, that *force majeure* may also have a role to play in situations of 'shared responsibility'. If two or more actors involved in a wrongful act can both rely on *force majeure*, the situation does not pose particular problems. As is the case with the other defences, difficult questions arise as soon as only one among a plurality of actors involved relies on *force majeure*.

If, in a group of states acting together (A, B, and C), only state A is absolved from responsibility due to the intervention of an irresistible and unforeseeable event, states B and C could find themselves in the situation that the injured state D would try to obtain compensation for the entire injury from them. At least, this would be a conceivable scenario if state D could hold states B and C jointly and severally responsible, i.e. if it could claim reparation for its entire injury from only one of the involved states (or two of the three, for that matter). This scenario shows that the adaptability of the circumstances precluding wrongfulness to situations of shared responsibility also depends on the manner in which other rules and principles of the law of international responsibility are applied and interpreted. It is a matter of debate whether the law of international responsibility includes a principle of joint and several liability.[91] In the absence of such a principle, states B and C would not be overly burdened by the reliance upon *force majeure* by state A. Depending on the facts of the case, it might then be problematic, however, to calculate the exact amount of reparation that state D can ask of states B and C. In many situations of shared responsibility, it will be difficult, if not impossible, to identify the exact contributions of the various actors involved. Judge

[89] Cf. Article 27(a) ARSIWA, n. 5.

[90] For an overview see Paddeu, 'A Genealogy of *Force Majeure* in International Law', n. 13, at 482–7.

[91] S. Besson, 'La Pluralité d'Etats responsable – Vers une solidarité internationale ?' (2007) 17 SZIER 13, at 15 et seq.; J. E. Noyes and B. D. Smith, 'State Responsibility and the Principle of Joint and Several Responsibility' (1988) 13 YJIL 225; decidedly in favour of the existence of such a principle: A. Orakhelashvili, 'Division of Reparation between Responsible Entities', in J. Crawford, A. Pellet, and S. Olleson (eds.), *The Law of International Responsibility* (Oxford University Press, 2010), p. 647, at p. 657; specifically on joint and several responsibility in situations of complicity see Aust, *Complicity and the Law of State Responsibility*, n. 47, pp. 288–95.

Simma dealt with a comparable question in his Separate Opinion in the *Oil Platforms* case, where he discussed the problem of 'factually indivisible acts'.[92]

The underlying rationale of *force majeure* in international law militates for a restrictive application of this circumstance. Its core requirement is the 'material impossibility' for a state or international organisation to conform itself to an obligation. If two or more actors act together in a group, it appears that this material impossibility should be assessed for each and every actor independently. This holds especially true for integral as opposed to reciprocal or interdependent obligations, if we follow the terminology of Sir Gerald Fitzmaurice, ILC Special Rapporteur on the law of treaties.[93] This may be illustrated by an example pertaining to shared responsibility arising out of situations where there is no concerted action. If we take, for instance, obligations in the context of climate change governance, such as goals for the reduction of greenhouse gases, why should states B and C profit from the material impossibility of state A to comply with its obligation? An extension of *force majeure* to other states would considerably weaken the normative pull of the obligation in question. In fact, this example may show that *force majeure* will always only be available for the specific state or international organisation which found itself in a situation where it was materially impossible to live up to its international obligations.

Finally, the defence of *force majeure* has a problematic relationship with a particular form of shared responsibility, i.e. the coercion of another state under Article 18 of the ARSIWA.[94] This provision provides for attribution of responsibility and is 'concerned with the specific problem of coercion deliberately exercised in order to procure the breach of one state's obligation to a third state'.[95] From the perspective of the coerced state, it can be said that the situation is not very different from one of *force majeure*. Indeed, the Commentary of the ILC acknowledges that 'coercion for the purpose of article 18 has the same essential character as *force majeure* under article 23. Nothing less than conduct which forces the will of the coerced State will suffice, giving it no effective

[92] *Oil Platforms* (*Islamic Republic of Iran* v *United States of America*), Judgment, ICJ Reports 2003, 161, Separate Opinion by Judge Simma, para. 78.

[93] Sir G. Fitzmaurice, 'Second Report on the Law of Treaties', ILC *Yearbook* 1957/II, at 30–1 and 35.

[94] See Chapter 4 of this volume, Fry, 'Attribution of Responsibility', n. 11, pp. 120–1.

[95] ARSIWA Commentary, n. 18, Article 18, para. 1.

choice but to comply with the wishes of the coercing State.'[96] It has been noted in the literature that this construction leads to an intricate conceptual problem. If the effect of *force majeure* as a circumstance precluding wrongfulness is to protect the coerced state against all claims of wrongfulness, there remains no wrongful act for which responsibility can be attributed to the coercing state.[97] The ILC took that problem into account and argued in its Commentary for a differentiation between the preclusion of wrongfulness for the coerced state, but not for the coercing state, pointing to the social necessity that the injured state must be able to hold one state responsible.[98] Conceptually, this is not very convincing, because the ultimate basis for the attribution of responsibility becomes blurred if one follows this approach. Instead, this scenario seems to provide an argument for a differentiation between circumstances precluding wrongfulness and other forms of defences which would merely excuse the coerced state or, more generally, the state that is faced with a situation of *force majeure*. Such a construction would ensure that the coerced state faces no claims of reparation for conduct which it was not effectively in a position to control. At the same time, its conduct would continue to be characterised as wrongful and responsibility could thus be attributed to the coercing state.[99]

3.5 Distress

The defence of distress addresses the specific situation in which an individual acting as a state organ, or in any other way that is attributable to a state or an international organisation, finds him or herself in a situation of peril and thus has no other reasonable way of 'saving the author's life or the lives of other persons entrusted to the author's care'.[100] Accordingly, distress is a highly personalised notion, implying almost by definition that it will only work with respect to the conduct attributable to an individual state or international organisation. If a group of states or international organisations cooperate in a certain way and one of the individuals involved finds him or herself in a situation of distress, only the state or

[96] Ibid., para. 2.
[97] Paddeu, 'A Genealogy of *Force Majeure* in International Law', n. 13, at 398 with footnote 104.
[98] ARSIWA Commentary, n. 18, Article 18, para. 4.
[99] Paddeu, 'A Genealogy of *Force Majeure* in International Law', n. 13, at 398.
[100] Article 24 ARSIWA/ARIO, n. 5.

international organisation to which the conduct in question is attributed can rely on the defence of distress. Difficult questions may once again arise due to uncertainties with respect to other questions of the law of international responsibility. If we consider a multiple attribution of conduct to, for instance, one state and an international organisation[101] to be possible, the underlying rationale of distress would seem to speak for the assumption that both this state and the international organisation could exculpate themselves.

In cases of complicity, things might be more complicated again. Considerations of fairness would encourage us to look more closely at the intent of the aiding/assisting state: did it merely wish to support the relevant individual to save his or her life? Or did it have further motives, possibly exploiting the situation of peril in which the person in question found him or herself? Such a situation could then border on a case of direction or control. These considerations may appear to be rather academic at first sight, but they might help to show how difficult it will be for the law of international responsibility to arrive at solutions that are considered fair and equitable in situations of shared responsibility.

3.6 Necessity

Among the circumstances precluding wrongfulness that are acknowledged by the ILC's work, necessity[102] has a particularly poor reputation as an antithesis to the rule of law as such.[103] It is associated with one state placing its interests above the obligation to comply with international law, and acting ruthlessly to the detriment of other states.[104] The ILC tried to restrict the scope of its application as much as possible, which becomes evident from a number of limiting conditions, as well as from

101 See the contribution of F. Messineo in Chapter 3 of this volume, 'Attribution of Conduct', n. 10, pp. 67–83.

102 Article 25 ARSIWA/ARIO, n. 5.

103 Cf. *Case concerning the difference between New Zealand and France concerning the interpretation or application of two agreements concluded on 9 July 1986 between the two States and which related to the problems arising from the Rainbow Warrior Affair*, Decision of 30 April 1990, (1990) 20 RIAA 217, at 254; P. Allott, 'State Responsibility and the Unmaking of International Law' (1988) 29 Harv Int LJ 1, at 17; Gaja, 'Fourth Report on the Responsibility of International Organizations', n. 51, para. 35; Okowa, 'Defences in the Jurisprudence of International Tribunals', n. 7, p. 398.

104 Cf. C. Tomuschat, 'Conclusions général', in Société française pour le droit international (ed.), *La Nécessité en droit international* (Paris: Pedone, 2007), p. 377, at p. 380.

the negative formulation of Article 25 ('necessity may not be invoked . . . unless').[105] In the ARIO, its scope of application was further reduced because there was a lack of practice indicating that international organisations could rely on necessity to the same extent as can states. According to Article 25 of the ARIO, an international organisation may only invoke necessity for the protection of an interest of one its member states, or of the international community as a whole, when the organisation has the function to protect that interest.[106]

A central requirement for the applicability of Article 25 is that the act in question 'is the only means for the State to safeguard an essential interest against a grave and imminent peril'. This formulation could be read to imply that among a group of states or international organisations acting together, necessity will only be available as a defence for one state or international organisation that can point to such an essential interest. However, such a reading of Article 25 would overlook the fact that the ILC has also considered it possible that an essential interest of 'the international community as a whole' is covered by this provision.[107] Therefore, Article 25 itself allows for cooperative efforts of states to rely on a state of necessity, if they deem it necessary to protect an essential interest of the international community. Therefore, a plurality of states acting together may potentially rely on Article 25 of the ARSIWA.

A case in point is the 1999 Kosovo intervention by several NATO member states, which argued that an 'overwhelming humanitarian necessity' required them to use armed force against the Former Federal Republic of Yugoslavia. In the course of the ICJ proceedings brought against eleven NATO members, Belgium defended its conduct, among other grounds, by relying on then Draft Article 33 as adopted on first reading.[108] Various arguments militate against such an approach. Article 25(1)(b) of the ARSIWA sets out that the act to be justified by necessity would not 'seriously impair an essential interest of the State or States towards which the obligation exists'. In light of the importance of the

[105] See on these limiting conditions T. Christakis, '"Nécessité n'a pas de loi?" Rapport général sur la nécessité en droit international', in Société française pour le droit international (ed.), *La Nécessité en droit international* (Paris: Pedone, 2007), pp. 11, at pp. 23–30.

[106] ARIO Commentary, n. 71, Article 25, para. 4.

[107] ARSIWA Commentary, n. 18, Article 25, para. 15.

[108] *Legality of Use of Force* (*Serbia and Montenegro* v. *Belgium*), Oral Pleadings of Belgium, CR 1999/15, ICJ Pleadings 1999, at. 17 et seq.

prohibition of the use of force under Article 2(4) of the UN Charter, such an essential interest is probably given. Since Article 2(4) of the UN Charter only knows two generally accepted exceptions – self-defence and authorisations of the UN Security Council under Chapter VII of the Charter – it would also seem to be the case that Article 25(2)(a) of the ARSIWA would speak against the possibility of relying on necessity here because 'the international obligation in question excludes the possibility of invoking necessity'. Finally, attention needs to be paid to Article 26 of the ARSIWA, which sets out the boundary of peremptory norms under general international law for the applicability of the circumstances precluding wrongfulness.[109] The Kosovo case may nonetheless show that a group of states could feel compelled to act in situations of necessity.

Furthermore, however, what practical relevance will the necessity construction have in situations such as the Kosovo intervention? The notion of 'essential interests' is ill-defined even with respect to the interests of individual states. The ILC has not offered any guidance with respect to what might be essential interests of the international community in this context. The Commentary only states that '[t]he extent to which a given interest is "essential" depends on all the circumstances and cannot be prejudged.'[110] A systematic take on the ILC's work could assimilate this notion to the regime of 'serious breaches of peremptory norms under general international law', as set forth in Articles 40 and 41 of the ARSIWA. The debates on the scope of the obligation of cooperation in Article 41(1) of the ARSIWA,[111] the lack of clarity with respect to the taking of collective countermeasures,[112] the disputed range of the obligation to prevent genocide under Article 1 of the Genocide Convention,[113] and finally, the possibly emerging

[109] On these issues see also O. Corten, 'La Nécessité et le *jus ad bellum*', in Société française pour le droit international (ed.), *La Nécessité en droit international* (Paris: Pedone, 2007), p. 127, at pp. 145–9; in general, Special Rapporteur James Crawford also appeared to be sceptical of such an argument: see Summary Record of the 2587th meeting of the ILC, UN Doc. A/CN.4/SR.2587 (1999), para. 27.

[110] ARSIWA Commentary, n. 18, Article 25, para. 15.

[111] S. Villalpando, *L'Émergence de la communauté internationale dans la responsabilité des Etats* (Paris: Presses Universitaires de France, 2005), pp. 379 et seq.

[112] Tams, *Enforcing Obligations Erga Omnes in International Law*, n. 78, passim.

[113] O. Ben-Naftali, 'The Obligations to Prevent and Punish Genocide', in P. Gaeta (ed.), *The UN Genocide Convention – A Commentary* (Oxford University Press, 2009), pp. 27–57. Convention on the Prevention and Punishment of Genocide, Paris, 9 December 1948, in force 12 January 1951, 78 UNTS 277 (Genocide Convention).

'responsibility to protect'[114] – all these issues show that the enforcement of community interests is a protracted and complicated matter.[115]

In various contexts, international law provides for different substantive and procedural hurdles before states and other actors can take up the role of 'guardians of the community interest'.[116] It would be very questionable if the balancing exercise between competing interests necessitated by Article 25 of the ARSIWA and the ARIO could bypass the more special rules concerning the enforcement of community interests in international law.[117] Hence, the addition of necessity into the toolbox for the enforcement of the community interest may not necessarily be a promising suggestion for the advancement of the international rule of law.

More specifically with respect to situations of shared responsibility, this assessment should caution us, as a matter of policy, to construe Article 25 of the ARSIWA and the ARIO in a manner that would make it easier for groups of states and/or international organisations to rely on this provision. If the contribution that necessity can make for the enforcement of the international community interest is limited, it can be argued that the 'personalised' character of necessity as an exception for a specific state and/or international organisation should be stressed.

In this context, we should not lose sight of the power dynamics. Shared responsibility is a natural consequence of cooperation among states, which by this very cooperation enhance their clout. States cooperate in order to achieve goals that they could not achieve when acting alone. If we take into account that the intervention of necessity does not presuppose any form of previous wrongful conduct on the part of the state against which the measure in question has been taken, it is questionable whether a potentially large number of 'third states' and/or international organisations should benefit from the intervention of this defence. Construing Article 25 of the ARSIWA and the ARIO in a way that would invite such wider participation in measures of necessity

[114] M. Vashakmadze, 'Responsibility to Protect', in B. Simma, D.-E. Khan, G. Nolte and A. Paulus (eds.), *The Charter of the United Nations – A Commentary*, 3rd edn. (Oxford University Press, 2012), p. 1201.

[115] On the inter-relatedness of these questions see C. J. Tams, 'Individual States as Guardians of Community Interests', in U. Fastenrath et al. (eds.), *From Bilateralism to Community Interest. Essays in Honour of Judge Bruno Simma* (Oxford University Press, 2011), p. 379.

[116] Ibid. [117] See also Christakis, '"Nécessité n'a pas de loi?"', n. 105, p. 26.

would work to the detriment of the affected state, which in itself has not set any legally relevant cause for an infringement of its interests.

4. Challenges for the circumstances precluding wrongfulness in situations of shared responsibility

After having gone through the individual circumstances precluding wrongfulness, it is notable that, in general, the circumstances precluding wrongfulness are oriented towards bilateral situations. With the possible exception of self-defence, all the circumstances precluding wrongfulness included in the ILC's work were conceived with a bilateral type of situation in mind. It can thus be presumed that as such they work only to the benefit of individual states or international organisations that can point to the fulfilment of the criteria laid down in Articles 20 to 27 of the ARSIWA and the ARIO. There is no automatic extension of the circumstances to other states or international organisations cooperating with states or international organisations that can rely on the defences.

Difficult situations can arise in virtually all modes of shared responsibility. In cases of multiple attribution, it is conceivable that the two or more states or international organisations to which the conduct or omission is attributed are not in the same legal position so as to avail themselves of the very same circumstance precluding wrongfulness. Multiple attribution of a given course of conduct may thus lead to diverging legal consequences depending on, for instance, the question of whether or not all states implicated in the taking of countermeasures are injured states under Article 42 of the ARSIWA. Joint responsibility between states which act together on the same footing may bring about situations in which only one of them can rely on a circumstance precluding wrongfulness. Complicity situations may lead to difficult exercises of determining whether conduct is lawful support for the acts taken by another state or international organisation, and thus benefiting from a circumstance precluding wrongfulness, or whether it entails an independent violation of the law which would need a justification in its own right – thus making it difficult for involved states and international organisations to determine whether or not they can support an actor who is relying on a circumstance precluding wrongfulness.

It appears that the circumstances are more severely tested by situations of shared responsibility arising out of concerted action than by shared responsibility arising out of situations where there is no concerted action. The absence of a link between the conduct in the latter case makes it reasonable to apply the circumstances with respect to all implicated actors individually. It is in the nature of such shared responsibility that the conduct of each contributing state or international organisation is assessed on its own merits. Shared responsibility arising out of concerted action poses more difficult questions, because the link between the conduct of the various actors involved makes it look more problematic if, more by chance than by design, suddenly only one actor benefits from a defence. Situations exhibit features of such shared responsibility because of the very fact that states and/or international organisations act together. Some kind of commonality between them may thus be said to be a defining feature of these situations. The intervention of a defence that only works to the favour of one among a group of states or international organisations potentially disintegrates this commonality.

In contrast, the circumstances can all cope reasonably well with the situation in which a group of states is acting together and all the states involved can rely on the circumstance precluding wrongfulness. Whether this is the case, however, may give rise to intricate questions (as was illustrated for the defences of consent and the taking of countermeasures). The application of the circumstances precluding wrongfulness becomes problematic when, among a group of involved states and/or international organisations, not all of the involved actors can rely on a circumstance precluding wrongfulness. While there may be good reasons to limit the reach of the circumstances to only some of the actors involved in cooperative conduct, it is equally conceivable that the circumstances may instead randomly apply in favour of one state and/or international organisation and not the other.

Furthermore, uncertainties with respect to other questions of the law of international responsibility impact upon the assessment of how well-equipped the regime of the circumstances precluding wrongfulness is. There are borderline cases where it is fairly unclear whether conduct qualifies as aid or assistance, or as independent violations of international obligations. This might make it difficult to foresee whether or not an aiding or assisting state will benefit from the circumstance precluding wrongfulness which works in favour of a cooperating actor. Also, the ongoing debate about the admissibility of countermeasures in the collective interest impacts upon the application of Article 22 of the ARSIWA and the ARIO to situations of shared responsibility.

Likewise, uncertainties pertaining to the division of reparation between several actors will be decisive with respect to the question of whether the application of the circumstances precluding wrongfulness will produce reasonable results. If, for instance, a group of states bears responsibility for given conduct and only one of the states is exculpated due to a situation of distress, the other states could find themselves in a situation in which they face a reparation claim which exceeds their own contribution to the wrongful conduct. Technically, this situation could be remedied by the disclaimer included by the ILC in Article 27 of the ARSIWA and the ARIO, according to which 'the invocation of a circumstance precluding wrongfulness … is without prejudice to (b) the question of compensation for any material loss caused by the act in question'.

At first sight, this disclaimer could be understood as, once again, challenging the ILC's decision to focus only on the codification of the secondary rules of international responsibility. If, after all, the effect of the circumstances precluding wrongfulness is taken seriously, there would be no basis to hold them responsible and order them to pay compensation for conduct which is, due to the intervention of the respective defence, perfectly lawful.[118]

The ILC was obviously mindful of this conceptual problem and observed in the Commentary that:

> (a)lthough article 27(b) uses the term 'compensation', it is not concerned with compensation within the framework of reparation for wrongful conduct, which is the subject of article 34. Rather it is concerned with the question whether a State relying on a circumstance precluding wrongfulness should nonetheless be expected to make good any material loss suffered by any State directly affected.[119]

The ILC further observed that Article 27(b) would not attempt to specify the conditions under which an affected state could obtain compensation. Instead it would be for the states involved to agree on the 'possibility and extent of compensation payable in a given case'.[120] Just how convincing this conceptual construction is remains an open question.[121] In a rather

[118] See ibid., pp. 51–4. [119] ARSIWA Commentary, n. 18, Article 27, para. 4.

[120] Ibid., para. 6.

[121] In this context, it can also be noted that it is unclear why other forms of the content of international responsibility are not also covered by this 'without prejudice' clause. For instance, it can be asked why reparation or satisfaction are not featured. In particular, satisfaction might be a particularly appropriate consequence of an act of necessity which is characterised by the fact that it is targeting an 'innocent' party. On these questions see also Christakis, 'Les "Circonstances excluant l'illicéité"', n. 27, p. 241.

laconic manner, the Commentary to the parallel provision in the ARIO observes that the question is simply left open by the 'no prejudice' clause. This would be the correct solution, as 'it would be difficult to set a general rule concerning compensation for losses caused by an act that would be wrongful, but for the presence of a certain circumstance'.[122] Somewhat indirectly, this formulation engages with the criticism the ILC has encountered after the inclusion of Article 27(b) of the ARSIWA. In the literature, it has been questioned whether the ILC was not effectively providing for a 'liability without wrongfulness' regime by the inclusion of this provision.[123]

In this context, once again a differentiation between circumstances precluding wrongfulness and defences that might merely excuse the state or international organisation in question might have helped to clarify this matter. In fact, the Draft Articles as adopted by the ILC on first reading in 1996 contained such a recognition *in nuce*, with a Draft Article 35 stating that the intervention of the circumstances of consent, *force majeure* and fortuitous event, distress, and necessity would 'not prejudge any question that may arise in regard to compensation for damage caused by that act'.[124] For the cases of countermeasures and self-defence, however, this 'without prejudice' clause did not apply. This solution was, however, somewhat at odds with the consistent affirmation of the ILC that it would *not* differentiate between circumstances precluding wrongfulness and responsibility.

The problems associated with Article 27(b) of the ARSIWA and the ARIO become even more complex for the type of situations which interest us here. The absence of a clearly defined system of joint and several responsibility, and the lack of procedural mechanisms for questions of internal redress among a group of states and/or international organisations finding themselves in a situation of shared responsibility arising out of concerted action, are likely to complicate situations of shared responsibility even further. This also holds true for the suggestion of the ILC that the states involved should negotiate the amount of compensation owed. Such negotiations will most likely become more protracted if they go beyond a purely bilateral framework.

122 ARIO Commentary, n. 71, Article 27, para. 2.

123 Christakis, 'Les "Circonstances excluant l'illicéité: une illusion optique?"', n. 27, p. 237.

124 Article 35 of the Draft Articles on State Responsibility adopted on first reading, ILC *Yearbook* 1996/II(2) 58, at 62.

5. Rethinking the conceptual basis of defences in the law of international responsibility

In the light of these difficulties, it may be asked how the state of the law could be improved. This question is legitimate despite the strong normative pull that the work of the ILC has exerted so far in the field of international responsibility. Despite the unsettled issue of the final legal status of the two sets of Articles, both – but so far, especially the ARSIWA – have been relied on to a large extent in international practice, and this holds true also for the circumstances precluding wrongfulness.[125] While not all of the circumstances have been applied in judicial practice since their adoption in 2001, at least the defences of countermeasures, *force majeure*, and necessity have been relied upon by international courts and tribunals.[126] A realistic proposal to improve the state of the law will thus have to take the defences as codified in Articles 20 to 27 of the ARSIWA and the ARIO as a starting point.

The main reason for conceptual difficulties with the defences appears to lie in them being lumped together into a single group, all of them bringing about a preclusion of wrongfulness. As already mentioned several times, this construction was never undisputed and a critical proposal for a conceptual reconfiguration of the defences could thus over time also become accepted in international practice.[127] Accordingly, it is suggested here to follow the differentiation between circumstances that preclude wrongfulness (consent, self-defence, countermeasures) and those that merely excuse the state and/or international organisation that invokes them (*force majeure*, distress, necessity).[128]

[125] See already J. Crawford and S. Olleson, 'The Continuing Debate on a UN Convention on State Responsibility' (2005) 54 ICLQ 959, at 966–8.

[126] See the case law referred to in the UN Materials, above n. 3.

[127] In fact, the critics of the ILC approach argue that a differentiation between differing degrees of wrongfulness would more closely mirror international practice than the all or nothing approach of the ILC: see Christakis, 'Les "Circonstances excluant l'illicéité"', n. 27, p. 226.

[128] This distinction follows the suggestion made by Special Rapporteur J. Crawford but not adopted by the ILC: see 'Second Report on State Responsibility', n. 29, paras. 228–9; a similar, but not identical distinction was suggested by Christakis, 'Les "Circonstances excluant l'illicéité: une illusion optique?"', n. 27, p. 244. Christakis argues to exclude consent altogether from the list of defences and distinguishes between *force majeure* and countermeasures, which would preclude wrongfulness on the one hand, and necessity and distress, on the other hand, which would exclude or attenuate responsibility. On self-defence as an attenuating circumstance, see Christakis and Bannelier, 'La Légitime défense en tant que "circonstance excluant l'illicéité"', n. 53, p. 256.

What would this change? For situations of shared responsibility, this differentiation could indicate that the presence of a circumstance truly precluding wrongfulness also impacts upon other implicated states, such as states that aid or assist the main actor. When the lawfulness of the conduct in question is clearly established, other states implicated in this conduct should benefit from this assessment. An argument in this regard is also the consistency with primary rules; this construction would follow the UN Charter law on self-defence, for instance. Also with respect to consent, it can be said that the structural similarity of this defence, with the conclusion of an agreement between the involved actors, indicates that it is really lawfulness that is established. In contrast, the latter group of circumstances have a more 'personal' and extrinsic character,[129] and have in and of themselves no connection to the existence of the breached obligation. Rather, they concern the particular situation in which the state and/or international organisation organ that acted found itself when the relevant conduct was committed. Accordingly, it is more apt to speak of 'excuses' here. The 'personalised' character of these circumstances militates against their transmission to other states that find themselves implicated in the conduct in question.

In addition, a difference between self-defence and countermeasures, on the one hand, and the circumstances of *force majeure*, distress, and necessity, on the other, may also be seen in the fact that the former group of circumstances come to be applied as a response to a wrongful act of the state against which measures of self-defence or self-help are taken. By contrast, *force majeure*, distress, and necessity all do not presuppose any form of wrongful conduct on the part of the state whose rights are ultimately infringed.

The law of international responsibility has various functions. Its main function still lies in providing a framework for the provision of reparation.[130] While injury is a precondition for a claim of reparation, responsibility arises regardless of the question of whether there is material damage of a state or another actor protected by international law. This signals that the law of international responsibility has developed

[129] Okowa, 'Defences in the Jurisprudence of International Tribunals', n. 7, at p. 409: 'external circumstances beyond its control'.

[130] *Factory at Chorżow (Germany v. Poland)*, Jurisdiction, 1927 PCIJ Series A – No. 9, 21; *Barcelona Traction, Light and Power Company, Limited*, n. 82, para. 36; on the traditional focus of this field of law on reparation see also G. Nolte, 'From Dionisio Anzilotti to Roberto Ago: The Classical International Law of State Responsibility and the Traditional Primacy of a Bilateral Conception of Inter-State Relations' (2002) 13 EJIL 1083.

into a more general tool for the upholding of international legality.[131] This rule of law-related function of the law of international responsibility[132] is an important conceptual factor for our subject. Among the three defences that we suggest grouping into the former category (preclusion of wrongfulness), self-defence and countermeasures are especially concerned with means to ensure a return to legality. Some would critically say that they do so in a rather archaic and primitive manner, both being forms of 'self-help' and thus remnants of an 'old' international law which was characterised by the absence of judicial and other institutionalised forms of dispute settlement.[133] Yet, in the still imperfectly centralised international legal system of today, their importance remains unchallenged by states whose views cannot be disregarded in this respect. These considerations do not apply for the second group of defences ('excuses'). *Force majeure*, distress, and necessity deal with external factors impacting on states and/or international organisations and their officials in concrete situations. It does not seem to be warranted to expand the group of actors who can rely on these ad hoc mechanisms.

In this context, it can be considered how this differentiation should be further developed. In terms of process, there are various possible avenues. Given the still insecure final status of the ARSIWA, it is a possible scenario that states could return to this issue when setting up a multilateral convention on state responsibility. As this prospect is rather unrealistic and – in light of possible interests of states to lower standards of responsibility – also undesirable, it can be left to the practice of states and international, as well as domestic, courts and tribunals to develop this field of the law further. As the ARSIWA are meant to be evidence of customary international law on the matter, states are also free to engage in new forms of practice that might change existing customary law. This practice could materialise in diplomatic contexts as well as in the form of agreements in specific sub-fields and regimes of international law. As the

[131] Cf. P.-M. Dupuy, 'A General Stocktaking of the Connections between the Multilateral Dimension of Obligations and the Codification of the Law of Responsibility' (2002) 13 EJIL 1053, at 1057.

[132] On the relationship between state responsibility and the rule of law, see A. Watts, 'The International Rule of Law' (1993) 36 GYIL 15, at 39; I. Brownlie, *The Rule of Law in International Affairs* (The Hague, Nijhoff: 1998), p. 79; A. Gattini, 'Post 1945 German International Law and State Responsibility' (2007) 50 GYIL 407; Aust, *Complicity and the Law of State Responsibility*, n. 47, pp. 83–9.

[133] Cf. B. Fassbender, *The United Nations Charter as the Constitution of the International Community* (Leiden: Nijhoff, 2009), p. 128.

state of the law is also not completely settled, there is considerable leeway for courts and tribunals to apply the circumstances along the lines suggested here.

In terms of substance, it then needs to be asked which states should be allowed to join forces for the 'return to legality'. Here, the distinction suggested by Nollkaemper and Jacobs between public and private functions of the law of international responsibility[134] might potentially be useful. To a certain extent, this distinction is an abstraction of the already existing differentiation between different kinds of obligations in international law, i.e. obligations owed only in bilateral pairings and obligations owed to a broader group of states and/or international organisations, in some cases even *erga omnes*. The categories of obligations *erga omnes partes* and obligations *erga omnes* will be especially decisive for establishing which states may take part in measures aimed at inducing a state and/or international organisation to return to legality.

Beyond this field of obligations, the rule on complicity will have to establish what forms of support third states might render to a state invoking a circumstance precluding wrongfulness. If the conduct in question would 'only' result in responsibility for complicity *in the absence* of the intervention of the defences of consent, self-defence, and the taking of countermeasures, such forms of support may lawfully be rendered by third states and/or international organisations. If, however, the conduct would result in an independent breach of the obligation concerned, third states and/or international organisations are not entitled to this conduct, if not for the violation of an obligation *erga omnes* or *erga omnes partes*.

With respect to excuses, this approach would make it clear that third states and/or international organisations could only rely on those excuses if the conditions are met for them individually. In some cases, cooperation with conduct that is merely excused may nonetheless still be carried out in a lawful manner. In this respect, Article 6 of the ARSIWA and Article 7 of the ARIO would allow states and/or international organisations to place an organ at the disposal of another state and/or international organisation. If the rather limiting conditions for this operation are met, conduct of the organ which has thus been placed at the disposal of the receiving state and/or international organisation would only be attributed to the latter.

[134] Nollkaemper and Jacobs, 'Shared Responsibility in International Law: A Conceptual Framework', n. 4, 400 et seq.

It is not submitted here that this suggested differentiation between two types of circumstances would solve all the problems we have encountered in this chapter. Almost by definition, situations of shared responsibility will, by virtue of their complex character, stress-test existing rules pertaining to the responsibility of states and international organisations. The complexities of international cooperation are an ever-creative force for the challenging of abstract rules conceived before a concrete dispute arises. This points towards the need for an integrated approach to questions of shared responsibility. Finding a seemingly convincing solution with respect to one question may entail problematic consequences in other respects. The problems pertaining to questions of reparation have shown this interdependence of the various parts of the law of international responsibility.[135]

6. Conclusions

In sum, a mixed balance can be drawn for the suitability of the circumstances precluding wrongfulness for situations of shared responsibility. Generally speaking, the suitability of the rules decreases to the extent that the complexity of the factual situation, i.e. the number of actors involved, increases. This is due to the design of the defences, which are modelled on bilateral situations. The circumstances precluding wrongfulness can cope reasonably well with situations in which all actors within a group can rely on the same circumstance precluding wrongfulness. If, however, only some of the states and/or international organisations acting together can rely on circumstances precluding wrongfulness, difficult questions arise pertaining to the issue of whether cooperating states and/or international organisations also benefit from the defence, and the problem of how to partition possible claims of reparation among the cooperating states and/or international organisations. This contribution has argued that these problems are partly caused by the approach underlying the ILC's work in this field, which consisted of lumping together all defences in a group of circumstances precluding wrongfulness. A more differentiated approach that distinguishes between circumstances precluding wrongfulness and mere excuses could help to remedy at least some of these problems.

[135] See Chapter 7 of this volume, P. d'Argent, 'Reparation, Cessation, Assurances and Guarantees of Non-Repetition'.

7

Reparation, Cessation, Assurances and Guarantees of Non-Repetition

PIERRE D'ARGENT

1. Introduction

Reparation, cessation, and assurances and guarantees of non-repetition form part of the 'content' of the international responsibility of a state or of an international organisation.[1] All three are commonly envisaged as new, 'secondary',[2] international obligations owed by the responsible international entities to other subjects of international law. Although those secondary obligations stem directly from customary rules of international law and do not need to be contractually established,[3] it is important to recall that each of them is not automatically owed by each responsible entity. Indeed, if responsibility (under either the rules on attribution of

Pierre d'Argent is Professor at the University of Louvain (UCL); Guest Professor, University of Leiden; Member of the Brussels Bar; formerly, First Secretary of the International Court of Justice. The research leading to this chapter has received funding from the European Research Council under the European Union's Seventh Framework Programme (FP7/2007–2013)/ERC grant agreement n° 249499, as part of the research project on Shared Responsibility in International Law (SHARES), carried out at the Amsterdam Center for International Law (ACIL) of the University of Amsterdam. All websites were last accessed on 20 March 2014.

1 See the titles of Part Two and Part Three of, respectively, the Articles on Responsibility of States for Internationally Wrongful Acts, ILC *Yearbook* 2001/II(2) (ARSIWA) and the Articles on the Responsibility of International Organizations, ILC Report on the work of its sixty-third session, UNGAOR 66th Sess., Supp. No. 10, UN Doc. A/66/10 (2011) (ARIO). Commentary to the Articles on Responsibility of States for Internationally Wrongful Acts, ILC *Yearbook* 2001/II(2) (ARSIWA Commentary); Commentary to the Articles on the Responsibility of International Organizations, ILC Report on the work of its sixty-third session, UNGAOR 66th Sess., Supp. No. 10, UN Doc. A/66/10 (2011) (ARIO Commentary).

2 The concept of 'secondary obligations' has been used throughout the ILC's work on international responsibility; see e.g. G. Arangio-Ruiz, 'Second Report on State Responsibility', ILC *Yearbook* 1989/II(1), 42, para. 144; ARSIWA Commentary, n. 1, 95, para. 4.

3 As opposed to the early conception expressed by H. Kelsen, 'Unrecht und Unrechtsfolge im Völkerrecht' (1932) 12 ZöR 481.

conduct or under the rules on attribution of responsibility) is a necessary condition for those secondary obligations to arise, it is nevertheless not a sufficient condition: cessation is owed only if the internationally wrongful act is of a continuing character;[4] appropriate assurances and guarantees of non-repetition must only be offered 'if circumstances so require';[5] and the 'obligation to make full reparation' arises under general international law only when an internationally wrongful act has caused an injury.[6] None of the secondary obligations addressed here are thus co-existent with international responsibility, since neither the continuing character of the breach, the need for guarantees and assurances, nor the injury are constitutive elements of responsibility under Article 1 of the Articles on Responsibility of States for Internationally Wrongful Acts (ARSIWA) and the Articles on the Responsibility of International Organizations (ARIO).[7]

The aim of this chapter is to enquire into the adequacy of the ARSIWA and the ARIO to address those 'secondary obligations' arising from internationally wrongful acts in situations of shared responsibility under international law. As defined in this volume, international responsibility is said to be 'shared' when multiple actors are responsible for their contribution to a single harmful outcome.[8] For reasons of coherence and available space, this chapter will assume that the multiple actors at stake are states and international organisations (only), and not (also) individuals or other non-state actors. When the conduct of individuals or other non-state actors results in a harmful outcome – together with the wrongful act(s) for which states or international organisations bear international responsibility – the first issue to address is whether those individuals or non-state actors have breached a rule of international (rather than domestic) law that they are bound to respect, and the second is to know whether the claim relating to their responsibility is made under domestic or international law.[9] The latter issue exists even when the conduct of the individual or non-state actor constitutes a breach of an international obligation, since one can be responsible under domestic law for such breaches. In such a case, the law applicable to the responsibility relationship will, at least in part, be domestic rather than international. Since the complexity stemming from the questions mentioned

4 Article 30(a) ARSIWA/ARIO, n. 1. 5 Article 30(b) ARSIWA/ARIO, n. 1.
6 Article 31 ARSIWA/ARIO, n. 1. 7 See ARSIWA and ARIO, n. 1.
8 See Chapter 1 of this volume, P. A. Nollkaemper, 'Introduction', p. 1, at pp. 6–12; and P. A. Nollkaemper and D. Jacobs, 'Shared Responsibility in International Law: A Conceptual Framework' (2013) 34(2) MIJIL 359, especially at 366–8.
9 See Chapter 2 of this volume, A. Gattini, 'Breach of International Obligations', p. 25.

would merit a separate chapter, they are not going to be addressed here. However, it is hoped that the present chapter will also help with mapping those issues.

The difficulty of addressing international responsibility when it is shared by states or international organisations results from the fact that documented international practice in that regard, in the form of reported case law or settlements, is extremely scarce, if not non-existent. As a result, the work of the International Law Commission (ILC) relating to the 'plurality of responsible States' has remained rather limited in scope and, as will be seen, is deliberately inconclusive in certain aspects. One is thus left with trying to develop some convincing answers based on legal logic and what can be understood as being the fundamentals of the law of international responsibility. The purpose of this exercise is to try to shed some light on this complex issue and to show how its complexity can be addressed in a rather simple way, provided that the various concepts at stake are correctly grasped.

In order to address the complexity resulting from situations of shared responsibility as defined above, and to determine who owes what to whom in terms of cessation, non-repetition, and reparation, the intrinsic legal and factual reasons for such complexity will first be recalled (section 2), before we turn to situations where a plurality of states or international organisations are responsible for several wrongful acts (section 3), or for the same wrongful act (section 4). Subsequently, the issues of co-perpetration (section 5), and of joint and several responsibility (section 6), will be addressed.

2. Reasons for complexity

Two main sets of reasons explain the complexity of shared responsibility situations in international law. They are intertwined but must nevertheless be distinguished. The first set of reasons stems from the various legal grounds for international responsibility (section 2.1), which directly impact upon the understanding of the facts themselves (section 2.2).

2.1 Two types of attribution

According to the ARSIWA and the ARIO, responsibility is established under international law either as a matter of attribution of conduct, or as a matter of attribution of responsibility.

Under the rules on attribution of conduct, an internationally wrongful act materially committed by a natural person is – by application of those specific rules which make up the gist of the law of international responsibility[10] – attributed to a legal person (a state or an international organisation), which is therefore considered to be internationally responsible for such an act. Under the rules on attribution of responsibility, a state or an international organisation is held responsible 'in connection with' the act of another state or organisation. This 'connection' may result from a situation of aid or assistance, direction and control, coercion, or, in the case of an international organisation, circumvention of international obligations.[11] It is beyond the scope of this chapter to review and critically assess the ARSIWA and ARIO rules on attribution of conduct and attribution of responsibility, as other chapters in this volume are concerned with their meaning and application in situations of shared responsibility.[12] For the purpose of this chapter, international responsibility is assumed to have been established under (one of) those rules that are considered to be correct and complete.

2.2 Several wrongful acts or the same wrongful act

It is submitted that an essential distinction between two hypothetical situations must be made in order to understand and 'read' the various instances of shared responsibility. The contribution of multiple actors to a single harmful outcome can either result from separate wrongful acts or from the same wrongful act. The essential *summa divisio*[13] is thus as follows.

First, under the first hypothetical situation ('A-type'), a plurality of subjects is responsible for *several* wrongful acts which result in an injury.[14] This situation is the easiest to imagine and to understand, as

[10] Articles 4–11 ARSIWA, n. 1; Articles 6–9 ARIO, n. 1.

[11] Articles 16–18 ARSIWA, n. 1; Articles 14–18, and 58–62 ARIO, n. 1.

[12] See Chapter 3 of this volume, F. Messineo, 'Attribution of Conduct', p. 60; and Chapter 4, J. D. Fry, 'Attribution of Responsibility', p. 98.

[13] S. Besson, 'La Pluralité d'Etats responsables – Vers une solidarité international?' (2007) 17 SZIER/RSDIE 13, suggests the division between *le fait conjoint* and *le fait distinct*.

[14] Sometimes, one entity (state or international organisation) is responsible for a plurality of separate wrongful acts resulting in a single harmful outcome. However, such a situation does not raise any issue of shared responsibility as only one entity bears responsibility for all the different wrongful acts. Nor is there a situation of shared responsibility when the (single or)

it is probably the most common, not only in domestic law, but also in international law. For instance, one state abducts a foreign national abroad and transfers that person to a third state where he or she is tortured by the local authorities. In this scenario, several wrongful acts were committed by different states; one state abducted and transferred a person; another state tortured the same person. Each state is clearly responsible for its own conduct, but it remains to be seen to what extent each state's responsibility triggers the secondary obligations of cessation, assurances and guarantees of non-repetition, and reparation, and whether international law provides for some rule according to which one of the states might be responsible for the conduct of the other.

Second, under the second hypothetical situation ('B-type'), several subjects are responsible for the *same* wrongful act that results in a single injury. One can, for instance, imagine that two riparian states are responsible for having polluted a river because the body in charge of managing it, and which authorised or failed to supervise harmful discharges – being deprived of a separate international legal personality – is to be considered as their common organ. If each state is responsible for the same wrongful act, it also remains to be seen in such a situation to what extent each state is bound by the same secondary obligations of cessation, assurances and guarantees of non-repetition, and reparation; and again, if one of the two states can be held accountable for the other one.

Of course, reality is sometimes even more complex and cannot be easily squeezed into those two separate hypothetical situations, so that they must be combined in order to correctly analyse a factual situation. For instance, if the abducting state directs and controls the torturing state in the example used above to illustrate an 'A-type' situation, a 'B-type' situation will arise within the 'A-type' situation as far as torture is concerned by application of the rule enshrined in Article 17 of the ARSIWA. Thus, in such a case, the abducting state will be responsible for its own conduct (abducting and transferring), but it will also be held responsible in connection with the torture committed by the other state, for which that last state will also be held responsible. Despite the complexity resulting from this combination, or superposition of the hypothetical situations of types A and B, it is submitted that distinguishing

separate wrongful act(s) committed by a single actor injure(s) a plurality of victims. In case of a plurality of injured states or international organisations, each of them may separately invoke the responsibility of the responsible entity; see Article 46 ARSIWA, n. 1 and Article 47 ARIO, n. 1.

between them remains crucial in order to conduct a sound legal analysis of the allocation of the secondary obligations at stake. The distinction between situations where the damage results from separate wrongful acts or from the same wrongful act is reflected in the work and Commentaries of the ILC,[15] even if the ARSIWA and the ARIO do not contain any specific provisions relating to shared responsibility situations stemming from a plurality of wrongful acts.

If the difference between the two hypothetical situations is fairly easy to understand, it might seem difficult to classify cases of co-perpetration as pertaining to 'A-type' or 'B-type' situations. For instance, if two states together wage an armed attack against a third state, is it the case that each of them has separately breached Article 2(4) of the United Nations (UN) Charter[16] and that several wrongful acts have occurred, or are they responsible for the same and single wrongful act? Does co-perpetration amount to a plurality of breaches of the same primary obligation ('A-type'), or to the commission by several subjects of the same wrongful act ('B-type')? As will be argued later (in section 5), situations of co-perpetration should, as a matter of principle, be considered as 'A-type' situations.

3. Several wrongful acts

Under the first, A-type hypothetical situation, a plurality of states and/or international organisations is responsible for several wrongful acts.

3.1 Possibilities

It will most often be the case that the international responsibility of each subject for each wrongful act will be established as a matter of attribution of conduct, as illustrated in the above example relating to abduction and torture. One state is responsible because its organs have abducted a person and handed him or her over to another state, and one state is responsible because its organs have tortured that person.

It is, however, also possible that the responsibility of one of the responsible entities is established 'in connection with the act' of another actor, as a matter of attribution of responsibility, because of the aid or assistance

[15] ARSIWA Commentary, n. 1, 125, para. 8.

[16] Charter of the United Nations, San Francisco, 26 June 1954, in force 24 October 1945, 1 UNTS 16.

given by the former to the latter. According to Article 16 of the ARSIWA (and Articles 14 and 58 of the ARIO), the state (or organisation) that aids or assists another state (or organisation) in the commission of a wrongful act is not responsible 'for that act', but rather 'for doing so', i.e. for aiding or assisting. Aiding or assisting is thus considered as a wrongful act distinct from the one that has been aided or assisted.[17] In such a situation, two different wrongful acts, for which two different entities bear responsibility, contribute to the harmful outcome. In the abduction and torture example given above, one can, for instance, imagine that the territorial state where the abduction and torture took place was instrumental in aiding or assisting. The territorial state would bear responsibility for having done so, its wrongful act (and responsibility) adding to the ones of the abducting state and of the other torturing state; three states would bear responsibility for three separate wrongful acts on the basis of different notions of attribution.

Articles 17 and 61 of the ARIO envisage other cases of responsibility 'in connection' with the conduct of another subject. Under Article 17, an international organisation 'incurs international responsibility if it circumvents one of its international obligations' by adopting a decision binding its members (be they states or organisations) to commit an act that would be internationally wrongful if committed by itself, or by authorising its members to commit an act that would be internationally wrongful if committed by the organisation itself 'and the act in question is committed because of that authorization'. Under Article 61 of the ARIO, a state member of an organisation

> incurs international responsibility if, by taking advantage of the fact that the organization has competence in relation to the subject matter of one of the State's international obligations, it circumvents that obligation by causing the organization to commit an act that, if committed by the State, would have constituted a breach of the obligation.

In each of these cases, the international organisation (Article 17) or the member state (Article 61) incurs responsibility, irrespective of the wrongfulness of the conduct of the members of the organisation (Article 17) or of the organisation (Article 61) resulting from the circumvention (Article 17(3); Article 61(2)). If the latter bear no responsibility for their

[17] ARSIWA Commentary, n. 1 67, para. 10; H. P. Aust, *Complicity and the Law of State Responsibility* (Cambridge University Press, 2011), p. 487; see also Chapter 5 of this volume, V. Lanovoy, 'Complicity in an Internationally Wrongful Act', p. 134, at p. 150.

own conduct, the situations under Articles 17 and 61 of the ARIO do not give rise to any 'shared' responsibility, as the circumvention will be the only behaviour triggering responsibility. But if the act ordered, authorised, or undertaken as a result of the circumvention is internationally wrongful for its author, a plurality of wrongful acts will exist, since the attribution of responsibility for circumvention is a 'for doing so' responsibility – circumvention is, as such, considered wrongful under Articles 17 and 61. In such a case, a plurality of wrongful acts exists and the situations envisaged by Articles 17 and 61 of the ARIO belong to the 'A-type' category.

3.2 *Solution*

In all those situations of shared responsibility where several actors are responsible through different and separate wrongful acts for their contribution to a single harmful outcome, the questions are how to allocate to the different responsible states (or organisations) the obligations to cease the respective wrongful acts (section 3.2.1), how to offer appropriate assurances and guarantees of non-repetition (section 3.2.2), and how to make reparation (section 3.2.3).

3.2.1 Cessation

When several subjects bear responsibility on the basis of attribution of conduct for several ongoing wrongful acts resulting in a single harmful outcome, it seems quite indisputable that each of those responsible subjects is bound to cease committing their respective wrongful acts. Of course, if one of the wrongful acts is not of a continuing character, cessation will not be required from the entity responsible for that past act. For instance, in the scenario sketched above, if the abduction and transfer are over, cessation will only be owed by the torturing state. But if the organs of that state are torturing in a facility situated in a third state, which would then be separately responsible for an illegal detention (and probably aid or assistance in the torture), that third state must also cease its own wrongful act by freeing the detainee.

When several subjects bear responsibility on the basis of attribution of responsibility, the situation deserves some clarification, because the ARSIWA and the ARIO seem to assume that cessation (together with assurances and guarantees of non-repetition and reparation) are part of the 'content' of international responsibility, irrespective of the nature of the attribution – of conduct or of responsibility – under which responsibility is established. It is, however, certain that it is not for the aiding or assisting state or international organisation[18] to cease committing the wrongful act that it has aided or assisted; in such circumstances, cessation of the continuing breach is solely owed by the state or the organisation responsible for it under the rules of attribution of conduct. This is quite obvious in cases of aid or assistance, as the aiding or assisting state (or organisation) is only responsible for such conduct, and not for the wrongful act that it has aided or assisted.[19] This being said, the assisting or aiding state (or organisation) is also bound by the obligation of cessation and must stop its aid or assistance if it is continuing to render it, simply because such aid or assistance constitutes a separate wrongful act attributable, as a matter of conduct, to that state (or organisation). In such a case, cessation of the aid or assistance is owed to the victim of the wrongful conduct of the aided or assisted subject, and not to the latter.

In a case of circumvention of international obligations by an organisation through a binding decision (or authorisation) that results in member states committing wrongful acts,[20] not only must those members stop their breaches from having a continuing character, but the organisation will also have to achieve cessation in relation to its own act, and on that basis eventually rescind its decision that led its members to commit wrongful acts.[21]

3.2.2 Assurances and guarantees of non-repetition

When shared responsibility results from a plurality of wrongful acts, the question of assurances and guarantees of non-repetition is not very different from that of cessation. It will be in light of each separate wrongful act – whether responsibility exists for each of them as a matter of attribution of conduct or attribution of responsibility – that an assessment will have to be made in order to decide whether the 'circumstances' require from each of the responsible subjects such assurances and guarantees, and what kind of assurances and guarantees must be made. Because one can only offer assurances and guarantees for one's own future behaviour, there is indeed no reason to believe that assurances and guarantees of non-repetition

[18] Article 16 ARSIWA, n. 1; Article 14 ARIO, n. 1. [19] See above, n. 17.

[20] Article 17(1)–(2) ARIO, n. 1.

[21] On the use of cessation, rather than restitution, to rescind legal acts and the differences of approaches by the ICJ in the *Arrest Warrant* judgment and *Wall* advisory opinion, see P. d'Argent, 'Compliance, Cessation, Reparation and Restitution in the Wall Advisory Opinion', in P.-M. Dupuy, B. Fassbender, M. N. Shaw, and K.-P. Sommermann (eds.), *Völkerrecht als Wertordnung – Common Values in International Law, Festschrift für/ Essays in Honour of Christian Tomuschat* (Kehl: N. P. Engel Verlag, 2006), p. 463.

would not have to be offered by some of the wrongdoers if one of them has already offered them in relation to its own wrongful act. In certain situations, no assurances and guarantees will be required at all; in others, some will have to be offered by certain subjects bearing responsibility and not by others; and in other cases, all of the responsible entities will be required to offer assurances and guarantees, each in relation to their own responsibility.

The nature of the obligation breached (is it a peremptory norm?) and the character of the breach (is it an egregious or grave breach?) are most likely to influence the understanding of the necessity, under those 'circumstances', to offer assurances and guarantees of non-repetition. For instance, assuming for the sake of argument that the prohibition on abductions is not considered as *jus cogens* while the prohibition on torture is, the abducting state may not be called upon to offer such assurances, whereas the torturing state might well be called upon to do so. Conversely, the *jus cogens* nature of one of the obligations breached might lead to consideration that the entities bearing responsibility for each of the wrongful acts must all offer assurances and guarantees, despite the different character of those acts and/or the difference in the nature of the obligations infringed.

3.2.3 Reparation

The ARSIWA and the ARIO only address situations of multiple responsible states or international organisations when those entities bear responsibility 'for the same internationally wrongful act'; the rule provided for by Article 47 of the ARSIWA and Article 48 of the ARIO relates to 'B-type' situations and will be analysed later in this chapter. It does not concern a situation of shared responsibility stemming from a plurality of separate and different wrongful acts, each triggering the international responsibility of several states or organisations. Nothing is said in the ARSIWA or the ARIO about 'A-type' situations. This silence is best explained by the fact that no specific rule is actually required in such cases and that the question of the allocation of the obligation to make reparation is simply governed by the orderly and reasoned application of the usual rules. Before justifying that statement (section 3.2.3(a)), some fundamental points relating to the obligation to make reparation must be recalled (section 3.2.3(a)).

3.2.3(a) The obligation to make full reparation

The 'obligation to make full reparation' is a positive obligation requiring action that can be classified as an obligation of result. As an obligation, it exists as long as it has not been fully and properly performed, or as long as the legal subject to whom it is owed has not renounced (partly or fully) its benefit. The obligation to make reparation is thus controlled by its debtor through its very performance, and by its creditor through a possible waiver.

The obligation to make full reparation may be owed to one or several 'injured' states and/or international organisations within the meaning of Article 42 of the ARSIWA and Article 43 of the ARIO. Thus, together with 'the character and content of the international obligation' that has been breached, 'the circumstances of the breach' have to be taken into account[22] in order to determine to whom the obligation is owed. It is, however, doubtful that the obligation to make reparation – in contrast to cessation and assurances and guarantees of non-repetition[23] – could be owed 'to the international community as a whole',[24] unless one considers that the breach of an *erga omnes* obligation entails an injury of a purely legal nature[25] to each subject of the international community. Such a view should logically lead to the consideration that reparation in the form of (at least) satisfaction must be offered to every subject of the international community when a breach of an *erga omnes* rule occurs. However, this does not seem to correspond to current international law, as clearly illustrated by the *Belgium* v. *Senegal* case, where the findings of the International Court of Justice (ICJ or Court), according to which Senegal was in breach of several of its obligations, were not made in response to a claim by Belgium for reparation in the form of satisfaction.[26] Although the Court ruled that Belgium had standing to invoke the responsibility of Senegal because of alleged breaches of *erga omnes partes* rules,[27] and considered at the request of Belgium that the breaches by Senegal existed and had to cease,[28] it never suggested that Belgium had suffered an injury that had to be made good. The findings of a continuing violation by Senegal were necessary to order cessation, but did not constitute a form of satisfaction. Thus, the 'character and content of

[22] Article 33(1) ARSIWA/ARIO, n. 1.

[23] Article 48(2)(a) ARSIWA, n. 1; Article 49(4)(a) ARIO, n. 1.

[24] Article 33(1) ARSIWA/ARIO, n. 1.

[25] See B. Stern, 'Et si on utilisait la notion de préjudice juridique? Retour sur une notion délaissée à l'occasion de la fin des travaux de la C.D.I. sur la responsabilité des États' (2001) 47 AFDI 3.

[26] *Questions relating to the Obligation to Prosecute or Extradite (Belgium* v. *Senegal)*, Judgment, ICJ Reports 2012, 422, at paras. 118–22.

[27] Ibid., para. 70. [28] Ibid., para. 121.

the international obligation' only has a bearing on the enlargement of the category of the non-injured subjects that may invoke the responsibility of the responsible entity in order to claim from it cessation and assurances of non-repetition. If non-injured subjects may not claim reparation for themselves, they may nevertheless claim from the responsible subject the performance of the obligation of reparation 'in the interest of the injured [state(s) or international organisation(s)] or of the beneficiaries of the obligation breached'.[29] The ARSIWA and the ARIO are indeed 'without prejudice to any right, arising from the international responsibility . . . which may accrue directly to any person or entity other than a [state or an international organisation]'.[30] To determine whether the obligation to make reparation could also be owed under general international law to individuals, or whether individuals have a right to reparation under general international law, is, however, outside the scope of this study.[31]

It is important to stress that the particular nature of the obligation breached has no bearing on the nature of the secondary obligation to make reparation stemming from that breach when it has caused an injury. The internationally wrongful act may consist of the infringement of a multilateral, *erga omnes* or even *jus cogens* obligation; the secondary obligation to make reparation will only be owed by the entity responsible for that breach to each entity actually injured, and not to the international community as a whole. Moreover, the obligation to make reparation is of a dispositive nature and can always be waived by its beneficiary.[32] Thus, when several states or international organisations have been injured

[29] Article 48(2)(b) ARSIWA, n. 1; Article 49(4)(b) ARIO, n. 1.

[30] Article 33(2) ARSIWA/ARIO, n. 1.

[31] See 'Basic Principles and Guidelines on the Right to a Remedy and Reparation for Victims of Gross Violations of International Human Rights Law and Serious Violations of International Humanitarian Law', UN Doc. A/RES/60/147 (2005); P. d'Argent, 'Le Droit de la responsabilité internationale complété? Examen des "Principes fondamentaux et directives concernant le droit à un recours et à réparation des victimes de violations flagrantes du droit international des droits de l'homme et de violations graves du droit international humanitaire"' (2005) 51 AFDI 27; d'Argent, 'Compliance, Cessation, Reparation and Restitution in the Wall Advisory Opinion', n. 21, at pp. 473–7.

[32] In cases of breaches relating to rules protecting individuals, a disputed point is to know whether the state can dispose of the rights – assuming they exist; see d'Argent, 'Le Droit de la responsabilité internationale complété?', n. 31 – of its nationals and waive or bar claims in that regard; see P. d'Argent, *Les Réparations de guerre en droit international public – La Responsabilité de l'Etat à l'épreuve de la guerre* (Brussels: Bruylant-LGDJ, 2001), at pp. 761–74; contra: Dissenting Opinion of Judge Cançado Trindade, *Jurisdictional Immunities of the State (Germany* v. *Italy: Greece intervening)*, Judgment, ICJ Reports 2012, 99, at pp. 19–24.

by an internationally wrongful act, each of the injured subjects may 'separately'[33] invoke the responsibility of the subject bearing responsibility for that act and claim reparation. The obligation to make reparation is established on a bilateral basis, between each responsible subject and each of the injured claimants.

The reason, but also the object, of the obligation to make full reparation is the injury. An injury is a legal construct in two respects.[34] First, intrinsically, it must consist of a harm to an interest considered as legitimate by the legal order that governs the obligation to make reparation. In other words, in order for a harm to be an injury capable of being the object of the obligation to make reparation under international law, such harm must concern a legitimate interest under international law. As far as states are concerned, it is generally understood that they have three main categories of legitimate interests under international law: they have a legitimate interest in the protection of their sovereignty, their property, and their nationals.[35] Second, extrinsically, such harm to a legitimate interest must be linked to the wrongful act by a causal relationship: the injury must be the consequence of the wrongful act. In other words, causality triggers the obligation to make reparation regarding certain harms, i.e. those that can be said to be the result of the breach. Causality is therefore of paramount importance when it comes to the obligation to make reparation. Even if a wrongful act has occurred, if the injury cannot be considered as having been caused by that act, the state or organisation bearing responsibility for it will not have to make reparation for that injury.[36] As will be seen below, causality not only governs the existence of the obligation to make reparation, but also the allocation of its performance, since it is on the basis of causality that, notably, apportionment is decided.

According to the obligation to make full reparation, 'reparation must, as far as possible, wipe out all the consequences of the illegal act and re-establish the situation which would, in all probability, have existed if that act had not been committed'.[37] To make reparation is thus, as far as

[33] Article 46 ARSIWA, n. 1; Article 47 ARIO, n. 1.

[34] J. Combacau and S. Sur, *Droit international public*, 7th edn (Paris: Montchrestien, 2006), p. 528.

[35] Ibid., at pp. 529–30.

[36] See e.g., *Application of the Convention on the Prevention and Punishment of the Crime of Genocide (Bosnia and Herzegovina* v. *Serbia and Montenegro)*, Judgment, ICJ Reports 2007, 43, at 233–4, para. 462 (*Bosnian Genocide* case).

[37] *Factory at Chorzów (Germany* v. *Poland)*, Merits, Claim for Indemnity, Judgment No. 13, 1928 PCIJ Series A – No. 17, at p. 47. See, on the notion of reparation, d'Argent, *Les Réparations de guerre en droit international public*, n. 32, at pp. 662–9.

possible, to 're-establish the situation which *would*, in all probability, have existed' in the absence of the wrongful act. To make reparation is *not* to re-establish the situation that *existed* just before the breach (status quo ante), but to establish the injured subject in the situation in which it would, 'in all probability', be at the time of the performance of the obligation to make reparation. This is why loss of profits can be claimed as part of the injury to be made good[38] and why restitution – which allows for the re-establishment of 'the situation which existed before the wrongful act was committed'[39] – is but one *form* of reparation, and not reparation itself.

Next to restitution, the other forms of reparation are compensation[40] and satisfaction.[41] In order to provide 'full reparation', those various forms of reparation are due 'either singly or in combination'[42] according to their own legal conditions and the nature and extent of the injury suffered that has to be made good. It is entirely possible that no compensation is owed as reparation for material damage following a wrongful act because it is considered that this breach is not causally linked to that damage, whereas satisfaction is owed as reparation for the non-material injury resulting from the same wrongful act. For instance, the ICJ rejected the compensation claim presented to it by Bosnia following the breach by Serbia of the obligation to prevent genocide for lack of a 'sufficiently direct and certain causal nexus'[43] between that wrongful act and the injury suffered by Bosnia. It ruled that 'it [was] however clear' that Bosnia was 'entitled to reparation in the form of satisfaction'[44] by a declaration of the Court. Moreover, as the ICJ stressed in the *Pulp Mills* case, the forms of reparation (whether restitution, compensation, or satisfaction) 'must be appropriate to the injury suffered, taking into account the nature of the wrongful act having caused it'.[45] Hence, it is possible to reject a claim for restitution or compensation despite the

[38] Article 36(2) ARSIWA/ARIO, n. 1. [39] Article 35 ARSIWA/ARIO, ibid.

[40] Article 36 ARSIWA/ARIO, ibid. [41] Article 37 ARSIWA/ARIO, ibid.

[42] Article 34 ARSIWA/ARIO, ibid.

[43] *Bosnian Genocide* case, at 36, pp. 233–4, para. 462. For critical appraisals of the strict causality test used by the ICJ in relation to the breach of an obligation to prevent, see A. Gattini, 'Breach of the Obligation to Prevent and Reparation Thereof in the ICJ's Genocide Judgment' (2007) 18 EJIL 695; P. d'Argent, 'Reparation and Compliance', in K. Bannelier, T. Christakis, and S. Heathcote, *The ICJ and the Evolution of International Law – The Enduring Impact of the Corfu Channel Case* (London: Routledge, 2012), p. 335.

[44] *Bosnian Genocide* case, n. 36, at 234, para. 463.

[45] *Pulp Mills on the River Uruguay (Argentina* v. *Uruguay)*, Judgment, ICJ Reports 2010, 14, at 104, para. 274.

injury being caused by the wrongful act for the reason that such form of reparation is not appropriate to the actual injury.

Ensuring full reparation by way of compensation may also require the payment of interest on any principal sum due,[46] either because such sum has been evaluated at a moment in time prior to the authoritative determination of the obligation to make reparation (compensatory interest), or because effective payment is posterior to such determination (interest on arrears).

Finally, 'full' reparation can be tempered by the contribution to the injury 'by wilful or negligent action or omission' of the injured state or organisation, or of 'any person or entity in relation to whom reparation is sought'.[47]

3.2.3(b) Allocating the obligation to make reparation

When several states and/or international organisations are responsible for a plurality of separate wrongful acts, the respective causal links between each act and the injury need to be assessed. Here is not the place to dwell on theories of causality.[48] Assuming one accepted understanding of what 'direct', 'certain', and not too 'remote' causality amounts to, what is important for the purpose of this analysis is to acknowledge that if one of the wrongful acts cannot be said to be in a causal relationship with the injury, the entity responsible for that act will not be bound by the obligation to make reparation for that injury, despite the breach and its responsibility for it. If that is the case, the obligation to make reparation will only concern the other wrongdoer(s). For instance, if one state (or one international organisation) is found to be in breach of the obligation to prevent genocide, while – presumably – another state has actually committed the said genocide through its armed forces, the obligation to make reparation in the form of compensation for the material injury will be owed by the latter state only if the breach of the obligation to prevent is found to lack 'a sufficient direct and certain causal nexus'[49] with the injury at stake. However, this does not mean that the entity responsible for the breach of the obligation to prevent genocide does not bear any responsibility for that breach, nor that it does not owe reparation in the form of satisfaction for the non-material injury

[46] Article 38 ARSIWA/ARIO, n. 1. [47] Article 39 ARSIWA/ARIO, ibid.

[48] See Chapter 2 of this volume, Gattini, 'Breach of International Obligations', n. 9. Gattini addresses causation in section 2.2, at pp. 28–31.

[49] *Bosnian Genocide* case, n. 36, at 234, para. 462.

resulting from its breach.[50] Causality in law – which is never a natural science appraisal, but always reflects human choices and understanding of what can be required from individuals or collective entities[51] – thus plays a crucial role in the limitation and the distribution of the secondary obligation stemming from the plurality of separate wrongful acts.

Once several separate wrongful acts are each considered to have a causal nexus with the injury that is the object of the reparation claim, which of the various wrongdoers is to make reparation? This question lies at the core of the complexity of shared responsibility as it relates to the issue of the distribution, or apportionment, of the obligation to make reparation. This, however, requires clarification of the various understandings of the relationship between multiple causes.

There are different ways to understand the relationship between multiple wrongful acts that are each considered to be potentially causally linked with the injury. In her seminal book, Brigitte Stern identified four possible situations where an injury seems to result from a plurality of events.[52] The first situation relates to a fake, or only apparent, plurality of causes; while the injury apparently resulted from several causes, it actually stems from one single cause, which is said to be 'exclusive'. The second situation arises when 'parallel', or 'coincidental',[53] causes exist. In such a situation, a wrongful act could by itself have produced the injury, but it actually occurred due to another event (*force majeure* or the – whether lawful or not – act of another subject), independently from the wrongful act. In the third situation, several injuries result from concurring causes and their addition seems to create a single injury. The various causes are then said to be 'complementary' of each other. The fourth situation arises when each cause is by itself insufficient to produce the single harmful outcome as it occurred. In such a situation, the different causes are said to be 'cumulative'.

The first and second situations – of 'exclusive' and 'parallel' (or 'coincidental') causes – are not shared responsibility situations for several wrongful acts. In the first situation, if the exclusive cause is a wrongful act, its author will have to make reparation alone for the entire injury. Of course, if several entities bear responsibility for that single act,

50 Ibid., para. 463.

51 D'Argent, *Les Réparations de guerre en droit international public*, n. 32, at pp. 624–6.

52 B. Bollecker-Stern, *Le Préjudice dans la théorie de la responsabilité internationale* (Paris: Pedone, 1973), pp. 267 et seq.

53 According to the terminology of J. Personnaz, *La Réparation du préjudice en droit international public* (Paris: Sirey, 1939), at p. 142.

a 'B-type' situation will emerge. In the second situation, the wrongful act is actually indifferent, as the injury occurred in spite of it; as a consequence, the wrongdoer will not be bound to make reparation.

In contrast, the third and fourth situations – of 'complementary' and 'cumulative' causes – are shared responsibility situations for several wrongful acts, and therefore deserve a closer analysis.

3.2.3(b)(i) Complementary causes

The 'complementarity' of causes can be illustrated by the hypothetical situation presented above, relating to the abduction and transfer by one state of a suspect who is then tortured by a third state. In such a situation, the globally harmful outcome of those different wrongful acts is actually made up of an accumulation of injuries, each produced by one of the acts; the abduction is an injury distinct from the torture. If only the abduction and transfer had taken place, an injury would have existed as such; if only the torture had occurred, another injury would have existed as such. In the sequence of events, the various successive wrongful acts have complemented each other to produce the apparently global harmful outcome. Such a situation calls for a rather simple solution, based on the fundamental principle according to which each entity must be responsible for the consequences of its own wrongful act (either as a matter of attribution of conduct or attribution of responsibility), but not for the consequences of the acts of another wrongdoer: 'the general principle in case of a plurality of responsible States is that each State is separately responsible for the conduct attributable to it'.[54] Hence, the responsibility of each wrongdoer can be separately invoked, to the extent of the causal importance of its own wrongful act in relation to the global injury. Since the unity of the harmful outcome is only apparent, the contribution of each wrongdoer to the reparation must be proportional to the actual effect that its own wrongful act has had on the injury as a whole. In other words, a situation of 'complementary' causes calls for the apportionment of the obligation to make reparation in due proportion to the causal influence of each wrongful act on the apparently global harmful outcome. Each wrongdoer will thus be bound to make reparation, but only proportionally to what can be considered as being its own share of the damage.

[54] J. Crawford, *The International Law Commission's Articles on State Responsibility, Introduction, Text and Commentaries* (Cambridge University Press, 2002), p. 272; ARSIWA Commentary, n. 1, 124, para. 3.

In his second report, Special Rapporteur Gaetano Arangio-Ruiz qualified as 'concomitant causes' the situation labelled here as 'complementarity', and also called for the apportionment of the obligation to make reparation for reasons of equity and 'a proper application of the causal link criterion'.[55] His suggestion was followed by the ILC as a whole, with the Commentary to (then) draft Article 44 reading as follows:

> The solution should be the payment of damages in proportion to the amount of injury presumably to be attributed to the wrongful act and its effects, the amount to be awarded being determined on the basis of the criteria of normality and predictability. In view of the diversity of possible situations, the Commission has not attempted to find any rigid criteria applicable to all cases or to indicate the percentages to be applied for damages awarded against an offending State when its action has been one of the causes, decisive but not exclusive, of an injury to another State.[56]

The apportionment solution was later criticised by Special Rapporteur James Crawford in his third report when discussing what he called 'cases of concurrent causes'.[57] According to him, the apportionment would not be consistent with international practice and the decisions of courts and tribunals. The Special Rapporteur referred for that purpose to the *Corfu Channel* case[58] and the *Diplomatic and Consular Staff* case.[59] In the first case, Albania had to pay the full amount of compensation claimed by the United Kingdom (UK) for having wrongfully failed to warn passing British warships of the presence of mines, despite the fact that the actual laying of the mines in the Corfu Channel was probably the action of Yugoslavia. In the second case, Iran was solely responsible for the hostage-taking because of its early failure to protect the foreign personnel from revolutionary students. In the opinion of the Special Rapporteur, the fact that, in this last case, the United States (US) had no claim under international law against the captors themselves made little difference, since the

[55] Arangio-Ruiz, 'Second Report on State Responsibility', n. 2, p. 14, para. 44.

[56] ILC *Yearbook* 1993/II(2), 70.

[57] J. Crawford, 'Third Report on State Responsibility', ILC *Yearbook* 2000/II(1), 19, paras. 31 and 34.

[58] *Corfu Channel (United Kingdom of Great Britain and Northern Ireland* v. *Albania)*, Merits, ICJ Reports 1949, 4 (*Corfu Channel*).

[59] *United States Diplomatic and Consular Staff in Tehran (United States of America* v. *Iran)*, Judgment, ICJ Reports 1980, 3. Together with the *Corfu Channel* case, ibid., this case is also referred to in the ARSIWA Commentary relating to Article 31, n. 1, 93, para. 12.

breach of the obligation by Iran necessarily triggered its duty to make full reparation.[60]

However, it is submitted that the *Corfu Channel* case – the only one of the two cases that is relevant for this discussion[61] – does not correspond to the situation of 'complementary' causes, but rather to 'cumulative' and converging causes (the fourth situation, which will be discussed below). Indeed, both the laying of the mines and the absence of warning were necessary to produce the damage suffered by the Royal Navy as it occurred. However, the laying of mines, if considered wrongful as such, was not harmful by itself (in contrast to abduction in the example given, which, by itself, is illegal *and* harmful) in the absence of ships in the Channel. Therefore, it seems that no real contradiction actually exists between the ILC's approaches under Arangio-Ruiz and under Crawford; the differences are more terminological than substantial once concepts and words are bridged. In that regard, it is quite significant that the last Special Rapporteur labelled causes that are 'both efficient causes of the injury, without which it would not have occurred'[62] as 'concurrent'. Such a notion actually corresponds to the concept of 'cumulative' causes in Stern's terminology (the fourth situation, as will be discussed in the next section). Moreover, Crawford had no difficulty with admitting that 'cases can occur where an identifiable element of harm can properly be allocated to one of several concurrently[63] operating causes alone'.[64] This situation corresponds to the 'complementarity' discussed here, because in such a case 'some part of the harm can be shown to be severable in causal terms from that attributed to the responsible State'.[65] Crawford also opined that this state should be held responsible for the consequences of its wrongful act in due proportion to its effects.

[60] Crawford, 'Third Report on State Responsibility', n. 57, 19, para. 34.

[61] As argued by S. Wittich, 'Joint Tortfeasors in Investment Law', in C. Binder, U. Kriebaum, A. Reinisch, and S. Wittich (eds.), *International Investment Law for the 21st Century. Essays in Honour of Christoph Schreuer* (Oxford University Press, 2009), p. 712, the breach by Iran of the obligation to protect the US Embassy premises necessarily presupposes that some troubling action that had to be prevented actually occurred. In this sense, there must have existed, from a material point of view, an 'inherent concurrent cause'. But this does not mean that a situation of shared responsibility resulted from such occurrence, because the Iranian failure to act was the only internationally wrongful act as such.

[62] Crawford, 'Third Report on State Responsibility', n. 57, at 17, para. 31.

[63] It is unfortunate and confusing to use also the adverb 'concurrently' in this context when the term is elsewhere used with another meaning.

[64] Crawford, 'Third Report on State Responsibility', n. 57, at 19, para. 35.

[65] Ibid., at 20, para. 35. See also ARSIWA Commentary, n. 1, Article 31, 93, para. 13.

As simple as it may seem at first sight, the apportionment of the obligation to make reparation in situations of complementary causal wrongful acts is far from being so. It calls indeed for some rather subjective, and sometimes agonising, evaluation of the respective influence that each wrongful act had on the outcome. In any event, such a solution can only be implemented on a case-by-case basis, as facts – or rather, what can be known about the facts, i.e. proven – are always of paramount importance. The knowledge of the facts will not only influence the apportionment in a situation of 'complementary' causes, but it may also eventually change that qualification into a 'cumulative' causes situation. The abduction and torture example used above could indeed be envisaged as a situation of 'cumulative' causes, if it were established that the abducting state was fully aware[66] and intended that the person it transferred to the detaining state would be tortured by the latter. In such a case, the transfer could be seen as wrongful aid or assistance in the commission of torture without which torture would not have been possible,[67] so as to consider this specific wrongful act of aiding or assisting as a 'cumulative' cause of torture. Yet another situation would exist if the transferring state had directed and controlled the torture by the detaining state. As mentioned above, the two states would then be responsible for the same wrongful act on the basis of Article 17 of the ARSIWA, and a 'B-type' situation would exist as far as torture is concerned.

3.2.3(b)(ii) Cumulative causes

A 'cumulative' intervention of several wrongful acts exists when each of them is causally linked to the injury, but none of them is by itself sufficient to produce the harmful outcome as it occurred. In this rather more exceptional situation, the injury is not severable into different harmful outcomes adding to each other, which can be allocated in causal terms to the separate wrongful acts. The injury cannot be linked, either exclusively (the first and second situations of, respectively, 'exclusive' or 'parallel'

66 By referring to the awareness of the wrongful act, it is not at all suggested that 'the requirement of awareness is to be preferred to the requirement that the aiding or assisting State be bound by the obligation breached by the recipient State'; A. Orakhelashvili, 'Division of Reparation between Responsible Entities', in J. Crawford, A. Pellet, and S. Olleson, *The Law of International Responsibility* (Oxford University Press, 2010), p. 646, at p. 653. The awareness criteria used here refers to the 'knowledge' mentioned in Article 16 ARSIWA, n. 1, coupled with the intention that the aid or assistance facilitates the wrongful act expected from the recipient state.

67 ARSIWA Commentary, n. 1, 67, para. 10.

causes) or partially (the third situation of 'complementarity', as discussed above), to one or several distinct wrongful acts. The injury is an indivisible totality that results from the addition of the various causal wrongful acts. Apportionment according to the causal effect of each wrongful act –which is possible when several wrongful acts, each having its harmful effect, complement each other so that an apparent global injury results from their accumulation – would be inadequate at the stage of the allocation of the obligation to make reparation, and is to be left until the issue of the eventual right of recourse arises[68] (see below, in section 6). Cumulative situations are therefore quite peculiar. For instance, as stated above, if the territorial state where the abduction took place has been instrumental in aiding or assisting the abduction, the separate wrongful act of aiding or assisting can be viewed as being a 'cumulative' cause of the illegal abduction committed by another state. Since the aid or assistance does not produce any harmful outcome severable from the abduction itself, but was necessary for it to happen, those two causes (aid or assistance by one state, actual abduction by another) can be understood as being 'cumulative' rather than 'complementary', at least 'when the assistance is a necessary element of the wrongful act in absence of which it could not have occurred'.[69] Thus, the complexity resulting from this example combines a situation of two cumulative wrongful acts (the aid or assistance and the abduction) complemented by another wrongful act (the torture itself).

[68] In domestic law, the issue of a right of recourse tailored according to the causal influence of the respective wrongful acts has led to debate over the foundation of *in solidum* obligations on the basis of the theory of causality, and to prefer an explanation of such 'solidary responsibility' between debtors on the basis of the protection of the creditor; see in French law, M. Bacache-Gibeili, 'Les Obligations – La Responsabilité civile extracontractuelle', in C. Larroumet (dir.), *Droit civil* (London: Economica, 2007), vol. V, p. 462 et seq.

[69] ARSIWA Commentary, n. 1, 67, para. 10 (strangely enough, and despite having clearly mentioned the fact that aiding or assisting is a wrongful act distinct from the aided or assisted act, the ILC Commentary refers in footnote 284 to Article 47, which is a situation where several states incur responsibility for one and the same wrongful act (see below)). If the aid or assistance is not of such effect, it would have to be considered as a 'complementary', rather than 'cumulative' cause: 'In other cases, however, the difference may be very material: the assistance may have been only an incidental factor in the commission of the primary act, and may have contributed only to a minor degree, if at all, to the injury suffered. By assisting another State to commit an internationally wrongful act, a State should not necessarily be held to indemnify the victim for all the consequences of the act, but only for those which, in accordance with the principles stated in Part Two of the articles, flow from its own conduct' (ibid.). Earlier, the same Commentary suggests that 'in cases where that internationally wrongful act would clearly have occurred in any event, the responsibility of the assisting State will not extend to compensating for the act itself' (ibid., at 66, para. 1). This would amount to a situation of 'parallel' or 'coincidental' causes.

Now, if the abducting state transfers the abducted person to the torturing state with full knowledge of the forthcoming torture, another situation of 'cumulative' causes could exist as far as torture is concerned, on the basis of that other aiding or assisting wrongful act. Another example of wrongful acts articulated as 'cumulative' causes of a single injury is to be found in the *Corfu Channel* case.[70]

There are two ways to analyse and solve such a shared responsibility situation.[71] First, despite the cumulative effect of the causal wrongful acts, one can decide nevertheless to identify and isolate one of them as being the most important and deciding one, considered to be the 'adequate cause'. The adequate cause will often be the one most proximate in time to the injury, occurring just before it. The entity responsible for the adequate, deciding (or sometimes called 'efficient') cause will then bear alone the obligation to make full reparation vis-à-vis the injured party (subject to a possible right of recourse against the other wrongdoers). Such analysis reduces the plurality into a singularity and tends to solve an inherently complex situation by making it simple. The 'cumulative' situation is reduced somehow to an 'exclusive' situation.

The second approach tends to take the shared situation of 'cumulative' causes for what it is: all the causal wrongful acts must be put on the same footing because the injury would not have occurred, as it occurred, without each and every one of them. The wrongful acts are said to be 'equivalent' to one another; they are each a *sine qua non* condition of the injury. In French-speaking countries, that approach of causality in 'cumulative' situations is known as the theory of *l'équivalence des conditions* and is derived from the philosophical writings of J. S. Mill.[72] It favours the victim as it considers that any of the wrongdoers is fully responsible for the injury because no causal wrongful act can be considered as more important than another, and that

[70] See section 3.2.3(b)(i), text to n. 61.

[71] The issue is well known in domestic law. For instance in French law, see generally on the difference between the adequate cause theory and the *équivalence des conditions* theory, G. Viney and P. Jourdain, *Traité de droit civil, Les Conditions de la responsabilité*, 3rd edn (Paris: LGDJ, 2006), p. 187 et seq.

[72] J. S. Mill, *A System of Logic, Ratiocinative and Inductive, Being a Connected View of the Principles of Evidence, and the Methods of Scientific Investigation*, 8th edn (New York: Harper, 1882), Book III, Chapter V, pp. 396 et seq.; Chapter X, pp. 537 et seq. On the appropriation of Mills' conceptions of logic by lawyers, see A. M. Honoré, 'Causation and Remoteness of Damage' (1971) 11 IECL, Chapter 7, at p. 203, para. 52. On the theory of *l'équivalence des conditions* as distinct from the adequate or efficient cause theories, see R. O. Dalcq, *Traité de la responsabilité civile* (Brussels: Larcier, 1962), vol. II, p. 102, paras. 2351 et seq.

each of them was necessary to produce the injury as it occurred. The obligation to make reparation is therefore borne equally and entirely by each of the wrongdoers,[73] the injured party being free to decide (for reasons of personal convenience or expediency) to present its full reparation claim to any one of them. Of course, double recovery of reparation by way of compensation is prohibited because the right to reparation is limited to full reparation and nothing more. As mentioned above, the object of the obligation to make full reparation is the injury, and nothing but the injury.

It is quite difficult to know which of these two approaches is favoured by international practice in 'cumulative' situations. This is because practice is extremely scarce and, when it exists, it is rarely explicit on the theoretical foundations of the decisions taken. Not only is the difference between 'complementary' and 'cumulative' situations rarely noticed and made, but the choice between the adequate cause and the equivalent causes theories does not appear to be consciously made in practice. In both the reasoning and the operative clauses of the judgment on the merits in the *Corfu Channel* case, the Court found Albania 'responsible under international law for the explosions [of 22 October 1946] and for the damage and loss of human life that resulted from them'.[74] This might be explained by the fact that no state other than Albania was respondent in the case brought before the ICJ. Such finding of responsibility is, however, not so much based on a logic of attribution,[75] but rather on a hidden understanding of causality. Because the Court was not explicit about that understanding, it is difficult to identify precisely the theory of causality it applied. What may be inferred from the judgment, however, is that all the damage suffered by the United Kingdom was considered to be a normal and foreseeable consequence of Albania's omission, as if that wrongful act was the only cause of the entire damage. This may lead one to think that the Court relied on some form of adequate or efficient causality; among the various possible causes, the most decisive one is selected, and the author of the illegal act constituting that cause must make reparation for all the damage. However, one may also think that the Court considered that the damage suffered by the United Kingdom would not have occurred, as it occurred, if it were not for the unlawful

[73] In French law, the obligation is said to be *in solidum*.

[74] *Corfu Channel*, n. 58, at 36.

[75] By definition, a failure to act never raises any question of attribution, not even 'negatively'; pointing out a failure to act requires one to identify who had to act, so that the 'subjective' element at stake in the search for attribution is always satisfied by finding the wrongful omission.

failure to warn of the presence of the mines, despite the fact that their laying was not (proven to be) attributable to Albania. The Court might thus have had in mind something like the theory of *l'équivalence des conditions*,[76] since the failure of Albania to warn the Royal Navy of the presence of the mines was a *sine qua non* condition of the explosions.

Be that as it may, the *équivalence des conditions* theory seems to have to be preferred, so that the obligation to make reparation for the whole injury is equally owed by each of the responsible entities. This is clearly the solution supported by Special Rapporteur Crawford[77] on the basis of, most notably, the *Corfu Channel* case. Since then, it seems to have been followed in some cases.[78] Of course, that solution must only be applied in a situation correctly analysed as relating to 'cumulative' – rather than 'complementary' – causes. However, the choice between the adequate cause theory and the equivalent causes theory in 'cumulative' situations will most likely be done in practice for reasons of expediency or some perceived sense of fairness for the victims. Because often the result considered desirable will somehow dictate the choice between the available theoretical approaches, one should not have too many illusions about the false security that apparently logical classifications provide.[79] This is especially the case since the a posteriori analysis of causality always boils down to hypothetical reconstructions of past events where their absence is posited in turn, in order to imagine possible different outcomes and gauge their respective influence and articulation. One element that can also be influential in this choice is jurisdictional considerations. Since there is no compulsory court or tribunal in general international law, the adequate cause theory may be overly restrictive in that regard, not to speak of the effects that the *Monetary Gold* doctrine[80]

[76] See on this d'Argent, 'Reparation and Compliance', n. 43, at pp. 344–5.

[77] See Crawford, 'Third Report on State Responsibility', n. 57, at 19, para. 34.

[78] See *CME Czech Republic BV (The Netherlands* v. *Czech Republic)*, Partial Award on Merits, (2001) 9 ICSID Reports 113, quoting the ARSIWA Commentary on Article 31, n. 1, and deciding that the responsibility of the respondent state was not diminished by the fact that its conduct was not the sole cause of the injury due to the concurrent acts of an individual. On this point, the award is far from being convincing, as argued by Wittich who considers that the joint responsibility issue has been addressed by the Arbitral Tribunal in a 'sloppy manner': S. Wittich, 'Joint Tortfeasors in Investment Law', n. 61, at p. 722.

[79] J. Verhoeven, *Droit international public* (Brussels: Larcier, 2000), p. 630.

[80] *Monetary Gold Removed from Rome in 1943 (Italy* v. *France, United Kingdom of Great Britain and Northern Ireland and United States of America)*, Preliminary Question, ICJ Reports 1954, 19, at 32; *Certain Phosphate Lands in Nauru (Nauru* v. *Australia)*, Preliminary Objections, ICJ Reports 1992, 240, at 261, para. 55 (*Nauru*).

might have if the equivalent conditions approach is rejected. The form of reparation claimed could also be an influential element in that regard. For instance, the adequate cause theory might be preferred just because restitution appears to be the most appropriate form of reparation and only one of the wrongdoers is in a position to make reparation through restitution.

4. The same wrongful act

Under the second hypothetical situation ('B-type'), several states and/or international organisations are responsible for the same wrongful act.

4.1 Possibilities

Such a situation exists when a common organ of several states carries out a wrongful act[81] or when responsibility is attributed to a state or an international organisation because it directed and controlled, or coerced,[82]

[81] ARSIWA Commentary, n. 1, 124, para. 2; Crawford, *The International Law Commission's Articles on State Responsibility*, n. 54, at 272. In its 1978 Report, following the work of R. Ago, the ILC already considered that the wrongful conduct of an organ common to two states is a case of 'parallel attribution of a single course of conduct to several States' so that such 'conduct of the common organ cannot be considered otherwise than as an act of each of the States whose common organ it is'. However, the ILC concluded at that time that such a situation resulted in a plurality of wrongful acts: 'If that conduct [of the common organ] is not in conformity with an international obligation, then two or more States will concurrently have committed separate, although identical, internationally wrongful acts', see ILC *Yearbook* 1978/II(2), 99. It is, however, suggested that, as only one course of action existed from a material point of view, it is correct to consider that states incur responsibility for *one* same wrongful act when that act is the conduct of a common organ. The *Eurotunnel Arbitration (The Channel Tunnel Group Ltd & France-Manche S.A.* v. *the Secretary of State for Transport of the Government of the United Kingdom of Great Britain and Northern Ireland and le ministre de l'équipement, des transports, de l'aménagement du territoire, du tourisme et de la mer du Gouvernement de la République française)* offers an example of a 'joint organ' triggering the responsibility of two states, namely France and the UK. In the Partial Award, (2007) 132 ILR 1 (also available at www.pca-cpa.org), the Arbitral Tribunal found that the Intergovernmental Commission (IGC) created by the Canterbury treaty was a 'joint organ' of France and the UK and opined that '[w]hat the IGC failed to do, the Principals [i.e. the two states] in whose name and on whose behalf the IGC acted equally failed to do' (at 103, para. 317).

[82] The coerced state could 'plead force majeure as a circumstance precluding the wrongfulness of its conduct', therefore possibly leaving the coercing state as the only responsible entity for that act; see Crawford, 'Third Report on State Responsibility', n. 57, at 73, para. 267.

the commission of an internationally wrongful act by another state or international organisation.[83] Breaches of mixed external agreements of the European Union (EU) are mentioned by the ILC's ARIO Commentary as examples of the responsibility of the EU and its member states for the same wrongful act when 'such agreements do not provide for the apportionment of the responsibility between the Union and its member States'.[84] 'B-type' situations also include cases of attribution of responsibility to a member (be it a state or an international organisation) of an international organisation for the wrongful act committed by that organisation when the member has accepted responsibility for it[85] or when the injured party was led to rely on its responsibility.[86] In that case (and apparently in that case only), the

[83] Articles 17–18 ARSIWA, n. 1; Articles 15–16, and 59–60 ARIO, n. 1.

[84] ARIO Commentary, n. 1, 142, para. 1. Discussing the Third Report by Special Rapporteur J. Crawford, members of the ILC raised doubts about the appropriateness of using the EU mixed agreements as an example of a shared responsibility under draft Article 47 ARSIWA, n. 1; ILC *Yearbook* 2000/II(2), 49, para. 274.

Under Article 3(7) of the protocol on the EU accession to the European Convention on Human Rights, the joint responsibility of the EU and member states for the same wrongful act is envisaged under the co-respondent procedure as a default rule: 'If the violation in respect of which a High Contracting Party has become a co-respondent to the proceedings is established, the respondent and the co-respondent shall be jointly responsible for that violation, unless they have jointly requested the Court that only one of them be held responsible and the Court decides that only one of them be held responsible.' Council of Europe, Meeting report, Fifth Negotiation Meeting between the CDDH ad hoc Negotiation Group and the European Commission on the Accession of the European Union to the European Convention on Human Rights, Final report to the CDDH, 3–5 April 2013, 47+1 (2013) 008rev2.

[85] An example of such an acceptance can be found in the draft Regulation of the European Parliament and the Council 'establishing a framework for managing financial responsibility linked to investor–state dispute settlement tribunals established by international agreements to which the European Union is party' (COM(2012) 335 final). Under Articles 3 and 207 of the Treaty on the Functioning of the European Union (available at http://eur-lex.europa.eu/), the EU has exclusive competence for a common commercial policy, including for foreign direct investment. As a consequence, the future international agreements on trade liberalisation will most likely include investment protection provisions and be concluded by the Union alone. International responsibility for alleged breaches of those agreements lies with the Union and not, as is the case of mixed agreements, together with member states. Under the draft Regulation, a member state shall nevertheless bear 'internal' financial responsibility if the illegal treatment was afforded by it, unless that treatment had been required by EU law (Article 3). If the external agreement provides for such possibility, the member state may act as respondent in the dispute resolution procedure, under certain circumstances (Article 8). Even when the Union is defendant, the member state may 'accept any potential financial responsibility arising from the arbitration' (Article 11).

[86] Articles 62 and 18 ARIO, n. 1.

responsibility of the member is 'presumed to be subsidiary'[87] in the sense that it 'may be invoked insofar as the invocation of the primary responsibility has not led to reparation'[88] since 'the international responsibility of the international organization of which the State [or the other organisation] is a member remains unaffected'.[89]

The ARSIWA Commentary also mentions the situation where 'two or more States ... combine in carrying out together an internationally wrongful act in circumstances where they may be regarded as acting jointly in respect of the entire operation'.[90] The section of this chapter dealing with co-perpetration (section 5) will examine whether such joint operation is indeed to be considered as pertaining to a 'B-type' or, rather, an 'A-type' situation, but the example referred to in the ARSIWA Commentary calls for an immediate clarification of the very notion of 'the same wrongful act'. The question is whether it means that only one wrongful act occurred while two or more states (or organisations) incur responsibility for it on the basis of one of the reasons recalled above, or eventually also that two or more actions by several states (or organisations) are similarly wrongful because they each breached the same international law rule. It is suggested that the singular as used in Articles 47 of the ARSIWA and 48 of the ARIO is to be taken seriously, so as to exclude from the notion of 'the same wrongful act' situations where several subjects incur responsibility for distinct, but similar, wrongful acts. 'The same wrongful act'[91] implies 'a single course of conduct'[92] and is not to be confused with similar (or identical) wrongful acts. When several states or organisations incur responsibility for a plurality of identical wrongful acts, an 'A-type' situation exists.

4.2 *Solution*

How should the basic principle of independent responsibility, according to which each state is separately responsible for the conduct attributed to it,[93] be applied in a situation 'where a single course of conduct is at

[87] Article 62(2) ARIO, n. 1. [88] Article 48(2) ARIO, n. 1.
[89] ARIO Commentary, n. 1, 164, para. 13.
[90] ARSIWA Commentary, n. 1, 124, para. 2.
[91] In French: 'du même fait internationalement illicite'.
[92] ARSIWA Commentary, n. 1, 124, para. 3.
[93] Ibid.; Crawford, *The International Law Commission's Articles on State Responsibility*, n. 54, at p. 272.

the same time attributable to several States [or organisations] and is internationally wrongful for each of them'?[94] The answer given by Article 47(1) of the ARSIWA and Article 48(1) of the ARIO is very simple, as it reflects the principle of independent responsibility: 'the responsibility of each State [or organisation] may be invoked in relation to that [same internationally wrongful act]'. In order to justify this rule, the ARSIWA Commentary refers to the *Nauru* case and recalls that the ICJ rejected the Australian argument, according to which its responsibility could not be raised separately from one of the two other states (the United Kingdom and New Zealand) that made up together the Administering Authority under the Trusteeship Agreement, and which were not parties to the case.[95] After having affirmed that 'Australia had obligations under the Trusteeship Agreement', the judgment on preliminary objections stressed that 'there [was] nothing in the character of that Agreement which debar[red] the Court from considering a claim of a breach of those obligations by Australia'.[96] By referring to the 'character'[97] of the Trusteeship Agreement, the Court was careful enough to avoid any over-generalisation of the solution it came to, by allowing for contractual derogation – even if it was only based on the general economy of a treaty, its 'character', and not its wording as such. This being said, in the absence of such contractual derogation, the responsibility of each state (or organisation) for the same internationally wrongful act may be invoked separately in relation to that act.

The ARSIWA Commentary labelled such a principle as being one of 'separate'[98] responsibility of each responsible entity, whereas the ARIO Commentary, ten years later, called it 'joint responsibility'.[99] Beyond the words, it is important to see that under that principle 'responsibility is not diminished or reduced by the fact that one or more other States [organisations] are also responsible for the same act'[100] and that each 'injured State [organisation] can hold each responsible State [organisation] to account for the wrongful conduct as a whole'.[101] But what does this mean in terms of cessation (section 4.2.1), assurances and guarantees of non-repetition (section 4.2.2), and reparation (section 4.2.3)?

[94] ARSIWA Commentary, n. 1, 124, para. 3. [95] *Nauru*, n. 80, at 258–9, para. 48.
[96] Ibid., at 259. [97] 'Nature', in the French version of the judgment.
[98] ARSIWA Commentary, n. 1, 125.
[99] ARIO Commentary to Article 48, 76, para. 1.
[100] ARSIWA Commentary, n. 1, 124, para. 1. [101] Ibid., para. 2.

4.2.1 Cessation

When several states (or organisations) are responsible for one same wrongful act having a continuing character, it is quite obvious that not every one of them is in a position to cease it. Everything will depend on the legal ground for which each of them incurs responsibility. If the wrongful act is being committed by a common organ, all the responsible entities will be bound by the obligation of cessation through the conduct of the common organ. If responsibility for the wrongful act results from direction and control, or coercion, the directing and controlling, or coercing, state (or organisation) cannot stop by itself the ongoing wrongful act. In such a situation, cessation will be owed by the subject that has been directed and controlled, or coerced, and to which the wrongful act is attributable as a matter of conduct. Is the directing and controlling, or coercing, state (or organisation) also bound (vis-à-vis the victim of the wrongful act) to cease its direction and control, or coercion, if it is ongoing? A positive answer would logically require that the direction and control, or coercion, be considered wrongful as such. This is not what the ARSIWA and the ARIO provide for, in contrast to situations of aid or assistance.[102] This being so, it seems, however, counter-intuitive and legally unsound to consider that the directing and controlling, or coercing, state (or organisation) is under no obligation to cease its 'negative' influence on the wrongdoer while being at the same time responsible, by attribution of responsibility, for the wrongful act resulting from it. On the other hand, it is far from certain that the directing and controlling, or coercing, state (or organisation) is also under the duty to 'virtuously' direct and control, or coerce, the author of the continuing wrongful act to cease committing it – no more at least than any other state (or organisation) is bound to 'cooperate to bring to an end through lawful means any serious breach'[103] of an obligation arising under a peremptory norm of general international law, when such breach exists. In all those situations, cessation of the direction and control, or coercion, is most likely to entail the cessation of the wrongful act itself, without great effort on the part of the directed and controlled, or coerced, wrongdoer, since it would probably not have wrongfully acted in the absence of such outside influence.

[102] See section 3.1, n. 17. [103] Article 41(1) ARSIWA, n. 1; Article 42(1) ARIO, n. 1.

4.2.2 Assurances and guarantees of non-repetition

When responsibility is shared 'for the same wrongful act', which of the responsible states (or international organisations) has to offer assurances and guarantees of non-repetition if the circumstances so require? As in 'A-type' situations, where several subjects incur responsibility for a plurality of separate wrongful acts, it is simply not possible to allocate in advance the burden of the assurances and guarantees of non-repetition on some of the responsible subjects in 'B-type' situations, nor to exclude that several such assurances and guarantees ought to be offered by several of the subjects bearing responsibility. Similarly, it is impossible to decide *in abstracto* which type of assurances and guarantees should be offered by each responsible state or organisation. Everything will depend on the circumstances, the nature of the obligation breached, the character of the breach, and the legal ground triggering shared responsibility for the same wrongful act. It cannot be excluded that every responsible state or organisation is individually called upon to offer assurances and guarantees of non-repetition.

4.2.3 Reparation

In the *Nauru* judgment on preliminary objections, after having rejected the objection of Australia according to which its responsibility could not have been invoked separately from the responsibility of the United Kingdom and of New Zealand, the ICJ made clear that its ruling did

> not settle the question whether reparation would be due from Australia, if found responsible, for the whole or only for part of the damage Nauru alleges it has suffered, regard being had to the characteristics of the Mandate and Trusteeship Systems ... and, in particular, the special role played by Australia in the administration of the Territory.[104]

As the case was amicably settled[105] and discontinued,[106] there is no authoritative answer to that question. This led the ILC to consider that

[104] *Nauru*, n. 80, p. 262, para. 56.

[105] See the Agreement between Australia and the Republic of Nauru for the Settlement of the Case in the International Court of Justice concerning *Certain Phosphate Lands in Nauru*, Nauru, 10 August 1993, in force 20 August 1993, 1770 UNTS 379. Australia agreed to pay the full amount claimed by Nauru by instalments, while the UK and New Zealand later agreed to contribute to the settlement; Crawford, 'Third Report on State Responsibility', n. 57, at 74, para. 271.

[106] *Nauru*, n. 80 Provisional Measures, Order of 13 September 1993, ICJ Reports 1993, 322.

the rule of separate invocation of responsibility provided in Article 47 of the ARSIWA

> neither recognizes a general rule of joint and several responsibility, nor does it exclude the possibility that two or more States will be responsible for the same internationally wrongful act. Whether this is so will depend on the circumstances and on the international obligations of each of the States concerned.[107]

Despite a rather obscure beginning,[108] the last sentence of this quote clearly refers to the passage of the *Nauru* judgment introduced by 'regard being had to . . .'. One must therefore understand that the rule of separate invocation of responsibility when several states or organisations are responsible for the same wrongful act is just what it is: a rule relating to the invocation of responsibility and not a substantive rule of responsibility, let alone a principle governing reparation. Indeed, Article 47 of the ARSIWA and Article 48 of the ARIO are each to be found under the first Chapter ('Invocation of responsibility . . . ') of the respective Part of each set of Articles dealing with 'the implementation of the international responsibility of a [state or international organisation]'. Hence, if an injury – or several injuries – results from the wrongful act for which several states or organisations are responsible, there is no doubt that the responsibility of each of them can be invoked for the purpose of claiming reparation.[109]

It seems difficult to argue that reparation for the whole injury could not be claimed from any of the various states or organisations responsible for the same wrongful act. From a causal point of view, the wrongful act is the only cause of the injury, even if several subjects bear responsibility for it. It is simply impossible to apportion those responsibilities according to the causal influence of the wrongful act on the injury, because that influence has been, by definition, exclusive. Since apportionment cannot be made on the basis of some quantitative appraisal of the causal influence of the wrongful act on the injury – as it presumptively resulted from one breach only – it could only be made by reference

107 ARSIWA Commentary, n. 1, 125, para. 6.

108 The sentence says that Article 47 of the ARSIWA does not 'exclude the possibility that two or more States will be responsible for the same internationally wrongful act', while the condition for its application is precisely a situation where several states are responsible for the same wrongful act.

109 See Chapter 8 of this volume, A. M. H. Vermeer-Künzli, 'Invocation of Responsibility', p. 251, at pp. 259–1.

to some qualitative evaluation of the legal reasons founding the responsibility of each of the several responsible states or organisations. In other words, it is the influence of each responsible subject in the wrongful act itself that would have to be taken into account and measured in proportional terms, rather than the influence that each wrongful act had on the injury. For instance, depending on the circumstances, one could consider that the coercing state is somehow 'more' responsible for the wrongful act committed by the coerced state, than that state itself. Such appreciation would be made in light of some 'sanctioning' policy reflecting the perceived gravity of the various grounds for responsibility.

However, it is submitted that the apportionment of what can be called the 'legal structure' of the causal wrongful act cannot be opposed to the injured party in order to limit its reparation claim addressed to any of the responsible states or organisations. Any apportionment on the basis of the 'legal structure' of the wrongful act and the grounds of responsibility for it is a matter between the responsible entities only, to be addressed if the issue of the right of recourse arises. After all, those reasons are indifferent as far as the injury is concerned, while the responsibility incurred by each state or organisation is 'not diminished or reduced by the fact that one or more other States [organisations] are also responsible for the same act'.[110] If indeed, as recalled above, each 'injured State [organisation] can hold each responsible State [organisation] to account for the wrongful conduct as a whole',[111] it would be contradictory to suggest that full reparation may not be claimed by the injured party from any of the states or organisations responsible for the same wrongful act. It is only if specific 'international obligations of each of the [entities] concerned'[112] impose a restriction on the right to invoke their respective responsibilities, and that those obligations are opposable to the victim, that a claim for full reparation could not be presented to any of them.[113] Absent such (opposable) obligations, the apportionment is only relevant as far as the right of recourse that the state or organisation which has provided reparation 'may have against the other responsible'[114] entities. The existence and legal basis of such a right of recourse will be addressed when discussing the issue of joint and several responsibility.[115]

[110] ARSIWA Commentary, n. 1, 124, para. 1. [111] Ibid., para. 2.
[112] Ibid., at 125, para. 6.
[113] This would be the case when an external agreement concluded by the EU and its member states provides for the apportionment of their respective responsibilities.
[114] Article 47(2)(b) ARSIWA, n. 1 and Article 48(3)(b) ARIO, n. 1.
[115] See section 6 below.

This being said, two provisos must be made at this juncture. The first relates to the forms of reparation, and the second to the prohibition of double recovery.

First, if full reparation may be claimed from, and is owed by, any of the states or organisations responsible for the same wrongful act, it might be the case that only one or some of them are in a position to actually perform the obligation to make reparation under the specific form of restitution. If restitution is considered in a specific instance to be the appropriate form of reparation, it could well be impossible for one wrongdoer, while possible for another. In particular, this would be the case if an object has to be returned and is in the possession of one of the wrongdoers, or if an internal act has to be repealed. In such a situation, the nature of the appropriate form of reparation will considerably influence the useful exercise of the right to invoke the responsibility of any of the responsible states or organisations, and will allocate the actual performance of the obligation to make reparation to a specific responsible entity, while discharging to a great extent the others from doing so. Of course, when reparation takes the form of compensation, these particularities do not arise. Also, as far as satisfaction is concerned, there does not seem to be any reason to require it specifically from one of the responsible entities in particular.

The second proviso relates to the prohibition of double recovery. As already mentioned in relation to the *équivalence des conditions* theory, in the case of shared responsibility where multiple wrongful acts are considered to be 'cumulative' causes of the injury, the prohibition of double recovery derives from the fact that the obligation to make reparation, and the right to get full reparation, 'is limited by the damage suffered'.[116] Article 47(2)(a) of the ARSIWA and Article 48(3)(a) of the ARIO recall the prohibition of double recovery as a proviso to the principle of separate invocation of responsibility when several states or organisations are responsible for the same wrongful act. Such a prohibition is found in many domestic legal systems and can most probably be considered as a general principle of law within the meaning of Article 38(1)(c) of the ICJ Statute, or even as an axiological principle inherent to the very notion of reparation. The prohibition is limited, as underlined by Articles 47 of the ARSIWA and 48 of the ARIO, to reparation 'by way of compensation'. Therefore, it cannot be excluded that satisfaction may be ordered from

[116] ARSIWA Commentary, n. 1, 125, para. 9. The report refers in footnote 720 to the *Factory at Chorzów* case, n. 37, where the PCIJ held that it could not grant a remedy sought by Germany because 'the same compensation would be awarded twice over'.

several responsible states or organisations. This is certainly the case when several injuries to different parties have resulted from the same wrongful act for which several entities are responsible, but it might also be the case when there is only one injured party.

The prohibition of double recovery reinforces the argument about the possibility of claiming full reparation from any of the states or organisations responsible for the same wrongful act. Indeed, there would be no need to recall such prohibition if the principle enshrined in Article 47 of the ARSIWA and Article 48 of the ARIO meant that full reparation for the injury could not be claimed from, and were not owed by, each state or organisation responsible for the same wrongful act. If apportionment according to (what has been called above) the 'legal structure' of the wrongful act were the rule in a situation of shared responsibility for the same wrongful act, there could be no risk of double recovery.[117]

5. Co-perpetration

When two or several states or international organisations simultaneously breach the same international rule binding each of them, are they separately responsible for different, though similar, wrongful acts ('A-type' situation), or for one and the same wrongful act ('B-type' situation)?

Situations of co-perpetration exist in international practice. For instance, it can be argued that through the Berlin Pact of Assistance of 27 September 1940,[118] the Axis Powers proceeded in concert and decided to wage jointly the Second World War. The decision of the US and the UK governments to use force against Iraq in 2003 could also be seen as a wrongful co-perpetration situation, if that use of force is considered illegal.

As these examples suggest, situations of co-perpetration do not raise many difficulties as far as attribution of conduct is concerned. Usually, it will be fairly easy to consider that, despite having proceeded in concert, each state (or organisation) has separately acted through its organs, so that the states (or organisations) concerned are each responsible for their own course of conduct. The fact that the rule breached is identical is actually quite irrelevant, since respect for that rule was separately owed

[117] Besson, 'La Pluralité d'Etats responsables', n. 13, at 21.

[118] Berlin Pact of Assistance, 27 September 1940, Hudson, International Legislation, vol. VIII, no. 591.

as a binding international obligation by each of the states (or organisations) concerned. What is important is to see that each state (or organisation) has acted by itself, even if they had decided to act together. The common intent of the responsible states (or organisations), or the fact that they acted in concert, does not transform their similar wrongful acts into one single wrongful act. As the ILC wrote in its 1978 Commentaries, '[i]f, for example, State A and State B are allies and proceed in concert to make an armed attack on a third State, each acting through its own military organs, two separate acts of aggression are committed by the two States'.[119] Hence, situations of co-perpetration should, as a matter of principle, be considered under the 'A-type' situation and analysed as such.[120] Any other solution would be quite unfair: if state A commits 100,000 soldiers and state B only 5,000 troops, to consider that they are separately responsible for one same wrongful act would not correspond to any politically and materially sound analysis of the situation.

If co-perpetration is an 'A-type' situation, should the several similar wrongful acts be considered as 'complementary' or 'cumulative' causes of the harmful outcome? It is impossible to give a definite answer to that question *in abstracto*, as it is only in light of the precise factual circumstances that the articulation of the wrongful acts can be adequately qualified, knowing that the default qualification should be 'complementary'. War – to refer again to the most-used illustration of co-perpetration – is indeed a harmful global outcome, made so by the addition of injuries resulting from specific, even if they are similar, wrongful acts. Despite their wilful and concerted co-belligerency, the responsibility of the Axis Powers after the Second World War was established, through peace treaties and other post-war arrangements, on an individual basis. None was held responsible for all the damage resulting from the war.[121] The 'complementary' articulation has thus prevailed. It is only as a matter of expediency and common sense that the former Axis Powers have exceptionally been made responsible for the conduct of one of their co-belligerents, for instance when the defeated territorial state had to make restitution for objects found on its territory and eventually displaced

119 ILC *Yearbook* 1978/II(2), 99. Those words are reproduced from R. Ago, 'Seventh Report on State Responsibility', ILC *Yearbook* 1978/II(1), 54, para. 59.

120 D'Argent, *Les Réparations de guerre en droit international public*, n. 32, at p. 547.

121 I. Brownlie, *System of the Law of Nations, State Responsibility, Part I* (Oxford: Clarendon, 1983), p. 189; d'Argent, *Les Reparations de guerre en droit international public*, n. 32, at p. 747 and references.

by its wartime ally from foreign occupied countries.[122] In contrast, Germany was made responsible, by Articles 231 and 232 of the Versailles Treaty, for all the damage resulting from the First World War, which was the result of its own military action or the actions of its co-belligerents. Not only did those provisions contractually establish Germany's legal responsibility for the war that did not exist in general international law at the time[123] (except vis-à-vis Belgium, whose neutrality had been wrongfully breached by Germany, as it admitted during the war), but they also created a regime of solidary responsibility that somehow reflected a 'cumulative' articulation of *ex post facto* declared aggressions. Such a contractually established (solidary) responsibility resulted in an enormous debt to be paid by Germany; it soon appeared financially impossible to implement, and economically destructive for the creditors themselves. That *in solidum* regime was definitively abolished by the Young Plan of 1930.[124]

A decisive element – though difficult to establish – in departing from the default qualification of situations of co-perpetration as made up of several 'complementing' wrongful acts would be to assess whether the participation of state B in the war was considered by state A to be a *sine qua non* condition to wage it. If that were the case, the similar wrongful acts could be considered as 'cumulative'. This would be more than a concerted action of the wrongdoers; it requires that one wrongdoer conditions its own conduct on the action of its partner. If that is the case, the two wrongful acts could be seen as 'cumulative' causes of the war, and each of the aggressors could be held responsible on the basis of the *équivalence des conditions* theory. If not, it would be more reasonable and closer to reality to consider those two breaches of Article 2(4) of the UN Charter as 'complementary' causes of the war. Neither the nature of the obligation breached nor the character of the breach should influence the way the articulation of identical causal wrongful acts is qualified.

However, as noted above, the 2001 ILC Commentary illustrated Article 47 of the ARSIWA by referring to a situation where 'two or more States ... combine in carrying out together an internationally wrongful act in circumstances where they may be regarded as acting

[122] See d'Argent, ibid.

[123] The responsibility established by Article 231 of the Versailles Treaty raised the notoriously contentious *Kriegsschuldfrage* which was debated not just in legal circles; see ibid., at pp. 72–81.

[124] On The Hague Agreement of 20 January 1930 constituting the Young Plan, its history, content, articulation with the Dawes Plan, and implementation, see ibid., at pp. 95–100 and references.

jointly in respect of the entire operation'.[125] According to the ILC, this would amount to several states being responsible for the same wrongful act. It is suggested that this assertion by the ILC does not contradict what has been argued above about co-perpetration as being a situation where several wrongful acts have been committed by a plurality of states or organisations. By referring to the joint action of states 'in respect of the entire operation', the ILC envisaged a very peculiar situation made up of exceptional circumstances that are usually not present in regular situations of co-perpetration. Be that as it may, the rather esoteric debate about one same wrongful act or several identical wrongful acts in such exceptional circumstances does not have much practical implication as far as making reparation is concerned. If the usual plurality of co-perpetration is favoured, the causes should certainly be considered as 'cumulative' when states have acted jointly 'in respect of the entire operation' and the *équivalence des conditions* theory is applied, so that full reparation can be indifferently claimed from any of the wrongdoers, as in a situation where a plurality of entities are responsible for the same wrongful act. In some cases, situations of an 'A-type' or 'B-type' do not make much difference for the injured party.

6. Joint and several responsibility

6.1 *The domestic law analogy*

As commonly understood, the responsibility of a plurality of subjects is said to be 'joint and several' when each of them is responsible for the acts of the others ('joint') and may be individually asked to make full reparation ('several').[126] In French law, the corresponding notion is *obligation in solidum*, and in German law, *Gesamtschuld*. In domestic legal systems, this form of responsibility is usually instituted in order to sanction the responsible entities for having joined in concert in their harmful courses of conduct – as opposed to accidental concurrent actions – and to protect the injured party by allowing it to claim full reparation from any of them. It is also usually provided by the law that the responsible entity providing full reparation at the request of the injured party has a right of recourse against the other responsible entities for their own contribution to the

[125] ARSIWA Commentary, n. 1, 124, para. 2. Also above, n. 90.
[126] See Crawford, 'Third Report on State Responsibility', n. 57, at 74, para. 272.

harmful outcome. Such right of recourse can easily be exercised by resorting to domestic courts and tribunals.

Joint and several responsibility has been debated in legal doctrine, with some authors clearly favouring it,[127] and others being hesitant[128] or even critical[129] about its existence and transposition to international law. Those debates are shaped by a real lack of practice[130] and the usual reference to some specific treaty provisions,[131] which are nevertheless insufficient to give rise to customary rules. In addition to the lack of practice, it is quite indisputable that the policy reasons which usually explain the existence of joint and several responsibility under domestic law are not the same under international law, while the necessary conditions for its fair implementation are absent. In a legal order primarily made up of juridical persons like states and international organisations, most of their concurrent courses of action are usually in concert; bureaucracies, which both states and organisations are, rarely act by accident and certainly not when they act together or at the same time.

[127] J. E. Noyes and B. D. Smith, 'State Responsibility and the Principle of Joint and Several Liability' (1988) 13 YJIL 225 (arguing *de lege ferenda*); A. Orakhelashvili, 'Division of Reparation between Responsible Entities', n. 66, at pp. 647–65; Separate Opinion of Judge Simma, *Oil Platforms (Islamic Republic of Iran* v. *United States of America)*, Judgment, ICJ Reports 2003, 161, at 353–9, paras. 63–78.

[128] I. Brownlie, *Principles of Public International law*, 6th edn (Oxford University Press, 2003), p. 440; S. Besson, 'La Pluralité d'Etats responsables', n. 13, at 13–38; B. Graefrath, 'Complicity in the Law of International Responsibility' (1996) 29 RBDI 370.

[129] Crawford, 'Third Report on State Responsibility', n. 57, at 74, para. 275; Wittich, 'Joint Tortfeasors in Investment Law', n. 61, at pp. 712–22; d'Argent, *Les Réparations de guerre en droit international public*, n. 32, at pp. 746–52.

[130] This was already noted by Brownlie some thirty years ago (*System of the Law of Nations, State Responsibility, Part I*, n. 121, at p. 189), but not much has changed since.

[131] The most often-quoted example, including by the ILC and the Special Rapporteurs, relates to the non-fault contractual regime of joint and several liability established by Articles IV and V of the Convention on International Liability for Damage Caused by Space Objects, London, Moscow, and Washington DC, 29 March 1972, in force 1 September 1972, 961 UNTS 187. Another example of conventional joint and several responsibility can be found in Article VIII(5)(e)(iii) of the Agreement between the Parties to the North Atlantic Treaty Organization regarding the Status of their Forces, London, 19 June 1951, in force 23 August 1953, 199 UNTS 67. Under that provision, the individuals injured in peacetime by the conduct of the armed forces of any of the North Atlantic Treaty Organization members may claim reparation from any of those states (the provision protects civilians in case of harmful joint military exercise when the identity of the army having caused the injury is not ascertainable). That right is to be exercised in accordance with the applicable domestic law provisions, so that the international law source and character of the joint and several regime established between states must be tempered accordingly. On these two references, see d'Argent, *Les Réparations de guerre en droit international public*, n. 32, at pp. 747–8.

What explains joint and several responsibility for individuals in domestic law can barely be transposed when it comes to the joint actions of entities like states or organisations in international law. As most concurrent actions by states or organisations are always, in one way or another, in concert, they would have to be 'sanctioned' by a joint and several responsibility mechanism; but this is clearly not what can be gathered from practice. It must also be recalled that the international law of responsibility is based on the attribution (of conduct or of responsibility) of internationally wrongful acts, rather than on some form of fault or malevolent intention. Moreover, and at least when injured parties are equal sovereign states (or equal autonomous international organisations), the international community has not been very preoccupied with the fate of victims of wrongful acts,[132] so that the need for a protective mechanism by which a full claim of reparation can be addressed to any of the wrongdoers is not as pressing as it has been in domestic legal orders. Finally, while the right of recourse is usually provided under domestic law by explicit statutory provisions and easily implemented in courts, nothing comparable exists under current international law. Any right of recourse is still in search of a solid legal ground in the absence of treaty provisions, while the lack of compulsory jurisdiction renders its exercise uncertain anyway – so much so that the very existence of joint and several responsibility may result in creating real injustices in the pursuit of justice. Therefore, resorting to comparative law in order to affirm the existence of a 'general principle of law'[133] of joint and several responsibility is hasty in light of the specificities of each national tradition, and unconvincing due to the structural differences between the domestic and international legal orders.[134]

6.2 *Solutions and problems*

Be that as it may, the developments discussed in this chapter have to a large extent deflated the debate about joint and several responsibility in

[132] Verhoeven, *Droit international public*, n. 79, at p. 633.

[133] Within the meaning of Article 38 of the ICJ Statute: see Separate Opinion of Judge Simma, *Oil Platforms*, n. 127, at 353–9, paras. 63–78.

[134] ARSIWA Commentary, n. 1, 124, para. 3: 'analogies [with 'joint and several responsibility' or 'solidary responsibility' in domestic law] must be applied with care'. See also Brownlie, *Principles of Public International Law* and Besson, 'La Pluralité d'Etats responsables', n. 13; Crawford, 'Third Report on State Responsibility', n. 57; and d'Argent, *Les Réparations de guerre en droit international public*, n. 32.

international law, as they have established that the practical benefit of such a regime, i.e. the possibility for the injured party to claim full reparation from any of the responsible states or organisations, actually exists in two specific situations: when several wrongful acts are considered to be 'cumulative' causes of the injury; or when shared responsibility stems from the same wrongful act. However, this does not mean that those situations should be labelled as 'joint and several responsibility' cases,[135] nor that they prove the existence of such a regime under general international law. This would be misleading for two reasons at least. First, the temptation would then be great to overlook the rather exceptional character of those two situations and extend their specific outcome in the more frequent situations where it would be totally inappropriate to do so, namely when several wrongful acts are considered to be 'complementary' causes of the injury. It simply cannot be the case, under general international law and in the absence of any contrary treaty provision, that a state (or an organisation) should be responsible for the specific harmful consequences of a distinct wrongful act for which it does not bear any responsibility. The basic principle remains that 'each State [or organisation] is separately responsible for the conduct attributable to it'.[136] As shown in the developments discussed above, this principle is not departed from in situations of 'cumulative' wrongful acts or of shared responsibility for the same wrongful act. Second, a joint and several responsibility regime worthy of its name would need to be more sophisticated than what has been concluded in terms of causality and wrongfulness in the two situations referred to above. For instance, what about the effect of a waiver by the injured party in favour of one of the responsible entities? Does it benefit the others, as it usually does in domestic law, in the absence of a specific provision to the contrary? Would the intrinsic logic of the international legal order not command the opposite conclusion? How is it possible to legitimately decide these kinds of issues in the absence of practice from which customary rules can be positively deduced, or when treaty provisions do not exist?

Another major point of uncertainty relates to the right of recourse, i.e. the contribution of the other responsible entities to the compensation

135 Crawford, 'Third Report on State Responsibility', n. 57, at 75, para. 277, noting about Article 47 ARSIWA that 'there is no need to identify this situation with "joint and several liability" as it is understood in certain national legal systems'.

136 Crawford, *The International Law Commission's Articles on State Responsibility*, n. 54, at p. 272; ARSIWA Commentary n. 1, 124, para. 3.

paid by one of them in favour of the injured party. It has already been mentioned that its effective exercise is rendered uncertain by the absence of a system of compulsory jurisdiction in general international law, but, more fundamentally, its existence and legal foundation are also far from being clear. Commenting on Article 47(2)(b) of the ARSIWA, the ILC Commentary considers that this proviso is, as its text makes clear, a 'without prejudice' clause and that 'there may be cases where recourse by one responsible State against another should not be allowed'.[137] With that general statement echoing the views of Special Rapporteur Crawford,[138] the ILC leaves it for future practice to decide what those cases should be, but also what could be the legal ground for the right of recourse outside those cases, and how to apportion the various contributions.

In domestic legal systems, the right of recourse between joint wrongdoers is essentially based on the mechanism of subrogation, by which the entity that has performed reparation in favour of the victim is subrogated in its rights.[139] But in civil law countries, subrogation must usually be established contractually or be provided under statutory provisions and does not similarly exist, as it does in common law, as a principle of equity.[140] In the absence of contractual or statutory provisions, it has been argued in civil law systems that the right of recourse could also be founded, as a last resort, on principles of unjust enrichment.[141] Even if this is not the place to engage in a comparative law exercise,[142] the domestic

[137] ARSIWA Commentary, n. 1, 125, para. 10.

[138] Crawford, 'Third Report on State Responsibility', n. 57, at 76, para. 275: 'there may be cases where as a matter of equity a court disallows any contribution, e.g. on the basis of the maxim *ex turpi causa non oritur actio*. In such cases the victim is compensated, but as between the joint wrongdoers the loss lies where it falls.' Reasons of policy are also advanced by H. P. Aust in order to question the appropriateness of a right of recourse when it could amount to sanctioning a 'pact of unlawfulness': Aust, *Complicity and the Law of State Responsibility*, n. 17, at p. 294.

[139] The mechanism is a standard feature in the insurance industry.

[140] During the ILC debate on the Third Report of Crawford, 'it was observed that the requirement for contribution was a common law notion not a civil law one'; ILC *Yearbook* 2000/II(2), 49, para. 280

[141] See in French law, P. Canin, *Les Actions récursoires entre coresponsables* (Paris: Litec, 1996), p. 278. On unjust enrichment in general, see J. W. Neyers, M. McInnes, and S. G. A. Pitel, *Understanding Unjust Enrichment* (Oxford: Hart, 2004), p. 415; C. Binder and C. Schreuer, 'Unjust Enrichment', in *Max Planck Encyclopedia of Public International Law* (Oxford University Press, 2007) (available at www.mpepil.com).

[142] See D. Friedman and N. Cohen, 'Adjustment among Multiple Debtors' (1989) *International Encyclopedia of Comparative Law*, Vol. X, Chapter 11, pp. 6–92. On subrogation in English law, see C. Mitchell, *The Law of Subrogation* (Oxford: Clarendon, 1994), p. 192.

law analogies could here again prove to be a difficult path that would not meet all expectations. It is therefore submitted that a 'general principle of law' in the sense of Article 38 of the ICJ Statute could only be 'discovered' in that regard with a certain degree of legal creativity and a spirit of progressive development.

Regarding the apportionment of the contributions claimed from the other responsible entities on the basis of some form of subrogation or unjust enrichment, it has already been argued that the situation is different when several wrongful acts are considered to be 'cumulative' causes of the injury or when shared responsibility stems from the same wrongful act. In a situation of cumulative wrongful acts, the apportionment will somehow be based on their respective quantitative causal influence. This might prove impossible to decide, if not contradictory with the causal theory that considers all cumulative wrongful acts as *sine qua non* conditions of the injury, and by holding them to be equivalent, this allows full reparation to be claimed from any of the responsible states or organisations. Therefore, for reasons of equity and logic, a default apportionment at the contribution stage might just be a strictly equal one between wrongdoers. In a situation of shared responsibility for the same wrongful act, any causal apportionment is strictly impossible. Hence, as argued above, it could only be based on some qualitative appraisal of what has been called the 'legal structure' of the wrongful act, i.e. the perceived gravity of the respective legal reasons triggering the responsibility of each entity for the same wrongful act. But here again, in the absence of a sure guide in that regard, equal apportionment could well be the outcome by default.

7. Conclusions

It can be concluded from this analysis that the ARSIWA and the ARIO only partly address the complexity stemming from situations of shared responsibility when it comes to the allocation of the secondary obligations of reparation, cessation, and assurances and guarantees of non-repetition. By limiting the 'plurality of responsible States' (or organisations) to cases where such responsibilities exist 'for the same internationally wrongful act', they fail to consider cases where the harmful outcome is the result of several wrongful acts for which several subjects are responsible. This focus on a single type of situation of shared responsibility can be explained by the specificity of the particular rule governing it. However, it would be a mistake to either ignore other forms of multiple responsibilities, or to apply that particular rule to those other forms. This chapter has tried to shed light on the various possible outcomes of shared responsibility situations. It remains to be seen whether their intrinsic complexity will be explicitly addressed and answered in practice, or if it will be blurred in settlements, whether agreed by the parties or imposed upon them by a tribunal or a court.

8

Invocation of Responsibility

ANNEMARIEKE VERMEER-KÜNZLI

1. Introduction

Under the system of the law of international responsibility as codified by the International Law Commission (ILC), the existence of responsibility is determined on the basis of two elements: breach and attribution. This requires an answer to the question of whether the conduct of a state or international organisation[1] is attributable to it and contrary to an international obligation binding upon that state or international organisation. The regime thus created is often called an 'objective regime' or 'objective responsibility'.[2] It is 'objective' in the sense that only attribution and wrongfulness are considered in the determination of responsibility - not causality, damage, negligence, culpa, intent, and other issues that relate to questions as to why the responsible state acted in the way it did. The notion that international responsibility is important for the effectiveness of international law hardly requires elaboration here.[3] Nevertheless, the

Annemarieke Vermeer-Künzli is Legal Counsel at the Ministry of Foreign Affairs, the Netherlands; associated researcher at the Amsterdam Center for International Law (ACIL), and Expert Associate, Research Project on Shared Responsibility in International Law (SHARES), University of Amsterdam. The author wishes to thank André Nollkaemper and Arnold Pronto for their useful comments and suggestions. The opinions in this chapter are solely the author's and do not necessarily represent those of the Kingdom of the Netherlands. All errors, of course, remain the author's. The research leading to this chapter has received funding from the European Research Council under the European Union's Seventh Framework Programme (FP7/2007–2013)/ERC grant agreement n° 249499, as part of the research project SHARES, carried out at the ACIL of the University of Amsterdam. All websites were last accessed on 20 March 2014.

1 The terms 'international organisation' and 'organisation' are used interchangeably. They are meant to refer to an international organisation to which the ARIO are applicable, hence an international organisation with separate legal personality.

2 A. Pellet, 'The Definition of Responsibility in International Law', in J. Crawford, A. Pellet, and S. Olleson (eds.), *The Law of International Responsibility* (Oxford University Press, 2010), p. 3, at p. 9.

3 Ibid., at p. 3.

actual implementation of such responsibility will depend upon its invocation. Without invocation, international responsibility will by and large remain unaddressed. Invocation, therefore, is essential for giving effect to international law in addition to the mere existence of international responsibility.

The rules on invocation were shaped by the traditional situation in which one state or international organisation acted independently from other entities and whose conduct and obligations could be individualised. In such situations, only the responsibility of that state or organisation required invocation to address responsibility for the breach. This context – responsibility of a single state or organisation – is also the basis for the rules on invocation as laid down by the ILC.

Situations of shared responsibility, with a plurality of responsible states or organisations,[4] may involve invocation of the responsibility of more than one state or international organisation. It is, however, by no means clear what the structure and implications of such invocation will be. The ILC demonstrated its awareness of the matter by including Article 47 in the Articles on Responsibility of States for Internationally Wrongful Acts (ARSIWA) and Article 48 in the Articles on the Responsibility of International Organizations (ARIO),[5] which will serve as the point of departure for the present analysis. As the ILC recognised, more than one state may be responsible for the same wrongful act, but neither the text of Article 47 of the ARSIWA nor the Commentaries provide any elucidation as to how such a situation will be analysed. The Commentaries stated that '[w]hether this is so will depend on the circumstances and on the international obligations of each state concerned'[6] and 'where there is more than one responsible state in respect of the same injury, questions of contribution may arise between them ... paragraph (b) [of Article 47] does not

[4] See for a discussion of the concept of shared responsibility, P. A. Nollkaemper and D. Jacobs, 'Shared Responsibility in International Law: A Conceptual Framework' (2012) 34(2) MIJIL 359; and Chapter 1 of this volume, P. A. Nollkaemper, 'Introduction', p. 1, at pp. 6–12.

[5] See Articles on the Responsibility of States for Internationally Wrongful Acts, ILC *Yearbook* 2001/II(2), 26, Article 47 (ARSIWA), and Articles on the Responsibility of International Organizations, ILC Report on the work of its sixty-third session, UNGAOR 66th Sess., Supp. No. 10, UN Doc. A/66/10 (2011) (ARIO), Article 48. Commentary to the Articles on Responsibility of States for Internationally Wrongful Acts, ILC *Yearbook* 2001/II(2), (ARSIWA Commentary); Commentary to the Articles on the Responsibility of International Organizations, ILC Report on the work of its sixty-third session, UNGAOR 66th Sess., Supp. No. 10, UN Doc. A/66/10 (2011) (ARIO Commentary).

[6] ARSIWA Commentary to Article 47, ibid.; ARIO Commentary to Article 48, ibid.

address the question of contribution'.[7] If the Commentaries to Article 47 of the ARSIWA seem short, the Commentaries to Article 48 of the ARIO are even shorter. They contain several *renvois* to the ARSIWA and their Commentaries, the only difference being the issue of subsidiary responsibility, which does not concern us here. Both provisions maintain the concept of 'objective responsibility', as is explained in the Commentary to Article 47 of the ARSIWA: '[t]he general rule in international law is that of separate responsibility of a State for its own wrongful acts'.[8] In other words, for each member of the plurality, attribution and breach must be determined separately, in line with the general approach in the law on international responsibility as designed by the ILC.[9]

These provisions of the ARSIWA, as will be demonstrated throughout this chapter, leave many issues unanswered. This raises two issues that must be borne in mind. With respect to invocation of shared responsibility, the ILC Articles put forward some measure of silence: that is, under-regulation or even absence of regulation, as will be explained in the following sections. This presents us, first, with a methodological problem. The present analysis of invocation of the responsibility of a plurality of states and/or international organisations will necessarily infer conclusions from this silence, but some of the conclusions will be somewhat speculative, even if they are based on well-informed speculation. It is perhaps tempting to criticise the ILC for a failure to formulate principles on this topic, but it is not particularly helpful. Not only is it rather unlikely that the Articles will change anytime soon, but the ILC also had very little to no practice at its disposal upon which to base its principles. Second, and related to the previous issue, it is important to bear in mind that invocation of responsibility of a plurality of responsible states (Article 47) and standing to invoke responsibility *erga omnes* (Article 48) were not dealt with in the Draft ARSIWA adopted on first reading.[10] Articles 47 and 48 of the ARSIWA have not benefited from the comments of governments, as they were included after the finalisation of

[7] ARSIWA Commentary to Article 47, para. 6, n. 5. [8] Ibid.

[9] See also Chapter 10 of this volume, C. J. Tams, 'Countermeasures against Multiple Responsible Actors', p. 312, at p. 316, for more analysis of Article 47 ARSIWA and Article 48 ARIO, n. 5.

[10] J. Crawford, *The International Law Commission's Articles on State Responsibility, Introduction, Text and Commentaries* (Cambridge University Press, 2002), p. 45. Obviously, Article 48 ARSIWA came less as a surprise, to replace former Article 19 on crimes of states, and benefited from more conceptual groundwork, but the fact remains that it was not part of the first set of Draft Articles.

the process of consultation, and were only reviewed in the plenary and the drafting committee of the ILC. It also means that the rules on invoking the responsibility of a plurality of states have not been part of the founding debates in the ILC between 1947 and 1996. Subjecting the draft to governments for their comments obviously is no guarantee for improvement. Yet, in combination with the thoughts and efforts of the various Special Rapporteurs in their reports, the discussions in the plenary and drafting sessions that culminated in the adoption on first reading of a set of Articles in 1996, and the scholarly debates that they have triggered, most earlier provisions have gone through substantial fine-tuning and clarification. One of the results is that Articles 47 and 48 remain somewhat disconnected from the rest of the ARSIWA. Many questions of the extent to which other parts of the ARSIWA apply to situations falling within the scope of Articles 47 and 48 remain unaddressed.[11]

As may have been expected, they were not fundamentally revisited in the ARIO project. This might be taken as a sign that their content was acceptable to states. It is submitted that such an assumption is difficult to justify. The aura of authority attached to the ARSIWA and the perceived necessity of finalising the ARIO quickly have both contributed to some measure of overenthusiasm for copying provisions of the ARSIWA into the ARIO.[12] While it is not necessarily the case that invocation of shared responsibility should be dealt with differently in the case of international organisations, copying Article 47 of the ARSIWA into the ARIO as Article 48 included copying the under-regulation and the silences. For the sake of clarity and the quality of the ARIO the ILC at least could, and perhaps should, have taken this opportunity to reconsider its rules on

[11] The present analysis will focus on invocation of a plurality of states (and/or organisations) and Article 48 will only be discussed in the context of providing standing. However, a clear example of 'disconnection' or under-regulation with respect to Article 48 is the issue of whether Article 44 (nationality of claims and exhaustion of local remedies) is applicable to claims involving injury to individuals under Article 48. For this discussion see A. M. H. Vermeer-Künzli, 'A Matter of Interest, Diplomatic Protection and State Responsibility *Erga Omnes*' (2007) 56 ICLQ 553, and E. Milano, 'Diplomatic Protection and Human Rights before the International Court of Justice: Re-Fashioning Tradition?' (2004) 35 NYIL 85, at 103–8.

[12] For an evaluation of this problem in general see C. Ahlborn, 'The Use of Analogies in Drafting the Articles on the Responsibility of International Organizations – An Appraisal of the "Copy–Paste Approach"' (2012) 9(1) IOLR 53; see also N. Blokker and R. Wessel, 'Introduction: First Views at the Articles on the Responsibility of International Organizations' (2012) 9(1) IOLR 1 and references therein.

invocation of shared responsibility.[13] In all fairness, we should perhaps be reminded, though, that the ILC was not providing for the most complex of cases, but creating a general framework for the law on responsibility, to be refined and adjusted as required by subsequent practice.

The result is that the Commentaries, statements of the drafting committee, and the parts of relevant reports by the last ILC Special Rapporteur treat the subject rather lightly, without much detail. The particulars of these will be discussed in the course of the analyses below, but the impression is unavoidable that the matter was not one of great doctrinal importance. Articles 47 of the ARSIWA and 48 of the ARIO specify that the general regime applicable to invocation in situations of only one responsible state or organisation also applies to situations involving a plurality of responsible states and/or international organisations. Yet, in suggesting that the 'normal' regime is applicable without any adjustment, they fail to provide for the inherent differences that exist between situations with one responsible state or international organisation and situations involving a plurality of responsible states and/or international organisations. While it is perhaps understandable that the ILC did not elaborate on the matter, as noted above, it is thus clear that these provisions leave important questions unanswered. In particular, the fundamental question of the extent to which invocation of the responsibility of a plurality of states and/or organisations is the same as invocation of the responsibility of a single state or international organisation is not addressed.

This chapter will approach this question in three parts. First, invocation relies on standing, or *locus standi* – that is, the right to invoke responsibility – which evidently may be more complicated to establish in cases of multiple responsible parties (section 2). This section will analyse both standing of injured states or international organisations and standing of non-injured states or international organisations with a legal interest (claims *erga omnes (partes)*).[14] Even if it is possible to establish injury or to derive standing based on the *erga omnes (partes)* nature of the norm, the next issue to be discussed will be that of admissibility of the claim (section 3). This section will address, first, the implications of the

[13] It did 'fix' the issue noted above in n. 11; Article 49(5) of the ARIO limits the application of Article 45 (nationality of claims and local remedies) to an injured state.

[14] For brevity's sake, these will be called injured states or international organisations, and states or international organisations with a legal interest. This is without prejudice to the fact that injured states obviously also have a legal interest in the claim, but the reverse is not the case. Also note that injury is not limited to material injury: legal or non-material injury may also give standing.

traditional requirements for admissibility of indirect claims (the nationality of claims rule and the local remedies rule) in situations of shared responsibility. The traditional rules do not provide for adjustment in case of a plurality of responsible states and/or international organisations, which may lead to rather absurd results that can only be prevented by modifying the rules. Second, it will address the fact that when a claim involves more than one responsible entity, admissibility will become more complicated due to specific requirements of admissibility applicable to the various international tribunals. Finally, section 4 will turn to the question of whether the fact that it may not be possible to actually invoke the responsibility of all parties involved in the breach, which may be due to rules of admissibility, standing, or both, has implications for the very responsibility of the parties whose responsibility is not invoked. This will be followed by some concluding observations (section 5).

2. Standing

Conceptually, invocation is preceded by the notion of standing, or *locus standi*. As will be explained in this section, standing is required for the right to invoke responsibility to materialise. In other words, a state or organisation wishing to invoke international responsibility must have standing to do so. Standing, then, gives the right to invoke responsibility. Between standing and invocation, standing is in this context perhaps the more important term. Once standing is secured, the right to invoke necessarily follows. It should be added that the actual invocation may depend on whether the state or international organisation with standing decides to exercise its right to invoke responsibility, whereas it cannot decide not to have standing. Whether invocation is successful may further depend on issues of admissibility. Invocation does not necessarily depend on access to a particular court or tribunal, and can be achieved through diplomatic channels. In the context of courts and tribunals, however, there is a further difference between invocation and standing. Standing is not influenced by issues of admissibility and jurisdiction of a particular court or tribunal. In the *East Timor* case, Portugal had standing to invoke the responsibility of Australia, but the claim was inadmissible due to the operation of the *Monetary Gold* rule,[15] thereby denying Portugal the

[15] *Monetary Gold Removed from Rome in 1943 (Italy* v. *France, United Kingdom of Great Britain and Northern Ireland and United States of America)*, Preliminary Question, ICJ Reports 1954, 19 (*Monetary Gold*).

opportunity to invoke Australia's responsibility before the International Court of Justice (ICJ or Court).[16] Before courts and tribunals, standing is a necessary but not a sufficient requirement for bringing a claim. Standing in itself, therefore, does not guarantee admissibility. It is possible to discuss invocation without resort to standing, since one could envisage a direct link between injury and legal interest *erga omnes (partes)* and invocation. Once injury or legal interest is established, the right to invoke follows. However, conceptually, the interjection of standing fulfils the important function of stabilising the legal framework: standing follows when certain conditions are met. These conditions may be the same as those applicable to invocation, but whether invocation also follows depends on whether the relevant state or international organisation chooses to exercise this right. In other words, standing refers to a qualification, whereas invocation is an entitlement.

International law and the ILC's Articles on responsibility of states and international organisations recognise two bases for standing. First, and most importantly, standing is derived from injury: the injured state or international organisation can invoke responsibility.[17] Second, non-injured states or organisations with a legal interest have standing due to the *erga omnes partes* or *erga omnes* nature of the obligation breached.[18] This distinction will be maintained in the present chapter. Criticism has been raised against the ILC's approach to injured states versus non-injured states with a legal interest.[19] However, this distinction, which is so essential to the ILC's approach, may play a decisive role in the context of invocation of the responsibility of a plurality of states and/or international organisations. Additionally, at present, the distinction matters because injured states and organisations have more rights with respect to claiming reparation than non-injured states and organisations.[20] Whether standing is based on injury or on a legal interest will largely be determined by the norm breached. When this norm creates a bilateral obligation, and when the breach specially affects the invoking state or

[16] *East Timor (Portugal* v. *Australia)*, Judgment, ICJ Reports 1995, 90 (*East Timor*).

[17] Article 42 ARSIWA and Article 43 ARIO, n. 5.

[18] Article 48 ARSIWA and Article 49 ARIO, ibid.

[19] For a critical note on this distinction, see B. Stern, 'The Obligation to Make Reparation', in J. Crawford, A. Pellet, and S. Olleson (eds.), *The Law of International Responsibility* (Oxford University Press, 2010), p. 563, at pp. 567–9. Given the unlikelihood of a complete revision of the ARSIWA and ARIO in this respect, this discussion will not be pursued here.

[20] See Article 48(2) ARSIWA and Article 49(4) ARIO, n. 5.

creates an interdependent regime, its breach leads to injury.[21] When it applies *erga omnes (partes)*, it gives non-injured states a legal interest. Since the primary obligations of the various members of the responsible plurality of states and/or international organisations often differ, in content and kind, the consequence is that in a complex situation involving several responsible states and/or international organisations, a state wishing to invoke the responsibility of more than one state and/or international organisation may have standing on a different basis vis-à-vis different members of this plurality. An example may be the situation of the Quartet for the Middle East: its conduct is attributable to the United States, the United Nations, Russia, and the European Union (EU) collectively. Yet, the extent to which, for instance, the ICJ's *Wall* advisory opinion[22] or the Geneva Conventions[23] are binding on each of the Quartet's members differs,[24] which may give different grounds of standing for the invocation of responsibility for the Quartet's conduct. Grave breaches of the Geneva Conventions may give standing based on legal interest, whereas non-compliance with the *Wall* advisory opinion may lead to injury. This complexity, while perhaps rare, challenges the distinction between standing based on injury and standing based on legal interest in cases involving a plurality of states with diverging primary obligations. What purpose does it serve to maintain a system in which a state or organisation, with respect to the same conduct, can be injured by one part of the plurality and affected in its legal interest by another?

[21] For the distinction between these different obligations see also section 2.1 below. On the different kinds of obligations see G. G. Fitzmaurice, ILC *Yearbook* 1957/II, 52–4; L.-A. Sicilianos, 'The Classification of Obligations and the Multilateral Dimension of the Relations of International Responsibility' (2002) 13 EJIL 1127; and C. J. Tams, *Enforcing Obligations Erga Omnes in International Law* (Cambridge University Press, 2010).

[22] *Legal Consequences of the Construction of a Wall in the Occupied Palestinian Territory*, Advisory Opinion, ICJ Reports 2004, 136 (*Wall* advisory opinion).

[23] Geneva Convention for the Amelioration of the Condition of the Wounded and Sick in Armed Forces in the Field, Geneva, 12 August 1949, in force 21 October 1950, 75 UNTS 31; Geneva Convention for the Amelioration of the Condition of the Wounded, Sick and Shipwrecked Members of Armed Forces at Sea, Geneva, 12 August 1949, in force 21 October 1950, 75 UNTS 85; Geneva Convention relative to the Treatment of Prisoners of War, Geneva, 12 August 1949, in force 21 October 1950, 75 UNTS 135; Geneva Convention relative to the Protection of Civilian Persons in Time of War, Geneva, 12 August 1949, in force 21 October 1950, 75 UNTS 287.

[24] For a more detailed analysis see J. Dugard and A. M. H. Vermeer-Künzli, 'The Elusive Allocation of Responsibility to Informal Organizations: The Case of the Quartet on the Middle East' in M. Ragazzi (ed.), *The Responsibility of International Organizations: Essays in Memory of Sir Ian Brownlie* (Leiden: Martinus Nijhoff, 2013), p. 261.

2.1 *Standing based on injury*

The structure of the law on responsibility defines three groups of injured states or organisations: the directly injured state or organisation; states or organisations that are specially affected by a breach owed to a group including that state or international organisation; and states or international organisations whose position is radically changed with respect to the further performance of the obligation due to the breach.[25] In drafting its provisions on injury, the ILC was clearly thinking of situations involving one responsible state or organisation only. While this does not necessarily disqualify the application of its rules on injury to situations involving more than one state and/or organisation, the fact remains that the two sets of Articles lack clear guidelines for situations involving a plurality of states and/or international organisations. The Commentary to Article 42 of the ARSIWA, for instance, refers exclusively to the invocation of the responsibility of *one* state. It is stated that:

> If one State violates an obligation the performance of which is owed specifically to another State, the latter is an 'injured State' in the sense of article 42. Other examples include binding unilateral acts by which one State assumes an obligation *vis-à-vis* another State; or the case of a treaty establishing obligations owed to a third State not party to the treaty.[26]

The frequent use of 'one' in this text suggests, at least, that the examples the ILC had in mind when drafting this Commentary were those involving a bilateral invocation. The Statement of the Chairman of the Drafting Committee in 2001 does not elucidate the matter. The part of the Statement on Article 43 (now Article 42) of the ARSIWA provides no explanation on whether injury can be caused by a wrongful act of more than one state. In the Statement of the Chairman of the Drafting Committee on the ARIO, it is merely mentioned that Article 42 of the ARSIWA served as a model and was used with minor linguistic

[25] Articles 42(a), 42(b)(i) and 42(b)(ii) ARSIWA; and 43(a), 43(b)(i) and 43(b)(ii) ARIO, n. 5, respectively. For the purposes of the present chapter, these three instances of injury as defined by the ILC will be followed. One could question whether cases falling under Article 42(b)(ii) ARSIWA and 42(b)(ii) ARIO really are instances of injury. As I have explained elsewhere, the distinction between injury under Article 42(b)(ii) and legal interest under 48(1)(b) is not as clear as the ILC presents it to be, which would apply *mutatis mutandis* to the relevant provisions of the ARIO. See A. M. H. Vermeer-Künzli, 'A Matter of Interest, Diplomatic Protection and State Responsibility *Erga Omnes*', n. 11, at 573–4.

[26] ARSIWA Commentary, n. 5, Article 42, at 118, para. 7.

changes.[27] Since Article 43 of the ARIO was not changed on second reading, the Statement on the final version of the ARIO does not discuss the provision.[28] Through Articles 47 of the ARSIWA and 48 of the ARIO, this framework then also applies to situations involving a plurality of responsible states and/or organisations. However, this similitude cannot be too easily presumed. Particular complexities will arise in determining the extent to which a state or organisation is individually injured, specially affected, or brought into a radically changed position due to the individualised conduct of each and every member of the plurality that is responsible for the breach. The ILC's Articles both for states and for organisations contain no indication that the rules on the determination of injury will be applied differently or less stringently in cases of a plurality of responsible states and organisations. This means that, if we assume that these Articles represent the law, standing to invoke responsibility will require a demonstration that the conduct of each and every member of the responsible plurality constitutes injury, providing the invoking state with standing. Or, as the ILC stated, 'the general principle in the case of a plurality of responsible States is that each State is separately responsible for conduct attributable to it in the sense of article 2'.[29]

Articles 47 of the ARSIWA and 48 of the ARIO complement Articles 42 of the ARSIWA and 43 of the ARIO, which provide for invocation for the injured state or organisation. Within this context, as will be explained below, the invocation of direct injury caused by the conduct involving a plurality of responsible states and/or organisations generates most complexities. The requirements of attribution of conduct and breach of an obligation for each member of the plurality of states and/or international organisations individually create a rather high threshold. Situations involving a plurality of states and/or international organisations are prone to include elements of aid and assistance, coercion, the creation of joint organs, direction and control, and composite acts. It is uncommon for states or organisations to act wrongfully in the context of a plurality without any form of coordination or cooperation. And even if

[27] Statement of the Chairman of the Drafting Committee, Mr Pedro Comissário Alfonso, 4 June 2008, at 3–4, available at http://legal.un.org/ilc/sessions/60/2008_DC_Chairman_RIO.4June2008.pdf.

[28] Statement of the Chairman of the Drafting Committee, 3 June 2011, at 28, available at http://legal.un.org/ilc/sessions/63/DCResponsibilityofInternationalOrganizations2011.pdf.

[29] ARSIWA Commentary, n. 5, Commentary to Article 47, para. 2.

that is the case, the chances of the conduct constituting a composite act are rather high.

Before we turn to the particular complexities of such a situation, it should be noted that invoking the responsibility of a plurality of states and/or international organisations may be less complicated in the event of injury based on the status of a specially affected state or organisation, or based on the radical change of the position (Article 42(b)(i) and (ii) of the ARSIWA and 43(b)(i) and (ii) of the ARIO, respectively). Interdependent regimes usually involve more than two states and/or international organisations, which necessarily increases the likelihood of a plurality of responsible entities. Especially when the regime is created for the protection of a particular area or species, the combination of obligations of prevention and obligations of result may easily lead to a plurality of responsible states and/or organisations. As an illustration, consider the following scenario, which will be referred to as scenario A: the activities of upstream states Arcadia and Utopia and possibly an international organisation contribute to pollution in downstream Ruritania. Demonstrating that the joint activities of Arcadia and Utopia in this scenario caused environmental pollution that especially affected Ruritania, because it is the downstream state of the polluted river, may be easier than proving direct injury. An obligation not to pollute rivers obviously causes the downstream state to be specially affected in case of breach, whereas it is less obvious, although not unthinkable, that it is also directly injured because of the bilateral nature of the obligation.

Returning to direct injury, the complexities of implementing responsibility for direct injury in situations involving a plurality of states and/or international organisations will affect, or even deny, standing to invoke the responsibility of all members of the plurality responsible for the breach. Requiring the individualisation of responsibility leads to particular complexities in cases involving aid and assistance, coercion, the creation of joint organs, direction and control, and situations of composite acts – especially when the accumulation of conduct is wrongful, but the separate and individual contributions are not.[30] In such cases, it is possible that various actors contribute by various courses of conduct to an outcome that is wrongful, with each member of the plurality being responsible for a piece of the puzzle which in and of itself may or may not

[30] Article 15 ARSIWA and Article 16 ARIO, n. 5.

be wrongful. Obviously, the conduct of joint organs is attributable to the creators of the organ in question, but the question of breach may still be complex when the joint organ is involved in a composite act. In such situations, it will often not be possible to hold all members involved in the situation equally responsible.

To illustrate the complexity of situations involving aid and assistance, let us consider the following scenario, which we will call scenario B. An international organisation, of which the relevant states are members, has issued a resolution obliging these states to take measures against terrorism, both in the form of prevention and the actual prosecution of terrorist suspects. An individual is captured in the territory of Arcadia and, without any form of due process, is transferred by Arcadian officials to the territory of Ruritania. Here, she is detained and tortured by officials from Arcadia and Utopia, with the knowledge of Ruritanian officials and in Ruritanian detention facilities. The individual has the nationality of Bellaria. The state aiding or assisting in the wrongful act of another state, as is the case of Ruritania,[31] can only be held responsible for its aid and assistance, and not for the conduct of the aided or assisted states. Under the present rules, Bellaria is not injured by a breach of the prohibition on torture by Ruritania. For composite acts, consider scenario A, described above, as one not involving a specially affected state, but one of direct injury. To invoke the responsibility of Arcadia and Utopia for the pollution, Ruritania has two options. It can either demonstrate that this is a case of a composite act, or that each and every act by Arcadia and Utopia in itself is wrongful. It has been argued that a composite act requires intent,[32] which, if applied to two or more responsible parties, will present an important hurdle, especially for the purpose of proof. These examples demonstrate the difficulty of invoking the responsibility of all members of a plurality for the situation as a whole. The pertinent question is, of course, whether that is problematic. To the extent that we may know what the ILC considered when it drafted the Articles on Responsibility, its work does not show much concern with this consequence, so perhaps it did not think it was a problem. The

[31] For the sake of argument, the obvious obligation of due diligence resting on Ruritania with respect to its territory and harmful effects on other states will be left aside, since the focus is on responsibility for the act of torture.

[32] J. Salmon, 'Duration of the Breach', in J. Crawford, A. Pellet, and S. Olleson (eds.), *The Law of International Responsibility* (Oxford University Press, 2010), p. 383, at p. 392.

consequence logically follows from Article 2 of the ARSIWA, which arguably provides the very foundation of international responsibility.

Even so, it is submitted that the system as designed in the ARSIWA and the ARIO is too crude. Chopping up a claim into its different parts may diminish the weight of the claim as a whole. This is somewhat analogous to composite breaches, where the sum of the conduct is more than each of the parts taken together. In other words, the Bellarian national in scenario B has suffered an extraordinary accumulation of injuries and it would seem somewhat to miss the magnitude of the breach if, due to requirements of standing, admissibility, and jurisdiction, Bellaria could only invoke the responsibility of Ruritania for its aid and assistance. It is admittedly difficult to envisage a system that provides for such scenarios. The solution could be found in changing the rules on invocation, for instance by weakening the requirement of 'individualisable' conduct. A stronger version of Article 16 of the ARSIWA would be another solution, lowering the threshold of complicity. Finally, a stricter regime included in primary obligations, lowering the threshold of the breach in the first place, might make it easier to invoke the responsibility of each member of the plurality. All of these solutions, however, are not to be expected to develop soon.

2.2 *Standing* erga omnes (partes)

In addition to standing derived from injury, non-injured states and international organisations with a legal interest have standing to invoke responsibility when the obligation is one owed *erga omnes partes* or *erga omnes*, as provided for in Articles 48 of the ARSIWA and 49 of the ARIO.[33] While the notion of obligations *erga omnes (partes)* is firmly established in international law,[34] the instances of successful invocation of responsibility by a state or international organisation deriving standing on this basis are

[33] It should be noted that standing *erga omnes* and *erga omnes partes* for international organisations is governed by the principle of speciality and is thus limited to obligations falling within the function of the international organisation (Article 49(3) ARIO, n. 5). While this may in fact limit the possibilities of an international organisation to invoke responsibility *erga omnes (partes)*, this issue will not be further discussed.

[34] *Barcelona Traction, Light and Power Company, Limited (Belgium* v. *Spain)*, Second Phase, ICJ Reports 1970, 3 (*Barcelona Traction* case); *Questions Relating to the Obligations to Prosecute or Extradite (Belgium* v. *Senegal)*, Judgment, ICJ Reports 2012, 422 (*Belgium* v. *Senegal* case).

few.[35] This, however, is not caused by the particular intricacies of the rules on invoking injury based on a breach of an obligation *erga omnes (partes)*, but rather by disputes on the status of the rule granting standing *erga omnes (partes)* as such,[36] the fact that most forums in which responsibility may be invoked (courts and tribunals) raise procedural obstacles to such invocation,[37] and perhaps because of a reluctance of states and international organisations to instigate procedures when they are not (directly) injured. For the purpose of invocation of responsibility of a plurality of states and/or international organisations, standing based on the nature of the obligation breached is, perhaps unexpectedly, less complicated than standing derived from injury. Standing in the former scenario is based on the nature of the norm breached and the membership of the relevant group or the international community, which for all intents and purposes will be easier to establish than injury. Once it has been determined that the relevant primary norm is one that applies *erga omnes* or *erga omnes partes*, all that is left is the determination of whether the state or international organisation invoking responsibility is part of the relevant *omnes*,[38] and the complexities will primarily relate to determining the contribution to the breach. Consider the situation in which a military operation organised by an international organisation and Arcadia and/or Utopia causes damage that cannot be justified under international humanitarian law to the civilian population, the cultural heritage, or the natural resources of Bellaria.[39] In this scenario, which will be referred to as scenario C, any

[35] This section will not distinguish between obligations *erga omnes* and obligations *erga omnes partes*. For an analysis of this distinction see Tams, *Enforcing Obligations Erga Omnes*, n. 21.

[36] While Article 48 ARSIWA and Article 49 ARIO, n. 5, were introduced in an exercise of progressive development, the notion of standing *erga omnes (partes)* was hardly new, nor particularly contested. Standing *erga omnes* was confirmed in the *Barcelona Traction* case, n. 34, (para. 3 of the judgment) and in *East Timor*, n. 16 (para. 29 of the judgment). For confirmation of the concept of standing *erga omnes (partes)* see the *Belgium* v. *Senegal* case, n. 34, in which the Court acknowledged the legal interest of all states parties to observance of the relevant obligation (paras. 68–9 of the judgment). See generally Tams, *Enforcing Obligations Erga Omnes*, n. 21.

[37] *Armed Activities on the Territory of the Congo (New Application: 2002) (Democratic Republic of the Congo* v. *Rwanda)*, Jurisdiction and Admissibility, ICJ Reports 2006, 6; *Arrest Warrant of 11 April 2000 (Democratic Republic of the Congo* v. *Belgium)*, Judgment, ICJ Reports 2002, 3; *East Timor*, n. 16. See also below section 3.2.

[38] See on invocation *erga omnes* and *erga omnes partes* generally Vermeer-Künzli, 'A Matter of Interest, Diplomatic Protection and State Responsibility *Erga Omnes*', n. 11.

[39] Although it is too early to assess the situation, it is possible that the crisis in Mali of 2013 would result in shared responsibility between France, the Economic Community of

state will have standing to invoke the responsibility of Arcadia, Utopia, and the international organisation for serious violations of international humanitarian law, if it can be proven that the conduct is attributable to all three of them.

In the ILC Articles on Responsibility, Articles 47 of the ARSIWA and 48 of the ARIO on the invocation of shared responsibility precede the provisions on invocation *erga omnes (partes)*. On that basis, the argument could be made that the ILC did not envisage invocation by a non-injured state with a legal interest in responsibility of a plurality of states and/or international organisations. Yet that is an overly enthusiastic exercise on close reading. Bearing in mind that both Article 47 and Article 48 were added after the adoption on first reading, the order in which they appear now in the ARSIWA is probably not intended to express the view that the responsibility of a plurality of states and/or international organisations cannot be invoked on the basis of a legal interest. Another round of revisions would perhaps have changed the order or otherwise have clarified that under Article 48, invocation is also possible against a plurality, for instance by expressly saying so in the Commentaries.

3. Admissibility

Under international law, invocation of responsibility is not limited to judicial procedures. Even though there seems to be some disagreement in the ILC as to what constitutes the presentation of a claim, it is clear that invocation can be done through diplomatic channels.[40] Thus, for invocation, the establishment of injury or standing based on the *erga omnes (partes)* nature of the norm may be sufficient. In practice, however, state responsibility finds implementation through judicial procedures. In such situations, the rules of courts and tribunals on jurisdiction and admissibility may influence the possibility of invoking responsibility. In addition, international claims are not limited to direct claims, but may involve the invocation of responsibility for injury inflicted upon individuals, which have their own additional rules on admissibility.

West African States, and the African Union, if their conduct were to constitute a breach of their international obligations.

[40] See the discrepancy between the Commentary to Article 42 of the ARSIWA, n. 5, which in paragraph 2 states that 'protest as such is not an invocation of responsibility', and the Commentary to Article 1 of the Draft Articles on Diplomatic Protection, ILC *Yearbook* 2006/II(2), which, in paragraph 8, explicitly includes protest as a way to exercise diplomatic protection, which it defines as the invocation of state responsibility.

The following discussion will be limited to those issues of admissibility that are particularly relevant in the context of shared responsibility. First, international law imposes additional conditions for the admissibility of claims based on indirect injury: the nationality of claims rule and the exhaustion of local remedies rule. Second, particular courts and tribunals have rules on admissibility that may complicate claims against a plurality of respondent states or organisations. In this part, the focus will be on the ICJ and the European Court of Human Rights (ECtHR), with a short section on the World Trade Organization (WTO) dispute settlement system.

3.1 Admissibility of indirect claims

In suggesting that the general rules of invocation are applicable also to claims involving a plurality of responsible states and/or international organisations, the ILC in its relevant Articles has not considered the effect of these rules on such claims. This becomes acutely relevant in the case of indirect claims.[41] These are usually presented in the exercise of diplomatic protection by states on behalf of their nationals. This section will therefore be limited to inter-state claims.[42] Indirect claims must comply with two additional rules that do not apply to direct claims: the

[41] In this section, indirect claims will refer to claims made by states against states and/or international organisations for injury inflicted on the former's nationals.

[42] International organisations are capable of protecting their 'nationals', i.e. their officials, but this is usually called functional protection (see *Reparation for Injuries Suffered in the Service of the United Nations*, Advisory Opinion, ICJ Reports 1949, 174). In such cases, there cannot be a nationality of claims rule and the local remedies rule is inapplicable due to the immunities available for the officials of international organisations. They cannot commence resorting to local remedies to present their claim. For international organisations, there is in this respect no distinction between direct and indirect claims. On the other hand, states have increasingly attempted to protect their nationals against acts of international organisations, especially in the context of the listing of suspected terrorists. While this is sometimes called diplomatic protection, it is hardly comparable. In these cases, the nationality of claims rule will apply, but not the local remedies rule, since the injured individual cannot present a claim under domestic law against the international organisation, again due to its immunity. In this context, see the *Sayadi & Vinck* cases concerning Belgian nationals on the terrorist lists imposed by the UN Security Council (*Sayadi & Vinck* v. *l'Etat Belge*, Tribunal de première instance de Bruxelles, decision of 18 February 2005) and the various *Kadi* cases before the European Court of Justice, *Kadi and Al Barakaat International Foundation* v. *Council of the European Union and Commission of the European Communities*, joined cases C-402/05 P and C-415/05 P, [2008] 3 CMLR 41.

nationality of claims rule and the local remedies rule,[43] which will be discussed in this order.

The nationality of claims rule restricts the invocation of responsibility to the state of nationality of the injured individual. While the nationality of claims rule has evolved to increase the number of eligible individuals, particularly with respect to multiple nationals in claims against a state of nationality and *mutatis mutandis* with respect to stateless persons and refugees, some restrictions still apply.[44] In particular, states may not exercise protection against the predominant state of nationality. Increasing the number of responsible states will increase the likelihood of claims against a state of nationality. This, in turn, may render claims against a plurality of states inadmissible with respect to the state part of the plurality of which the injured individual is a national. Under normal circumstances, however, that should not affect the remainder of the claim and the responsibility of the other members of the plurality. In addition, it also has no effect on the *responsibility* of the state of nationality against which the claim is presented. The nationality of claims rule is not a substantive requirement of responsibility. Although the doctrine of non-responsibility for injury against nationals enjoyed some support in the past, this doctrine has now by and large been abandoned, especially in light of the emergence of human rights law. Torture is prohibited, regardless of against whom it is committed.[45] Therefore, it will affect the admissibility of the claim, and thus prevent invocation of responsibility, yet will not affect the responsibility as such.

With respect to the local remedies rule, when it is applied strictly, increasing the number of responsible states will increase the number of national remedies to be exhausted in equal measure. In the concrete example of scenario B, the tortured Bellarian national would be required to exhaust local remedies in Ruritania, Arcadia, and Utopia before her state of nationality could espouse the claim. This, however, may be contrary to the notion of reasonableness on which the rule arguably relies and which limits exhaustion to remedies that are reasonably available to the injured individual.[46] The lack of detail in the ARSIWA

[43] See Article 44 ARSIWA and Article 44 ARIO, n. 5.

[44] See A. M. H. Vermeer-Künzli, 'Nationality and Diplomatic Protection, a Reappraisal', in S. Forlati and A. Annoni (eds.), *The Changing Role of Nationality* (London: Routledge, 2013), p. 76.

[45] Ibid.

[46] See Article 15 of the Draft Articles on Diplomatic Protection and accompanying Commentary, paragraph 3, n. 40. See also J. Paulsson, *Denial of Justice in International*

and the ARIO[47] concerning admissibility of indirect claims in the case of a plurality of responsible states is particularly problematic in this regard. There is no obvious solution. Some measure of exhaustion of local remedies must be retained, but to require complete exhaustion vis-à-vis all entities involved would be too demanding. It should be noted here that, contrary to the nationality of claims rule, the ARIO also contain a requirement regarding exhaustion of remedies. Before a claim against an international organisation is admissible, the injured individual is required to exhaust 'any available and effective remedy provided by that organization'.[48]

If we assume that exhausting all available remedies is too much to ask in the light of some measure of reasonableness in the application of the local remedies rule, there are theoretically two ways in which the number could be brought down. First, some of the states and/or organisations against which the claim was brought could waive the requirement to exhaust local remedies. This would be highly unlikely. The case law of the ICJ and the ECtHR shows that the requirement to exhaust local remedies is not taken lightly, and that respondent states usually try to object to admissibility for failure to comply with this requirement.[49] The only way to achieve a limiting of the number of instances to be exhausted would be to oblige some states to waive the requirement to exhaust local remedies in cases of invocation of shared responsibility, but it would be challenging to determine which state must waive its right. It is far from clear what criteria should be applied for such determination. One could think of limiting exhaustion of local remedies to the state on the territory of which the injury was inflicted, to the state whose remedies would be most easily accessible to the individual, to the state whose breaches were

Law (Cambridge University Press, 2005), p. 118, and A. M. H. Vermeer-Künzli, 'As If: The Legal Fiction in Diplomatic Protection' (2007) 18 EJIL 37, at 52–5.

47 Articles 44 and 45 respectively, n. 5. Please note that this discussion will not address the question of whether international organisations can exercise diplomatic protection, or whether that should be termed functional protection (see Draft Articles on Diplomatic Protection, Introduction to the Commentary, para. 2, n. 40). Since the issue is not whether they can exercise protection, but what the conditions are for invoking responsibility against a plurality of responsible states, this question is not an essential one to answer.

48 Article 44(2) ARIO, n. 5.

49 See *Interhandel (Switzerland* v. *United States of America)*, Preliminary Objections, ICJ Reports 1959, 6; *Elettronica Sicula S.p.A (ELSI) (United States of America* v. *Italy)*, Judgment, ICJ Reports 1989, 15; *Ahmadou Sadio Diallo (Republic of Guinea* v. *Democratic Republic of the Congo)*, Preliminary Objections, ICJ Reports 2007, 582. See also *Akdivar and others* v. *Turkey*, App. No. 21893/93 (ECtHR, 16 September 1996).

most serious, and perhaps to states on yet other grounds. Even so, there is no international rule, principle, or even practice to provide a foundation for such limitation. Second, the states and/or organisations involved in an indirect claim could agree to join the cases and submit to the jurisdiction of one of the states. Thus the domestic courts of one of the states included in the plurality would entertain a case also involving the claims against the other states and/or international organisations. This is also a very unlikely scenario, especially in light of the continuing importance attached to immunities.[50] In scenario B, the conduct of all entities is connected to such an extent that prioritising is difficult, and even if prioritising were possible, all entities would still be entitled to claim immunities.

International law does offer some exceptions to the requirement to exhaust local remedies. They are listed in Article 15 of the ILC Draft Articles on Diplomatic Protection (ADP).[51] Apart from the waiver provided for in Article 15(e), the only exception that could possibly be of some avail is the one based on the absence of a relevant connection, Article 15(c) of the ADP. The example given in the Commentaries to this provision is one of transboundary pollution, more specifically the nuclear fallout after the Chernobyl accident. Assuming that the accident constituted a breach of Russia's obligations, it would be unreasonable to require Scottish farmers whose crops were contaminated by the nuclear fallout to exhaust local Russian remedies.[52] Similarly, in scenario A described above, should the injury be indirect, the injured individuals arguably would not have to exhaust local remedies in Arcadia and Utopia. However, these exceptions provide no solution to the issue of a multiplicity of local judicial systems to which to resort: it will depend on the facts of the case. If the individual in scenario B happened to have

[50] See *Jurisdictional Immunities of the State (Germany* v. *Italy: Greece intervening)*, Judgment, ICJ Reports 2012, 99.

[51] Draft Articles on Diplomatic Protection, ILC *Yearbook* 2006/II(2) (ADP).

[52] Commentary to Draft Articles on Diplomatic Protection, Article 15(c), para. 7, n. 40. This case may to some extent be a mixed claim, in the sense that the United Kingdom could argue direct injury resulting from the environmental damage. In a mixed claim, the part that addressed individual, indirect injury still requires compliance with the local remedies rule and the nationality of claims rule. Article 15(c) was specifically designed to address situations in which the connection between the wrongdoer and the injured individual was absent or very weak, because the law on diplomatic protection does not otherwise recognise exceptions such as one based on the fact that there is a difference here between the place of origin of the injury and the place of the resulting damage.

some connection to Utopia, Article 15(c) of the ADP would not apply and she would be required to exhaust local remedies there, too. A judge confronted with this issue would have very little choice. The requirement of reasonableness in the application of the local remedies rule is not hierarchically superior to issues such as immunities. The availability of any exception to the local remedies rule will depend on whether the facts allow this.

As this section has demonstrated, the rules on admissibility of indirect claims, particularly the nationality of claims rule and the local remedies rule, have not been adapted to situations involving more than one responsible state and/or international organisation. At the same time, they have the potential for creating nigh insurmountable hurdles for invoking the responsibility of all members of the plurality of states and/or organisations responsible for the internationally wrongful act(s). The rules and principles on international responsibility of states and international organisations and general principles of international law, however, do not at present offer a clear path towards a lessening of these hurdles.

3.2 Admissibility before international courts and a plurality of respondent states

The rules of jurisdiction and admissibility applicable to international courts and tribunals may further complicate invocation of responsibility of a plurality of states and/or international organisations.[53] The *Monetary Gold* principle is a clear example of such a rule. While invocation is not limited to judicial settlement and can also be effectuated through diplomatic channels, the obstacles applicable to invoking the responsibility for a plurality of states and/or international organisations in established dispute settlement mechanisms will affect the implementation of state responsibility most obviously.[54] Although this contribution is not concerned with

[53] In this section, the focus will be on respondent states, since the practice of international courts and tribunals of adjudicating claims involving international organisations is almost non-existent. The exception is the WTO dispute settlement system, which will be discussed. The ICJ and the ECtHR have as yet no jurisdiction to entertain claims against international organisations.

[54] Taken more broadly, the *Monetary Gold* rule (see n. 15) could be applicable to diplomatic settlement as well: in scenario B, Arcadia could raise objections against a diplomatic settlement between Ruritania and Bellaria including a statement on the (il)legality of Arcadia's conduct.

procedural aspects of shared responsibility,[55] some discussion on the extent to which these aspects affect invocation as such is necessary.

It will be impossible to discuss all relevant courts and tribunals, and therefore the discussion will be limited to the ICJ and the ECtHR. A few comments will also be made on the WTO dispute settlement system.

3.2.1 The ICJ

At the ICJ, no inherent obstacles exist to invoke the responsibility of more than one state. Yet, the ICJ Statute and rules and procedures contain no special rules for cases involving a plurality of states. States are free to join cases in the sense that they may bring an application against more than one state. The rules do not provide for *ex post* joinder by states, although such joinder will probably be feasible with the consent of all parties involved.[56] Article 47 of the Rules of the Court does allow the Court to join cases, and gives it some margin of discretion in deciding whether or not to join two or more cases.[57]

The question that concerns us here will involve the application of one state against two or more co-responsible states. Practice until now has actually demonstrated that such an injured state wishing to invoke the responsibility of more than one state can bring multiple applications, rather than one case against a plurality of respondents. An example of this practice is the *Legality of Use of Force* case, brought by Serbia and Montenegro against ten different states that had all participated in the North Atlantic Treaty Organization (NATO) bombings of the former Yugoslavia. While Serbia and Montenegro mentioned the other applications in each of them, it did not join these applications.[58] Also, the Democratic Republic of the Congo (DRC) launched three separate cases,

[55] On this, see the collection of papers in the *Themed Section: Procedural Aspects of Shared Responsibility in International Adjudication* (2013) 4(2) JIDS 277.

[56] Although this is not specifically provided for, this can be derived *a contrario* from the decision of the Court not to join in the face of objections of the parties. See M. Paparinskis, 'Procedural Aspects of Shared Responsibility in the International Court of Justice' (2013) 4(2) JIDS 295, at 304.

[57] Ibid., at 303–5. Serbia and Montenegro could perhaps not have joined all cases, since the alleged basis for jurisdiction differed for some states. The Court could have joined some of the cases as well, but apparently did not see the need.

[58] E.g. *Legality of Use of Force (Federal Republic of Yugoslavia* v. *United States of America)*, Application of the Federal Republic of Yugoslavia, ICJ Reports 1999, p. 1. Serbia and Montenegro could perhaps not have joined all cases, since the alleged basis for jurisdiction differed for some states. The Court could have joined some of the cases as well, but apparently did not see the need.

against Rwanda, Uganda, and Burundi respectively, concerning the ongoing armed hostilities on its territory in the late 1990s; Libya had two cases, against the United States and the United Kingdom, concerning the Lockerbie incident of 21 December 1988; and Nicaragua brought one claim against Honduras and one against Costa Rica for armed activities at its borders in the 1980s. This shows that the relevant applicants apparently felt the need to bring individual cases, whereas they all referred to the same underlying conflict involving a plurality of parties. The Court has approached such issues on a case-by-case basis.

In the *Legality of Use of Force* cases, the hearings were held together, but the various states involved submitted individual memorials and the Court issued individual decisions, even though these were often identical. Arguably, this is the case that comes closest to a 'real' shared responsibility case, because the NATO member states had acted together with a single wrongful outcome. This was actually used as an argument against the jurisdiction of the Court. The Netherlands argued that NATO's actions were collective, and that any determination on the lawfulness of the Netherlands' participation 'will necessarily, unavoidably and logically involve a determination by the Court of the alleged unlawfulness of the action of an international organization or of States which are not present before the Court'.[59] The ICJ eventually declined to exercise its jurisdiction on other grounds and thus did not consider this argument.

In the cases concerning the DRC, the Court issued three separate judgments. This was, amongst other reasons, due to the fact that the bases for jurisdiction of the Court vis-à-vis Rwanda, Uganda, and Burundi were not identical. The DRC relied on a number of treaties, including the Genocide Convention,[60] in its case against Rwanda;[61] it relied on its declaration under Article 36(2) of the Statute of the Court in the case against Uganda; and it invited Burundi to accept the jurisdiction for this case under what is

[59] *Legality of Use of Force* case *(Federal Republic of Yugoslavia* v. *The Netherlands)*, Preliminary Objections of the Kingdom of The Netherlands, ICJ Reports 2000, para. 7.2.13.

[60] Convention on the Prevention and Punishment of the Crime of Genocide, Paris, 9 December 1948, in force 12 January 1951, 78 UNTS 277 (Genocide Convention).

[61] It should be added that the initial proceedings against Rwanda were identical to those against Burundi, but in light of Rwanda's memorial and the apparent futility of the case, the DRC instituted new proceedings in 2002, this time based on a number of specific treaties, including the Genocide Convention. *Armed Activities on the Territory of the Congo (New Application: 2002) (Democratic Republic of the Congo* v. *Rwanda)*, n. 37.

known as *forum prorogatum*, where it concerned the use of force, and under the CAT[62] and the Montreal Convention,[63] which include dispute settlement clauses.[64] The DRC started each of the three applications with a reference to the fact that it was also bringing a claim against the other two states.[65] However, since Rwanda, Uganda, and Burundi allegedly supported different armed groups engaged in the use of force on the territory of the DRC, the question of whether the acts complained of were attributable to the relevant states required separate analyses. It is difficult to say whether this informed the DRC's decision to submit three different cases. It would perhaps be somewhat of a stretch to prove that the governments of Rwanda, Burundi, and Uganda conspired in an attempt to attack the Congo to add an element of joint wrongful enterprise, and the DRC chose to argue that they independently sought to benefit from the lack of control of the Congolese authorities over the eastern part of this vast country. In the applications, the arguments were limited to the individual states, except for the note on the first page that applications had been brought against the two other states as well. In the memorials on behalf of the DRC, the individuality of the applications was emphasised to avoid the implications of the *Monetary Gold* rule: they presented arguments on the alleged wrongful conduct of one respondent only.[66] The wrongful conduct of Rwanda, Uganda, and Burundi was perhaps not shared, and the DRC did not try to make it seem that way.

These examples clearly support the individualised approach to responsibility as found in the work of the ILC. The responsibility of each participant is invoked separately and determined on the basis of an individual analysis of attribution of conduct and breach. In none of these cases did the fact that other parties were involved influence the standing of the applicant. On the basis of this observation, however, the only valid

[62] Convention Against Torture and Other Cruel, Inhuman or Degrading Treatment or Punishment, New York, 10 December 1984, in force 26 June 1987, 1465 UNTS 85 (CAT).

[63] Montreal Convention for the Unification of Certain Rules for International Carriage by Air, Montreal, 28 May 1999, in force 4 November 2003, 2242 UNTS 309.

[64] *Armed Activities on the Territory of the Congo (Democratic Republic of the Congo* v. *Burundi)*, Application of the Democratic Republic of the Congo, ICJ Reports 1999, at 11.

[65] Ibid., at 2; *Armed Activities on the Territory of the Congo (Democratic Republic of the Congo* v. *Rwanda)*, Application of the Democratic Republic of the Congo, ICJ Reports 1999, p. 2; *Armed Activities on the Territory of the Congo (Democratic Republic of the Congo* v. *Uganda)*, Application of the Democratic Republic of the Congo, ICJ Reports 1999, at 2.

[66] *Armed Activities on the Territory of the Congo (Democratic Republic of the Congo* v. *Uganda)*, Mémoire de la République Démocratique du Congo, Vol. I, July 2000, para. 0.29.

conclusion is that states have not brought cases against more than one state invoking shared responsibility. It does not allow for the conclusion that they cannot do so, nor inform us about any additional rules, such as a different approach to the exhaustion of local remedies, that may apply in such cases. This lack of practice adds to the silence in the Articles of the ILC and emphasises the difficulty in clarifying the implications of 'shared-ness' for the invocation of responsibility.

The only case that was brought against a plurality of respondents in fact provided the most important obstacle to the invocation of shared responsibility. In the *Monetary Gold* case, Italy brought a complaint against France, the United Kingdom, and the United States, but not Albania.[67] The Court considered that Albania's 'legal interests would not only be affected by a decision, but would form the very subject-matter of the decision', and for that reason declined to give judgment.[68] Without entering into a discussion on the rule itself, some aspects of it must be discussed here.[69] While highly relevant for the jurisdiction of the ICJ, the importance of the rule outside this context must not be over-estimated, because the application of the *Monetary Gold* rule does not bear on the international responsibility of the members of the plurality. However, in cases of truly shared responsibility, a decision on the merits of the claim will necessarily involve a statement on the legality of the conduct of other members of the plurality. Returning to scenario B, a finding that Ruritania is responsible for violating its due diligence obligation not to allow torture to occur on its territory requires a determination of Arcadia and Utopia's conduct as being contrary to the prohibition of torture. Given the limited number of states that have accepted the Court's compulsory jurisdiction, it will usually be the case that an injured state or a state with a legal interest cannot force all members of the plurality to appear at the ICJ. The application of the *Monetary Gold* rule in cases involving shared responsibility, which, as stated above, will usually necessitate a statement on the wrongfulness of the conduct of other members of the responsible plurality, will then effectively prevent the entire case from proceeding to the merits, as happened in the *East Timor* case.[70]

[67] *Monetary Gold*, n. 15. [68] Ibid., at 32.

[69] For more details see Paparinskis, 'Procedural Aspects of Shared Responsibility in the International Court of Justice', n. 56, at 305–17.

[70] *East Timor*, n. 16, at 393.

As the practice before the ICJ also shows, this outcome can only be avoided if the situation can be broken down into smaller parts, as the DRC did in its claims on the war fought on its territory. If a claimant can thus invoke the responsibility of one member of the plurality for one aspect of the situation only, the *Monetary Gold* rule will not constitute a fatal obstacle. Nevertheless, as with the issue of injury described above in section 2.1, if the situation is divided into different smaller claims this may, and often will, fail to do justice to the situation as a whole, especially when some aspects remain beyond the reach of the Court. If, in scenario B, for reasons of consent to jurisdiction, the ICJ could only hear a case against Ruritania, it would be difficult to envisage any meaningful substance brought to the dispute. Any claim not addressing the issue of torture would fail to address the essence of the case. The conclusion is therefore inevitable that the operation of the *Monetary Gold* rule will have serious consequences for the scope of the dispute before the Court *ratione materiae* in cases of shared responsibility and, with that, for the invocation of responsibility more generally. Claims, or parts thereof, may be declared inadmissible and responsibility for the relevant wrongful act cannot be invoked. Unlike in cases before the ECtHR, which will be explained below, the effect of the rule may be that a matter that falls within the jurisdiction of the ICJ *ratione materiae* and *ratione loci* cannot be heard because one member of the plurality of responsible states has not consented to the jurisdiction. Some have expressed more optimism. For instance, Paparinskis wrote, in the context of the ICJ's handling of cases involving shared responsibility, that 'one hopes that future developments will display greater sensitivity to these matters'.[71] He argued that '[p]ositive law permits certain improvements, particularly regarding joinders and *Monetary Gold*, and an appreciation of the systemic perspective might lead to gradual reordering of these rules.'[72] The author is unable to share this optimism. States rarely subject themselves to the jurisdiction of the ICJ if they are not required to[73] and they will seize any opportunity to dispute admissibility. At present, plenty of opportunities to do so are available. A joinder of cases will provide no solution when the *Monetary Gold* rule applies and the hesitancy of the

[71] Paparinskis, 'Procedural Aspects of Shared Responsibility in the International Court of Justice', n. 56, at 318.

[72] Ibid.

[73] Witness the only case relying on *forum prorogatum* being the case between Djibouti and France. See *Certain Questions of Mutual Assistance in Criminal Matters (Djibouti* v. *France)*, Judgment, ICJ Reports 2008, 177.

Court to join cases does not bode well for the future.[74] With the Court's continuing emphasis on consent to jurisdiction, this situation is unlikely to change.[75]

3.2.2 The ECtHR

The situation at the ECtHR, though better than at the ICJ, is far from perfect when it comes to appreciating the special nature of cases involving a plurality of responsible states.[76] The ECtHR's statutes and rules of procedure, like the ICJ, contain no inherent prohibition on claims against more than one state, and in fact it has decided cases against more than one state[77] and even held one or both states responsible.[78] However, it has little to no separate provisions for claims involving a plurality of respondent states.[79] Although some rules of procedure exist to facilitate claims involving a plurality of respondent states – such as the appointment of one judge to represent all instead of multiple judges ad hoc and the possibility of joining complaints – it has not developed any rules that address the fundamental issues of standing, admissibility, and

[74] The Court did join two cases relatively recently, but that example is irrelevant for the present purposes: it concerned the joinder of a case brought by Nicaragua against Costa Rica and a case brought by Costa Rica against Nicaragua. These cases could relatively easily be construed as a claim and a counterclaim. This is hardly comparable to joining claims of one applicant against a plurality of states. See International Court of Justice, Press Release no. 2013/10 of 23 April 2013, *Certain Activities carried out by Nicaragua in the Border Area (Costa Rica* v. *Nicaragua) Construction of a Road in Costa Rica along the San Juan River (Nicaragua* v. *Costa Rica) The Court joins the proceedings in the two cases*, available at www.icj-cij.org.

[75] See e.g. *Armed Activities on the Territory of the Congo (New Application: 2002) (Democratic Republic of the Congo* v. *Rwanda)*, n. 37, Separate Opinion Judge ad hoc John Dugard, at 86–94.

[76] M. den Heijer, 'Procedural Aspects of Shared Responsibility in the European Court of Human Rights', SHARES Research Paper 17 (2012), ACIL 2012, available at www.sharesproject.nl; also published in the *Themed Section: Procedural Aspects of Shared Responsibility in International Adjudication*, (2013) 4(2) JIDS 361.

[77] Most prominently, with respect to the application and the number of respondents, is perhaps the *Banković* case: *Banković a.o.* v. *Belgium and 16 other states*, App. No. 52207/99 (ECtHR, 2 May 2007).

[78] See *Ilaşcu a.o.* v. *Moldova and Russia*, App. No. 48787/99 (ECtHR, 8 July 2004); *M.S.S.* v. *Belgium and Greece*, App. No. 30696/09 (ECtHR, 21 January 2011); and *Rantsev* v. *Cyprus and Russia*, App. No. 25965/04 (ECtHR, 7 January 2010) (*Rantsev*).

[79] This section will not include a discussion on the co-respondent mechanism, which is being developed to address cases involving claims against the EU and its member states. For an analysis see Den Heijer, 'Procedural Aspects of Shared Responsibility in the European Court of Human Rights', n. 76.

responsibility. It will usually consider admissibility, both on the merits and on issues such as the local remedies rule, separately for all respondent states and apply the same standards as in cases against one respondent. In the *Stojkovic* case, which involved a claim against Belgium and France, this resulted in the inadmissibility of the claim against Belgium and the admissibility of the claim against France, which was eventually upheld.[80] In the *Rantsev* case, the ECtHR also considered the complaints against Russia and Cyprus separately. The ECtHR has even joined cases that had some connection, such as the cases of *Behrami* and *Saramati*, but in its consideration dealt with each claim and each respondent separately.[81] Especially in cases involving complex coordination of activities, such as aid and assistance, where one state inflicts the actual injury, but other states significantly contribute by assisting in the wrongful act, the ECtHR will often decline to exercise its jurisdiction against the aiding or assisting state due to its admissibility requirements. Most importantly, such cases will fail on the question of jurisdiction *ratione personae*, since the aiding or assisting state will successfully argue that it lacked effective control over the conduct resulting in injury and that it, therefore, did not fall within the ECtHR's jurisdiction under Article 1 of the European Convention on Human Rights (ECHR).[82]

The jurisdiction of the ECtHR is, like the ICJ's, based on consent. This consent is obtained when states ratify the ECHR and thereby consent to the ECtHR's jurisdiction. Therefore, the indispensable third party rule also applies, because the ECtHR will not exercise its jurisdiction over a state that has not consented to it and thus the rule will also influence the admissibility of cases brought to this Court. However, for our present purposes, it is not particularly significant. This has two causes. First, due to the compulsory jurisdiction of the ECtHR over all contracting parties to the ECHR, complainants can always present their claim against as many of the contracting parties to the Convention as they wish, which will prevent the exclusion of any indispensable third party. To some extent, it is thus up to the applicant to make sure that all relevant states are included in the application. Second, if the claim involves conduct of a

80 *Stojkovic* v. *France and Belgium*, App. No. 25303/08 (ECtHR, 27 October 2011), para. 40, on the non-admissibility against Belgium, and para. 57, for the finding that France had violated the Convention.

81 *Agim Behrami and Bekir Behrami* v. *France* and *Ruzhdi Saramati* v. *France Germany and Norway*, App. No. 71412/01 and App. No. 78166/01 (ECtHR, 2 May 2007).

82 See *Tugar* v. *Italy*, App. No. 22869/93 (ECtHR, 18 October 1995) and *Aziz* v. *Cyprus, Greece, Turkey and the United Kingdom*, App. No. 69949/01 (ECtHR, 23 April 2002).

non-contracting party, this part of the claim will be inadmissible, because the ECtHR obviously has no jurisdiction.[83] While this may in individual cases result in the inadmissibility of the entire claim, especially when the contracting party involved was aiding or assisting the non-contracting party, this is inevitable since international law in general does not allow the imposition of treaty obligations on non-parties to the treaty. No responsibility will arise. This is different from preventing a complaint against a state that is bound by the obligation, but has not consented to the relevant dispute settlement mechanism, because such a state is responsible under international law. In this sense, the effect of the rule is perhaps less frustrating. As long as the claimant ensures that it includes all relevant states in the application, the claim will only be declared inadmissible because of the *Monetary Gold* rule when entertaining the claim would mean holding a state responsible for breach of an obligation that was not binding upon that state.

In conclusion, the case law of the ECtHR has not provided much guidance on the particular issue of invoking shared responsibility. It receives complaints against a plurality of responsible states, but discusses the complaints on an individualised basis and has thereby not developed a special approach, such as a lowering of the number of local remedies to be exhausted, because of the number of respondents. For all intents and purposes, it would have been the same had the applicant brought separate cases.

3.2.3 The WTO

The WTO dispute settlement system is perhaps the least problematic of the three.[84] Complaints against more than one respondent are not uncommon.[85] For instance, India brought a complaint against the EU and the Netherlands on the seizure of generic drugs,[86] and the United

83 See *Tugar* v. *Italy*, n. 82, concerning a complaint against Italy, which allegedly failed to prevent the sale of mines to Iraq, which subsequently led to injury, in Iraq, of an individual. The conduct of Iraq was obviously beyond the Court's reach and the situation was considered not to fall within the jurisdiction of Italy.

84 See generally, Y. Iwasawa, 'WTO Dispute Settlement as Judicial Supervision' (2002) 5 JIEL 287.

85 It should be noted that the vast majority of cases involving more than one respondent concern the EU. See L. Bartels, 'Procedural Aspects of Shared Responsibility in the WTO Dispute Settlement System' (2013) 4(2) JIDS 343.

86 Complaint by India, DS408, in consultation at the time of writing. Brazil has brought a similar complaint, DS409, also currently in consultation.

States started procedures against the EU and some of its member states on civil aviation.[87] The WTO system seems to be rather open to such procedures. In fact, in the *Turkey – Textiles* case, the Appellate Body dismissed an appeal to the indispensable third party rule by the European Communities (EC), despite its obvious interest in the case, and narrowed down its decision to Turkey's measures.[88] One of the arguments of the Appellate Body to reject the argument that the case should be dismissed was that the EC could have joined the case, but chose not to.[89] Although the WTO's website states that 'countries bring disputes to the WTO if they think their rights under the agreements are being infringed',[90] suggesting that it requires injury for claims to be admissible, cases may in fact also be based on 'serious prejudice' to the interests of the member states.[91] The WTO dispute settlement body has admitted complaints by states that were arguably not specially affected by the alleged breach of WTO law – for instance because they did not export the goods subject to unlawful tariffs – on the basis that the measures complained of harmed global trade and therefore also the complainant state. The *locus classicus* here is the *EC – Bananas* case, in which the United States was allowed to join, despite the fact that it scarcely produced or exported bananas.[92] Complaining against a plurality of responsible states and/or organisations is thus less complicated, since it is not necessary to prove injury vis-à-vis all respondents.

[87] *European Communities – Measures Affecting Trade in Large Civil Aircraft*, Report of the Appellate Body of 18 May 2011, AB-2010-1. In this case, the United States not only objected to distortion of trade between it and the European Union due to subsidies in the EU for its own aircraft industries, but also the potential harm to trade with third countries: see para. 14. Some of these claims were rejected, but only for the failure of the United States to substantiate the claims.

[88] *Turkey – Restrictions on Imports of Textile and Clothing Products*, Report of the Panel of 31 May 1999, WT/DS34/R. The measures complained of by India were implemented by Turkey following an agreement with the European Community. A determination of their lawfulness arguably required a determination of the lawfulness of the agreement between Turkey and the European Communities.

[89] Ibid., para. 9.11.

[90] See World Trade Organization, 'Understanding the WTO: What We Do,' available at http://wto.org/english/thewto_e/whatis_e/what_we_do_e.htm.

[91] See e.g. *European Communities and Certain Member States – Measures Affecting Trade in Large Civil Aircraft*, Report of the Panel of 30 June 2010, WT/DS316/R, at 833, para. 7.1610.

[92] *European Communities – Regime for the Importation, Sale and Distribution of Bananas*, Report of the Appellate Body of 9 September 1997, AB-1997-3.

In conclusion, in the context of the WTO, invoking the responsibility of a plurality of states and/or international organisations is not subjected to major procedural obstacles raised by the mere fact that there is a plurality of respondents. There are probably various explanations for this, many of them not inherent in principles on invocation and in any event including the defined nature of the primary norms subjected to WTO dispute settlement.

4. The consequences of non-invocation

As the analysis above has demonstrated, the invocation of the responsibility of all the members of a plurality of states and/or organisations when responsibility is shared is fraught with obstacles. In many cases, this will mean that the responsibility of some, the majority, or even the most important members will not be invoked. This raises the question of whether non-invocation of responsibility in cases of shared responsibility affects the very responsibility of the state or organisation whose responsibility is not invoked.

A preliminary answer is that it does not, since responsibility as such does not depend on invocation but only on the existence of a breach of an obligation that is attributable to the relevant state and/or organisation. This answer must be further refined, though, because non-invocation may have effects on the realisation of responsibility. The first, and obvious, effect will be on reparation. The obligation to make reparation is inherent in responsibility, but this obligation is impossible to implement without invocation, if only because the injured state or organisation must indicate the kind and amount of desired reparation. As has been discussed in Chapter 7 of this volume, reparation in situations of shared responsibility has its own complexities. These may constitute a real disadvantage for the member of the plurality of responsible states or organisations whose responsibility is invoked, because it may be liable to provide reparation in full also on behalf of the members whose responsibility is not invoked, without being able to reclaim part of what it paid from its partners in crime.[93] As already stated, the objectivity of international responsibility dictates that whether or not responsibility is actually invoked does not affect the very existence of responsibility of the

[93] For more details, see Chapter 7 of this volume, P. d'Argent, 'Reparation, Cessation, Assurances and Guarantees of Non-Repetition', p. 208, at pp. 244–49.

members of the responsible plurality not involved in the process of invocation. Even so, this may not contribute to the perceived fairness of the process.

A further effect of non-invocation is that it may affect the allocation of responsibility. The state or international organisation that is part of the responsible plurality, but not part of the process in which responsibility is invoked, is both at an advantage and a disadvantage. The advantage is that its responsibility, and its contribution to the injury, will not be identified. The disadvantage, though, is that it will be unable to argue its position, or bring additional evidence, and so on, to clear its name without compromising its position as a non-participant in the procedures. Actively participating would trigger the principle of *forum prorogatum*, while it may be entitled to abstain under the principle of consent. Apart from situations in which such abstention renders the entire claim inadmissible due to the *Monetary Gold* rule, absence of one or more of the relevant parties may have implications for the distribution of responsibility. The ICJ has settled disputes and issued advisory opinions without the contribution of an essential party.[94] While the Court has been criticised in such instances for having proceeded without having at its disposal all the relevant facts and arguments,[95] it has not subjected a state to its jurisdiction without the consent of that state. There is therefore some validity in the argument that abstaining is at the risk of the abstaining state. In the cases that concern us here, the absence of a participant has serious consequences. The absence of necessary evidence provided by the non-participant(s) that could exonerate them or indeed the respondent is to some extent a practical problem that could be solved by finding some of the evidence elsewhere, but if that is impossible, it has more fundamental consequences. The court will be unable to consider the very allocation of responsibility between the members of this plurality or determine causality, complicity, and participation. To illustrate this, let us assume that in scenario A, Arcadia and Utopia dump the prohibited substances x and y in the river. Combined, and due to the chemical reaction that follows, they cause aggravated

[94] See *United States Diplomatic and Consular Staff in Tehran (United States of America* v. *Iran)*, Judgment, ICJ Reports 1980, 3; *Military and Paramilitary Activities in and against Nicaragua (Nicaragua* v. *United States of America)*, Jurisdiction and Admissibility, ICJ Reports 1984, 392, in which the respondent did not appear; and the *Wall* advisory opinion, n. 22, in which Israel refused to participate.

[95] See e.g. *Wall* advisory opinion, n. 22; Separate Opinion of Judge Higgins, at 217–18; and Declaration of Judge Buergenthal, at 240–5.

pollution, seriously damaging downstream Ruritania. Without the participation of Utopia, a court will be unable to determine the extent of responsibility of Arcadia, even without the operation of the *Monetary Gold* rule. It is possible to declare that Arcadia is responsible for dumping one of the substances, but not to consider the aggravated effect due to the combination with the other substance. Similarly, in scenario B, Ruritania's conduct is only wrongful because it facilitated wrongful conduct against the Bellarian national by Arcadia and Utopia, but without the participation of Arcadia and Utopia, a court cannot determine this wrongfulness. Again, in theory this does not affect responsibility, in the sense that its existence does not depend on invocation. In reality, however, it makes meaningful implementation of shared responsibility fiendishly difficult.

5. Conclusions

This chapter has used the fictitious states of Arcadia, Utopia, Ruritania, and Bellaria, the names of which remind us perhaps of Elysian Fields or paradise, to illustrate the complexities of invoking shared responsibility. Sadly, we cannot discard these complexities as attached to a non-existent fantasy. The above analysis has demonstrated that the invocation of shared responsibility suffers from under-regulation and silences. Standing to invoke responsibility requires injury or legal interest on the basis of individualised and separate responsibility of each of the members of a plurality of responsible states and/or international organisations. This is irrespective of the number of responsible states or organisations, and will often force an injured state or organisation, or a non-injured state or organisation with a legal interest, to fragment its claim into the smaller pieces that fit this mould. Even if there is standing to present a claim against all participants in the wrongful conduct, this claim will still not address the aggravating circumstance that the injured entity suffered breaches caused by a plurality of states and/or international organisations. The claim will only address the individualised responsibility of each member of the plurality. The totality will be lost.

The actual implementation of shared responsibility by means of invocation is further complicated by specific requirements applicable to claims. These range from issues of admissibility of indirect claims (the nationality of claims and local remedies rules) to issues of admissibility before international courts and tribunals (the *Monetary Gold* rule). All of these have sound rationales and are firmly established in international law. However, their unaltered application to situations involving more than one respondent state or international organisation often presents fatal obstacles to the claim. This outcome is undesirable. The chances of success should not depend so much on the number of respondents. The solution is far from obvious. Regimes of strict(er) liability, automatic waivers of criteria of admissibility, compulsory dispute settlement, and more sophisticated primary rules, especially on issues of complicity and causation, would all address parts of the problems of invoking shared responsibility. However, none of these are particularly appealing to states and international organisations, reducing the likelihood of their implementation.

The analysis of invocation of shared responsibility has revealed an important disconnect between the legal regime of invocation of responsibility and the situation to which it should apply. Development and refinement may come from subsequent practice and perhaps a revision of the ILC's work on international responsibility. To avoid the travails of Bellaria and its real-life counterparts, it is to be hoped that regulating the invocation of shared responsibility will be considered more seriously than it has been in past efforts.

9

Serious Breaches of Peremptory Norms

ERIC WYLER AND LEÓN CASTELLANOS-JANKIEWICZ

1. Introduction

The law of international responsibility attaches special consequences to serious breaches of obligations arising under peremptory norms of general international law.[1] This aggravated regime was introduced to respond to internationally wrongful acts breaching the right to self-determination of peoples, the prohibitions of aggression, genocide, apartheid, torture, the slave trade and racial discrimination, war crimes, and crimes against humanity.[2] Like other obligations, these norms are susceptible to being breached by multiple actors resulting in a single harmful outcome through joint or cumulative action.[3]

Serious breaches require a high threshold of gravity to engage the international responsibility of wrongdoers and are more likely to involve multiple actors in their commission than other violations of international law. The indeterminacy of this gravity threshold is especially problematic

Eric Wyler is Lecturer at the Graduate Institute of International and Development Studies, Geneva, and Visiting Professor at the Université Paris 2 Panthéon – Assas. León Castellanos-Jankiewicz is a PhD Candidate and Teaching Assistant at the Graduate Institute of International and Development Studies (Geneva). He is a former member of the SHARES Research Project (2010–2011). The authors would like to thank Francesca Scalco for her valuable research assistance and the members of the SHARES Research Project at the Amsterdam Center for International Law (ACIL) for insightful comments. The research leading to this chapter has received funding from the European Research Council under the European Union's Seventh Framework Programme (FP7/2007–2013)/ ERC grant agreement n° 249499, as part of the research project on Shared Responsibility in International Law (SHARES), carried out at the ACIL of the University of Amsterdam.

[1] Hereinafter 'serious breaches' or 'serious breaches of peremptory norms'.

[2] See Roberto Ago, 'Fifth Report on State Responsibility', ILC *Yearbook* 1976/II(1), at 32.

[3] See P. A. Nollkaemper and D. Jacobs, 'Shared Responsibility in International Law: A Conceptual Framework' (2013) 34 MIJIL 359.

when the conduct of several actors produces serious breaches.[4] The tragic events in Syria make this painfully clear in light of the war crimes and crimes against humanity committed by government forces and anti-government armed groups.[5] Within Syria, no less than three entities have been exercising varying degrees of control over extensive swathes of the territory where the violations occurred.[6] Beyond Syrian borders, regional actors have continuously provided military and financial support to the parties involved.[7] But taken individually, these contributions may not meet the required gravity threshold to trigger their international responsibility for serious breaches.[8] An important objective of this chapter is to provide solutions for these sub-threshold situations, which are a major challenge for the grave breaches regime in the context of shared responsibility.[9]

This chapter will proceed as follows. It first considers the extent to which the aggravated regime of international responsibility accommodates the scenario of several entities involved in the commission of serious breaches. We explore this question by examining issues of shared responsibility in light of structural, substantive, and procedural aspects

4 See J. Salmon, 'Les Métamorphoses de la gravité', in M. Kohen (ed.), *Promoting Justice, Human Rights and Conflict Resolution through International Law: Liber Amicorum Lucius Caflish* (Leiden: Nijhoff, 2007), p. 1175. Salmon demonstrates that the degree of required gravity varies across primary rules. The plot thickens when the law of international responsibility requires a 'gross and systematic failure by the responsible State to fulfil the obligation' to engage responsibility for serious breaches. See Article 40(2) ARSIWA, n. 10.

5 'Report of the independent international commission of inquiry on the Syrian Arab Republic', UN Human Rights Council, UN Doc. A/HRC/24/46 (2013), at 23, paras. 192–4.

6 These are the government, the Syrian National Coalition, and the Kurdish Supreme Council. See 'Report of the independent international commission of inquiry on the Syrian Arab Republic', ibid., at 4, paras. 15–17.

7 Hizbullah and Iraqi Shiites fight alongside the government, which recently secured a USD 3.6 billion credit line from Iran and is negotiating a loan from Russia. In turn, influential Sunni clerics from Arab states have declared a jihad against the Syrian government. See 'Report of the independent international commission of inquiry on the Syrian Arab Republic', n. 5, at 5, paras. 18–22.

8 Lack of political will also explains the gap in accountability, as shown by the failed attempts in the Security Council to refer the violations in Syria to the International Criminal Court. See the press release of the Swiss Federal Department of Foreign Affairs, 'Switzerland asks UN Security Council to refer the serious crimes committed in Syria to the International Criminal Court', 14 January 2013.

9 See Chapter 1 of this volume, P. A. Nollkaemper, 'Introduction', at p. 12: 'even though the current international law of responsibility may not address sub-standard causal contributions, they may well be relevant in regulatory schemes that seek to prevent questions of shared responsibility *ex post facto* arising in the first place'.

of the serious breaches regime (section 2). Section 3 outlines the shared obligations of cooperation, non-recognition, and non-assistance aimed at ending serious breaches and wiping out their effects. We enquire whether third parties and principal wrongdoers can be jointly responsible when breaching these communitarian obligations. Finally, we suggest that the *erga omnes* dimension of such norms entails a shared duty to invoke serious breaches in diplomatic relations and international dispute settlement (section 4).

2. Serious breaches of peremptory norms and shared responsibility

This section describes the relationships between the serious breaches regime and forms of shared responsibility. Section 2.1 briefly outlines the special character of peremptory norms, the interests they protect, and how this is relevant for instances of multiple wrongdoers. It then asks whether the grave breaches regime as it stands today can generate shared forms of responsibility, and concludes that the system allows this, as shown in the cases of aggression and genocide (section 2.2). But it becomes evident that most problems of shared responsibility for serious breaches are procedural, and section 2.3 is devoted to describing the challenges and exploring solutions.

2.1 The scope and content of peremptory norms

Peremptory norms of general international law include the prohibition of aggression, genocide, slavery, racial discrimination, crimes against humanity, and the right to self-determination.[10] The proscription of crimes against humanity and war crimes are also considered as peremptory.[11] More recently, the International Court of Justice (ICJ or Court) has elevated the prohibition of torture to the category of a peremptory norm,

[10] Articles on Responsibility of States for Internationally Wrongful Acts, ILC *Yearbook* 2001/II(2) (ARSIWA); Commentary to the Articles on Responsibility of States for Internationally Wrongful Acts, ILC *Yearbook* 2001/II(2) (ARSIWA Commentary), Commentary to Article 26, para. 5.

[11] *Legality of the Threat or Use of Nuclear Weapons*, Advisory Opinion, ICJ Reports 1996, 226, at 257, para. 79: 'these fundamental rules are to be observed by all States whether or not they have ratified the conventions that contain them, because they constitute intransgressible principles of international customary law'.

which is presumably binding on states and international organisations.[12] This is a significant development since the affirmation of torture as an international crime attracting individual criminal liability,[13] and may result in joint responsibility between states and individuals.[14] To a lesser extent, it has been argued that terrorism constitutes a discreet international crime, although scant state practice supports this contention, and scholars have not arrived at a definite conclusion.[15]

The prohibition of serious breaches of peremptory norms is the normative response to protect and safeguard the most essential values of the international community. These values were enshrined in the United Nations (UN) Charter in 1945[16] and have evolved ever since by attaining greater legal protection than other norms in international law. Rules prohibiting the breach of peremptory norms form part of *jus cogens*, a higher body of law of overriding importance from which no derogation is permitted. The concept of *jus cogens* was first embodied in Article 53 of the 1969 Vienna Convention on the Law of Treaties, which provides that a treaty is void if, at the time of its conclusion, it conflicts with a peremptory norm of general international law recognised by the international community of states as a whole.[17] Few norms are recognised as such, but peremptory norms have all attained *jus cogens* status.

Peremptory norms bind states, international organisations, and individuals alike. States are held responsible under the law of international

[12] *Questions relating to the Obligation to Prosecute or Extradite* (*Belgium* v. *Senegal*), Judgment, ICJ Reports 2012, 422, at 457, para. 99: 'the prohibition of torture is part of customary international law and it has become a peremptory norm (*jus cogens*)'.

[13] *Prosecutor* v. *Furundžija*, Judgment, ICTY Case No. IT-95-17/1-T, 10 December 1998, paras. 139–42. See E. de Wet, 'The Prohibition of Torture as an International Norm of *Jus Cogens* and its Implications for National and Customary Law' (2004) 15 EJIL 97.

[14] On the alleged responsibility of individual agents of the United States government for torture in Guantánamo Bay see P. Sands, *Torture Team: Deception, Cruelty and the Compromise of Law* (London: Allen Lane, 2008).

[15] The US Court of Appeals of the Second Circuit held in *US* v. *Yousef* that, given the absence of an agreed-upon definition of terrorism as an international crime, it does not attract universal jurisdiction for prosecution in domestic courts: *US* v. *Yousef and Others*, 327 F 3d 56 (2d Cir. 2003). See A. Cassese, 'Terrorism as an International Crime' in A. Bianchi (ed.), *Enforcing International Law Norms against Terrorism* (Oxford: Hart, 2004), p. 213, and A. Cassese, 'The Multifaceted Criminal Notion of Terrorism in International Law' (2006) 4 J Int Crim Just 1. See also C. Damgaard, *Individual Criminal Responsibility for Core Crimes: Selected Pertinent Issues* (Berlin: Springer, 2008), p. 359.

[16] Charter of the United Nations, San Francisco, 26 June 1954, in force 24 October 1945, 1 UNTS 16 (UN Charter).

[17] Vienna Convention on the Law of Treaties, Vienna, 23 May 1969, in force 27 January 1980, 1155 UNTS 331.

state responsibility, and individuals are accountable under the law of individual criminal liability. For their part, the growing body of rules governing the responsibility of international organisations is applicable to intergovernmental bodies and the acts of their member states in their institutional framework. In addition, rules proscribing the commission of peremptory norms are called to operate in different bodies of law: international humanitarian law, international criminal law, and human rights law. States, international organisations, and individuals have positive obligations to respect and ensure compliance with these international norms.[18]

States cannot be held criminally liable under the law of international state responsibility, although an attempt was made within the International Law Commission (ILC) to create an aggravated responsibility regime for the commission of so-called state crimes.[19] Roberto Ago, the second Special Rapporteur on state responsibility, introduced this proposal in 1976.[20] Despite the advantage of recognising a higher level of protection for the most important norms within the international community, state crimes were discarded from the Articles on Responsibility of States for Internationally Wrongful Acts (ARSIWA)[21] and the 'crime of state' was substituted with an aggravated regime whereby states may be held responsible for serious breaches of obligations under peremptory norms of general international law.[22] As will be seen below, special consequences attach to the breach of these rules, with important legal ramifications involving injured and responsible entities, but also the international community as a whole.

[18] P. A. Nollkaemper, 'Introduction' in P. A. Nollkaemper and H. van der Wilt (eds.), *System Criminality in International Law* (Cambridge University Press, 2009), p. 12.

[19] R. Ago, 'Fifth Report on State Responsibility', ILC *Yearbook* 1976/II(2), 95.

[20] Ibid. According to Ago's proposal, crimes of state constituted a serious breach of an international obligation of essential importance for safeguarding any of the following: the maintenance of international peace and security, such as the prohibition of aggression; the right to self-determination of peoples, such as the prohibition of the establishment or maintenance by force of colonial domination; the prohibition of slavery, genocide, and apartheid; and the preservation of the human environment, such as norms prohibiting massive pollution of the atmosphere or of the seas.

[21] See n. 10; J. Crawford, 'First Report on State Responsibility', ILC *Yearbook* 1999/II(1), 1.

[22] E. Wyler, 'From "State Crime" to Responsibility for "Serious Breaches of Obligations under Peremptory Norms of General International Law"' (2002) 13 EJIL 1147, at 1158. For a pertinent account of the legislative history of crimes of state and different opinions, see J. H. H. Weiler et al. (eds.), *International Crimes of States: A Critical Analysis of the ILC's Draft Article 19 on State Responsibility* (Walter de Gruyter: Berlin and New York, 1989).

2.2 *Shared responsibility for serious breaches of peremptory norms*

It is increasingly acknowledged that international responsibility is shared when the consequences of harm can be distributed among wrongdoers.[23] This means that responsibility for joint wrongful conduct – whether cooperative or cumulative – resulting in a single harmful outcome should be apportioned in a manner facilitating recovery by injured parties.[24] This hypothesis envisages the commission of an internationally wrongful act by more than one state.[25]

As it stands today, international law accepts the possibility of attributing the same wrongful conduct to several responsible entities: this much is noted in the context of state responsibility and that of international organisations.[26] Multiple states or international organisations are concurrently responsible when a joint operation results in wrongful conduct committed via their own agencies or common organs.[27] The same applies when one state or international organisation has directed or controlled another in the commission of an internationally wrongful act,[28] or when

[23] P. A. Nollkaemper, 'Aspects of Shared Responsibility in International Adjudication' (2013) 4 JIDS 280.

[24] In *Certain Phosphate Lands in Nauru* (*Nauru* v. *Australia*), Preliminary Objections, ICJ Reports 1992, 240, at 258–9, the International Court of Justice found that Australia alone could be sued on the basis of the Mandate Agreement for Nauru undertaken jointly with the United Kingdom and New Zealand: 'The Court does not consider that any reason has been shown why a claim brought against only one of the three States should be declared inadmissible *in limine litis* merely because that claim raises questions of the administration of the Territory, which was shared with two other States.'

[25] J. Crawford, *State Responsibility: The General Part* (Cambridge University Press, 2013), p. 333.

[26] The latter body of law covers the joint responsibility of states and international organisations for the same internationally wrongful act. See Article 47 ARSIWA, n. 10, entitled 'plurality of responsible states', and Article 48 of the Articles on the Responsibility of International Organizations, ILC Report on the work of its sixty-third session, UNGAOR 66th Sess., Supp. No. 10, UN Doc. A/66/10 (2011) (ARIO) on 'responsibility of an international organization and one or more States or international organizations'.

[27] See Article 47 ARSIWA, n. 10, and Chapter 3 of this volume, F. Messineo, 'Attribution of Conduct', p. 60.

[28] ARSIWA Commentary, n. 10, Commentary to Article 17, para. 9: 'As to the responsibility of the directed and controlled State, the mere fact that it was directed to carry out an internationally wrongful act does not constitute an excuse ... The defence of "superior orders" does not exist for States in international law. This is not to say that the wrongfulness of the directed and controlled State's conduct may not be precluded under Chapter V, but this will only be so if it can show the existence of a circumstance precluding wrongfulness, e.g. *force majeure*.' See also Chapter 4 of this volume, J. D. Fry, 'Attribution of Responsibility', p. 98, at pp. 117–20.

concurrent responsibility is engaged on the basis of aid and assistance.[29] Similarly, the law of international responsibility envisages holding a plurality of entities responsible for the same internationally wrongful act. Although it does not transpose the legal principles of joint and several liability that are common in domestic legal systems, the law of international responsibility does not exclude the possibility 'that two or more States will be responsible for the same internationally wrongful act'.[30]

Breaches of peremptory norms carry special consequences for responsible states, but also entail a series of joint obligations addressed to the international community as a whole that do not otherwise arise. When confronted with serious breaches, the law of international responsibility operates on three levels. First, responsible states must comply with the obligations of cessation, non-repetition, and reparation in accordance with the general rules applicable to every internationally wrongful act.[31] Second, all states must cooperate to bring the serious breach to an end, while refraining from recognising its lawfulness and providing aid and assistance in maintaining the situation.[32] This has been called the aggravated regime of international responsibility. Finally, because of their communitarian character and *erga omnes* dimension, every state has the right to invoke a violation of serious breaches because they are owed to the international community as a whole.[33] We discuss the extent of these obligations for third states in section 3 below, where we enquire whether their violation entails the joint responsibility between the principal wrongdoer and the entity that fails to align itself within the aggravated regime.

For a breach to be serious, it must transgress a peremptory norm and be carried out in a gross or systematic way. That is, the violation must be 'of a flagrant nature, amounting to a direct and outright assault on the values protected by the rule . . . carried out in an organised and deliberate

[29] Article 16 ARSIWA, n. 10. See also Chapter 5 of this volume, V. Lanovoy, 'Complicity in an Internationally Wrongful Act', p. 134.

[30] See ARSIWA Commentary, n. 10, Commentary to Article 47, para. 6, and Article 48 ARIO, n. 26. See generally Chapter 8 of this volume, A. M. H. Vermeer-Künzli, 'Invocation of Responsibility', p. 251.

[31] As outlined in Articles 28–33 ARSIWA, n. 10.

[32] See Articles 40–1 ARSIWA, n. 10, and our discussion in section 3.1: 'The aggravated regime of responsibility and shared obligations'.

[33] See Article 48 ARSIWA, n. 10: 'Any State other than an injured State is entitled to invoke the responsibility of another State in accordance with paragraph 2 if: (b) the obligation breached is owed to the international community as a whole.' See our discussion in section 3.2: 'A shared duty to invoke serious breaches?'

way'.[34] An important question to be determined is how and when this required threshold of gravity is met through the conduct of multiple entities causing damage together or cumulatively.

The required parameters of seriousness restrict the scope of the aggravated regime to the most blatant violations, and may represent an obstacle for the application of the aggravated regime when a multiplicity of actors is involved at different levels. For instance, in situations of cumulative responsibility,[35] each independent wrong must arguably present a gross or systematic character in order to trigger the aggravated regime. Therefore, joint acts of torture and serious violations of international humanitarian law that cumulatively reach the required threshold of gravity cannot attract responsibility for serious breaches if each individual violation does not present a gross and systematic character. Consequently, these acts will not enjoin the international community as a whole to react against the wrongdoers. This is problematic, because serious breaches are hardly ever committed single-handedly, and often involve a host of actors to plan and execute or stand idly by.[36] Varying degrees of involvement can be envisaged that will not reach the required threshold, and minor violations cannot in principle be assimilated to the conduct of the principal wrongdoer for the purposes of responsibility.

The fact that multiple actors cannot be held jointly and severally liable for the harmful outcomes they collectively cause is due to the principle of individual attribution, which is the dominant approach for the determination of international responsibility predicated on the notion that each entity is responsible for the wrongful acts it commits, regardless of whether multiple actors are involved in a single injury. This leads to the observation that the secondary rules of responsibility are too narrow in scope to cover serious breaches reached by multiple actors cumulatively. A possible solution is to attribute conduct for serious breaches in light of harmful outcomes.[37] In this sense, shared responsibility can be considered

[34] ARSIWA Commentary, n. 10, Commentary to Article 40, para. 8.

[35] Cumulative shared responsibility originates when there is no formalised concerted action between the wrongdoers: Nollkaemper and Jacobs, 'Shared Responsibility in International Law', n. 3, at p. 368.

[36] P. A. Nollkaemper, 'Dual Attribution: Liability of the Netherlands for Conduct of Dutchbat in Srebrenica', (2011) 9 J Int Crim Just 1143.

[37] On the notion of harmful outcome, see Nollkaemper and Jacobs, 'Shared Responsibility in International Law', n. 3, at p. 367. To these authors, the notion of injury in state responsibility as an element of the internationally wrongful act 'is not easily combined with a concept of injury that captures acts by multiple actors contributing to outcomes that affect many states or the international community as a whole'.

as a parameter to assess the gravity of the breach outside the traditional formula of individual attribution. Instead, causation can play a major role in the context of joint breaches involving peremptory norms.[38]

In light of the preceding remarks, we shall consider discrete breaches activating the aggravated regime and their implications for shared responsibility. In what follows, we deal with the specific examples of aggression and genocide.[39]

2.2.1 Aggression

The uncertain world order emerging from the 1919 peace saw the outlawing of aggressive war in a string of instruments, inaugurated by the Briand-Kellogg Pact and Article 10 of the League Covenant in 1928 and 1929, respectively.[40] After war ravaged Europe twice over, this culminated in the adoption of Article 2(4) of the UN Charter, which categorically proscribed the use of force. The ICJ qualified the provision as a 'fundamental or cardinal principle' of customary international law in the *Nicaragua* case.[41] More recently, in the *Wall* advisory opinion, the Court concluded that the illegality of territorial acquisition resulting from the threat or use of force reflected customary international law.[42]

[38] See our discussion at section 2.3.2: 'The irrelevance of damage and causal analysis in the determination of responsibility.'

[39] The present chapter does not cover war crimes and crimes against humanity as distinct categories owing to lack of space, but it should be mentioned that pursuant to Common Article 1 of the Geneva Conventions of 1949, all states parties are bound to the shared obligation to guarantee their observance: 'The High Contracting Parties undertake to respect and to ensure respect for the present Convention in all circumstances.' Convention for the Amelioration of the Condition of the Wounded and Sick in Armed Forces in the Field, Geneva, 12 August 1949, in force 21 October 1950, 75 UNTS 31, Article 1. According to the ICJ in *Nicaragua*, this provision is a general principle of humanitarian law to which the Conventions merely give specific expression. *Military and Paramilitary Activities in and against Nicaragua (Nicaragua* v. *United States of America)*, Merits, ICJ Reports 1986, 14, at 114, para. 220. It follows that several states, whether or not parties to a conflict, can take action to ensure compliance with principles of international humanitarian law, and may also react against breaches of this law.

[40] General Treaty for the Renounciation of War as an Instrument of National Policy (Kellogg–Briand Pact), Paris, 27 August 1928 94 LNTS S7; Covenant of the League of Nations, 28 June 1919, in force 1 October 1920, 225 Parry 195. See also United Nations General Assembly Resolution 3314 (XXIX) of 14 December 1974.

[41] *Military and Paramilitary Activities in and against Nicaragua*, n. 39, at 100, para. 190. See also the Declaration on Principles of International Law concerning Friendly Relations and Co-operation among States in accordance with the Charter of the United Nations, General Assembly Resolution 2625 (XXV) of 24 October 1970, Annex, para. 1.

[42] *Legal Consequences of the Construction of a Wall in the Occupied Palestinian Territory*, Advisory Opinion, ICJ Reports 2004, 136, at 171, para. 87 (*Wall* advisory opinion).

Shared responsibility in this context is exemplified by joint military action amounting to aggression by a coalition of states against a third state in violation of Article 2(4) of the UN Charter. This was argued by Yugoslavia in the *Legality of Use of Force* cases against the North Atlantic Treaty Organization (NATO) coalition, when it stated that '[a]cts of NATO are imputable to the Respondents'. The argument was pleaded under the assumption that 'NATO acts under the political and military guidance and control of its Member States, each separately and all together'.[43] With this, Yugoslavia argued that the acts of NATO were imputable to each respondent state, admitting the possibility of multiple attribution for the same internationally wrongful act. It is of course unnecessary for each wrongdoing state to perform the wrongful act in its entirety, and the extent of responsibility will depend on the degree of participation, such as co-authorship or mere assistance.[44] Another possible example of joint attribution is the invasion of Iraq by the United States and the United Kingdom in 2003,[45] although the role of the United Kingdom has been described as an instance of assistance by some.[46]

Pursuant to the Rome Statute of the International Criminal Court (ICC),[47] an individual may be responsible for aggression in conjunction with the state. Article 8 *bis* of the Rome Statute, adopted by the Assembly of States Parties in 2010, defines aggression as:

> the planning, preparation, initiation or execution, by a person in a position effectively to exercise control over or to direct the political or military action of a State, of an act of aggression which, by its character, gravity and scale, constitutes a manifest violation of the Charter of the United Nations.

[43] *Legality of Use of Force (Serbia and Montenegro* v. *Belgium)*, Preliminary Objections, ICJ Reports 2004, 279. See the Memorial of the Applicant, 'Law Related to the Issue of Imputability' at p. 327. The Memorial outlines the relevant rules laid down in the NATO Handbook of 1998: 'All nations opting to be members of the military part of NATO contribute forces which together constitute the integrated military structure of the Alliance ... the integrated military structure remains under political control and guidance at the highest level at all times.' On this basis, Serbia argued that any NATO military plan 'has to be endorsed by each Member State participating in it'.

[44] C. Dominicé, 'Attribution of Conduct to Multiple States and the Implication of a State in the Act of Another State', in J. Crawford, A. Pellet, and S. Olleson, *The Law of International Responsibility* (Oxford University Press, 2010), p. 281, at p. 282.

[45] H. P. Aust, *Complicity and the Law of State Responsibility* (Cambridge University Press, 2011), at pp. 219–20.

[46] The Anglo-American invasion has been discussed as an instance of aid and assistance and not outright co-authorship. See *Edward Horgan* v. *An Taoiseach* (2003) 132 ILR 407, 429–31.

[47] Rome Statute of the International Criminal Court, Rome, 17 July 1998, in force 1 July 2002, 2187 UNTS 3 (Rome Statute).

This definition covers situations where multiple states are involved in proscribing the 'action of a State in allowing its territory, which it has placed at the disposal of another State, to be used by that other State for perpetrating an act of aggression against a third State'.[48] This opens the door to situations of shared responsibility between states and individuals for the crime of aggression under the ordinary rules of attribution codified in Article 4 of the ARSIWA.[49] In sum, the prohibition of aggression is an obligation that must be observed by states and its individual organs. It is proscribed under treaty law and customary international law. The recent criminalisation of aggression by the ICC will potentially give rise to state responsibility and individual criminal liability for the same factual complex, albeit within different regimes of law.

2.2.2 Genocide

The prohibition of genocide is a peremptory norm of general international law.[50] Article III of the Genocide Convention[51] prohibits several forms of shared conduct in relation to genocide. These are conspiracy to commit genocide, direct and public incitement to commit genocide, attempt to commit genocide, and complicity in genocide. At first glance, the Genocide Convention seems to be an instrument whose primary objective is to hold private individuals liable for the commission of genocide, while obliging states to cooperate in punishing and preventing the crime.[52] However, the Convention's dispute settlement clause obliges states to abide by all of the Convention's provisions. Article IX reads as follows:

48 Rome Statute, ibid., Articles 8 *bis* (1) and 2(f). The amendments to Article 8 are contained in depositary notification C. N.651.2010 Treaties-6, dated 29 November 2010.

49 Pursuant to Article 4(1) ARSIWA, n. 10: 'The conduct of any State organ shall be considered an act of that State under international law, whether the organ exercises legislative, executive, judicial or any other functions, whatever the position it holds in the organization of the State, and whatever its character as an organ of the central government or of a territorial unit of the State.'

50 *Application of the Convention on the Prevention and Punishment of the Crime of Genocide (Bosnia and Herzegovina* v. *Serbia and Montenegro)*, Judgment, ICJ Reports 2007, 43, at 110–11, para. 161 (*Genocide* case); *Application of the Convention on the Prevention and Punishment of the Crime of Genocide (Bosnia and Herzegovina* v. *Serbia and Montenegro)*, Provisional Measures, Order of 13 September 1993, ICJ Reports 1993, 325 (Separate Opinion Judge Lauterpacht, at 440).

51 Convention on the Prevention and Punishment of the Crime of Genocide, Paris, 9 December 1948, in force 12 January 1951, 78 UNTS 277 (Genocide Convention).

52 P. Gaeta (ed.), *The UN Genocide Convention – A Commentary* (Oxford University Press, 2009), Part III: Individual Criminal Responsibility for Genocide.

> Disputes between the Contracting Parties relating to interpretation, application or fulfillment of the present Convention, including those relating to the responsibility of a State for genocide or any other acts enumerated in Article III, shall be submitted to the International Court of Justice at the request of any of the parties to the dispute.[53]

It is unusual for a dispute settlement clause to determine the scope of application of a treaty. However, the ICJ interpreted this disposition as widening the Convention's scope of application to states in the preliminary objections phase of the *Bosnian Genocide* case, where it found that Article IX 'does not exclude any form of State responsibility'.[54] In its judgment on the merits, the Court stated: 'it would be paradoxical if States were thus under an obligation to prevent . . . but were not forbidden to commit such acts through their own organs, or persons over whom they have such firm control that their conduct is attributable to the State concerned under international law'.[55] The Court concluded that the contracting parties 'may be responsible for genocide and other acts enumerated in Article III of the Convention'.[56] This gives way to the possibility of invoking state responsibility for genocide under the Convention, whereas individuals will be held liable through international criminal law.

The ICJ has recognised that the principles underlying the Genocide Convention are binding on states, even without any conventional obligation.[57] Customary international law prohibits the commission of genocide on the part of states and distinguishes itself in content from the norms primarily oriented towards establishing individual criminal liability in the Genocide Convention. This customary rule for states is evidenced by the work of the ILC on state responsibility, which provides that nothing precludes the wrongfulness of a state's obligation arising under peremptory norms of general international law.[58] Moreover, the ICJ recognised that the prohibition of genocide is a peremptory norm of general international law having a *jus cogens* character in the *Armed Activities on the Territory of the Congo* case.[59]

53 Article IX, Genocide Convention, n. 51.

54 *Application of the Convention on the Prevention and Punishment of the Crime of Genocide (Bosnia and Herzegovina* v. *Serbia and Montenegro)*, Preliminary Objections, ICJ Reports 1996, 595, at 616, para. 32.

55 *Genocide case*, n. 50, at 113, para. 166. 56 Ibid., para. 169.

57 *Reservations to the Convention on the Prevention and Punishment of the Crime of Genocide*, Advisory Opinion, ICJ Reports 1951, 15, at 23.

58 ILC *Yearbook* 2001/II(2), 84.

59 *Armed Activities on the Territory of the Congo (New Application: 2002) (Democratic Republic of the Congo* v. *Rwanda)*, Jurisdiction and Admissibility, ICJ Reports 2006, 6,

State responsibility may therefore be concurrent with individual criminal liability for genocide. The ICJ noted that this duality of responsibility was a 'constant feature of international law'[60] when responding to the Federal Republic of Yugoslavia (FRY)'s arguments to the effect that the Convention dealt exclusively with individual criminal conduct. It went on to recall Article 25(4) of the Statute of the ICC, whereby '[n]o provision in this Statute relating to individual criminal responsibility shall affect the responsibility of States under international law', and Article 58 of the ARSIWA, which provides that the Articles are 'without prejudice to any question of the individual responsibility under international law of any person acting on behalf of the State'. Thus understood, conclusive criminal responsibility of an individual organ is not a necessary requirement to engage state responsibility for genocide. The respondent in the *Bosnian Genocide* case argued that such a finding was a condition *sine qua non* for establishing state responsibility, but the Court found no legal bar under this heading to restrain it from exercising its jurisdiction, and added that the absence of a prior conviction had little to do with whether or not an act of genocide has actually been committed.[61]

Another important issue of shared responsibility arose in the *Bosnian Genocide* case in the context of complicity between states and non-state actors. Bosnia argued that the FRY[62] was complicit in the commission of genocidal acts perpetrated by the Republika Srpska, an armed group that was a party to the internal armed conflict that dismembered Yugoslavia during the 1990s. Although complicity is not a category recognised by the law of international responsibility, the Court saw no reason 'to make any distinction of substance between "complicity in genocide", within the meaning of Article III, paragraph (e), of the [Genocide] Convention, and the "aid or assistance" of a State in the commission of a wrongful act by another State within the meaning of Article 16 [ARSIWA]', and focused on 'the provision of means to enable or facilitate the commission

para. 64. See also the Individual Opinion of Judge ad hoc Dugard expounding on the notion of *jus cogens* in international litigation, ICJ Reports 2006, at 86.

60 *Genocide* case, n. 50, at 116, para. 173.

61 *Genocide* case, n. 50, at 119, para. 181. At para. 182, the Court described possible reasons why such a conviction may not exist: 'genocide has allegedly been committed within a State by its leaders but they have not been brought to trial because, for instance, they are still very much in control of the powers of the State including the police, prosecution services and the courts and there is no international penal tribunal to exercise jurisdiction over the alleged crimes'.

62 This was the name of Serbia and Montenegro between 27 April 1992 and 3 February 2003. *Genocide* case, n. 50, at 46.

of the crime'[63] in assessing the required threshold. It should be recalled that Article 16 of the ARSIWA establishes that responsibility for aid and assistance is engaged when the assisting state is aware of the circumstances of the internationally wrongful act.[64] The ARSIWA Commentary elaborates on this point: 'If the assisting or aiding State is unaware of the circumstances in which its aid or assistance is intended to be used by the other State, it bears no international responsibility.'[65] The Court reasoned that the FRY's responsibility could only be engaged had it been aware of the perpetrators' specific intent (*dolus specialis*) to commit genocide,[66] and concluded that the condition had not been met because 'it was not conclusively shown that the decision to eliminate physically the adult male population of the Muslim community from Srebrenica was brought to the attention of the Belgrade authorities when it was taken'.[67] This was despite the Court acknowledging that there was 'little doubt' that the atrocities were committed with resources facilitated by the FRY.[68] Had the Court determined that this requirement was fulfilled, it would have doubtless found the FRY responsible for aiding and assisting the Republika Srpska in the commission of genocide.

2.3 Limits to multiparty adjudication for serious breaches

2.3.1 Procedural issues

The main problems that lie along the road towards shared responsibility for serious breaches are procedural, and arise in the adjudicative phase. Although peremptory norms are also *erga omnes* and are owed to the international community as a whole, tribunals cannot adjudicate their breach without a jurisdictional link between the parties to a dispute.[69]

[63] *Genocide* case, n. 50, at 217, para. 420: 'The Court sees no reason to make any distinction of substance between "complicity in genocide", within the meaning of Article III, paragraph (e), of the [Genocide] Convention, and the "aid or assistance" of a State in the commission of a wrongful act by another State within the meaning of the aforementioned Article 16.'

[64] Article 16 ARSIWA, n. 10. The second requirement is that the act would be internationally wrongful if committed by the assisting state.

[65] ARSIWA Commentary, n. 10, Commentary to Article 16, para. 4.

[66] *Genocide* case, n. 50, at 218, para. 421: 'If that condition is not fulfilled, that is sufficient to exclude categorization as complicity.'

[67] Ibid., at 218, para. 423. [68] Ibid., para. 422.

[69] J. Crawford, 'Responsibility for Breaches of Communitarian Norms: An Appraisal of Article 48 of the Articles on Responsibility of States for Internationally Wrongful Acts',

Indeed, having the relevant entitlements does not suffice: they must also extend the procedural right to institute proceedings.[70] This is paradoxical, because international law gives all states a legal interest to claim against breaches of peremptory norms regardless of whether they are parties to the relevant instruments.[71] This feature is exclusive to peremptory norms, but it does not follow that such a dispute is justiciable in international adjudication. Absent a dispute settlement clause, enforcement of these obligations is problematic, and this holds especially true for multiparty proceedings.

In the *Armed Activities* case, the ICJ recalled that 'the mere fact that rights and obligations *erga omnes* or peremptory norms of general international law (*jus cogens*) are at issue in a dispute cannot in itself constitute an exception to the principle that its jurisdiction always depends on the consent of the parties'.[72] In effect, the ICJ confined its evaluation of legal interests within its jurisdictional competence. In the *Genocide* case, it constrained its findings to the limits of the Genocide Convention, upon which its jurisdiction was founded:

> The jurisdiction of the Court in this case is based solely on Article IX of the Convention. It follows that the Court may rule only on the disputes between the Parties to which that provision refers . . . It has no power to rule on alleged breaches of other obligations under international law, not amounting to genocide, particularly those protecting human rights in armed conflict. That is so even if the alleged breaches are of obligations

in U. Fastenrath et al. (eds.), *From Bilateralism to Community Interest: Essays in Honour of Bruno Simma* (Oxford University Press, 2011) p. 224, at p. 239: 'A corresponding procedural framework for the invocation of responsibility for breaches of communitarian norms remains to be developed, for example, one permitting the invocation by more than one member of the international community in multiparty proceedings, instead of the traditional approach of joining related proceedings.'

70 F. Matscher, 'Standing before International Courts and Tribunals', in R. Benhardt (ed.), *Encyclopedia of Public International Law*, Vol. IV (Amsterdam: Elsevier, 2000), p. 594, at p. 594.

71 See C. J. Tams, *Enforcing Obligations Erga Omnes in International Law* (Cambridge University Press, 2005); and S. Villalpando, *L'Émergence de la communauté internationale dans la responsabilité des États* (Paris: Presses Universitaires de France, 2005).

72 *Armed Activities on the Territory of the Congo (New Application: 2002)*, n. 59, at 52, para. 125. See also in respect to obligations *erga omnes* the judgment in *East Timor*: 'the Court considers that the *erga omnes* character of a norm and the rule of consent to jurisdiction are two different things. Whatever the nature of the obligations invoked, the Court could not rule on the lawfulness of the conduct of a State when its judgment would imply an evaluation of the lawfulness of the conduct of another State which is not a party to the case'. *East Timor (Portugal* v. *Australia)*, Judgment, ICJ Reports 1995, 90, at 102, para. 29.

> under peremptory norms, or of obligations which protect essential humanitarian values, and which may be owed *erga omnes*.[73]

What transpires from these passages is that grave breaches may give rise to many independent legal interests, but these are not a substitute for standing and jurisdiction. To prove standing, an applicant must first fall within the definition of those who are entitled to appear before the tribunal.[74] Second, it must demonstrate a jurisdictional link with the respondents in regard to the dispute. Inevitably, the principle of consent to jurisdiction plays a major role as to whether responsibility can be distributed among multiple wrongdoing actors in the adjudicative phase.

It is problematic that breaches of communitarian obligations can be invoked by any state interested in their compliance, whereas their enforcement remains a different matter. Invocation has its *sedes materiae* on entitlements, but enforcement is predicated on procedure. The possibility of invoking serious breaches has widened the spectrum of states entitled to respond to violations, but the procedural requirements to protect these rights have not responded in kind.

A related difficulty is the high standard of proof that is required in international proceedings to establish the commission of serious breaches. Further, obtaining conclusive evidence demonstrating shared responsibility for serious breaches can be challenging when wrongful conduct has been cumulative. The standard of proof for serious breaches was restated by the ICJ in the *Bosnian Genocide* case when it required 'that it be fully convinced that the allegations [of genocide] made in the proceedings ... have been clearly established. The same standard applies to the proof of attribution for such acts'.[75] To the Court, therefore, there should be no room for doubt as regards the factual accuracy of the allegations. Interestingly, the Court will apply the same test for the process of attribution, although no such requirement exists in the ARSIWA, thereby

[73] *Genocide* case, n. 50, at 104, para. 147.

[74] C. F. Amerasinghe, *Jurisdiction of Specific International Tribunals* (The Hague: Kluwer, 2009), p. 318.

[75] *Genocide* case, n. 50, at 129, para. 209. Similarly, the Eritrea–Ethiopia Claims Commission 'required clear and convincing proof of liability ... because the Parties' claims frequently involved allegations of serious – indeed sometimes grave – misconduct by a State. A finding of such misconduct is a significant matter with serious implications for the interests and reputation of the affected State. Accordingly, any such finding must rest upon substantial and convincing evidence.' Eritrea's Damages Claims Eritrea–Ethiopia Claims Commission, Final Award, at 10, para. 35 (see www.pca-cpa.org).

leaving little room for the determination of shared forms of responsibility that do not conform to the general principle stated in Article 1 of the ARSIWA.[76] One could ask whether this high threshold of proof is called for when multiple actors are involved in the commission of serious breaches.

The reluctance of states to spell out the consequences of joint breaches in conventional law has prompted states to develop procedures allowing for multiparty adjudication. This is true for arbitral procedures, provided the required provisions are specified in the special agreement,[77] and for the World Trade Organization.[78] The imminent accession of the European Union (EU) to the European Convention on Human Rights will allow EU member states and the Union to appear as co-respondents before the European Court of Human Rights.[79] However, serious breaches of peremptory norms face a procedural gap in this regard. The overwhelming majority of inter-state claims for serious breaches are brought to the ICJ, where proceedings are eminently adversarial and bilateral.[80] An exception is the Eritrea–Ethiopia Claims Commission, which worked under the aegis of the Permanent Court of Arbitration and decided claims for loss, damage, or injury by one government against the other resulting from violations of international humanitarian law.[81]

[76] As stated in Article 1 ARSIWA, n. 10: 'Every internationally wrongful act of a State entails the international responsibility of that State.'

[77] F. Baetens, 'Procedural Issues Relating to Shared Responsibility in Arbitral Tribunals' (2013) 4 JIDS 319.

[78] L. Bartels, 'Procedural Aspects of Shared Responsibility in the WTO Dispute Settlement System' (2013) 4 JIDS 343.

[79] Council of Europe, Report to the Steering Committee for Human Rights of 10 June 2013, 47+1(2013)008rev2, Commentary to draft Article 3 on the co-respondent mechanism, at 7, para. 7: 'If the violation in respect of which a High Contracting Party is a co-respondent to the proceedings is established, the respondent and the co-respondent shall be jointly responsible for that violation, unless the Court, on the basis of the reasons given by the respondent and the co-respondent, and having sought the views of the applicant, decides that only one of them be held responsible.'

[80] *Application of the International Convention on the Elimination of All Forms of Racial Discrimination (Georgia* v. *Russian Federation)*, Preliminary Objections, ICJ Reports 2011, 70; *Jurisdictional Immunities of the State (Germany* v. *Italy: Greece intervening)*, Judgment, ICJ Reports 2012, 99; *Genocide* case, n. 50; *Armed Activities on the Territory of the Congo (New Application: 2002)*, n. 59; *Armed Activities on the Territory of the Congo (Democratic Republic of the Congo* v. *Uganda)*, Judgment, ICJ Reports 2005, 168; *Legality of Use of Force*, n. 43; *East Timor*, n. 72; *Military and Paramilitary Activities in and against Nicaragua*, n. 39.

[81] *Guidance Regarding Jus ad Bellum Liability*, Eritrea–Ethiopia Claims Commission, Decision No. 7, (2007) 26 RIAA 1.

Although the ICJ Rules of Court envisage joint proceedings[82] and some cases have been joined in the past, experience shows that states are averse to multiparty dispute settlement in high-profile cases where responsibility for serious breaches is at stake. In the *Legality of the Use of Force* cases, the Presidency of the Court suggested joining the proceedings instituted by Serbia and Montenegro against several states that used force under the mandate of NATO.[83] Serbia and Montenegro noted that it had brought the cases on the basis of the same factual complex and was in favour of the joinder, but Belgium opposed this.[84] The judgment on preliminary objections notes that the Agents were 'informed that the Court had decided that a joinder of the proceedings would not be appropriate'.[85] Although the ICJ Rules do not require the Court to obtain the consent of the parties to join cases, it can be presumed that Belgium's objection played a major role.

2.3.2 The irrelevance of damage and causal analysis in the determination of responsibility

As noted above, international law does not exclude the establishment of shared responsibility when a plurality of wrongdoers has contributed to damage. But the law falls short of providing the procedural guarantees to enable injured parties to recover from responsible entities, since international responsibility is not based on the concept of damage, but relies instead on wrongfulness to attribute the relevant conduct.[86] This means that causal analysis linking conduct to wrongdoers is not required by international law in determining the extent of responsibility, because the process of attribution subsumes causation.[87] This reduces complex

[82] Article 47 of the Rules of the Court (as amended in 2005) provides: 'The Court may at any time direct that the proceedings in two or more cases be joined. It may also direct that the written or oral proceedings, including the calling of witnesses, be in common; or the Court may, without effecting any formal joinder, direct common action in any of these respects.'

[83] These included Belgium, Canada, France, Germany, Italy, the Netherlands, Portugal, and the United Kingdom.

[84] *Legality of Use of Force*, n. 43, at 286, para. 17.

[85] Ibid., at 287, para. 18.

[86] For a critique on this point see B. Stern, 'A Plea for "Reconstruction" of International Responsibility Based on the Notion of Legal Injury', in M. Ragazzi (ed.), *International Responsibility Today: Essays in Memory of Oscar Schachter* (Leiden: Brill, 2005), p. 93; and B. Stern, 'Et si on utilisait le concept de préjudice juridique? Retour sur une notion délaissée à l'occasion de la fin des travaux de la CDI sur la responsabilité des Etats' (2001) 47 AFDI 3.

[87] For a discussion of how attribution subsumes causation see L. Castellanos-Jankiewicz, 'Causation in International State Responsibility', SHARES Research Paper 07 (2012) ACIL 2012-07, at 11 (available at www.sharesproject.nl, last accessed on 20 March 2014).

liabilities involving multiple actors to bundles of bilateral relationships that do not always satisfy the jurisdictional requirements for adjudication.[88]

If causation were an element of international responsibility – indeed, if the starting point of responsibility were the outcome of damage, whether material or non-material – a jurisdictional link between the injured state and a single wrongdoer would suffice for the purpose of recovering the whole, because the conduct of other entities could be factored into the damage caused by the principal. But the paradigmatic structure of bilateral dispute settlement effectively prevents this from happening by ascribing responsibility individually,[89] which leads international tribunals to rely on the indispensable third party rule and related doctrines of judicial restraint to isolate the conduct of the principal wrongdoer from a broader factual complex.[90]

The absence of causal analysis from the determination of an internationally wrongful act inhibits the shared responsibility of multiple actors acting collectively or cumulatively in bilateral proceedings. The law of international responsibility places little reliance on primary norms to attribute wrongful conduct, focusing on agency and attribution instead. But the process of attribution is individual, making actors liable for their own wrong. Damage, on the other hand, allows for the consideration of causal analysis and the material damage sustained, which may or may not be inflicted by multiple wrongdoers.

The absence of damage in the determination of responsibility has a long history. Already in 1973, Roberto Ago considered that damage was not a necessary requirement for a finding of international responsibility.

[88] Simma treats the notion of multilateral treaties as 'bundles of bilateral rights and obligations'. See B. Simma, 'Bilateralism and Community Interest in the Law of State Responsibility', in Y. Dinstein and M. Tabory (eds.), *International Law at a Time of Perplexity: Essays in Honor of Shabtai Rosenne* (Dordrecht: Nijhoff, 1989), p. 821, at pp. 821–2.

[89] In *Corfu Channel*, the ICJ treated Albania's knowledge of the presence of mines that resulted in the destruction of a British vessel as separate from the responsibility for actually laying down the minefield, although both wrongful acts resulted in a single harmful outcome. *Corfu Channel (United Kingdom of Great Britain and Northern Ireland* v. *Albania)*, Merits, ICJ Reports 1949, 4, at 17: 'In light of the information now available to the Court, the authors of the minelaying remain unknown. In any case, the task of the Court, as defined by the Special Agreement, is to decide whether Albania is responsible, under international law, for the explosions which occurred.'

[90] *Monetary Gold Removed from Rome (Italy* v. *France, United Kingdom of Great Britain and Northern Ireland and United States of America)*, Preliminary Question, ICJ Reports 1954, 19; *East Timor*, n. 72.

In his view, there were internationally wrongful acts that did not result in injury, and while it was true that every failure to fulfil an obligation entailed injury, then the element of injury was already covered by the failure to fulfil the obligation.[91]

In private law, any act causing damage involves the responsibility of the person committing the act, and requires reparation to be made. In international law, a wrongful act entails the responsibility of the state, but reparation does not automatically follow. As noted by Ian Brownlie, 'the idea of reparation . . . tends to give too restrictive a view of the legal interests protected [by the law of state responsibility]. The duty to pay compensation is a normal consequence of responsibility, but is not conterminous with it'.[92] This is due to the public law overtones given by Roberto Ago to the content of responsibility, as expounded by Bilge, who stated that it was impossible to dissociate the internationally wrongful act from injury, thus concluding that damage could not be regarded as the third element of responsibility. As a corollary, causation plays no part in the determination of responsibility.[93]

In the ILC's public law view, the consequences of international responsibility give priority to the new legal relationships arising between the wrongdoing state and the international community, among which reparation to the injured state is but a single aspect. A wider consideration of the implications for injured states would render the aggravated regime for breaches more amenable to obtaining reparation for damage. Using causal analysis in the determination of an internationally wrongful act is a possible solution. This would imply taking higher account of material damage to establish responsibility. Currently, the role of primary rules in this process is residual, overshadowed by the notion of objective legal injury. This excludes the causal relationships linking the damage as a whole to multiple wrongdoers because the internationally wrongful act – not damage – gives an injured state the legal interest to institute proceedings.

Therefore, a state's responsibility is primarily circumscribed to its wrongful conduct. Moreover, the internationally wrongful act of a state must be the cause of the damage for which reparation is sought. The inevitable consequence is that serious breaches arising from the aggregated

[91] ILC *Yearbook* 1973/I, at 20.

[92] I. Brownlie, *Principles of Public International Law*, 6th edn (Oxford University Press, 2003) p. 421.

[93] ILC *Yearbook* 1973/I, at 25, para. 19.

conduct of multiple wrongdoers have little chance of becoming justiciable because the required jurisdictional link between an applicant and several wrongdoers is harder to assert. A broader consideration of causation would take the harm inflicted on the injured party as the point of departure to determine responsibility. Under the current system, determinations of wrongfulness and the process of attribution revolve around the wrongdoer and define the conditions upon which an injured party may claim reparations. The serious breaches regime would ensure more accountability if the interests of injured parties were taken into consideration in the determination of an internationally wrongful act and its attribution.

3. Consequences arising from a serious breach of peremptory norms: are they shared?

Serious breaches entail particular consequences for third states, in addition to the obligations set out for responsible states. First, third states must not provide aid or assistance that maintains the illegal situation, and must refrain from recognising the breach as lawful. These measures are designed to bring the breach to an end through cooperation. Second, any state can invoke responsibility for breaches of obligations owed to the international community as a whole.

3.1 The aggravated regime of responsibility and shared obligations

3.1.1 Cooperation

Pursuant to Article 41 of the ARSIWA, states must cooperate to bring grave breaches to an end through lawful means. A failure to do so will entail the international responsibility of the concerned entities. Whether this responsibility is shared will mainly depend on the extent of the breach, the means available to end it, and the degree of cooperation undertaken to restore legality. It is clear from the Commentary to Article 41 that the obligation to cooperate 'applies to States whether or not they are individually affected by the serious breach' and that this calls for 'a joint and coordinated effort by all States to counteract the effects of these breaches'.[94] Although this provision was acknowledged as a progressive

[94] ARSIWA Commentary, n. 10, Commentary to Article 41, para. 3.

development of international law by the ILC, it is clear that an international undertaking to counter serious breaches involving several actors can attract responsibility in case of default, especially if the breach is a continuing one.

The legal status of the duty of cooperation enshrined in Article 41(1) of the ARSIWA is rather indeterminate. On the one hand, the Declaration of Principles on Friendly Relations and Cooperation of States, adopted by the UN General Assembly in 1969,[95] describes this principle as one of the main pillars for the maintenance of international peace and security, and for the respect of human rights. On the other hand, 'it might be open to question whether general international law at present prescribes a positive duty of cooperation'.[96] Be that as it may, we can infer the presence of an obligation to cooperate within the institutional framework of the UN (particularly through the action of the Security Council) in Article 49 of the Charter, whereby member states shall afford mutual assistance in carrying out the measures decided upon by the Security Council. The recent pronouncement of the ICJ in the *Wall* advisory opinion clarifies matters further and reinforces the normative content of the obligation to cooperate. In that advisory opinion, the Court held that the UN should 'consider what further action is required to bring to an end the illegal situation resulting from the construction of the wall and the associated régime'.[97] The views of the Court and of the ILC appear to be the same. The latter, in the Commentary to Article 41(1) of the ARSIWA, refers to cooperation, especially in the framework of a competent international organisation: '[w]hat is called for in the face of serious breaches is a joint and coordinated effort by all States to counteract the effects of these breaches.'[98]

When a serious breach is non-continuing, the obligation of non-cooperation becomes redundant. When the illegal act does not extend in time, the serious breach can neither be strengthened nor brought to an end by the conduct of third states. In any event, the latter remain bound by the obligation of non-recognition for the purpose of contrasting the

[95] Although UN General Assembly resolutions do not have a binding character, the unanimous consent of states to their adoption, as occurred in the case of the Declaration of Principles on Friendly Relations and Cooperation of States, may be understood as a general acceptance of the validity of the rules declared therein. See *Military and Paramilitary Activities in and against Nicaragua*, n. 39, para. 188.

[96] ARSIWA Commentary, n. 10, Commentary to Article 41, para. 3.

[97] *Wall* advisory opinion, n. 42, at 200, para. 160.

[98] ARSIWA Commentary, n. 10, Commentary to Article 41(1), para. 3.

continuing effects that may be produced by the violation, as discussed in what follows.

3.1.2 Non-recognition

The principle of non-opposability of the consequences of unlawful acts finds its contemporary expression in the obligation not to recognise as lawful a situation created by a serious breach of international law.[99] After taking note of the Universal Declaration of Human Rights, alongside the binding Mandate for South West Africa and the UN Charter, the ICJ declared that South Africa's presence in Namibia was illegal and 'opposable to all States in the sense of barring *erga omnes* the legality of a situation which is maintained in violation of international law',[100] signaling that the principle of non-discrimination had become universal. The Court's finding was exceptionally far-reaching because it involved legal consequences for *all* states that relied on South Africa's discriminatory policy. In the *Wall* advisory opinion, the Court reaffirmed the obligation of non-recognition in light of 'the character and the importance of the rights and obligations involved'.[101] Having determined that Israel was in violation of the Palestinian peoples' right to self-determination and of certain rules of international humanitarian law, the Court decided that 'all States are under an obligation not to recognize the illegal situation resulting from the construction of the wall'.[102] Any subsequent conduct of other states validating the wall's construction would have engaged the responsibility of the recognising state. The same might be said in the context of Iraq's annexation of Kuwait in 1991: any state recognising the sovereignty of Iraq over the occupied territory of Kuwait would have incurred responsibility on the basis of consecutive obligations stemming from the aggravated regime. Whether this responsibility would have been shared with Iraq is doubtful, because any resulting damage would have been non-material and too remotely related to the initial act of aggression.

[99] Article 41(2) ARSIWA, n. 10.

[100] *Legal Consequences for States of the Continued Presence of South Africa in Namibia (South West Africa) Notwithstanding Security Resolution 276 (1970)*, Advisory Opinion, ICJ Reports 1971, 16, at 57, para. 126. The Court also qualified this principle by saying that 'the non-recognition of South Africa's administration of the Territory should not result in depriving the people of Namibia of any advantages derived from international co-operation and other official acts'. Ibid., at 56, para. 125.

[101] *Wall* advisory opinion, n. 42, at 200, para. 159. [102] Ibid.

A clearer case for shared responsibility between principal wrongdoers and third states for breaching the non-recognition obligation would involve an international organisation that validated the consequences of serious breaches through the conclusion of further agreements binding its members. In these cases, the conduct of the member states can be engaged independently from the responsibility of the organisation.[103] It is, of course, also possible that the joint responsibility of the organisation and its member states is engaged.[104]

3.1.3 Non-assistance

The third consequence of peremptory breaches is the obligation of third states not to provide assistance in the commission of the internationally wrongful act. When states assist the principal wrongdoer in strengthening the illegal situation created by the serious breach, they may be held responsible for a violation of the obligation of non-assistance. This situation could give rise to a cumulative shared responsibility between the primary and the secondary wrongdoers.

This possibility arose when the Security Council condemned apartheid in South Africa in 1977. A decade earlier, equality and non-discrimination had reached the status of international human rights norms recognised under international conventions, international custom, and general principles of law.[105] In Resolution 418 (1977), acting under Chapter VII of the UN Charter, the Security Council condemned the 'massive violence and killings' used by the South African government against civilians opposing apartheid, and determined that the acquisition of arms by South Africa constituted a threat to international peace and security. It instructed all states to cease providing it with weaponry and further enjoined them to refrain from any cooperation with South Africa in the manufacture and development of nuclear weapons.[106] The Council also called upon states that were non-members of the United Nations to comply with the aforementioned measures, suggesting that these obligations were owed to the international community as a whole, and that international responsibility attached to their violation.

In the context of the right to self-determination, the Council made similar pronouncements involving African territories under Portuguese

[103] Articles 17 and 62 ARIO, n. 26. [104] Article 48 ARIO, n. 26.

[105] *South West Africa* cases (*Ethiopia* v. *South Africa*; *Liberia* v. *South Africa*), Second Phase, ICJ Reports 1966, 4, at 300 (Dissenting Opinion Judge Tanaka).

[106] UN Doc. S/RES/418 (1977).

administration. Its Resolution 218 (1965) condemned Portugal's failure 'to recognize the right of the peoples under its administration to self-determination and independence' on the basis of previous Council and General Assembly Resolutions, and requested all states to refrain from offering the Portuguese government any assistance 'which would enable it to continue its repression'.[107] The question remains whether a violation of these rules would constitute a discreet breach of the non-assistance obligation, or if it would result in some form of shared responsibility. In most cases this will be a matter of degree: if the aid and assistance is substantial enough and satisfies the standards of Article 16 of the ARSIWA, the responsibility of two or more entities can be engaged.

3.1.4 Additional consequences

In this subsection we briefly discuss the additional consequences following the commission of a serious breach provided by the savings clause in Article 41 of the ARSIWA. This provision recognises that international law may provide for further consequences flowing from the commission of a serious breach. In this way, it becomes open to the simultaneous application of other international legal regimes and to any future developments of the international legal order. In fact, other international treaties may establish subject-specific provisions stemming from the breach of a particular peremptory norm.

For example, additional legal consequences flowing from the commission of the serious breach are applicable to all states under the regime of collective security when Chapter VII of the UN Charter binds them. The UN Security Council has a primary role in handling the consequences of threats to peace and security. It may offer solutions similar to those of the law of responsibility to bring to an end the serious breach and to neutralise its illegal effects,[108] and it represents the major institutional channel through which the international community can take action to stop the continuation of wrongful conduct. An eminent example is UN Security Council Resolution 687 (1991), adopted in the aftermath of Iraq's invasion of Kuwait and which created the UN Compensation Commission.[109] This body was established to deal with claims arising from loss, damage, or

[107] UN Doc. S/RES/218 (1965).

[108] The practice of the Security Council constitutes the main legal basis for upholding the customary status of both obligations under Article 41(2) ARSIWA, n. 10.

[109] UN Doc. S/RES/687 (1991).

injury to foreign governments, nationals, and corporations resulting from the unlawful invasion and occupation of Kuwait.[110] Resolution 687 held that Iraq was 'liable under international law' for all damage caused, although, controversially, it stopped short of qualifying Iraq's invasion as an act of aggression.[111] In light of its lack of judicial character, the Security Council's attribution of liability to Iraq is altogether questionable. But the scope of its Chapter VII powers is wide, and could possibly be used to hold several states responsible for the same wrongful act.

3.2 *A shared duty to invoke serious breaches?*

The inherent gravity of peremptory norms calls for concerted action to bring them to an end, as we have seen in the section above. It also gives standing to all states to invoke their breach in international adjudicative bodies, provided the necessary jurisdictional requirements are met.[112] Under its current formulation, the invocation of serious breaches by non-injured states is formulated as an entitlement to be exercised in a facultative manner. But we argue that the regime of responsibility for serious breaches would be much more effective if this constituted a shared obligation in view of the communitarian interest involved. This proposition is not a new one. In his Separate Opinion appended to the ICJ's judgment in the *Armed Activities* case, Judge Simma mentioned that Uganda had standing – and the duty – to invoke the violations of international humanitarian law and human rights law suffered by certain individuals in Ndjili International Airport in the hands of Congolese military personnel. This was regardless of whether the victims had Ugandan nationality.[113] The underlying rationality of this pronouncement, continued Judge Simma, is to eliminate gaps in the law where they can be avoided, especially when a positive rule provides for remedial action. We subscribe to this view as regards the serious breaches regime, while noting that the enforcement of the international rule of law can only gain from prospects such as this one.

[110] Ibid., para. 18. [111] Ibid., para. 16.

[112] Article 48 ARSIWA, n. 10: 'Any State other than an injured State is entitled to invoke the responsibility of another State in accordance with paragraph 2 if: (b) the obligation breached is owed to the international community as a whole.'

[113] *Armed Activities on the Territory of the Congo (Democratic Republic of the Congo* v. *Uganda)*, n. 80, at 338 (Separate Opinion Judge Simma).

4. Conclusions

Shared responsibility for crimes that destabilise the public order is an ancient notion, common to many traditions and cultures. The concept was well entrenched in the Western traditions of bygone times, when law and religion were hardly distinguishable from one another.[114] The Greek myths speak of maledictions attaching to criminals and their descendants, as revealed by the Atreidae's tragic destiny. The murder of Thyestes's three newborns at the hands of his brother Atreus was perpetrated throughout generations. It influenced the fate of Agamemnon – Atreus's son – who was moved to sacrifice his daughter Iphigenia to ensure his successful Trojan expedition, only to be assassinated by his wife Clytemnestra, aided by Aegisthus (fathered by Thyestes and his daughter Pelopia, whom he raped!). Thereafter, Orestes committed matricide to avenge his father, killing Clytemnestra. It was the goddess Athena who ended the curse by creating the Aeropagus, a tribunal composed of Athenian citizens called upon to pass judgment on Orestes. The votes being equally divided, the goddess decided to acquit him.[115]

History has also displayed the collective dimension of crime, as evidenced by the complex evolution of the customary right to vengeance. It suffices to recall that grave crimes, such as murder and rape, evoke communitarian dimensions from the perpetrator's standpoint and that of the victim.[116] The crime attaches to the guilty man, his family, and his descendants – 'until the 7th generation', biblically put – and authorises vengeance against his community. In turn, the victim's entourage, city, and allies are called to re-establish equilibrium through the legitimate exercise of violence.[117]

In this context, we may interpret the move from 'private' vengeance towards the exercise of the state's institutionalised right to punish as

[114] Some have dubbed these notions as pre-legal. L. Gernet, *Droit et institutions en Grèce antique* (Paris: Flammarion, 1968), especially Part I.

[115] See Aeschylus, *Les Eumenides* (Paris: Gallimard, 1967) p. 377.

[116] Gernet, *Droit et institutions en Grèce antique*, n. 114, p. 87. This tradition continued until the age of the modern state, as shown by literature dating back to the seventeenth and eighteenth centuries: in *The Cid* by Corneille, Rodrigue must avenge the affront against his father to avoid dishonour, and in Molière's *Don Juan*, Doña Elvire's brother hunts down the man who seduced, married, and abandoned his sister.

[117] The Iliad reminds us that the dishonour inflicted on Menelaus by the abduction of queen Helen, his wife, attracts the sympathy of Greek kings to his cause. The expedition mounted against Troy thus has an indisputable dimension of collective vengeance being exercised by a plurality of communities against the main wrongdoer – Paris – but also against his family and his entire city.

evidence of the prejudice borne by every member of society when grave crimes are committed. In other words, the law invests the public authority with the power to react against crimes in the name of every member of society.

This notion is translated in the international legal plane through Articles 48 and 41 of the ARSIWA: the former authorises every non-injured state to invoke the responsibility of the wrongdoer, whereas the latter requires that all states cooperate towards the re-establishment of the international public order.

Indeed, shared responsibility for grave breaches of peremptory norms, having translated an ancestral practice into the realm of international law, provides a restorative legitimacy that we are still surprisingly reluctant to recognise.

10

Countermeasures against Multiple Responsible Actors

CHRISTIAN J. TAMS

1. Introduction

1.1 The concept of countermeasures

Countermeasures are coercive measures taken by a responding state (or other actor) against a target state (or other actor) in response to a wrongful act for which the targeted actor bears responsibility. They have become fairly rare today, but remain a conceptually important feature of the arsenal of 'law enforcement concepts'.

As a broad rule, general international law permits countermeasures as a flexible means of responding to previous wrongful conduct,[1] but submits their exercise to a range of procedural and substantive conditions. If these conditions are met, the countermeasure functions as a 'justification' or – in the terminology of the International Law Commission (ILC) – a circumstance precluding the wrongfulness of the conduct. In the words of Article 22 of the 2001 Articles on Responsibility of States for Internationally Wrongful Acts (ARSIWA):[2]

Christian J. Tams is Professor of International Law at the University of Glasgow. The research leading to this chapter has received funding from the European Research Council under the European Union's Seventh Framework Programme (FP7/2007–2013)/ERC grant agreement n° 249499, as part of the research project on Shared Responsibility in International Law (SHARES), carried out at the Amsterdam Center for International Law (ACIL) of the University of Amsterdam.

1 For a useful overview see the chapters in Part V, Section III of J. Crawford, A. Pellet, and S. Olleson (eds.), *The Law of International Responsibility* (Oxford University Press, 2010); for details see O. Y. Elagab, *The Legality of Non-Forcible Counter-Measures in International Law* (Oxford: Clarendon Press, 1988).

2 Articles on Responsibility of States for Internationally Wrongful Acts, ILC *Yearbook* 2001/II(2) (ARSIWA).

> The wrongfulness of an act of a State not in conformity with an international obligation towards another State is precluded if and to the extent that the act constitutes a countermeasure taken against the latter State in accordance with chapter II of part three.

The essence of that provision is taken up in Article 22(1) of the 2011 Articles on the Responsibility of International Organizations (ARIO),[3] addressing countermeasures taken by international organisations. However, Article 22(2) ARIO adds that:

> an international organization may not take countermeasures against a responsible member State or international organization [under the conditions referred to in paragraph 1] unless:
>
> (b) the countermeasures are not inconsistent with the rules of the organization; and
>
> (c) no appropriate means are available for otherwise inducing compliance with the obligations of the responsible State or international organization concerning cessation of the breach and reparation.

This suggests that the general law of countermeasures – binding as customary international law and in many respects reflected in the ILC's two sets of Articles – interacts with special treaty regimes; it is subsidiary to treaty-specific 'means . . . for otherwise inducing compliance with the obligations of the responsible State or international organization'. Beyond that, as a feature of the general law of responsibility, countermeasures can be modified or contracted out by special treaties. Because '[c]ountermeasures are a feature of a decentralized system',[4] they are affected by processes of institutionalisation and/or centralisation. '[R]ules of the organization' (in the words of Article 22(2) of the ARIO) can no doubt impose restrictions. More generally, specific treaty regimes may add further conditions or may exclude countermeasures altogether.[5]

[3] Articles on the Responsibility of International Organizations, ILC Report on the work of its sixty-third session, UNGAOR 66th Sess., Supp. No. 10, UN Doc. A/66/10 (2011) (ARIO).

[4] Commentary to the Articles on Responsibility of States for Internationally Wrongful Acts, ILC *Yearbook* 2001/II(2) (ARSIWA Commentary), Introduction to Part Four Chapter II, para. 1.

[5] Both of the ILC's texts recognise the primacy of specialised regimes that seek to disapply the general rules. In the words of Article 57 ARSIWA, n. 2: 'These articles are without prejudice to any question of the responsibility under international law of an international organization, or of any State for the conduct of an international organization.' To give just two examples, 'sophisticated' regimes of dispute settlement, such as World Trade Organization (WTO) law and European Union law, are typically taken to have excluded the right to rely on countermeasures: see e.g. *United States – Sections 301/310 of the Trade*

1.2 Delimitation

The concept of countermeasures justifies a particular type of response against wrongful conduct (or, in the terminology that is used in this edited volume, against 'harmful outcomes').[6] While the lines may at times be difficult to draw in practice, countermeasures need to be distinguished from three cognate concepts.

First, as a 'responsibility concept', countermeasures are to be distinguished from responses against qualified wrongful conduct amounting to (material) breaches of a treaty in the sense of Article 60 of the Vienna Convention on the Law of Treaties (VCLT).[7] While the specific measures taken may be quite similar (e.g. the suspension of an agreement in response to a breach), international law establishes distinct legal regimes for 'treaty-based' and 'responsibility-based' responses. The former notably require a material breach and a focus on responses within one and the same treaty regime; what is more, they suspend the treaty obligation rather than providing a justification for its non-compliance.[8]

Second, intrinsically wrongful countermeasures (that thus require some justification) are to be distinguished from unfriendly acts below

Act of 1974, Panel Report of 22 December 1999, WT/DS/152/R, paras. 7.35–7.46 (arguing that WTO law 'prevent[s] member States from unilaterally resolving their disputes in respect of WTO rights and obligations'); and further Article 344 of the Treaty on the Functioning of the European Union; and *Commission of the European Economic Community* v. *Luxembourg and Belgium*, European Court of Justice, joined cases 90/63 and 91/63, (1964) ECR 626.

6 P. A. Nollkaemper and D. Jacobs, 'Shared Responsibility in International Law: A Conceptual Framework' (2013) 34(2) MIJIL 359, at 367.

7 Vienna Convention on the Law of Treaties, Vienna, 23 May 1969, in force 27 January 1980, 1155 UNTS 331 (VCLT).

8 ARSIWA Commentary, n. 4, Introductory Commentary, Part Three, Chapter II, para. 4: 'Countermeasures are to be clearly distinguished from the termination or suspension of treaty relations on account of the material breach of a treaty by another State, as provided for in article 60 of the 1969 Vienna Convention. Where a treaty is terminated or suspended in accordance with article 60, the substantive legal obligations of the States parties will be affected, but this is quite different from the question of responsibility that may already have arisen from the breach. Countermeasures involve conduct taken in derogation from a subsisting treaty obligation but justified as a necessary and proportionate response to an internationally wrongful act of the State against which they are taken. They are essentially temporary measures, taken to achieve a specified end, whose justification terminates once the end is achieved.' In practice, things may be much more complex than this suggests; but from a responding actor's perspective, the stringent conditions imposed by Article 60 of the VCLT mean that countermeasures are the far more attractive option. For details see B. Simma and C. J. Tams, 'Reacting against Treaty Breaches', in D. B. Hollis (ed.), *The Oxford Guide to Treaties* (Oxford University Press, 2012), p. 576.

the level of (prima facie) illegality.[9] Examples include protests, diplomatic demarches, support for resolutions condemning breaches, the decision to refrain from cooperation in other fields, the rupture of diplomatic relations, and all other forms of retorsions. Such unfriendly, but legal, conduct is typically the most obvious way of responding to 'harmful outcomes'; in practice it may well be decisive and constitute a highly efficient way of putting pressure on the wrongdoing actor. However, international law does not regulate responses below the threshold of 'prima facie illegality' in any detail. All states and all organisations can always protest, send letters, decide not to agree on treaties benefiting another state, etc. – they do not require a 'title' to respond.

Third, while permitting the use of coercion, countermeasures are today understood to refer to responses of a *non-forcible* nature. Whether forcible countermeasures can be justified at all is a matter for debate. In any event, forcible responses would be subject to the special regime regulating/limiting recourse to force in international relations, as set out in the United Nations (UN) Charter.[10]

More controversially, it is necessary to determine the relationship between the general concept of countermeasures and reactions based on specific treaties. This is not a case of clear-cut inclusion or exclusion. On the face of it, countermeasures constitute a 'private' response governed by general international law, and operate outside institutionalised contexts. However, in some instances institutionalised sanctions may provide evidence of a particular approach reflected (also) in general international law. Whether this is so depends on the level of specificity of the institutional regime, and in particular on whether it intends to derogate from the general framework.

9 Elagab, *The Legality of Non-Forcible Counter-Measures in International Law*, n. 1, at p. 4 and pp. 29–30. In its work on state responsibility, the ILC made a similar point when distinguishing formal ways of invoking responsibility (requiring some form of 'title') from informal representations (which were always acceptable). In its ARSIWA Commentary to Article 42, para. 2, n. 4, it observed: 'There is in general no requirement that a State which wishes to protest against a breach of international law by another State or remind it of its international responsibilities in respect of a treaty or other obligation by which they are both bound should establish any specific title or interest to do so. Such informal diplomatic contacts do not amount to the invocation of responsibility unless and until they involve specific claims by the State concerned, such as for compensation for a breach affecting it, or specific action such as the filing of an application before a competent international tribunal, or even the taking of countermeasures. In order to take such steps, i.e. to invoke responsibility in the sense of the articles, some more specific entitlement is needed.'

10 See Article 50(1)(d) ARSIWA, n. 2 and ARSIWA Commentary to Article 50(1)(d), n. 4.

1.3 *Essential features of the regime*

Drawing on international practice and case law, both the ARSIWA and the ARIO recognise a general right to resort to countermeasures,[11] subject to a number of conditions. For reasons of convenience, these can be presented in three 'clusters'.[12]

First, countermeasures can only be taken in response to a wrongful act. Subjective perceptions of wrongfulness are not sufficient. As, typically, international conduct triggering responses is not submitted to an objective, prior scrutiny, this means that the responding actor responds at its own risk.[13] The initial wrongful act must have also affected the responding actor to justify a response. This requirement is typically phrased as one of 'legal interest' or 'injury', both of which describe the relation between the initial breach and the responding actor. In the regular scenario, described in Article 42 of the ARSIWA and Article 43 of the ARIO, the responding actor acts as an 'injured State or international organization'; this is true, for example, where it has been individually affected by a breach. More controversial are responses in defence of general or 'public' interests. These are generally discouraged, as otherwise any state or international organisation – claiming to defend a greater good – could take countermeasures.[14] However, Article 54 of the ARSIWA and Article 57 of the ARIO leave some room for 'lawful measures', by 'an entity other than an injured State or international organization', against breaches of obligations protecting collective interests of the international community as a

[11] As noted above, this may be disapplied or modified by special rules.

[12] For details see notably the ARSIWA Commentary to Articles 49–54, n. 4.

[13] Pronouncements by the Arbitral Tribunal in the case concerning the *Air Service Agreement of 27 March 1946, (United States of America/France)*, (1978) 54 ILR 338 (*Air Service*), at para. 81, at some time gave rise to doubt, but the matter now seems settled. In its ARSIWA Commentary to Article 49, para. 3, n. 4, the ILC set out what seems the (now generally) accepted position: '*Paragraph 1* of article 49 presupposes an objective standard for the taking of countermeasures, and in particular requires that the countermeasure be taken against a State which is responsible for an internationally wrongful act in order to induce that State to comply with its obligations of cessation and reparation. A State taking countermeasures acts at its peril, if its view of the question of wrongfulness turns out not to be well founded. A State which resorts to countermeasures based on its unilateral assessment of the situation does so at its own risk and may incur responsibility for its own wrongful conduct in the event of an incorrect assessment. In this respect, there is no difference between countermeasures and other circumstances precluding wrongfulness' (footnotes omitted).

[14] See ARSIWA Commentary to Article 54, n. 4 and Article 56 ARIO, n. 3; and further C. J. Tams, *Enforcing Obligations Erga Omnes in International Law* (Cambridge University Press, 2010), pp. 198 et seq.

whole or of communities of treaty parties. Such 'lawful measures' can be taken to 'ensure cessation of the breach and reparation in the interest of the injured party or of the beneficiaries of the obligation breached'.

Second, before resorting to countermeasures, the responding actor must call upon the targeted actor to cease its wrongful conduct and notify it of its intention to resort to countermeasures. An exception to this general condition is recognised for so-called 'urgent countermeasures as are necessary to preserve [the responding actor's] rights'.[15] In its Commentary to Article 55 of the ARIO, the ILC formulated the underlying rationale in the following terms:

> The responsible international organization is thus given an opportunity to appraise the claim made by the injured State or international organization and become aware of the risk of being the target of countermeasures. By allowing urgent countermeasures, paragraph 2 makes it however possible for the injured State or international organization to apply immediately those measures that are necessary to preserve its rights, in particular those that would lose their potential impact if delayed.[16]

While the line between urgent and regular countermeasures may at times be difficult to draw in practice, it is not questioned as a matter of principle.

Third, as regards their scope, countermeasures must be proportionate, or – in the words of Article 51 of the ARSIWA and Article 54 of the ARIO – 'commensurate with the injury suffered, taking into account the gravity of the internationally wrongful act and the rights in question'.[17] This is the essential substantive limitation on countermeasures, which ensures that responses are not treated as a licence to punish the wrongdoing actor. Because countermeasures can affect a broad range of legal relations, 'judging the "proportionality" of countermeasures is not an easy task and can at best be accomplished by approximation'.[18] What is required is a comparison between the initial breach and the countermeasures; the latter must remain equivalent. In assessing proportionality, the impact of the measures needs to be taken into account, as must

[15] Article 55(2) ARIO, n. 3.

[16] Commentary to the Articles on the Responsibility of International Organizations, ILC Report on the work of its sixty-third session, UNGAOR 66th Sess., Supp. No. 10, UN Doc. A/66/10 (2011) (ARIO Commentary), Article 55(2).

[17] See e.g. Article 51 ARSIWA, n. 2. The notion of a 'commensurate' response goes back to the ICJ's judgment in *Gabčíkovo-Nagymaros Project (Hungary/Slovakia)*, Judgment, ICJ Reports 1997, 7, at 56, paras. 85–7 (*Gabčíkovo-Nagymaros*).

[18] *Air Service*, n. 13, para. 83.

the relevance of the underlying legal provision that has been violated.[19] Lastly, in order to be proportionate, countermeasures must in principle be temporary and reversible.[20]

It is clear from the preceding paragraphs that, as a general form of law enforcement applicable in a range of settings, countermeasures are regulated in a rather flexible way. From the perspective of shared responsibility as defined in this volume, this is an opportunity as much as a problem. It can be presented as a problem because applying the legal regime of countermeasures will often not yield 'obvious' or 'natural' results. Conversely, the flexibility inherent in such notions as 'legal interest', 'proportionality', and so on can be used to fine-tune the general legal regime of countermeasures to the specific problems of shared responsibility. This will be done in the subsequent sections, initially by mapping shared responsibility issues arising in relation to countermeasures (section 2), and then by suggesting how the general regime could be applied to the different settings that are identified (sections 3 to 5).

2. Questions and scenarios

2.1 Questions

The legal regime of bilateral, inter-state countermeasures has been discussed for decades. To date, it remains shaped by venerable awards such as *Naulilaa*,[21] or decisions in disputes about bilateral treaties (*Air Service*,[22] *Gabčíkovo-Nagymaros*).[23] Notwithstanding disagreement on some smaller issues, the traditional regime seems generally to be reflected in Part Three, Chapter II of the ILC's ARSIWA. As is clear from the introductory

[19] Hence in *Air Service*, the Tribunal suggested that it was 'essential, in a dispute between States, to take into account not only the injuries suffered by the companies concerned but also the importance of the questions of principle arising from the alleged breach'; see ibid.

[20] See notably Article 49(3) ARSIWA, n. 2 and Article 51(3) ARIO, n. 3. The ILC emphasises the temporary and reversible character of countermeasures on frequent occasions, but in the end recognises that 'the duty to choose measures that are reversible is not absolute. It may not be possible in all cases to reverse all of the effects of countermeasures after the occasion for taking them has ceased. For example, a requirement of notification of some activity is of no value after the activity has been undertaken. By contrast, inflicting irreparable damage on the responsible State could amount to punishment or a sanction for non-compliance, not a countermeasure as conceived in the articles'. ARSIWA Commentary to Article 49, para. 9, n. 4.

[21] *Responsabilité de l'Allemagne à raison de dommages causés dans les colonies portugaises du Sud de l'Afrique (Portugal* v. *Germany)*, Award, (1928) 2 RIAA 1011 (*Naulilaa*).

[22] *Air Service*, n. 13. [23] *Gabčíkovo-Nagymaros*, n. 17.

summary, it has been developed to fit bilateral inter-state relations and it is in this context that requirements such as prior notification or proportionality can be applied, and that a concept as general as proportionality could perhaps be concretised meaningfully.

The involvement of further actors tests the viability of the regime; it raises the question of whether the (traditionally bilateral) concept of countermeasures can be meaningfully adapted to fit multilateral settings. So far, this question has largely been addressed from the perspective of multiple *responding actors*. As hinted at in the preceding section, there is some debate about whether states that are not individually affected by a prior breach should be entitled to defend general or public interests by means of countermeasures – a matter left open by Article 54 of the ARSIWA and Article 57 of the ARIO – and if so, whether and how such responses ought to be coordinated.[24] The converse perspective – that of multiple actors responsible for the harmful outcome – seems not to have been analysed systematically thus far. Rather than looking at a broadening of the circle of responding actors, this would result in a multiplication of the potential targets. When addressing the matter in the following sections, from the perspective of shared responsibility, the crucial question is whether countermeasures can be *taken against each of the multiple actors* responsible for one 'harmful outcome'.

Allowing such responses against each of the responsible actors could enhance the effectiveness of the law of responsibility, as countermeasures might force each of them towards compliance. On the other hand, countermeasures might perhaps be too broad a concept to respect differentiated contributions to shared responsibility. It therefore also needs to be asked whether countermeasures *taken in response* to shared responsibility are subject to specific conditions. It is these two questions that the present inquiry seeks to address. It does so on the basis of responses given in the ILC texts of 2001 and 2011. At the outset, it should be noted that in many respects, answers remain tentative. There is fairly little solid practice that could help to ground responses. Very often, the international regime is developed by 'extrapolation' from bilateral rules, and the ILC's responses given in the Articles of 2001 and 2011 often reflect uncertainty about fundamental concepts of shared responsibility.

[24] See M. Akehurst, 'Reprisals by Third States' (1970) 44 BYIL 1; J. Charney, 'Third State Remedies in International Law' (1989) 10 MIJIL 57; Tams, *Enforcing Obligations Erga Omnes*, n. 14, pp. 198 et seq. See H. P. Aust's contribution in Chapter 6 of this volume, H. P. Aust, 'Circumstances Precluding Wrongfulness', p. 169, at p. 206.

2.2 *Scenarios*

In seeking to apply the regime of countermeasures to instances of shared responsibility, different forms of shared responsibility need to be distinguished. The conceptual framework on which this edited volume is based suggests a general distinction between cases in which the responsibility arises out of concerted action, and cases in which there is no concerted action.[25] Drawing on, and adapting, that distinction in the context of countermeasures, it seems possible to identify three scenarios of shared responsibility that focus on the degree of responsibility borne by the different actors that are responsible for harmful outcomes.[26]

2.2.1 Equally shared responsibility

Multiple actors can share responsibility for a harmful outcome as equals. If the 'harmful outcome' in question is one and the same wrongful conduct, it will often be based on some form of cooperation or joint omission. Joint, possibly collusive, active conduct in violation of international law would be the prime example in point: an armed attack by armies of more than one state would be a 'classic' example. This is by no means the only setting, though. Conduct through an organ established by a plurality of actors would be another example. What is more, where responsibility for omission within multilateral contexts (e.g. non-compliance with a duty to prevent a certain event from occurring) is concerned, shared responsibility would seem to be the normal case, and outside special settings (protecting powers, or guarantees) it will typically be equally shared. Finally, responsibility can be 'equally shared' even in the absence of coordinated action. A plurality of actors, acting independently of each other, could violate commitments under 'parallel' but not identical obligations, including where the obligation is of a different nature (e.g. an obligation of conduct and an obligation of result).[27] To take up an example referred to by the ILC, 'several States might contribute to polluting a river by the *separate* discharge of pollutants'.[28] In this

[25] See Chapter 1 of this volume, P. A. Nollkaemper, 'Introduction', p. 1, at pp. 6–12. Nollkaemper and Jacobs, 'Shared Responsibility in International Law', n. 6, at 360–70, especially 368–9.

[26] Admittedly, the line between the first two scenarios ('equally shared' and 'differentiated responsibility') is not always easy to draw. As principles of shared responsibility are only gradually established, it is still being negotiated.

[27] However, see below for a comment on the relationship between wrongful acts based on active conduct, and those based on omission.

[28] ARSIWA Commentary to Article 47, para. 8, n. 4 (emphasis added).

case, their contribution to the harmful outcome, while not coordinated and joint, could make each of the actors equally responsible as well.

2.2.2 Differentiated responsibility

Multiple actors may bear different degrees or forms of responsibility for one and the same harmful outcome. Most lawyers schooled in domestic law would think of the cooperation between the 'principal' and the 'accomplice' in the violation of the law, and the same scenario can of course be envisaged under international law.[29] In fact, the recognition, in Article 16 of the ARSIWA and international case law,[30] of a *general* concept of complicity in state responsibility makes this scenario increasingly relevant.[31] Complicity is not the only instance of differentiated – and 'derivative'[32] – responsibility, though. In a specific setting, states or other actors may be required not to instigate, or incite, wrongful conduct,[33] and special rules may preclude them from recognising the effects of certain grave breaches of other actors.[34] Beyond forms of active conduct, wherever international law has recognised a duty to prevent or suppress certain harmful outcomes,[35] it may be necessary to distinguish between (a) the responsibility for commission of a wrong, and (b) responsibility for failure to prevent it (a form of responsibility thrown into stark relief by the 2007 merits judgment of the International Court of Justice (ICJ or Court) in

[29] For many details see H. P. Aust, *Complicity and the Law of State Responsibility* (Cambridge University Press, 2011); for an earlier, cautious, assessment see B. Graefrath, 'Complicity in the Law of International Responsibility' (1996) 29 RBDI 370.

[30] See the ICJ's judgment in the *Application of the Convention on the Prevention and Punishment of the Crime of Genocide (Bosnia and Herzegovina* v. *Serbia and Montenegro)*, Judgment, ICJ Reports 2007, 43, para. 420 (*Bosnian Genocide* case) (where Article 16 ARSIWA is said to 'reflec[t] a customary rule').

[31] Curiously, the point is regularly ignored. Aust's study on *Complicity and the Law of State Responsibility*, n. 29, provides the clearest exposition of the applicable regime and highlights its practical relevance. See also Chapter 5 of this volume, V. Lanovoy, 'Complicity in an Internationally Wrongful Act', p. 134.

[32] Cf. Introductory ARSIWA Commentary to Part One, Chapter IV, para. 7, n. 4.

[33] See e.g. Article III(c) of the Convention on the Prevention and Punishment of the Crime of Genocide, Paris, 9 December 1948, in force 12 January 1951, 78 UNTS 277 (Genocide Convention), and Article 4 of the International Convention on the Elimination of All Forms of Racial Discrimination, New York, 21 December 1965, in force 4 January 1969, 660 UNTS 195.

[34] See e.g. Article 41(2) ARSIWA, n. 2 and Article 42(2) ARIO, n. 3.

[35] See e.g. Article I of the Genocide Convention, n. 33, and Article IV(a) of the International Convention on the Suppression and Punishment of the Crime of Apartheid, New York, 30 November 1973, in force 18 July 1976, 1015 UNTS 243.

the *Bosnian Genocide* case).[36] Where negative duties (to abstain) coexist alongside duties of prevention, the relationship between responsibility for conduct and responsibility for omission is more difficult to characterise. However, at least where the multiple responsible actors belong to the same category – e.g. where one state has committed a wrong that another state has failed to prevent – it is probably best viewed as a form of differentiated responsibility.[37]

2.2.3 Responsibility for conduct carried out in the framework of an international organisation

Even where responsibility is based on one single act, and no issue of differentiated responsibility arises, the uncertain rules governing the allocation of responsibility between states and international organisations may give rise to specific problems in relation to countermeasures. This is true irrespective of whether responsibility is equally shared or differentiated. In both instances, the link between the international organisation and its member states adds a further dimension to the 'shared responsibility puzzle'.

These three scenarios are not mutually exclusive, and can be combined. What is more, it may not always be obvious whether different forms of responsibility are equally shared or differentiated. Still, at the risk of a schematic assessment, the distinction will be applied in the following sections, as it allows for a relatively clear presentation of the material in this otherwise fairly 'hazy' area of international responsibility.

3. Countermeasures and equally shared responsibility

Of the three scenarios, the first – equally shared responsibility – is probably the least problematic in theory, even though applying the conditions limiting resort to countermeasures may pose practical challenges. In line

[36] See *Bosnian Genocide* case, n. 30, paras. 428–38. While the Court did not 'purport to establish a general jurisprudence applicable to all cases where a treaty instrument, or other binding legal norm, includes an obligation for States to prevent certain acts' (para. 429), aspects of its discussion of the requirements of responsibility for omission would seem to be capable of general application.

[37] The matter is certainly not obvious and requires much further discussion. One might also consider responsibility for an act and responsibility for an omission to be 'equal'. However, it is worth noting that in the *Bosnian Genocide* case, n. 30, the ICJ seems to have restricted the range of remedies available in case of breaches by omission.

with the questions identified in section 2.1, it needs to be asked whether each of the various actors that are equally responsible for a 'harmful outcome' can be targeted by countermeasures. The relevant legal texts would seem to answer this question in the affirmative.

3.1 *Responsibility triggered by independent wrongful acts*

Where different actors separately (i.e. without coordination) contribute to a harmful outcome, this in fact would seem to follow from the general principle of independent responsibility. The ILC Commentary notes – and the point of principle would not seem to be disputed – that '[i]n such cases, the responsibility of each participating State is determined individually, on the basis of its own conduct and by reference to its own international obligations.'[38] Examples mentioned by the ILC include 'the separate discharge of pollutants' eventually resulting in an oil spill; or the separate, and independent, violations of international law by Yugoslavia (laying of mines) and Albania (failure to warn) that formed the backdrop to the *Corfu Channel* case.[39] Notwithstanding the involvement of multiple actors, responsibility in these settings arises in the bilateral relations between the individual actors concerned. Each contributor is responsible only to the extent that it has violated international law: Albania for the failure to warn; Yugoslavia for the laying of mines. As long as the focus remains on these separate responsibility relationships – i.e. as long as an injured actor seeks to hold Albania responsible for its independent failure to warn, or Yugoslavia for its laying of the mines – the regular framework of responsibility can be applied. It is perfectly possible to treat the two breaches as self-standing, each triggering its own consequences, and each triggering a right of the injured actor to implement responsibility, including by means of countermeasures.

Thus 'bilateralised', responsibility can be addressed by the regular rules governing implementation as laid down in the respective Parts IV of the ARSIWA and the ARIO. An injured actor would need to establish some form of entitlement to act (legal interest) and comply with the conditions governing the admissibility of claims, and it could eventually enforce responsibility by means of countermeasures. In all this, responsibility remains limited to the bilateral relations. Notably, as regards the

[38] ARSIWA Commentary to Article 47, para. 8, n. 4.

[39] Ibid. Cf. *Corfu Channel (United Kingdom of Great Britain and Northern Ireland* v. *Albania)*, Merits, ICJ Reports 1949, 4.

consequences of a state's wrongful conduct, each of the independently responsible states has to make 'reparation [only] for the injury caused by [its] internationally wrongful act'.[40] This may be difficult to apply in practice – what, precisely, is the consequence of a failure to warn; how much of the harmful outcome has been caused by each individual contributor? – but, in principle, it is not disputed.

The independent character of responsibility is reflected in the rules on countermeasures, which, after all, are designed to implement claims to cessation and reparation, and only go so far as such claims exist.[41] In applying the rules on proportionality, a responding actor will therefore have to establish that its response is commensurate with the injury caused by the independent breach of the targeted actor. And in line with the general rules, countermeasures taken against one of multiple responsible actors engaged in independent conduct will have to cease when the particular independent breach stops.

All this suggests that where responsibility is triggered by independent wrongful acts, the general regime can be applied without major modification. There is no doubt a risk of artificial compartmentalisation when wrongful acts are treated as independent, even though they contribute to the same (harmful) outcome. Yet this compartmentalisation is the result of treating independent wrongful acts as separate (which is a basic assumption of Part One of the ARSIWA) and of requiring a causal link between wrongful conduct and injury for the purposes of reparation (a key decision informing Part Two of the ARSIWA). The regime of countermeasures merely follows suit. Designed to enhance the prospect of enforcing responsibility, it is instrumental.

3.2 *Responsibility triggered by interrelated wrongful acts*

Matters are more complex where equally shared responsibility is incurred in relation to the *same* wrongful act, and where the conduct of various actors is interrelated rather than separate. Still, in principle, the basic presumption is that each of the actors involved may face claims for responsibility, and none of them can hide behind the 'collective'. Article 47(1) of

[40] Article 31(a) ARSIWA, n. 2. See also Chapter 7 of this volume, P. d'Argent, 'Reparation, Cessation, Assurances and Guarantees of Non-Repetition', p. 208.

[41] For example, under Article 52(1)(a) ARSIWA, n. 2, the responding state must 'call upon the responsible State . . . to fulfil its obligations under part two'; this presupposes the existence of an obligation.

the ARSIWA and Article 48(1) of the ARIO are quite clear in fact: they both provide in near-identical terms that:

> Where several States [or: an international organisation and one or more States or other international organisations] are responsible for the same internationally wrongful act, the responsibility of each State [or organisation] may be invoked in relation to that act.

Article 48(2) of the ARIO moves beyond this by laying down a special rule for instances of 'subsidiary responsibility'.[42] Addressing 'subsidiarity', it would not seem to cover instances in which responsibility is equally shared.

The Commentaries on the respective Articles are not particularly detailed, but the Commentary to Article 47 of the ARSIWA identifies the key reasons supporting the position adopted. In the words of the ILC, the provision gives expression to

> the general principle that in such cases [of joint responsibility for the same internationally wrongful act] each State is separately responsible for the conduct attributable to it, and that responsibility is not diminished or reduced by the fact that one or more other States are also responsible for the same act.[43]

This view, while formulated in relation to the general concept of 'invocation of responsibility' underlying Part Three ARSIWA and Part Four ARIO, affects the position as to countermeasures. As Article 49 of the ARSIWA and Article 50 of the ARIO clarify, countermeasures are one particular way of invoking responsibility, and they are a generally available response against the responsible state or international organisation.[44]

International practice is by no means widespread, but it would seem to support the position taken by the ILC. Three examples can serve to illustrate the point.

First, the response by Western states against the imposition of martial law in Poland in 1981 highlights that, in the absence of indications to the contrary, responsibility triggered by conduct of two states will be perceived as 'equally shared', and will expose each of them to countermeasures.[45] In

[42] See section 5. [43] ARSIWA Commentary to Article 47, para. 1, n. 4.

[44] See ARSIWA Commentary, n. 4, Introductory Commentary to Part Three Chapter II, para. 3: countermeasures are 'instrumental in character and are appropriately dealt with in Part Three as an aspect of the implementation of State responsibility'.

[45] The case involved an instance of 'third party countermeasures', taken by states not injured in the traditional sense. As such, it supports the view that such 'third party countermeasures' are actually permitted.

response to the draconian measures adopted against dissidents and Solidarnosc activists, many Western states expressed concern, protested against violations of internationally protected human rights standards, and responded by way of retortions.[46] In some instances, countries such as the United States, Switzerland, and the United Kingdom decided to suspend bilateral aviation agreements with Poland (which needed to be justified as a countermeasure). For present purposes, what matters most is that in addition to Poland, responses also targeted the Soviet Union, which was perceived to have required and facilitated the imposition of martial law. Hence the United States suspended the landing rights of Aeroflot, safeguarded by international agreements, on American territory. This no doubt reflected power politics during the Cold War era, but was based on the reasoning underlying Article 47 of the ARSIWA. In the words of President Reagan, a response targeting the Soviet Union was justified as it bore 'a major share of the blame for the development in Poland'.[47] In short, below the level of rhetoric and clamour, the conduct was based on a principle of joint Soviet–Polish responsibility for the alleged violation of international human rights standards.

Second, when looking at other forms of invoking international responsibility, the position taken in Article 47 of the ARSIWA and Article 48 of the ARIO also finds affirmation in international case law. The ICJ's *Nauru* judgment[48] in fact would seem to be the clearest exposition of the principle of joint responsibility (and was drawn on in the ILC's work). The case concerned allegedly wrongful conduct by three states (through the vehicle of an international entity, the 'Administering Authority') of which one, Australia, was sued alone. Dismissing Australia's argument that it could not be 'singled out', the Court observed that there was no reason

> why a claim brought against only one of the three States should be declared inadmissible in *limine litis* merely because that claim raises questions of the administration of the Territory, which was shared with two other States. It cannot be denied that Australia had obligations under the Trusteeship Agreement, in its capacity as one of the three States

[46] For details see H. E. Moyer Jr and L. A. Mabry, 'Export Controls as Instruments of Foreign Policy: The History, Legal Issues and Policy Lessons of Three Recent Cases' (1983) 15 L & Pol Int Bus 1, at 63 ff.; Tams, *Enforcing Obligations Erga Omnes*, n. 14, at pp. 213–15.

[47] Statement of 28 December 1981, reproduced in M. Nash, 'Contemporary Practice of the United States Relating to International Law' (1982) 76 AJIL 374, at 380.

[48] *Certain Phosphate Lands in Nauru (Nauru* v. *Australia)*, Preliminary Objections, ICJ Reports 1992, 240 (*Nauru*).

> forming the Administering Authority, and there is nothing in the character of that Agreement which debars the Court from considering a claim of a breach of those obligations by Australia.[49]

While the modality of invoking responsibility is a different one from that encountered in the Polish–Soviet case referred to above, the two instances in fact complement each other rather well. The former concerns the broadening of the range of 'target states'; the latter clarifies that even where three states are cooperating in a structured way, each of them can be subjected to law enforcement measures. As countermeasures (per Article 49 of the ARSIWA and Article 51 of the ARIO) can be taken against all responsible states, the *Nauru* reasoning would seem to be of relevance.

Third, a brief passage from the European Court of Justice's (ECJ) case law can be taken to apply a parallel line of reasoning to the relations between member states and international organisations. Like *Nauru*, the case is not concerned with countermeasures, but it, too, is relevant as it indicates who bears responsibility (which then can be invoked by the generally available methods, including countermeasures). In *Parliament* v. *Council*, the ECJ analysed legal relations within mixed agreements concluded by the European Union and its member states. While some of them may contain special provisions, the ECJ noted that as a general rule,

> in the absence of derogations expressly laid down in the Convention, the Community and its member States as partners of the ACP States are jointly liable to those latter States for the fulfilment of every obligation arising from the commitments undertaken, including those relating to financial assistance.[50]

3.3 *The scope of responsibility*

The preceding discussion suggests that where responsibility is equally shared, each of the actors contributing to the (same) harmful outcome can be targeted by countermeasures. It remains to be seen whether the fact that a plurality of actors is responsible should affect the reach, or scope, of countermeasures taken against each single one of them. On the basis of the general rules outlined above, the answer should be in the affirmative. Just as in cases of independent responsibility mentioned

[49] Ibid., at para. 40.

[50] *Parliament* v. *Council*, European Court of Justice, case C-316/91, (1994) ECR I-653, at 660–1, para. 29.

above, the regime of countermeasures (requiring responses to be 'commensurate with the injury suffered')[51] is affected by rules on the *scope* of responsibility borne by each one of the multiple responsible actors. As an enforcement concept, countermeasures are restricted by rules determining the consequences of responsibility. Hence where one particular state bears the bulk of responsibility for a wrongful act, countermeasures directed against it can be more harmful than those directed against a state whose responsibility is more limited.

In theory, this seems rather clear. However, two concerns need to be addressed. First, where a particular harmful outcome is the consequence of interrelated conduct, there is much debate about the allocation of responsibility between the different responsible actors. The matter is typically addressed in terms of the domestic law concept of 'joint and several' responsibility, and it boils down to a straightforward question: should each of the equally responsible actors be individually liable for the entire injury caused by the breach of international law? The problem is much discussed,[52] but remains controversial. For present purposes, it is important to note that if international law were to accept a standard of joint and several responsibility, each responsible actor could be targeted by countermeasures commensurate with the harmful outcome in its entirety – which in turn should result in a greater tolerance of 'intrusive' countermeasures. This indeed would seem to follow from special treaty provisions that expressly declare each actor responsible for the harmful outcome in its entirety. For example, Article IV(2) of the Convention on International Liability for Damage Caused by Space Objects (while dealing with liability, and within a very specific setting) expressly reserves the right of claimants 'to seek the entire compensation due under this Convention from any or all of the launching States which are jointly and severally liable'.[53]

[51] Article 49 ARSIWA, n. 2; Article 51 ARIO, n. 3.

[52] See e.g. Aust, *Complicity and the Law of State Responsibility*, n. 29, pp. 274 ff; A. Orakhelashvili, 'Division of Reparation between Responsible Entities', in J. Crawford, et al. n. 1, p. 647; S. Besson, 'La Pluralité d'Etats responable' (2007) RSDIE 13; J. E. Noyes and B. D. Smith, 'State Responsibility and the Principle of Joint and Severable Liability' (1988) 13 YJIL 225 (all with further references). See also d'Argent, 'Reparation, Cessation, Assurances and Guarantees of Non-Repetition', n. 40, at pp. 244–49.

[53] Convention on International Liability for Damage Caused by Space Objects, London, Moscow, and Washington DC, 29 March 1972, in force 1 September 1972, 961 UNTS 187. Judge Simma's Separate Opinion in the *Oil Platforms* case might be interpreted similarly: see *Oil Platforms (Islamic Republic of Iran* v. *United States of America)*, Judgment, ICJ Reports 2003, 161, Separate Opinion by Judge Simma, paras. 60 ff.

By contrast, the general texts on responsibility are more guarded. Article 47(2) of the ARSIWA and Article 48(3) of the ARIO seek to ensure that a claimant ought not to be able to 'recover, by way of compensation, more than the damage it has suffered'. And even in the *Nauru* case, the ICJ was cautious to clarify that permitting recourse against Australia as one of the responsible states 'does not settle the question whether reparation would be due from Australia, if found responsible, for the whole or only for part of the damage Nauru alleges it has suffered'; this would require an analysis of 'the characteristics of the Mandate and Trusteeship Systems . . . and, in particular, the special role played by Australia in the administration of the Territory'.[54] In light of these statements, the existence of a general principle of joint and several responsibility should not simply be assumed.

The second concern is of more general relevance; it is based on the flexible nature of the proportionality test. As noted above, proportionality is the key criterion limiting the reach of countermeasures. It 'translates' rules on the division of responsibility between multiple actors into limits on countermeasures. And yet, while it is a crucial limit in theory, perhaps one should not place too much reliance on proportionality. There is no doubt a responding actor is required to tailor its countermeasures to be commensurate. However, in practice, the flexibility inherent in the proportionality test renders precise assessments rather illusory. If judging proportionality 'can at best be accomplished by approximation',[55] how should one determine whether a particular response (say, a travel ban imposed on government officials) would still be a commensurate response against one of multiple responsible actors? Also, given the dearth of authoritative assessments, could we really expect this particular assessment to depend on whether the targeted actor is responsible for the injury in its entirety, or merely for its share? It seems that proportionality will need to be specified much more before it can be seen as a real limit on countermeasures. This, one hastens to add, is not a problem of shared responsibility proper, but a weakness of the general regime, in which proportionality remains underdeveloped. In the presence of multiple responsible actors, it arises acutely. At the same time, pragmatically, one might say that precisely because proportionality is a flexible criterion, it can be applied to instances of equally shared responsibility.

[54] *Nauru*, n. 48, at p. 262, para. 56. [55] *Air Service*, n. 13, para. 83.

4. Countermeasures and differentiated responsibility

4.1 Introductory remarks

If responsibility is not equally shared, but differentiated, the application of countermeasures in response to harmful outcomes poses problems of a different nature. Matters are fairly straightforward if countermeasures are taken against the 'principal wrongdoer': i.e. the state or organisation that is directly responsible for a breach of international law. This possibility exists and is in no way affected by the illegal contribution, of a 'lesser degree', of another state or organisation, to the wrongful conduct. The real problem concerns not countermeasures against the 'principal wrongdoer', but those taken against other actors that bear responsibility in another role, namely as an accomplice in the wrongful conduct, or as an instigator, or as an actor who ought to have prevented another actor's wrongful conduct. These instances are not very common. Countermeasures are fairly rare to begin with, and if a state or organisation relies on them, it would normally be expected, as a matter of practice, to direct them against the 'principal' target. However, some practice exists, and as principles of derivative responsibility emerge and become more accepted, the legal questions arise more acutely. In this regard, it may be worth reiterating the recent trend towards an affirmation of a general rule against complicity in wrongfulness, of obligations of non-recognition, and the increasing debate about duties of prevention. As noted above, while raising different problems, all of these can be viewed as instances of differentiated responsibility.[56] As ancillary responsibility is triggered by separate forms of conduct (aid and assistance, recognition, failure to prevent), the better view is that Article 47(1) of the ARSIWA and Article 48(1) of the ARIO (envisaging implementation measures against each of a plurality of actors responsible for *the same unlawful act*) do not apply.[57]

Still, actors that illegally recognise, or aid and abet, wrongful conduct of course remain in breach of international law. Should other actors be entitled to respond to that illegality by resorting to countermeasures? Pragmatically, one might say that the problem is unlikely to be of practical relevance; if they decide to resort to countermeasures, it seems counter-intuitive that responding actors should target accomplices or other actors bearing lesser forms of responsibility. Yet this merely helps to put the problem in perspective, but does not solve it. When looking at the ILC's

[56] See section 2.2.2.

[57] Cf. Aust, *Complicity and the Law of State Responsibility*, n. 29, at pp. 288–90.

texts, the answer would seem rather clear. A violation of a rule against complicity, to take just one example, qualifies as an internationally wrongful act in the sense of the respective Articles 1 to 2 of the ARSIWA and the ARIO; and it is against wrongful conduct that countermeasures can be taken. In light of the previous discussion, it may be added that, at present, the countermeasure would have to be tailored to be commensurate with the effects of the particular wrongful conduct against which it is directed – i.e. the aiding and abetting, the illegal recognition, etc. – but could not be a blanket response against the harmful outcome as such.[58] In this setting, perhaps even a flexible criterion such as proportionality could be expected to act as a meaningful limitation. Yet all these may be said to be side issues. The real question is whether international law should accept a right to direct countermeasures against actors bearing lesser forms of responsibility. Would it not be sensible to limit, as a matter of law, the possibility of coercive responses, and to move to a system of 'staggered' responsibility that permits coercive responses only against the principal wrongdoers?

4.2 An emerging restriction on countermeasures against 'lesser wrongs'?

As forms of lesser, derivative responsibility – and principles of shared responsibility – are only gradually being developed, it would be wrong to expect international law to provide ready-made answers. In fact, present practice would not seem to yield clear indications at all. But, perhaps, change is underway. In retrospect, future generations of international lawyers may look back to the present decade as one in which – as part of a regime of differentiated responsibility – international law came to recognise restrictions on the availability of countermeasures against 'lesser wrongs'. Three rather different features of the present regime could be said to point in that direction, and could foreshadow the emergence of a more restrictive regime.

First, the legal regime governing claims before international courts might support a restrictive approach.[59] The ICJ in particular – applying the so-called 'indispensable third party rule' (or '*Monetary Gold* principle') – has long refused to entertain claims against states bearing

[58] Yet even that is discussed; cf. Aust, ibid., pp. 274 ff.

[59] See Chapter 8 of this volume, A. M. H. Vermeer-Künzli, 'Invocation of Responsibility', p. 251, at pp. 270–80, and the collection of papers on *Procedural Aspects of Shared Responsibility in International Adjudication*, published in a themed section in (2013) 4(2) JIDS 277.

ancillary responsibility if the principal actor has not consented to the jurisdiction of the Court, and if, in the course of the proceedings, the Court would be required to pronounce on the legality of that principal actor's conduct.[60] To be sure, the indispensable third party rule is controversial and is based on considerations of jurisdiction, not on a restriction of claims.[61] However, its application entails results rather similar to an exclusion of countermeasures against 'lesser wrongs': in specific settings, a form of enforcement that would otherwise be open becomes unavailable. One might readily say that the situations of heavily regulated judicial claims, on the one hand, and decentralised, 'private' countermeasures, on the other, are incomparable. But there is perhaps room for the argument that if, as a result, international courts have been hesitant to accept legal claims (which after all 'should not be considered an unfriendly act between States', but encouraged)[62] against 'side actors', there could perhaps be an argument also to restrict archaic responses by way of countermeasures.

Second, albeit more tentatively, there is at least some recent evidence that might suggest that responsibility for ancillary breaches should give rise to a more 'lenient' regime of remedies; this in turn might have repercussions at the level of law enforcement by way of countermeasures. The ICJ's merits judgment in the *Bosnian Genocide* case, while taking the notion of a 'duty to prevent' seriously, was cautious when pronouncing on the remedies triggered by such a breach by omission. Having determined the respondent state's responsibility for failure to prevent acts of genocide at Srebrenica, the Court needed to address the consequences of

[60] See the ICJ's *Monetary Gold* and *East Timor* cases, *Monetary Gold Removed from Rome in 1943 (Italy* v. *France, United Kingdom of Great Britain and Northern Ireland and United States of America)*, Preliminary Question, ICJ Reports 1954, 19, at 32; and *East Timor (Portugal* v. *Australia)*, Judgment, ICJ Reports 1995, 90, at 100–5, paras. 23–35, respectively. See further the discussion of the concept in the *Nauru* and *Nicaragua (Jurisdiction and Admissibility)* cases: see *Nauru*, n. 48, at 259–62, para. 55; *Military and Paramilitary Activities in and against Nicaragua (Nicaragua* v. *United States of America)*, Jurisdiction and Admissibility, ICJ Reports 1984, 392, at para. 35; as well as, more recently, *Armed Activities on the Territory of the Congo (Democratic Republic of the Congo* v. *Uganda)*, Judgment, ICJ Reports 2005, 168, at para. 38.

[61] For a succinct summary of the Court's jurisprudence see L. Caflisch, 'Cent ans de règlement pacifique des différends interétatiques' (2001) 288 RCADI 245, at 406 et seq.; C. F. Amerasinghe, *Jurisdiction of Specific International Tribunals* (Leiden: Martinus Nijhoff, 2009), pp. 13–14 and pp. 50 et seq.

[62] Manila Declaration on the Peaceful Settlement of International Disputes, UN Doc. A/RES/37/10 (1982), Annex, para. 5.

such a breach. It recalled the principle of reparation, but then went out of its way to make a specific point. In the words of the Court, while

> the Respondent did have significant means of influencing the Bosnian Serb military and political authorities which it could, and therefore should, have employed in an attempt to prevent the atrocities . . . it has not been shown that, in the specific context of these events, those means would have sufficed to achieve the result which the Respondent should have sought [i.e. the prevention of genocide].[63]

And further:

> Since the Court cannot therefore regard as proven a causal nexus between the Respondent's violation of its obligation of prevention and the damage resulting from the genocide at Srebrenica, financial compensation is not the appropriate form of reparation for the breach of the obligation to prevent genocide.[64]

This statement might be read to point towards a more general distinction between principal and ancillary breaches. And on that basis (which at present remains tentative), one might perhaps consider whether the regime of countermeasures should not also reflect the different levels of responsibility.

Third, within the framework of the ARIO, Article 48(2) provides the clearest indication of how a differentiated regime of responsibility could be 'translated' into the field of law enforcement. Notably, the provision distinguishes between 'primary' and 'subsidiary' levels of responsibility. For the purposes of implementation, Article 48(2) clarifies that '[s]ubsidiary responsibility may be invoked insofar as the invocation of the primary responsibility has not led to reparation.' As the Commentary suggests, this is designed to give effect, for the purposes of invocation, to provisions like Article 62 of the ARIO, which stipulates that under certain circumstances (dealt with separately in the subsequent section), member states can be subsidiarily responsible for conduct of an international organisation. The subsidiary character of a member state's responsibility, however, would seem to affect the regime of countermeasures. As the ILC's Commentary clarifies, while claims are being pursued against the primarily responsible organisation, those directed against the 'subsidiarily responsible entity' can only be made 'subject to the condition that the entity whose responsibility is primary fails to provide

[63] *Bosnian Genocide* case, n. 30, para. 462. [64] Ibid.

reparation'.[65] With respect to countermeasures, as long as that condition remains in place, no claim of reparation is due against the entity bearing subsidiary responsibility – and hence no countermeasures can be taken against it. In the end, then, the concept of subsidiary responsibility in the sense of Article 48(2) of the ARIO entails a result that is similar to that of the indispensable third party rule in ICJ proceedings: at least initially, law enforcement measures could only be taken against the principal wrong-doer, but not against those bearing lesser ('subsidiary') responsibility.

To summarise the preceding argument, perhaps there is room to consider whether in different fields of responsibility, concepts giving effect to differentiated regimes of responsibility are gaining ground. None of them concerns the regime of countermeasures directly, but for the reasons set out, they would seem to be related and perhaps merit consideration. To simply state that '[t]here are . . . no structural reasons which exacerbate the problem of countermeasures in the case of complicit States'[66] (or indeed other actors bearing ancillary responsibility) may thus be an oversimplification. Perhaps one might suggest that, taken together, the three tendencies point towards modifications of the traditional regime, which needs to be adapted to accommodate degrees of responsibility.

4.3 Counterarguments

Still, the considerations set out in the preceding section remain tentative, and need to be tested. Upon their own terms, they can be rebutted without much difficulty; all it takes would be to state that 'they prove little', as they do not concern countermeasures specifically. As regards judicial proceedings, and the indispensable third party rule more particularly, one might go further and note that the ICJ's approach is not derived from general concepts of responsibility, but from a specific reading of the rules of jurisdiction; certainly not a necessary implication of consensualism, but a deliberate extension, and a controversial one at that.

Perhaps more significantly, there is at least some international practice indicating that states and international organisations do at times take meaningful enforcement action against states bearing ancillary

[65] Article 48 ARIO, para. 3, n. 3. By contrast, the Commentary to the first reading provision had noted that 'Subsidiarity does not imply the need to follow a chronological sequence in addressing a claim', ARIO Commentary to Article 47(3) (first reading), para. 3, n. 16.

[66] Aust, *Complicity and the Law of State Responsibility*, n. 29, at p. 288.

responsibility. Research conducted does not yield examples of 'clear-cut' countermeasures proper. However, complicity, illegal recognition, and the like have at times been met with unfriendly acts or retorsions. Again, one might say that this does not offer conclusive proof in a debate intending to establish rules governing countermeasures. However, what seems clear is that some form of enforcement action against ancillary breaches of the law is considered. The following illustrative examples – each of which raises problems of its own – might thus be said to provide some evidence in point.

First, where collective sanctions have taken the form of boycotts against a certain state or practice in order to deprive it of international support, states violating the boycott have themselves been at times subjected to acts of retorsion and isolated themselves. Protests and boycotts against New Zealand following that country's sport exchanges with apartheid South Africa would provide such an example.[67]

Second, the recognition by a member state of what in the view of an organisation was an illegal situation has been met with sanctions. Egypt's suspension from the Arab League in the wake of the Israeli-Egyptian peace treaty[68] (pursuant to which in Annex III, Article 1, the parties 'agree[d] to establish diplomatic and consular relations and to exchange ambassadors upon completion of the interim withdrawal') might be read in that way.[69]

Third, where an international sanctions regime requires states to prevent the proliferation of certain risks, the implementation of the duty to prevent may take rather 'robust' forms. The US-sponsored 'Proliferation Security Initiative' – comprising voluntary agreements, but also assertions of a right to act unilaterally – could be seen as evidence of this.[70]

Finally, where a state is seen as supporting internationally wrongful conduct by a non-state actor (as opposed to another state or organisation), that state may be targeted by rather forceful international sanctions. By

[67] On the background see J. L. Chappelet and B. Kübler-Mabbott, *The International Olympic Committee and the Olympic System: The Governance of World Sport* (London: Routledge, 2008), at pp. 109–10.

[68] Peace Treaty between Israel and Egypt, 18 ILM 362 (1979), at 362.

[69] See K. D. Magliveras, *The Exclusion from Participation in International Organisations* (Dordrecht: Martinus Nijhoff, 1999), at pp. 237–8; and briefly B. Simma and C. J. Tams, 'Article 60 (1969/1986) [Commentary]', in O. Corten and P. Klein (eds.), *The Vienna Conventions on the Law of Treaties: A Commentary* (Oxford University Press, 2011), p. 1362.

[70] For details see Y.-H. Song, 'The U.S.-Led Proliferation Security Initiative and UNCLOS: Legality, Implementation, and an Assessment' (2007) 38 ODIL 101.

way of illustration, it suffices to refer to the range of enforcement measures (UN sanctions, countermeasures proper, ICJ proceedings) against the Federal Republic of Yugoslavia in relation to conduct, typically by Bosnian Serbs, within Bosnia and Herzegovina.

The preceding considerations suggest that at present, international law does not provide any clear-cut rules regarding countermeasures against ancillary breaches. International practice is sparse. Concepts or arguments that might justify a restriction of the right to take countermeasures are still in their infancy. Given that ancillary breaches are, after all, internationally wrongful acts in and of themselves, no such restriction should be presumed. It may be seen as a preferable approach *de lege ferenda*, but the ('preferable') regime has yet to crystallise. The better view is that, for the time being, countermeasures can be used in response to ancillary breaches of international law – that is, against states or international organisations that fail to prevent conduct that they ought to have prevented; against states or international organisations that recognise as legal a situation created by a 'serious breach ... of an obligation arising under a peremptory norm of general international law';[71] or against states and international organisations that aid and assist in the commission of a wrongful act.

It may be worth pausing to consider the implications of this assessment by considering hypothetical instances of violations of treaty-based duties to prevent genocide or racial discrimination. In the light of the ICJ's case law, for responsibility to arise, it 'does not need to be proven that the State concerned definitely had the power to prevent the genocide; it is sufficient that it had the means to do so and that it manifestly refrained from using them'.[72] Precisely how many states or actors bear such responsibility for failure to prevent depends on the facts of each case; however, often the circle will be rather large. The preceding considerations suggest that against all these ancillary breaches, countermeasures are, in principle, available. Of course, in line with the general rules, countermeasures would have to remain proportionate. However, while that is agreed in principle, perhaps not too much should be expected from the concept of proportionality as it is so flexible, and in the field of countermeasures it seems to be applied with particular flexibility. This in turn explains the 'appeal', *de lege ferenda*, of restrictions to the right to take countermeasures. As regimes of shared and differentiated responsibility

[71] Cf. Articles 40–1 ARSIWA, n. 2; Articles 41–2 ARIO, n. 3.
[72] *Bosnian Genocide* case, n. 30, para. 438.

emerge, we should not preclude that they will entail an exclusion of countermeasures against actors bearing 'lesser' forms of responsibility.

5. Countermeasures and responsibility for conduct carried out in the framework of an international organisation

Special problems arise if responsibility is shared between an international organisation and its member states. This scenario cuts across the two scenarios addressed so far, as responsibility may be shared equally or unequally. Clearly, it presents particular challenges, as the allocation of responsibility between an international organisation and its member states is difficult and controversial. Controversies about attribution of conduct, or about the proper object of legal claims, affect the legal regime of countermeasures, which presupposes the responsibility of the targeted actor and is designed to induce cessation/reparation. The scarcity of countermeasures taken against international organisations further complicates the assessment. All this suggests that the regime is still in flux.

That said, to a large extent, the particular challenges do not affect the regime of countermeasures proper. They need to be addressed within the framework of the rules of attribution, or in applying the principles of reparation to international organisations and their member states. As a law enforcement concept, countermeasures will 'implement' whatever result is reached. To take but one example, if the *Behrami*[73] decision was correctly decided, and the conduct in question could not be attributed to a European Convention on Human Rights member state, it would not be necessary to discuss coercive forms of law enforcement against member states; they had broken no law in the first place. The key question does not concern countermeasures, but the rules of attribution. By the same token, and in line with what has been suggested above, if member states are not liable for damage caused by 'their' international organisation, no reparation claims could be enforced against them, and countermeasures would have to be taken against the international organisation required to provide for reparation. All this suggests that there is limited room for legal argument about the regime of countermeasures. The real problems lie elsewhere.

Nevertheless, four points can briefly be made. First, Articles 13 to 18 and 57 to 61 of the ARIO do not endorse a 'blanket' responsibility of

[73] *Agim Behrami and Bekir Behrami* v. *France*, App. No. 71412/01 (ECtHR, 2 May 2007).

member states for activities of international organisations of which they are a member. However, they provide for rather broadly defined categories in which both member states and international organisations bear responsibility in relation to acts of the other. In the light of what has been stated above, this would need to be reflected in the rules on countermeasures.

Second, as a general rule, Articles 13 to 18 and 57 to 61 of the ARIO do not introduce a hierarchy between the different forms of responsibility of member states and international organisations. However, as noted above, Article 62(1) of the ARIO is the exception that proves the rule. It mentions two relatively narrowly defined instances in which 'a State member of an international organization is responsible for an internationally wrongful act of that organization', namely if:

(a) it has accepted responsibility for that act towards the injured party; or
(b) it has led the injured party to rely on its responsibility.

In these instances, as made clear by paragraph 2, '[t]he international responsibility of a State ... is presumed to be subsidiary.' As Article 62(2) of the ARIO is the only provision of the text that expressly uses this terminology ('subsidiary'), it may be assumed that in other instances of interaction between member states and international organisations (notably circumvention in the sense of Articles 17 and 61 of the ARIO), responsibility would not result in subsidiary responsibility. The exception set out in Article 62 of the ARIO therefore has a narrow scope of application.

Third, importantly, Article 48(2) applies the distinction between primary and subsidiary responsibility to the field of law enforcement. In no unclear terms, it notes that '[s]ubsidiary responsibility may be invoked insofar as the invocation of the primary responsibility has not led to reparation.' As noted above, this is an important provision that could guide the future development of the law in other areas of differentiated responsibility as well. However, in the absence of meaningful international practice, at present, its impact is uncertain.

Fourth, if it is accepted, then the distinction between primary and subsidiary responsibility might be of considerable relevance for the regime of countermeasures. Unlike other forms of law enforcement (notably proceedings before national or international courts), countermeasures are not subject to the complex limitations that in practice have complicated attempts to hold international organisations responsible. 'Immunity' is no bar; and unlike before some state-centred international courts, countermeasures can be taken against each international legal subject. This suggests that whereas with respect to judicial proceedings, international organisations may often not be promising targets, countermeasures could very well be directed against them. This in turn would mean that enforcing the law against the actor bearing primary responsibility could be quite meaningful – so that the subsidiary responsibility of member states in the sense of Article 62 need not become relevant.

6. Conclusions

The regime of countermeasures is characterised by its flexibility. While developed in the bilateral, inter-state setting, it can generally be applied to instances of shared responsibility. In fact, as shown in the preceding sections, where multiple actors bear responsibility for a harmful outcome, they can usually be targeted individually. This is notably due to the approach adopted in Article 47(1) of the ARSIWA and Article 48(1) of the ARIO, which for instances of equally shared responsibility is probably the correct one. Matters are more complex where responsibility is not shared equally, but in a differentiated way. In this scenario (i.e. scenario number 2 of the present chapter), one might well discuss whether countermeasures should be available against actors that are responsible for ancillary breaches. As a matter of principle, the two ILC texts do not impose any limitation; only for the rather special case of subsidiary responsibility as set out in Article 62 of the ARIO are some member states shielded from countermeasures until redress has been sought from international organisations.

The general impression gained is that where multiple actors bear some form of responsibility for a harmful outcome, the injured state (or indeed states other than injured states – if the restrictive reading of Article 54 of the ARSIWA and Article 57 of the ARIO is rejected) has a wide measure of discretion in deciding against whom to direct countermeasures. This further increases the already considerable flexibility of the concept of countermeasures. In this respect, the present discussion confirms how difficult it is to reach agreement on restricting the regime of countermeasures. At the same time, it must not be forgotten that, notwithstanding the regime's flexibility, countermeasures are used only rarely; the considerable academic debate masks their limited practical relevance in contemporary international law. This in turn affects the status of the two ILC texts on the matter: as far as shared responsibility is concerned, they do not provide much detail. And as far as countermeasures against multiple responsible states are concerned, the texts had to be drawn up on the basis of a very limited body of international practice. This makes them both more open to change, or more likely to channel developments – and it increases the need for a rigorous academic debate about the proper role of countermeasures.

11

Conclusions: Beyond the ILC Legacy

ANDRÉ NOLLKAEMPER AND ILIAS PLAKOKEFALOS

1. Introduction

In this concluding chapter we assess the extent to which, and how, the law of international responsibility as laid down in the ARSIWA[1] and the ARIO[2] provides a basis for determination and implementation of a responsibility that is shared by multiple states and/or international organisations.

One general conclusion can be stated up front. This is that, quite obviously, neither the ARSIWA nor the ARIO were designed and drafted with situations of shared responsibility in mind. In both texts, only one principle expressly addresses the possibility of the international responsibility of multiple wrongdoers. This is the principle that where several states and/or international organisations are responsible for the same internationally wrongful act, the responsibility of each state or organisation may be invoked in relation to that act.[3] This principle recognises that several states and/or international organisations can be responsible for the same wrongful act, without expressly stating this. However, taken strictly, it only applies to the question of invocation. As such it is not

André Nollkaemper is Professor of Public International Law at the Faculty of Law of the University of Amsterdam, and director of the SHARES Research Project. Ilias Plakokefalos is a post-doctoral researcher in the SHARES Project at the University of Amsterdam. The research leading to this chapter has received funding from the European Research Council under the European Union's Seventh Framework Programme (FP7/2007–2013)/ERC grant agreement n° 249499, as part of the research project on Shared Responsibility in International Law (SHARES), carried out at the Amsterdam Center for International Law (ACIL) of the University of Amsterdam.

[1] Articles on Responsibility of States for Internationally Wrongful Acts, ILC *Yearbook* 2001/II(2) (ARSIWA).

[2] Articles on the Responsibility of International Organizations, ILC Report on the work of its sixty-third session, UNGAOR 66th Sess., Supp. No. 10, UN Doc. A/66/10 (2011) (ARIO).

[3] Article 47 ARSIWA, n. 1, Article 48 ARIO, n. 2.

determinative of other questions of shared responsibility, and can at most be used in the construction of other principles – as most contributors to this volume have done.[4]

Apart from this principle on the same wrongful act, both the ARSIWA and the ARIO implicitly recognise the possibility of shared responsibility by their inclusion of 'without prejudice' provisions. These provisions stipulate that attribution to, or responsibility of, one state or international organisation is without prejudice to attribution to, or responsibility of, another actor and thus make clear that responsibility of one actor need not be exclusive.[5] However, they do not in themselves provide a basis for shared responsibility; nor do they provide direction for the scope and distribution of such responsibility. Moreover, these provisions are noteworthy for the fact that they have only been included in relation to some principles, and not to others. While an *a contrario* argument (for example, to the effect that it could be inferred from the absence of such provisions in relation to circumstances precluding wrongfulness that these provisions would *not* apply in situations of multiple wrongdoers) is unwarranted, this does confirm that neither the ARSIWA nor the ARIO were designed for addressing questions of shared responsibility.

It indeed appears from the chapters in this volume that application of the various principles to situations of shared responsibility is based more on their adaptability than on their design. The following comment by Tams in relation to countermeasures applies to most of the other chapters: since the regime has been developed to fit bilateral inter-state relations, '[t]he involvement of further actors tests the viability of the regime; it raises the question of whether the (traditionally bilateral) concept of countermeasures can be meaningfully adapted to fit multilateral settings.'[6]

The lack of specific guidance on questions of shared responsibility obviously is, at least in part, caused by the fact that the construction of the principles of international responsibility, in relation to questions of shared responsibility, could not be based on significant practice. On issues such as attribution of conduct, circumstances precluding wrongfulness, or countermeasures, hardly any practice exists in relation to multiple wrongdoers. Fry's comment with respect to attribution of responsibility is of

[4] E.g. Chapter 2, A. Gattini, 'Breach of International Obligations', p. 25; Chapter 4, J. D. Fry, 'Attribution of Responsibility', p. 98; Chapter 7, P. d'Argent, 'Reparation, Cessation, Assurances and Guarantees of Non-Repetition', p. 208.

[5] Articles 10(3), 19, 57, and 58 ARSIWA, n. 1; Articles 19, 63, and 66 ARIO, n. 2.

[6] Chapter 10 in this volume, C. J. Tams, 'Countermeasures against Multiple Responsible Actors', p. 312, at p. 319.

more general relevance: 'the points made here are somewhat theoretical and speculative'.[7]

Against the background of this general conclusion, we will (in line with the analytical framework set forth in Chapter 1)[8] assess the contributions from two angles. In section 2 we will determine the ways in which the law of international responsibility, often without expressly referring to it, may facilitate, guide, or limit the determination or implementation of shared responsibility. In section 3 we will assess the extent to which the law of responsibility as contained in the International Law Commission's (ILC) legacy allows for differentiation between different factual contexts in which questions of shared responsibility may arise. This may depend on the contents of the primary obligations, the (public or private) nature of the interests at stake, and the nature of the actors that contribute to harmful outcomes. In section 4 we will conclude with our assessment of the extent to which questions of shared responsibility can be resolved within the system of responsibility developed by the ILC, and argue that international law should move beyond the ILC legacy.

2. The enabling capacity of the ILC system

On the whole, the contributions to this volume demonstrate that the law of international responsibility is a highly flexible body of law that in many situations will allow for the determination and implementation of shared responsibility (section 2.1). However, in several respects, notably pertaining to the distribution of responsibility and reparation between multiple actors, the ILC Articles provide little guidance (section 2.2). Particular aspects of the law, including attribution of conduct and invocation, may be outright prohibitive of a determination or implementation of shared responsibility (section 2.3).

2.1 Facilitation

The fact that the ARSIWA and the ARIO rarely deal expressly with questions of shared responsibility does not mean that they do not allow for or support the determination or implementation of shared responsibility. The international law of responsibility proves to be a flexible body of

[7] Fry, 'Attribution of Responsibility', n. 4, at p. 100.
[8] P. A. Nollkaemper, 'Introduction', p. 1 at pp. 16–20.

law that can be applied in, and adjusted to, a wide variety of situations, including situations involving shared responsibility.

The flexibility of the law is in part due to its generality. This generality was a precondition for the ability of the ILC to finalise the ARSIWA in the first place,[9] thus influencing the ARIO, which were based on them. The fact that both sets of Articles were formulated in highly general terms, and do not offer much detail on the precise conditions and consequences of responsibility, was a condition for their acceptability. While this generality may be seen as a drawback by some, it turns out to be a virtue when the ILC Articles need to be adapted to situations which the drafters did not have in mind.

This flexibility is particularly evident in the Articles that deal with a breach of an international obligation. Gattini demonstrates that the ARSIWA do not pose serious problems in terms of shared responsibility.[10] Where multiple actors causally contribute to harm, this will only engage their shared responsibility if their conduct can be construed as a breach of an obligation. Whether or not this is the case depends, above all, on the type and nature of the primary obligation and on the question whether the relevant subjects are bound by the obligation breached. If so, 'the objective element of international responsibility, i.e. the breach of an international obligation, does not pose major problems'.[11]

Also, the principles relating to attribution generally are flexible and allow for a determination of shared responsibility. This holds both for attribution of conduct and attribution of responsibility. As to the former, Messineo argues that the provisions on attribution of conduct concerning a multiplicity of possibly responsible actors are largely unproblematic.[12] His proposition that the possibility of multiple attribution has to be considered as the default rule[13] may seem provocative insofar as there is hardly any practice to support the notion of dual attribution of conduct. Moreover, some of the rare instances that do exist, notably the *Srebrenica* judgments of the Dutch courts,[14] relate to a situation that

[9] J. Crawford, 'The ILC's Articles on Responsibility of States for Internationally Wrongful Acts: A Retrospect' (2002) 96 AJIL 874, at 879.

[10] Gattini, 'Breach of International Obligations', n. 4, at p. 59. [11] Ibid.

[12] The exception is transferred organs where international law does not recognise multiple attribution, see Chapter 3 of this volume, F. Messineo, 'Attribution of Conduct', p. 60, at pp. 83–96.

[13] Ibid., at pp. 62, 88, 97.

[14] *Hasan Nuhanović* v. *The Netherlands*, ECLI:NL:GHSGR:2011:BR0133 (5 July 2011), at para. 5.3; also ILDC 1742 (NL 2011). See B. Boutin, 'Responsibility of the Netherlands for the Acts of Dutchbat in *Nuhanović* and *Mustafić*: The Continuous Quest for a Tangible Meaning for "Effective Control" in the Context of Peacekeeping' (2012) 25

Messineo considers to be an exception to the presumption of dual attribution.[15] Nonetheless, his assessment is persuasive and indeed suggests that the ARSIWA and the ARIO are highly flexible and do not preclude shared responsibility. They enable, for instance, shared responsibility in situations involving joint organs (as supported by the *Nauru*[16] and *Eurotunnel*[17] cases), and in situations where both international organisations and their member states incur responsibility. Therefore, 'the answer to the "whodunit" question in international law often yields two or three results at once: someone can be wrongfully detained by an individual, two states, and an international organisation, all at the same time'.[18]

The picture for attribution of responsibility is no different. Both the ARSIWA and the ARIO leave open the possibility of attributing responsibility to one actor for internationally wrongful conduct committed by another actor. Indeed, it can be inferred from the very definition of attribution of responsibility, in terms of responsibility for the conduct of another, that there cannot be situations where all of the parties bear attributed responsibility. Fry thus observes that the 'combination of attributed responsibility to one state or international organisation, on the one hand, and attribution of responsibility or conduct to another, on the other, might lead to multiple attribution (of responsibility, conduct, or both)'.[19] It should be noted, however, as observed by Gattini, that 'the entire Part Five of the ARIO – with the exception of Article 62, which codifies the well-established rule of the subsidiary responsibility of member states for wrongful acts of an international organisation in some particular and well-defined instances – is more an abstract exercise *de lege ferenda* than *de lege lata*'.[20]

LJIL 521; P. A. Nollkaemper, 'Dual Attribution: Liability of the Netherlands for Conduct of Dutchbat in Srebrenica' (2011) 9 J Int Crim Just 1143; *The Netherlands* v. *Hasan Nuhanović*, ECLI:NL:HR:2013:BZ9225 (6 September 2013), at para. 3.11.2; see also para. 3.9.4.

15 Messineo, 'Attribution of Conduct', n. 12, at p. 83.

16 *Certain Phosphate Lands in Nauru (Nauru* v. *Australia)*, Preliminary Objections, ICJ Reports 1992, 240.

17 *Eurotunnel Arbitration (The Channel Tunnel Group Ltd & France-Manche S.A.* v. *the Secretary of State for Transport of the Government of the United Kingdom of Great Britain and Northern Ireland and le ministre de l'équipement, des transports, de l'aménagement du territoire, du tourisme et de la mer du Gouvernement de la République française)*, Partial Award, (2007) 132 ILR 1.

18 Messineo, 'Attribution of Conduct', n. 12, at p. 63.

19 Fry, 'Attribution of Responsibility', n. 4, at p. 99.

20 Gattini, 'Breach of International Obligations', n. 4, at p. 54.

The principle of complicity is the paradigmatic example of a principle that enables shared responsibility: indeed, shared responsibility is inherent in the very concept of complicity. Where the relevant criteria are satisfied, complicity will result in shared responsibility, even though, as Lanovoy demonstrates, the criteria leave open many questions.[21] The aid provided may rise to a level where the aiding state becomes co-perpetrator, and thus jointly responsible with the state or organisation that receives the aid.[22] If not, the aiding state will be responsible for a separate wrong. But, either way, responsibility will only arise when the receiving state indeed commits the wrong. Without prejudice to the ambiguities and obstacles discussed below,[23] complicity thus automatically results in shared responsibility.

The situation for circumstances precluding wrongfulness is quite different. Whereas complicity intrinsically involves shared responsibility, the circumstances precluding wrongfulness seem to pertain to the assessment of conduct of individual actors. As such, they can preclude rather than enable shared responsibility. Nonetheless, as Aust notes, the provisions on circumstances precluding wrongfulness in the ARSIWA and the ARIO are flexible and seem to cope, in general, rather well with situations of shared responsibility.

The principles pertaining to reparation appear to be similarly flexible. Apart from the case of responsibility 'for the same internationally wrongful act' (Article 47 of the ARSIWA and Article 48 of the ARIO), where the responsibility of each state or organisation may be invoked in relation to that internationally wrongful act, the Articles are silent in relation to shared responsibility stemming from different wrongful acts. However, this does not mean that the ARSIWA and the ARIO cannot accommodate such questions. D'Argent notes that '[t]his silence is best explained by the fact that no specific rule is actually required in such cases and that the question of the allocation of the obligation to make reparation is simply governed by the orderly and reasoned application of the usual rules'.[24]

A similar flexibility applies to invocation. Articles 47 of the ARSIWA and 48 of the ARIO expressly deal with invocation in a situation of shared responsibility, at least for the rare situation in which there is a single

[21] Chapter 5 in this volume, V. Lanovoy, 'Complicity in an Internationally Wrongful Act', p. 134, at p. 136.

[22] Fry, 'Attribution of Responsibility', n. 4 at p. 117.

[23] See sections 2.2 and 2.3.

[24] D'Argent, 'Reparation, Cessation, Assurances and Guarantees of Non-Repetition', n. 4, at p. 217.

wrongful act. Apart from this, the ILC drafted the Articles on invocation on the premise that these would arise in a bilateral setting.[25] However, as long as shared responsibility arises from a combination of conduct that leads to individual responsibility, this would, in principle, not seem to cause any problems: injured states or organisations can invoke the responsibility of each state or organisation individually.

Since the regime for countermeasures is largely based on the notion of injured states, what has just been said in relation to invocation also applies here. Tams notes that 'where responsibility is triggered by independent wrongful acts, the general regime can be applied without major modification'.[26] Similarly, countermeasures can be taken against states committing the same wrongful act.[27] Also in this context, flexibility is a virtue. Tams observes that as a general form of law enforcement applicable in a range of settings, countermeasures are regulated in a rather flexible way: '[f]rom the perspective of shared responsibility . . . this is an opportunity as much as a problem', as 'the flexibility inherent in such notions as "legal interest", "proportionality", and so on can be used to fine-tune the general legal regime of countermeasures to the specific problems of shared responsibility.'[28]

The regime of aggravated responsibility envisaged in Part Two of Chapter Three of the ARSIWA is also rather flexible. None of the Articles contained therein inherently precludes the possibility of the existence of a multiplicity of actors. Indeed, as Wyler and Castellanos-Jankiewicz argue, in practice it is often the case that breaches of these Articles involve multiple actors.[29] As long as each of the actors involved are shown to have engaged in serious breaches of the same or different obligations arising under a peremptory norm, there is no indication that each of the actors could not be held responsible for such a breach. An element of multiplicity, moreover, is present in Article 41 ARSIWA, where the cooperation to bring an end through lawful means to such a breach inherently involves multiple states.

Despite these enabling features of the regime, however, the ARSIWA leave open a number of questions in terms of the determination of

[25] Vermeer-Künzli points out that '[t]he frequent use of "one" in this text suggests, at least, that the examples the ILC had in mind when drafting this Commentary were those involving a bilateral invocation.' See Chapter 8 in this volume, A. M. H. Vermeer-Künzli, 'Invocation of Responsibility', p. 25, at p. 259.

[26] Tams, 'Countermeasures against Multiple Responsible Actors', n. 6, at p. 324.

[27] Ibid., p. ___. [28] Ibid., p. ___.

[29] Chapter 9 in this volume, E. A. Wyler and L. A. Castellanos-Jankiewicz, 'Serious Breaches of Peremptory Norms', p. 284, at p. 284.

responsibility by multiple actors and also raise some obstacles to an effective implementation.[30] A number of problems that seem to appear in relation to shared responsibility and the breach of peremptory norms are not directly related to the ILC Articles as such. The recurring problems of the nature and place of causal analysis within the system of responsibility, as well as jurisdictional hurdles, do persist in the case of aggravated responsibility.[31] They do not, however, stem from the nature of the Articles.

In sum, it would seem that most relevant parts of the law of international responsibility are flexible, and that rules which for the most part were designed for bilateral situations can largely be applied and adjusted in situations of shared responsibility. In principle, that would seem to apply to each of the three types of shared responsibility identified in Chapter 1; concurrent responsibility (through the operation of the principle of multiple attribution), cumulative responsibility (through the principles on aid and assistance and attributed responsibility), and joint responsibility (due to the operation of the principle concerning the same wrongful act).[32]

2.2 *Guidance*

The very flexibility of the law of international responsibility is as much a drawback as it is a virtue. Precisely because of the general nature of the provisions, the law rarely provides guidance on (often complex) questions of determination, allocation, and implementation in situations where responsibility is shared.

To some extent such lack of guidance is not due to the specific features of shared responsibility, but rather reflects the generality of the law of international responsibility as such. For instance, it remains an open question as to whether proportionality (as part of the regime on countermeasures) may complicate the application of countermeasures in situations of shared responsibility. Tams rightly observes that this is 'not a problem of shared responsibility proper, but a weakness of the general regime'.[33]

However, the specific nature of questions of shared responsibility, combined with the lack of practice, increases the uncertainty in the construction and application of principles of international responsibility.

[30] Ibid., at p. 291. [31] Ibid., at p. 301–4.
[32] Nollkaemper, 'Introduction', n. 8, at pp. 9–10.
[33] Tams, 'Countermeasures against Multiple Responsible Actors', n. 6, at p. 329.

Indeed, all of the chapters in the present volume raise a range of open questions – which defy easy solutions – that may arise when the principles are applied in situations of shared responsibility.

It would seem that the insistence on the principle of independent responsibility of states has led the ILC to close its eyes to the variety of questions that may arise in situations where there is a multiplicity of wrongdoing actors. Of course, this neglect was exacerbated and, to some extent, legitimised by the lack of practice, which stripped the element of urgency in the development of principles pertaining to shared responsibility.

In the absence of specific principles, the exercise of adaptation is largely a process of translating principles set up for a bilateral setting to a situation of multiplicity. It may be true that the Articles do not necessarily impede that translation. But they are not of much help either. Circumstances precluding wrongfulness offer a good example. Aust points out that 'in general, the circumstances precluding wrongfulness are oriented towards bilateral situations'.[34] The transition to situations of shared responsibility is not always obvious. For instance, how does the principle of consent apply where it has been initially accorded to one state or international organisation, but that state or international organisation is in turn assisted by another state or international organisation? No ready answers can be found in the Articles themselves. Similar questions can be raised for most of the other principles.

While in a number of chapters a wide variety of aspects have been identified where the ILC Articles give little guidance, in this section we will focus on one particular problem: the distribution of responsibility, and, in particular, reparation between multiple actors. This problem will present itself in particular in cases of cumulative responsibility and joint responsibility.[35]

In those cases where it can be determined that multiple states and/or international organisations are responsible, the question will arise whether they are then responsible for the same act or omission, and to the same degree. Most ILC Articles do not differentiate between degrees of responsibility. While this is consistent with the 'objective responsibility' regime the ILC sought to establish, in cases of multiple responsible states it suggested 'all or nothing' solutions that might be seen as too rigid.

[34] Chapter 6 in this volume, H. P. Aust, 'Circumstances Precluding Wrongfulness', p. 169, at p. 199.

[35] As defined in Chapter 1, see Nollkaemper, 'Introduction', n. 8, at pp. 9–11.

A key problem is the lack of a well-defined concept of causality. Of course, in the Articles as designed by the ILC, causation is not, strictly speaking, an element of responsibility. It does not fall under the general rubric of secondary rules. However, in actual determinations of (shared) responsibility, causation will frequently be decisive. Given the definition of shared responsibility as referring to situations where different actors contribute to a single harm,[36] the determination of degrees of contribution is key not only for defining whether or not the case at hand is a case of shared responsibility at all, but also for identifying degrees of responsibility. For instance, in a situation where some of the actors are bound by a negative obligation and some by a positive one, a concept of causality that would be varied according to the different kinds of obligations that were violated would permit better fine-tuning between the different responsibilities of different actors.[37] The possibility of different degrees of responsibility is also recognised by Fry, who observes that attribution of responsibility seems to be grounded on the notion of – varying – degrees of control. But it is somewhat unclear what this means, and whether there is a coherent basis for variation. Fry observes that since attribution of responsibility is being determined by different criteria than attribution of conduct, the two (or more) states that are linked through control will not bear responsibility on a coherent basis.[38]

A related problem is the lack of quantitative criteria for shared responsibility in the context of attribution of responsibility. Fry points out that the ILC approach does not allow the responsibility of the multiple authors to be quantified: the controlling and the controlled, and the coercing and the coerced are, once attribution of responsibility is established for the former and/or attribution of conduct leading to responsibility for the latter, treated only qualitatively if an action is brought against either one of them.[39]

As to complicity, profound questions remain as to what degrees of contribution actually trigger the responsibility of the aiding state, and thereby shared responsibility, and how the law deals with possible variations in responsibility between the aiding and the aided state. Lanovoy observes that 'the ILC's provisions on responsibility for complicity do not

[36] P.A. Nollkaemper and D. Jacobs, 'Shared Responsibility in International Law: A Conceptual Framework' (2013) 34 MIJIL 359, at 366–8; Nollkaemper, 'Introduction', n. 8, at pp. 6–12.

[37] Gattini, n. 4, at p. 30.

[38] Fry, 'Attribution of Responsibility', n. 4, at p. 127.

[39] Ibid., at pp. 128–129.

contain a content-based limitation. Any contribution insofar as it is clearly linked to the commission of the principal wrongful act would constitute aid or assistance'.[40] The question of responsibility then also revolves around the causal link, and the extent to which the specific aid or assistance facilitates the commission of an internationally wrongful act. Lanovoy also observes that this arguably includes omissions, but this point is controversial.[41]

While the question of distribution of responsibility is primarily relevant to distribution of reparation (a point to which we turn below), this is certainly not the only manifestation. One other manifestation arises in relation to countermeasures in cases where responsibility is not equally shared. Tams suggests that the main question here is whether countermeasures should be restricted in cases involving an aiding, assisting, or a coerced state, so as to reflect the different 'share' of responsibility.[42] International law does not provide a clear answer.[43]

Turning to distribution of reparation, the law is largely silent on how to determine shares of reparation in those situations where causation does not provide easy answers. This holds both in situations where there is a single wrongful act, and in situations of different wrongful acts (whether concurrent or cumulative responsibility). As to the former, Article 47(2) of the ARSIWA stipulates that the principle enunciated in paragraph 1 is without prejudice to allocation of reparation between the responsible parties, but neither the principle nor the Commentary provides the beginning of an analysis on how this allocation should proceed. As to the latter, d'Argent notes that the ARSIWA and the ARIO only partly address the complexity stemming from situations of shared responsibility when it comes to the allocation of the secondary obligations of reparation, cessation, and assurances and guarantees of non-repetition. Furthermore they fail to consider cases where the harmful outcome is the result of several wrongful acts for which several subjects are responsible.[44]

This also affects questions of reparation in relation to complicity. Lanovoy observes that 'the current regime of responsibility for complicity leaves little room for the injured party to obtain full reparation for the

[40] Lanovoy, 'Complicity in an Internationally Wrongful Act', n. 21, at p. 149. [41] Ibid.
[42] Tams, 'Countermeasures against Multiple Responsible Actors', n. 6, at pp. 331–7.
[43] Ibid., at p. 336.
[44] D'Argent, 'Reparation, Cessation, Assurances and Guarantees of Non-Repetition', n. 4, at p. 249.

injury that bears an imprint of complicity'.[45] He critiques the ILC for failing 'to provide guidance on the causal standards governing a third party's contribution to an internationally wrongful act'.[46] While d'Argent identifies several options for allocation of reparation,[47] it is difficult to know which of those approaches is favoured by international practice.

The absence of elaborate causal rules creates problems especially in the context of the regime of aggravated responsibility. If most breaches of peremptory norms usually require the participation of a number of actors, thus creating a complex relationship between them and the harmful outcome, a simplistic causal analysis would reduce the implementation of responsibility to a set of bilateral relationships.[48] Such a result would not reflect the complexity of the situation on the ground.

The regime of aggravated responsibility suffers from lack of guidance in another significant respect, namely regarding the consequences arising from a serious breach (i.e. cooperation, non-recognition, non-assistance). Wyler and Castellanos-Jankiewicz point out that 'an international undertaking to counter serious breaches that involves several actors can attract responsibility in case of default'.[49] There is surprisingly little guidance, however, on how these consequences are to be treated in international law, especially in the case of shared responsibility.

2.3 *Obstacles*

To some extent, the lack of guidance in practice noted above may turn into obstacles for the determination and implementation of shared responsibility. In addition to the points mentioned above, on a few points the law of responsibility contains outright limitations to such determination and implementation.

One set of limitations concerns contributions to harmful outcomes that remain below the threshold required to establish them as a wrongful act or to otherwise engage the responsibility of states. There will be cumulation,[50] but the individual contributions fall short of what is

[45] Lanovoy, 'Complicity in an Internationally Wrongful Act', n. 21, at p. 136. [46] Ibid.

[47] D'Argent, 'Reparation, Cessation, Assurances and Guarantees of Non-Repetition', n. 4, at pp. 229–2.

[48] Wyler and Castellanos-Jankiewicz 'Serious Breaches of Peremptory Norms', n. 29, at pp. 301–2.

[49] Ibid., at p. 305. [50] Compare Nollkaemper, 'Introduction', n. 8, at pp. 11–12.

required to trigger responsibility. Apart from lacunae in primary norms, this results from the high thresholds that are set for complicity (notably the possible requirement of intent)[51] and responsibility of international organisations in connection with acts of member states, and vice versa. The question is whether 'the assessment of an act or omission, attributed to a certain state, and per se lawful, would change on account of the fact of having been added up with other acts or omissions that are attributable to other states'.[52]

The law is ill-equipped to solve problems of cumulation that arise from contributions that, in whole or in part, may remain below the level of what is required for triggering responsibility. Gattini observes that 'there is no hint in the ILC Commentary that the single act or omission forming the composite wrongful act could be *per se* lawful',[53] and that outside the context of attribution of responsibility

> it is inconceivable that, through the concept of a composite act, a state could be made responsible only for the fact that an act or omission which is attributable to it, and which is *per se* perfectly lawful, is in a way causally linked to other wrongful acts or omissions attributable to other states.[54]

A particular limitation in this category concerns the possible exclusivity of attribution. Messineo and Fry both make the point that such exclusivity would only exist in a limited set of circumstances.[55] However, where such exclusivity does exist (in particular, with respect to the transferred organs rule), any contribution by other actors would remain without legal consequence. A related point is that the approach of the ILC accepts the existence of varying degrees of control which, as Fry suggests, if taken to an extreme, may lead to the dismantling of the sharing of responsibility of contributing states (e.g. in the case of coercion).[56] The fact that the controlling state will be responsible for the wrongful act committed by the controlled state leaves no room for discussion of the possibility that the controlled state may share responsibility, even in a limited fashion, for the act.[57]

[51] Lanovoy, 'Complicity in an Internationally Wrongful Act', n. 21, at p. 130.
[52] Gattini, 'Breach of International Obligations', n. 4, at p. 48. [53] Ibid.
[54] Ibid., at p. 49.
[55] Messineo, 'Attribution of Conduct', n. 12, at p. 62; Fry, 'Attribution of Responsibility', n. 4, at pp. 112–113.
[56] Fry, 'Attribution of Responsibility', n. 4, at pp. 120–1. [57] Ibid., at p. 119.

A further limitation noted here arises in situations of aid and assistance, where the aiding state is not bound by the same obligation as the state to which aid is given. The bilateral pull of the ARSIWA here manifests itself in the requirement that the assisting state must be bound by the obligation breached by the assisted state, which, as Lanovoy argues, would 'undermine the legality function of international responsibility'.[58]

A distinct possible set of limitations applies to invocation. Formally, it would seem that all conditions for invocation apply normally in situations of shared responsibility. However, in cases of multiple actors who engage in concerted action, it may be readily apparent that this could be burdensome for plaintiffs. Vermeer-Künzli observes that insisting on the requirement of local remedies in such cases may 'be contrary to the notion of reasonableness on which the rule arguably relies and which limits exhaustion to remedies that are reasonably available to the injured individual'.[59] Furthermore, the rules of jurisdiction and admissibility applicable to international courts and tribunals – though not belonging to the law of responsibility as such – may complicate or even impede the invocation and implementation of responsibility of a plurality of states and/or international organisations.[60]

A final limitation to note here, which does not, however, pertain to the rules of responsibility proper,[61] is the right of recourse in cases where there is joint and several liability. This is particularly relevant in relation to situations that in Chapter 1 we characterised in terms of joint responsibility.[62] In general international law there seems to be no clear legal basis for such a right that would resolve problems of allocation of the contributions, internally, among the wrongdoing states. This situation does not allow for a smoothly running system of joint and several liability to emerge.[63]

58 Lanovoy, 'Complicity in an Internationally Wrongful Act', n. 21, at p. 136.

59 Vermeer–Künzli, 'Invocation of Responsibility', n. 25, at p. 267; Article 15 of the Draft Articles on Diplomatic Protection and accompanying Commentary, ILC *Yearbook* 2006/II(2), paragraph 3. See also J. Paulsson, *Denial of Justice in International Law* (Cambridge University Press, 2005), p. 118 and A. M. H. Vermeer-Künzli, 'As If: The Legal Fiction in Diplomatic Protection' (2007) 18 EJIL 37, at 52–5.

60 See the collection of papers in the *Themed Section: Procedural Aspects of Shared Responsibility in International Adjudication* (2013) 4(2) JIDS 277.

61 It is a problem of the lack of a general compulsory dispute settlement, as well as of the development of international rules on the topic.

62 Nollkaemper, 'Introduction', n. 8, at pp. 9–10.

63 Such a general joint and several liability regime would, of course, be limited to cases of multiple entities breaching the same wrongful act.

3. Differentiation

Quite apart from the degree of guidance that is provided by the ARSIWA and the ARIO, the chapters demonstrate that they provide little basis for differentiation. In principle, they apply uniformly to all situations of shared responsibility. However, it seems quite obvious that in many parts they rely on arrangements that may differ, depending on the context. In this section we will assess the contributions from the perspective of differentiation on the basis of three aspects: first, the role of primary rules; second, the public/private distinction; and third, the diversity of actors.

3.1 Differentiation on the basis of primary rules

The ARSIWA and the ARIO leave much to the nature and content of primary rules. As noted in Chapter 1, this was not so much a conceptual choice as a pragmatic one that allowed the ILC to finish its work.[64] Understandable as that may be, it also means that solving any question of shared responsibility is only marginally aided by the ILC texts, as it will largely depend on the primary rules.

The question of whether, and on what grounds, multiple states can be held responsible at all in relation to a single harmful outcome is surprisingly open. In part, this relates to the contents and nature of primary obligations, for it may be unclear who has to do what, and whether it is at all possible for multiple states to be obliged to act (and can thus theoretically be in breach of their obligations). As Gattini points out, this is particularly unclear in cases of obligations to prevent and obligations *erga omnes*.[65] He notes that a differentiation according to the structure of the international obligations – an option discarded by the ILC – might well be useful or even necessary in the context of cases of shared responsibility.[66]

While it may be said that both sets of Articles are fine as long as the primary obligations are better defined, the end result still poses considerable uncertainty and possible arbitrariness in determinations of shared responsibility.

Leaving aside the question of time and feasibility, it would seem that more could have been done in terms of systematising and differentiating the various questions that may arise in the determination of shared

[64] Nollkaemper, 'Introduction', n. 8, at p. 18.
[65] Gattini, 'Breach of International Obligations', n. 4, at pp. 31–5, p. 37–46.
[66] Ibid., at pp. 25, 27, 59.

responsibility for a breach of particular obligations. The point was forcefully made by Gattini, who drew attention to the need to differentiate between obligations of result and obligations of means, and to the specific interpretative questions that may arise in relation to obligations to prevent.[67]

One particular source of uncertainty in this context, which in fact affects the entirety of shared responsibility, concerns the scope and content of the principle of causation. Gattini notes that the lack of a more nuanced and differentiated concept of causation will lead to problems in the application of a 'right *erga omnes*' as recognised by the International Court of Justice (ICJ) in the *East Timor* case.[68] The ICJ may, as Gattini observes, have brought us to the conclusion that such an obligation, by its very nature, may be simultaneously violated by all states – by some through positive acts, and by all the others through omissive conduct. If so, any breach of an *erga omnes* obligation could give rise to a shared responsibility. But '[i]n the absence of some corrective devices – one of which could be the choice of a particular causality theory, such as the adequate causality or the protective purpose causality – the application of the principles of shared responsibility would lead to unexpected, and possibly unwarranted, results.'[69]

It may, of course, be said that it was not for the ILC to provide clarity in areas where the relevant actors could not do so on the basis of primary norms. However, in our assessment of the ability of international law to address questions of shared responsibility, a blame-shifting game between the ILC and states is not of much interest. Indeed, the distinction between secondary and primary rules is neither consistent nor helpful.

The primary/secondary rule divide is problematic in two respects. On the one hand, some elements that are normally part of or associated with primary rules are to be found in the ARSIWA and the ARIO, raising questions of consistency. For instance, Fry observes that the requirement of knowledge common to attributed responsibility both in the ARSIWA and ARIO, may 'be seen as problematic, because incorporating subjective elements like knowledge into the constitutive elements of responsibility is a deviation from the basic premise of objective responsibility

[67] Ibid., at pp. 35–7, 37–46.
[68] *East Timor (Portugal* v. *Australia)*, Judgment, ICJ Reports 1995, 90.
[69] Gattini, 'Breach of International Obligations', n. 4, at p. 33.

underlying both the ARSIWA and the ARIO'.[70] This points not only to a fundamental conflict within the law of responsibility, but also to the need to consider primary and secondary rules in conjunction, where the requirement of fault is sometimes provided in the primary rules and sometimes in the secondary rules.

On the other hand, and more practically relevant, it follows that where the ARSIWA and the ARIO are silent, the resolution of particular questions of shared responsibility will frequently require that primary and secondary rules are considered together. The contributions thus support the argument for a holistic and integrated approach, irrespective of any primary/secondary categorisation, that looks at both the content of obligations and the rules that were treated as rules of responsibility by the ILC.[71]

3.2 *Differentiation on the public/private continuum*

Several contributions have drawn attention to the need to distinguish between the private and the public law dimensions of the law of international responsibility.

Gattini points out that *erga omnes* obligations may have distinct implications for shared responsibility.[72] This is even more true for *erga omnes* rights.[73] Another example is the way *erga omnes* are perceived through the prism of positive/negative obligations. If states are deemed to be bound by *erga omnes* obligations, in the sense of having an obligation to abstain from a specific act, the question arises whether these obligations are not merely shared but also joint, in the sense that they must be discharged in a concerted fashion.[74] While this is a possibly dangerous view, because it would render their performance rather cumbersome, it helps to show the implications that different interpretations of the public nature of (primary) rules may have in the determination of a breach from a shared responsibility viewpoint.

The public/private distinction also seems relevant for other parts of the ILC texts. Aust observes that the ILC considered it possible that an essential interest of 'the international community as a whole' is covered by the provision on necessity, and adds that 'Article 25 of the ARSIWA

[70] Fry, 'Attribution of Responsibility', n. 4, at pp. 121–2.
[71] Nollkaemper and Jacobs, 'Shared Responsibility in International Law', n. 36, at pp. 411–12.
[72] Gattini, 'Breach of International Obligations', n. 4, pp. 31–5. [73] Ibid., at pp. 32–3.
[74] Aust, 'Circumstances Precluding Wrongfulness', n. 34, at p. 200.

itself allows for cooperative efforts of states to rely on a state of necessity, if they deem it necessary to protect an essential interest of the international community. Therefore, a plurality of states acting together may potentially rely on Article 25 of the ARSIWA.'[75] The distinction also has immediate consequences for this assessment, as the defences that he groups as part of the category of 'preclusion of wrongfulness' (notably self-defence and countermeasures), which could be relied upon by a broader set of states, are especially concerned with means to ensure a return to legality. Given the frequent absence of alternative means of enforcement, these defences remain key to public law values of the system of international law. This does not apply to the group of defences that Aust groups as 'excuses': in these cases it 'does not seem to be warranted to expand the group of actors who can rely on these *ad hoc* mechanisms'.[76]

The regime of aggravated responsibility is specifically designed to target crimes that 'destabilize the public order', as Wyler and Castellanos-Jankiewicz point out. Notably, it is within this regime that the public/private distinction can be seen as breaking down when it comes to shared responsibility. As noted above, a breach of peremptory norms by a multiplicity of actors will be reduced to a number of bilateral relations of responsibility without giving full effect to the public dimension of that breach. What is more, the Articles that cover the consequences of such a breach, which are clearly designed to provide for a 'public' response to it, are not sufficiently clear.

Also, d'Argent notes that the nature of the obligation breached (whether or not a norm is a peremptory norm) and the character of the breach (whether or not it is an egregious or grave breach) 'are most likely to influence the understanding of the necessity, under those "circumstances", to offer assurances and guarantees of non-repetition'.[77]

All of this supports the argument that in considering how international law facilitates determination and implementation of shared responsibility, it may be necessary to draw a distinction between situations where responsibility maintains its usual 'private law model' and those situations where it acquires a public law dimension. Of course, we recognise that the dichotomy between public and private law models is not watertight, and to some extent they should be considered as a

[75] Ibid., at p. 196. [76] Ibid., at p. 205.

[77] D'Argent, 'Reparation, Cessation, Assurances and Guarantees of Non-Repetition', n. 4, at p. 217.

continuum with shades of grey, rather than as a black and white opposition. Indeed, to do otherwise would be to open ourselves to the compelling critique on the private/public dichotomy in international law.[78] Nonetheless, we submit that it is useful and possible to identify distinctions between public and private law dimensions of responsibility.[79] The nature of the obligation may determine the nature of corresponding responsibility. The increased differentiation of norms in the international legal order affects the nature of responsibility, whether these are construed in terms of *jus cogens* or *erga omnes*. We thus have to recognise the possibility of classifying obligations according to their nature and how this might affect the shared responsibility for their breach.

3.3 *Differentiation based on actors*

Finally, there may be a need to differentiate between situations of shared responsibility depending on the nature of the actors involved. In this volume we have been primarily concerned with the responsibility of states and international organisations. The analysis made clear that between these two actors, the law of responsibility needs to differentiate considerably, notwithstanding the often discussed 'copy and paste' approach of the ILC in the ARIO.[80]

Notably, the principles relating to international organisations are much more open to the possibility that one actor is responsible in connection with the act of another actor.[81] In this context, Gattini draws attention to the fact that the ILC – in contrast to what it had said in relation to the parallel Article 47 of the ARSIWA – considered joint responsibility to be the general rule, applicable in all cases of Part Two and Part Five of the ARIO. He observes that a possible explanation for this switch of perspective could be that joint responsibility as a general rule is easier to affirm when international organisations are involved:

78 See in a quite different context e.g. C. Chinkin, 'A Critique of the Public/Private Dimension' (1999) 10 EJIL 387.

79 Nollkaemper and Jacobs, 'Shared Responsibility in International Law', n. 36, at p. 415.

80 C. Ahlborn, 'The Use of Analogies in Drafting the Articles on the Responsibility of International Organizations – An Appraisal of the "Copy–Paste Approach"' (2012) 9(1) IOLR 53.

81 N. Nedeski and P. A. Nollkaemper, 'Responsibility of International Organizations "in connection with acts of States"' (2012) 9(1) IOLR 33.

> because in this context the application of joint responsibility does not touch upon the sensitive issue of sovereignty, i.e. making a state responsible for the acts or omissions of another, which is the major stumbling block for affirming joint responsibility as a general rule in all cases of shared state responsibility.[82]

That being said, the degree to which the conditions for, and consequences of, responsibility are indeed different between responsibility of states and responsibility of international organisations remains a subject of discussion. The difficulties of transposing principles from the ARSIWA to the ARIO are highlighted by Messineo in his critique on Article 7 of the ARIO. He argues that Article 7 of the ARIO was wrongly formulated, and that the criterion of 'effective control' – taken from the ARSIWA – in this context is misleading.[83] It should, of course, be recalled that the principles on attribution of responsibility in relation to international organisations are largely *de lege ferenda*.[84]

Also, Tams draws attention to the specific problems arising in cases of countermeasures in relation to international organisations. He observes that the allocation of responsibility between an international organisation and its member states is difficult and controversial, and that:

> Controversies about attribution of conduct, or about the proper object of legal claims, affect the legal regime of countermeasures, which presupposes the responsibility of the targeted actor and is designed to induce cessation/reparation . . . All this suggests that the regime is still in flux.[85]

Several chapters have also drawn attention to the specific questions that may arise when not only states and international organisations, but also other actors, contribute to a single harmful outcome. Lanovoy notes that the requirement of opposability in relation to complicity '[p]erpetuates a particular vision of reciprocal normativity in international law'[86] and '[s]huts the door to the development or extension of responsibility to wrongdoings committed in collaboration between states and entities other than states, which are rarely if ever bound by the same obligations'.[87]

82 Gattini, 'Breach of International Obligations', n. 4, at p. 51.
83 Messineo, 'Attribution of Conduct', n. 12, at pp. 91–3.
84 Gattini, 'Breach of International Obligations', n. 4, at p. 54.
85 Tams, 'Countermeasures against Multiple Responsible Actors', n. 6, at p. 337.
86 Lanovoy, 'Complicity in an Internationally Wrongful Act', n. 21, at p. 159.
87 Ibid.

Gattini argues that '[t]he main reason why it is difficult to envisage a general framework of shared responsibility between states and individuals is the uncertain state of the law on the issue of direct accountability of individuals for violations of customary international law, besides the already-mentioned and well-circumscribed instances of individual criminal responsibility',[88] as well as 'the difficulty in sensing the respective content of the obligations and the limits of the two kinds of responsibility'.[89] He critiques the ILC for not having thus far taken any opportunity to specify the possible interactions of state and individual responsibility, not only in relation to the saving clause of Article 56 of the ARSIWA, but also in relation to the codification of the prevention of transboundary harm from hazardous activities.[90]

As d'Argent points out, a comprehensive assessment of these problems not only involves an examination of different actors, but also of the relationship between different legal orders. For when conduct of individuals or other non-state actors combines with contributions by states or international organisations in creating a harmful outcome, the first question that needs to be asked is whether 'those individuals or non-state actors have breached a rule of international (rather than domestic) law that they are bound to respect, and the second is to know whether the claim relating to their responsibility is made under domestic or international law'.[91]

The complexity stemming from the questions raised is only illustrated by the examples discussed in this volume, and requires separate analysis at a later stage.

4. Beyond the ILC

It emerges from the preceding analysis that while the ARSIWA and the ARIO may not be problematic in some respects for the determination and implementation of shared responsibility, they also leave much to be desired. The recurring problems can be summarised as follows. First, the ILC Articles evade most questions of shared responsibility. The mantra of individual responsibility is hardly helpful for resolving the

88 Gattini, 'Breach of International Obligations', n. 4, at p. 54. 89 Ibid., at p. 56.
90 Ibid.
91 D'Argent, 'Reparation, Cessation, Assurances and Guarantees of Non-Repetition', n. 4, at p. 210.

straightforward question of whether and how a multiplicity of actors can be held responsible for producing a single harmful outcome. Second, the Articles that do more expressly envisage the possibility of shared responsibility (attribution of responsibility, aid and assistance) raise fundamental questions regarding their scope and content. Third, the adaptability of most Articles to situations of shared responsibility is to be found more in their unelaborated nature and less in their conscious design so as to adapt in such situations. Fourth, the approach of the ILC that excluded any meaningful discussion on causation or the elaboration of quantitative criteria for the implementation of responsibility is not helpful for an accurate apportionment of responsibility in the instances where multiple actors are involved. Fifth, part of the problem is that a single set of Articles can hardly do justice to the wide variety of contexts in which questions of shared responsibility do arise. In this respect, the relevance of the ILC Articles is hampered not only by the bilateral approach, but also by that fact that they do not differentiate between public and private aspects, that they exclude primary rules, and that they only address states and international organisations.

The question thus presents itself as to how to proceed from here. There are two main options. A first option is to make an effort to expand the existing Articles as much as possible so as to accommodate questions of shared responsibility. A second option is to look outside the ILC regimes for solutions to the challenges of shared responsibility.

A combination of the two approaches is the preferred solution. On the one hand, there are instances (particularly the Articles on breach, invocation, and countermeasures) where shared responsibility problems can be, with varying degrees of difficulty, accommodated. Whether this will be so depends largely on the nature of the shared responsibility – whether it is concurrent, cumulative, or joint). In cases where it consists of complementary separate wrongful acts, the Articles generally may accommodate most issues. There is no reason to devise different rules where the current ones can, for the most part, serve the purpose. The application and development of the existing Articles in relation to questions of shared responsibility may help develop a better fit between the existing law and the challenges of shared responsibility.

On the other hand, we have to recognise the limits of the possibility of solving problems of shared responsibility by a set of Articles that was not devised to deal with them. Answering questions (or solving problems) of shared responsibility will require stepping outside the normative framework of the ILC's work, by considering alternative grounds for the distribution of multiple actors in international law.[92] It will also require formulating specific solutions that take into account the context of particular issue-areas.[93]

Stepping outside the ILC regime does not necessarily set up a conflict with that regime. The ILC itself left enough open spaces for *lex specialis* to develop. The development of secondary rules in certain sectoral regimes that might deviate from the ILC Articles is perfectly possible. At least in the short term, it will, however, marginalise the relevance of the ILC Articles for solving problems of shared responsibility. The solutions will have to be found elsewhere. However, in the long run, this development, depending on its pace, intensity, and stability, can also have an effect on the *lex generalis*. It can be envisaged that at some point in the future the ILC rules can be changed, in critical details, so as to accommodate new state practice in the field of shared responsibility.

These two steps, which can run in parallel, thus require further study of the phenomenon of shared responsibility. This further study can be conceptualised on several levels. First, the structural problems of the ILC, as well as the silence on certain important issues (e.g. causation, quantification of responsibility, etc.), must be revisited so as to be fine-tuned with an eye to shared responsibility. Second, it should be considered what alternative normative bases can inform decisions on shared responsibility. Third, the practice of shared responsibility as it appears in various sectoral regimes must be mapped and documented. Finally, an effort to conceptualise shared responsibility on the basis of the findings regarding the state of the art, considerations of alternative normative grounds for distribution of responsibility, and the practice of shared responsibility, is in order. The inquiry in the present volume was the necessary first step in this long-term agenda.

[92] This will be aim of P. A. Nollkaemper and D. Jacobs (eds.), *Distribution of Responsibilities in International Law* (Cambridge University Press, 2015 *forthcoming*).

[93] This will be aim of P. A. Nollkaemper and I. Plakokefalos (eds.), *Practice of Shared Responsibility in International Law*, (Cambridge University Press, 2015 *forthcoming*).

INDEX